Ausgabe Nord

Context 21

Teacher's Manual

mit Vorschlägen zur Leistungsmessung

Cornelsen

Im Auftrag des Verlags herausgegeben von
Prof. Hellmut Schwarz, Mannheim, *unter Mitarbeit von* Mervyn Whittaker, Bad Dürkheim

Erarbeitet von
Ingrid Becker-Ross, Krefeld; Heiko Benzin, Neustrelitz; Peter Brünker, Bad Kreuznach; Barbara Derkow Disselbeck, Köln; Ulrike Elsäßer, Stuttgart; Dr. Tobias Franke, Münster; Jörg Hoch, Gettorf; Ulrich Imig, Wildeshausen; Dr. Annette Leithner-Brauns, Dresden; Dr. Paul Maloney, Hildesheim; Oliver Meyer, Buxheim; Kerstin Petschl, Wendlingen am Neckar; Angela Ringel-Eichinger, Bietigheim-Bissingen; Alexander Trost, Tübingen; Sabine Tudan, St. Georgen im Schwarzwald; Mervyn Whittaker, Bad Dürkheim; Allen J. Woppert, Berlin
sowie
Prof. Hellmut Schwarz, Mannheim (Vorwort)

Redaktion
Dr. Marion Kiffe (Projektleitung); Katrin Heinecke (verantwortlich); Katrin Gütermann, Solveig Heinrich, Neil Porter, Marc Proulx; Dr. Bettina Schaschke, Dr. Ilka Soennecken (Text- und Bildrechte); Kieran Breen, Katherine Glass, Lorna McGavigan, Constanze Schöder, Claudia Siebald und Ralph Williams (Assistenz)

Layoutkonzept und technische Umsetzung
zweiband.media, Berlin

Umschlaggestaltung
Klein & Halm Grafikdesign, Berlin

Weitere Bestandteile des Lehrwerks:
- **Schülerbuch** (ISBN 978-3-06-032331-9 broschiert; 978-3-06-032465-1 gebunden)
- **Audio-CDs** (ISBN 978-3-06-032239-8)
- **Video-DVD** (ISBN 978-3-06-032240-4)
- **Language, Skills and Exam Trainer**
  mit CD-Extra (ISBN 978-3-06-032415-6);
  Language, Skills and Exam Trainer with Answer Key
  mit CD-Extra inkl. Lösungen: ISBN 978-3-06-032361-6)
- **Interaktive Präsentationen für Whiteboard und Beamer** (ISBN 978-3-06-032475-0)

Website zum Lehrwerk: www.context21.de

Die Links zu externen Webseiten Dritter, die in diesem Lehrwerk angegeben sind, wurden vor Drucklegung sorgfältig auf ihre Aktualität geprüft. Der Verlag übernimmt keine Gewähr für die Aktualität und den Inhalt dieser Seiten oder solcher, die mit ihnen verlinkt sind.

1. Auflage, 3. Druck 2014

© 2010 Cornelsen Verlag, Berlin
© 2014 Cornelsen Schulverlage GmbH, Berlin

Das Werk und seine Teile sind urheberrechtlich geschützt. Jede Nutzung in anderen als den gesetzlich zugelassenen Fällen bedarf der vorherigen schriftlichen Einwilligung des Verlages.
Hinweis zu den §§ 46, 52 a UrhG: Weder das Werk noch seine Teile dürfen ohne eine solche Einwilligung eingescannt und in ein Netzwerk eingestellt oder sonst öffentlich zugänglich gemacht werden.
Dies gilt auch für Intranets von Schulen und sonstigen Bildungseinrichtungen. Die Kopiervorlagen dürfen für den eigenen Unterrichtsgebrauch in der jeweils benötigten Anzahl vervielfältigt werden.

Druck: H. Heenemann, Berlin

ISBN 978-3-06-032332-6

 Inhalt gedruckt auf säurefreiem Papier aus nachhaltiger Forstwirtschaft.

Inhaltsverzeichnis

Vorwort 5
Die Bestandteile von *Context 21* 7
Erläuterung der Symbole und Abkürzungen 12
Übersicht *Topics, text forms, skills, authors and levels* 14

Kapitel 1 The UK – Tradition and Change 19
Kopiervorlage 1: Evaluating a Presentation 45
Kopiervorlage 2: Listening to Music 46
Kopiervorlage 3: Take Back the City (Snow Patrol) 47
Topic Vocabulary Politics 48

Kapitel 2 The USA – Dreams and Struggles 51
Kopiervorlage 4: Lynching Will Maxie 79
Kopiervorlage 5: Issues in Evangelicalism 81
Kopiervorlage 6: Ignorant Citizens 83
Topic Vocabulary Religion 84

Kapitel 3 The Individual in Society 87
Kopiervorlage 7: Mediation: A Day for Blokes 109
Kopiervorlage 8: Roles for Project Work 110
Topic Vocabulary 111

Kapitel 4 National Identity and Diversity 113
Kopiervorlage 9: A Bicultural Upbringing 133
Kopiervorlage 10: Assimilation or Diversity? 134
Topic Vocabulary 135

Kapitel 5 India – Past and Present 137
Kopiervorlage 11: India Crossword Puzzle 156

Kapitel 6 The Media 157
Kopiervorlage 12: Media Log 174
Kopiervorlage 13: Media Log Evaluation Sheet 175
Kopiervorlage 14: Elements of a News Report 176
Kopiervorlage 15: Evaluation of Media Logs 177
Topic Vocabulary 178

Kapitel 7 Global Perspectives 181
Kopiervorlage 16: Map of the World 200
Kopiervorlage 17: Outsourcing 201
Kopiervorlage 18: More Globalization? 202
Topic Vocabulary 204

Kapitel 8 The World of Work and Business 205
Kopiervorlage 19: Reading Comprehension 225
Topic Vocabulary 226

Kapitel 9 Science, Technology and the Environment 229
Kopiervorlage 20: Climate Change – Global Processes and Effects 249
Kopiervorlage 21: Doing a SWOT Analysis 250
Kopiervorlage 22: Writing a Bibliography 251
Topic Vocabulary 253

Kapitel 10 The World of English 257

Kopiervorlage 23: Reading Comprehension 271
Topic Vocabulary 272

Kapitel 11 Shakespeare 273

Kopiervorlage 24: Phrases from Shakespeare 293
Kopiervorlage 25: 60-Second Shakespeare 294
Topic Vocabulary 295

Group Activities (Cooperative Learning Strategies) 297

Quellenangaben 300

Vorwort zum Teacher's Manual

Konzeption

Context 21 ist ein integriertes Lese- und Arbeitsbuch, das die Grundlage für den Englischunterricht an allgemeinbildenden und beruflichen Gymnasien sowie Gesamtschulen bildet. Es baut auf den in der Sekundarstufe I bzw. mit *Context 21 Starter* erworbenen Vorkenntnissen und Kompetenzen auf, konsolidiert und erweitert sie und führt die Schülerinnen und Schüler sicher zum Abitur.

Context 21 ist das Nachfolgewerk zu New Context und entwickelt dessen Vorzüge weiter. Es liegt in insgesamt zehn Regionalausgaben vor und setzt die länderspezifischen Lehrpläne und Abiturvorgaben jeweils punktgenau um.

Der Unterricht mit *Context 21* ruht auf fünf Säulen:
1. Textarbeit
2. Spracharbeit
3. Kompetenzschulung
4. Interkulturelles und themenorientiertes Lernen
5. Integrierte Übungen

1. Textarbeit

Das Lehrwerk zeichnet sich durch eine Fülle unterschiedlicher authentischer Texte und Textsorten aus. Deren Themen und Gestaltung wecken das Interesse der Schülerinnen und Schüler, erweitern ihr Wissen bzw. ihre Kompetenzen und fördern ihre interkulturelle Handlungsfähigkeit. Häufig bereiten sie die zunehmend selbstständige Lektüre von Ganzschriften vor oder runden diese ab.

Context 21 schult – den Zielen der Oberstufe entsprechend – den sachgemäßen und flexiblen Umgang mit Texten. Die Schülerinnen und Schüler lernen, Texte hörend und lesend zu erschließen, wobei die Verstehensschulung auf verschiedenen Anforderungsebenen durchgeführt wird: von einfachen zu zunehmend komplexeren Verständnisaufgaben bis hin zum Transfer auf andere Texte und die Lebenswelt der Schülerinnen und Schüler. Dabei werden unterschiedliche Analysetechniken vermittelt, die auch die stilistische Ebene einbeziehen.

Durch die konsequente Integration von sprach- und kompetenzorientierten Übungen in die Textarbeit beschreitet *Context 21* neue Wege (vgl. 5.).

Neben der rezeptiven Komponente der Textarbeit wird durchgängig die produktive berücksichtigt. Die Schülerinnen und Schüler werden angeleitet, Texte zu verfassen, z.B. in Analogie zu den vorgestellten Mustern oder auch im Sinne des *creative writing* und der mündlichen Textproduktion. Sprachliche bzw. inhaltliche und methodische Hilfen bieten die *Language help* in der Randspalte, das *Skills File* sowie das *Glossary*.

2. Spracharbeit

Durch die Verkürzung der Schulzeit bzw. der Wochenstundenzahlen in manchen Bundesländern sind die Voraussetzungen der Schülerinnen und Schüler beim Durchlaufen der Sekundarstufe II heterogener als früher. Daher müssen die zentralen Sprachmittel, die für die Bearbeitung der anspruchsvollen Aufgaben in der Oberstufe notwendig sind, zunehmend reaktiviert und konsolidiert werden.
Daneben zielt die Spracharbeit darauf ab, individuelle sprachliche Fehlerquellen und Defizite zu beseitigen und die allgemeine Sprachkompetenz zu verbessern. Integriertes und kontextbezogenes Üben spielt daher eine wichtige Rolle (vgl. 5.). Auch das Ausdrucksvermögen der Schülerinnen und Schüler (ihr „Stil") ist durch gezielte Übungen zu verbessern.

3. Kompetenzschulung

Entsprechend der Zielsetzung aller Lehrpläne und Curricula nimmt das Training der kommunikativen Kompetenzen einen zentralen Raum ein. Aufgaben und Übungen zu Hör- und Hör-/Sehverstehen, Leseverstehen, Sprechen, Schreiben und zur Sprachmittlung (*mediation*) sind in jedem Kapitel prominent vertreten und im *Skills File* verankert. Im Hinblick auf die neuen Formen der Abiturprüfung wird in *Context 21* nicht nur das Schreiben, sondern auch die Schulung der Mündlichkeit betont (vgl. dazu auch *Communicating across Cultures*, *Everyday English*, *Exam Practice – EP6: Speaking* sowie die Übungen im *Language, Skills and Exam Trainer*).

▶ TM S. 9

Gleichzeitig legt *Context 21* großen Wert auf die Ausbildung der methodischen Kompetenzen: Aufbauend auf den Grundlagen des vorangegangenen Unterrichts werden die Schülerinnen und Schüler durch das Training der *study skills* zu immer selbstständigerem Lernen geführt. Anregungen und Hilfen für Projekte und die Präsentation der Ergebnisse werden in jedem Kapitel gegeben. Die dabei erworbene Lernkompetenz ermöglicht es, immer effektiver und unabhängiger von der Lehrkraft zu arbeiten und damit die Schulzeitverkürzung zumindest teilweise zu kompensieren.

Zusätzlich werden in jedem Kapitel vertraute sowie neue Formen des kooperativen Lernens eingesetzt, die in einer größeren Interaktion der Schülerinnen und Schüler und einem besonders sprechaktiven Unterricht resultieren und gleichzeitig die Sozialkompetenz der Lernenden stärken.

4. Interkulturelles und themenorientiertes Lernen

Die Vermittlung der kulturellen Kompetenz, d.h. sowohl der Erwerb des grundlegenden soziokulturellen Wissens als auch der interkulturellen bzw. transkulturellen Handlungsfähigkeit, ist in der modernen Sprachdidaktik hoch angesiedelt, da sie für die übergeordneten Zielsetzungen des Fremdsprachenlernens wie Völkerverständigung und Toleranz unabdingbar ist.

Context 21 bringt Schülerinnen und Schülern das Leben und die Kultur englischsprachiger Länder auf anregende Weise näher und stellt dabei nicht nur Sachwissen bereit, sondern gewährt ihnen auch Einsichten in politisch-soziale und historische sowie ethische und kulturelle Zusammenhänge. Gleichzeitig regt das Lehrwerk immer wieder an, Vergleiche mit anderen Ländern bzw. der eigenen Lebenswelt zu ziehen, sich zu kontroversen Fragen zu positionieren und in Diskussionen einzutreten.

Context 21 leistet damit einen für diese Altersstufe besonders wichtigen Beitrag zur Werteerziehung und fördert gleichzeitig die Diskursfähigkeit.

5. Integrierte Übungen

Durch die vielfältige und konsequente Einbeziehung von sprach- und kompetenzorientierten Übungen unterscheidet sich *Context 21* grundlegend von anderen Oberstufenlehrwerken. Die Übungen tragen entscheidend dazu bei, die bereits konstatierten sprachlichen Defizite zu verringern und die sachgerechte Anwendung von Kompetenzen zu fördern.

Übungen spielen in vielen Teilen des Lehrwerks eine wichtige Rolle:
- In den **Kapiteln** ist in den auf die Texte folgenden Aufgaben mindestens eine sprachlich-stilistische oder eine auf die Schulung von Kompetenzen bezogene Übung integriert. Damit wird die Aufmerksamkeit der Schülerinnen und Schüler entweder auf grammatikalische bzw. lexikalische oder auf stilistische Phänomene des Texts gelenkt und ihre Verwendung nicht isoliert, sondern im Kontext des Themas bzw. des Texts trainiert. Auf diese Weise wird den Schülerinnen und Schülern der Nutzen dieser Sprachmittel unmittelbar einsichtig gemacht. Gleiches gilt auch für die Schulung bestimmter auf den Text bezogener Kompetenzen.
- Halten die Schülerinnen und Schüler oder die Lehrkraft weitere Übungen für sinnvoll, werden sie durch Querverweise in der Randspalte zur **Reference Section** geführt:
Die *Language Practice* umfasst neben notwendigen Erklärungen auch Übungen sowohl zu den fehlerträchtigsten lexikalischen und grammatikalischen als auch zu stilistischen Phänomenen.
Auch in der *Exam Practice* und im *Skills File* sind unter der Bezeichnung „Practice" (gelb unterlegte) Übungen zu den einzelnen Kompetenzen integriert.

Damit folgt in vielen Fällen auf die Beschreibungen der jeweiligen *skills* sofort deren praktische Anwendung.
- Weitere Übungen zu allen im Schülerbuch geübten Bereichen enthält der ***Language, Skills and Exam Trainer***.

Die Bestandteile von *Context 21*

- Schülerbuch (SB)
- vier Audio-CDs
- Video-DVD
- *Language, Skills and Exam Trainer* (LSET)
- Website
- Interaktive Präsentationen für Whiteboard und Beamer
- *Teacher's Manual* (TM) mit Vorschlägen zur Leistungsmessung

Das Schülerbuch

Das Schülerbuch besteht aus 11 Kapiteln, die oberstufengemäß in beliebiger Reihenfolge einsetzbar sind, und einer ebenfalls flexibel zu nutzenden *Reference Section*. Zur leichteren Handhabung enthalten die Kapitel Verweise auf
- Übungen in der *Language Practice*;
- Erläuterungen und Übungen zu den kommunikativen und methodischen Kompetenzen im *Skills File*;
- Fachtermini im *Glossary*.

Die Struktur des Schülerbuchs im Überblick

Chapters	Lead-in
	Words in Context
	Part A
	Part B etc.
	Communicating across Cultures

Reference Section						
Language Practice						
Vocabulary Matters		Grammar Matters	Style Matters		Everyday English	
Skills File						
Study and Language Skills	Listening and Viewing Skills	Speaking Skills	Reading Skills	Writing Skills		Mediating Skills
Exam Practice						
How to Do Exams in General	Analysis and Interpretation	Composition	Mediating/ Translating	Listening/ Viewing	Speaking	Standardized Test Formats
Glossary						
Language for Tasks ('Operatoren')						
Charts						
Historical Documents						

Der Aufbau des Schülerbuchs

Alle Kapitel enthalten die gleichen Bausteine, die wie die Kapitel selbst zumindest teilweise flexibel einsetzbar sind:

Lead-in Jedes Kapitel beginnt mit einem zweiseitigen Einführungsteil, der aus einer Kombination von Text- und Bildelementen besteht und die Lernenden in die Themen und Aufgaben des Kapitels einführt. Dieser Teil sollte am Anfang behandelt werden, da

Vorwort zum Teacher's Manual

er wichtige Aspekte des Kapitelthemas und die dazugehörige Lexik präsentiert und gleichzeitig an das Vorwissen und die Erfahrungswelt der Schülerinnen und Schüler anknüpft. Kooperative Arbeitsformen, wie z. B. *think–pair–share*, motivieren und regen die Interaktion der Schülerinnen und Schüler an.

Words in Context Auf diesen Teil sollte bei der Bearbeitung eines Kapitels besonderes Gewicht gelegt werden, da er nicht nur die Gesamtthematik umreißt, sondern auch grundlegenden Wortschatz vermittelt und übt. Der Text gibt einen Überblick über zentrale Themen des Kapitels, die anschließend in den authentischen Texten der *Parts A, B, usw.* entfaltet und diskutiert werden. Die im Text gelb unterlegten Wörter und Kollokationen stellen einen wesentlichen Teil des Lernwortschatzes des betreffenden Kapitels dar und werden von den Schülerinnen und Schülern in unterschiedlichen Übungen verwendet und dadurch verankert. Die sprachliche Fokussierung wird zusätzlich durch die Aufnahme grammatischer Übungen, die im Text benutzte Strukturen umwälzen, und durch Verweise auf Übungen in der *Language Practice* unterstrichen.

Die Vokabellisten *(Vocab Sheets)* mit dem Lernwortschatz aus *Words in Context* und den anderen Kapitelteilen werden sowohl auf der LSET-CD-Extra als auch auf der TM-DVD-ROM zur Verfügung gestellt. Durch Schreibräume, die von den Schülerinnen und Schülern individuell zu füllen sind, wird das eigenverantwortliche Lernen gefördert. Weitere Übungen zu diesem Wortschatz finden sich im *Language, Skills and Exam Trainer*.

Parts A, B, … Jedes Kapitel enthält zwei bis vier *Parts*. Sie bilden das Kernstück der Kapitel und illustrieren mit ihren Texten und dazugehörigen Aufgaben verschiedene Aspekte des jeweiligen Themas.

Die Texte tragen dem erweiterten Textbegriff Rechnung: Die Schülerinnen und Schüler arbeiten nicht nur mit fiktionalen Texten (Short Storys, Romanauszügen, Gedichten usw.), sondern auch mit Sachtexten wie Zeitungsartikeln und Reden, mit Diagrammen und Statistiken sowie mit Postern, Fotos und Gemälden. Darunter befinden sich auch relativ umfangreiche oder mehrfach kodierte Texte (z. B. Filme, Videos), wie sie für die Oberstufenarbeit typisch sind.

Hör- und Hör-/Sehtexte finden sich auf der Audio-CD bzw. der Video-DVD und werden durch Aufgaben im SB erschlossen und analysiert.

Die vielfältigen Aufgaben zu den Texten sind in der Regel als *tasks* mit den entsprechenden Operatoren (s. Übersicht im Anhang des SB) formuliert. Sie umfassen Verstehensübungen auf verschiedenen Anforderungsniveaus sowie Aufgaben zur inhaltlichen oder stilistischen Analyse und Interpretation. Daneben gibt es produktorientierte oder transferierende Aufgabenstellungen. Zu diesen Aufgaben werden in der Randspalte Redemittel *(Language help)* bereitgestellt, die die zügige und sprachlich angemessene Bearbeitung erleichtern.

Hilfe erhalten die Schülerinnen und Schüler auch in der Rubrik *Trouble spot*, die zur sprachlichen Bewusstmachung und zur Vermeidung von Interferenzfehlern beiträgt (z. B. „National Identity and Diversity", B3). Vertiefende Übungen zu einigen *Trouble spots* finden sich im LSET.

Ein wesentlicher Bestandteil der Kapitel sind die Übungen zur sprachlichen Festigung (z. B. „The USA – Dreams and Struggles", C3, Aufgabe 4, *-ing forms*), zur stilistischen Analyse (z. B. „The USA – Dreams and Struggles", A2, Aufgabe 2, *imagery*) und zum Kompetenztraining (z. B. „The USA – Dreams and Struggles", D5, Context Task „Writing an Essay"), die in den inhaltlichen Kontext des jeweiligen Kapitelteils eingebunden sind.

EXTRA Die Texte und Aufgaben berücksichtigen unterschiedliche Schwierigkeitsniveaus, sodass sowohl Lernstärkere als auch Lernschwächere angemessen gefordert bzw. gefördert werden. Zur Differenzierung dienen gleichfalls die als „Extra" ausgewiesenen Aufgaben, die zusätzliche Anforderungen v. a. an Leistungsstärkere stellen.

Vorwort zum Teacher's Manual

Context Task — Wesentliche im Kapitel vermittelte Inhalte werden nach dem letzten Part in der *Context Task* noch einmal reflektiert und praktisch umgesetzt. So verfassen die Schülerinnen und Schüler ein Bewerbungsschreiben (vgl. „The World of Work and Business", C3), beteiligen sich an einer Diskussion (vgl. „India – Past and Present", C4) oder gestalten eine Präsentation (vgl. „The UK – Tradition and Change", C4).

Communicating across Cultures — Die Mehrzahl der Kapitel enthält (meist vor oder nach dem letzten *Part*) den Abschnitt Communicating across Cultures, der die inter- bzw. transkulturelle Kompetenz der Schülerinnen und Schüler schult (z. B. in „Shakespeare", „Dealing with Different Cultural Values"). Er bereitet sie auf Begegnungen mit Englisch sprechenden Menschen vor und verbessert sowohl ihre kommunikativen Fertigkeiten als auch ihre zwischenmenschliche Sensibilität.

Die Audioaufnahmen in diesem Abschnitt verbessern nicht nur die Hörkompetenz der Lernenden, sondern stellen vor allem Gesprächsmodelle vor, die von den Schülerinnen und Schülern zu analysieren und auszuwerten sind. Diese Modelle werden dann in Rollenspielen umgesetzt (z. B. in „The USA – Dreams and Struggles" vor Part D zum Thema „Talking to Somebody about Their Country").

▶ Übersicht S. 7

Der Aufbau der Reference Section

Language Practice — Die Rubrik *Language Practice* ergänzt die sprachlichen Übungen in den Kapiteln und unterstreicht damit die große Bedeutung der Sprachschulung in *Context 21*. Sie ist untergliedert in:

- *Vocabulary Matters:* Dieser Abschnitt wendet sich besonders wichtigen bzw. fehlerträchtigen Bereichen der Wortschatzarbeit zu (z. B. *collocations* oder *false friends*), erklärt und übt sie. Auch die für das Leseverstehen essenziellen Wortbildungsregeln werden aufgegriffen und in Übungen umgesetzt.
- *Grammar Matters:* In diesem Abschnitt werden zentrale Phänomene der Grammatik nach einem vorbereitenden *Test-yourself*-Teil kurz auf Englisch erläutert und auf abwechslungsreiche Weise geübt. Dabei werden v.a. für die Textarbeit in der Oberstufe relevante Strukturen einbezogen (z. B. LP 16: *Using the passive*).
- *Style Matters:* Im Hinblick auf Klausuren und das Abitur, aber auch auf Anforderungen nach der Schulzeit ist die Schulung des Ausdrucksvermögens von besonderer Bedeutung. Daher enthält der Abschnitt *Language Practice* acht Seiten zum Thema *Style Matters*, deren Ziel die Verbesserung der stilistischen Kompetenz der Schülerinnen und Schüler ist. Dabei wird sowohl auf der Wortebene (z. B. *LP 21: Finding alternatives to over-used words*) und im syntaktischen Bereich (z. B. *LP 25: Expressing yourself concisely*) als auch satzübergreifend (z. B. *LP 26: Connecting your thoughts: linking words*) gearbeitet. Auch zum Thema *Using the appropriate register* (s. LP 22) finden sich Erklärungen und Übungen.
- *Everyday English:* Alltagsenglisch ist für die Kommunikation der Schülerinnen und Schüler bei Auslandsaufenthalten während und nach der Schulzeit unverzichtbar: Themen wie „Telephoning for accomodation" oder „Eating out" werden den Schülerinnen und Schülern durch eine Fülle von Hörbeispielen und anschließende Rollenspiele, die die aktive Beteiligung fordern, nahe gebracht. Wichtig ist dabei auch die zusätzliche soziokulturelle Information in den *Fact Files* und die sprachliche Unterstützung durch die in *Context 21* durchgängig verwendete *Language help*.

Die Lösungen der Aufgaben in der *Language Practice* stehen den Schülerinnen und Schülern auf der Schülerbuch-DVD-ROM zur Verfügung.

Skills File — Im *Skills File* werden die für *Context 21* prägenden kommunikativen und methodischen Kompetenzen in den Bereichen *Study and Language Skills, Listening and Viewing Skills, Speaking Skills, Reading Skills, Writing Skills* und *Mediating Skills* zusammengefasst und auf Englisch erläutert. Dabei wird auf das in der Sekundarstufe I Gelernte zurückgegriffen. Gleichzeitig werden neue oberstufenspezifische Teilkompetenzen, (z. B. *SF 13: Quoting*; *SF 25: Debating*; *SF 45: Writing a comment*) vermittelt. In den Abschnitten *SF 31: Reading poetry*; *SF 32: Reading/Watching drama*; *SF 33: Reading narrative prose* werden die für die Arbeit mit literarischen Texten notwendigen Kompetenzen vermittelt.

Auf alle *Skills*-Abschnitte wird aus den einzelnen Kapiteln heraus verwiesen. Querverweise innerhalb des *Skills File* stellen neue Zusammenhänge her.

Besonders hervorzuheben ist, dass den Erklärungen der Kompetenzen in vielen Fällen Übungen (unter der Bezeichnung „Practice") folgen, die den Schülerinnen und Schülern Sicherheit in der Anwendung der skills vermitteln. Zusätzliche Übungen finden sich im Language, Skills and Exam Trainer unter Skills Training, sodass die Schülerinnen und Schüler nicht nur im sprachlichen Bereich, sondern auch bei den skills eine optimale Übungsfrequenz erreichen können.

Exam Practice Eine der zentralen Innovationen im Lehrwerksverbund ist die intensive Vorbereitung auf Prüfungen bzw. Prüfungsformen und damit auch auf das Abitur. Der Abschnitt *Exam Practice* ist ins Schülerbuch integriert. Er bietet bundeslandunabhängige Hilfen und Übungen, wobei nicht nur auf typische Probleme beim Schreiben von Klausuren (einschließlich Sprachmittlung und Übersetzung), sondern auch auf neuere Formen der „Kommunikationsprüfung" und auf die in manchen Bundesländern eingeführten standardisierten Testformate eingegangen wird.

Darüber hinaus bereitet auch der regionalisierte *Language, Skills and Exam Trainer* intensiv auf die Prüfung vor. Dies geschieht durch die schrittweise Erläuterung und Einübung der für das betreffende Bundesland repräsentativen Abitur-Prüfungsformate sowie durch ein auf der *Context 21*-Website angebotenes *mock exam* (mit Musterlösung) zum Download.

Glossary Das *Glossary* umfasst ca. 100 Termini aus allen Bereichen der Textarbeit in alphabetischer Anordnung. Sie werden in knapper Form auf Englisch erklärt und veranschaulicht.

Operatoren *Language for Tasks*, eine Aufstellung der in den Kapiteln benutzten Arbeitsanweisungen (Operatoren), ist entsprechend den weithin gültigen Anforderungsbereichen der Oberstufe (*comprehension, analysis* und *comment/composition/evaluation, etc.*) untergliedert. Erklärt werden die Operatoren anhand von Definitionen, die sich nach den Vorgaben der verschiedenen Bundesländer richten, sowie anhand eines Anwendungsbeispiels.

Diese Doppelseite enthält damit auch die Aufgabenformulierungen, wie sie den Klausuren der Oberstufe bis hin zum Abitur zugrunde liegen. Im Sinne des autonomen Lernens können sich die Schülerinnen und Schüler dadurch selbstständig und gezielt auf Leistungsüberprüfungen vorbereiten.

Audio-CDs

Die *Audio-CDs* umfassen alle Hörtexte, u.a. Podcasts, Interviews, Reden und Musterdialoge; die Aufgaben für ihre Bearbeitung finden sich im SB.

Video-DVD

Die *Video-DVD* enthält alle Videoclips und relevanten Filmsequenzen zur Schulung des Hör-/Sehverstehens; die Aufgaben für ihre Bearbeitung finden sich im SB.

Language, Skills and Exam Trainer

Der *Language, Skills and Exam Trainer* (LSET) enthält sowohl zu jedem SB-Kapitel passgenaue Übungen zu Grammatik und Wortschatz als auch drei umfangreiche Teile kapitelübergreifender Übungen zum sprachlichen Ausdrucksvermögen (*Focus on Style*), zur gezielten Einübung, Anwendung und Wiederholung abiturrelevanter Fertigkeiten (*Skills Training*) und zur systematischen Prüfungsvorbereitung (*Exam Training*). Querverweise zwischen den Abschnitten des LSET sowie ein ausführliches Register (*Exercise Finder*) ermöglichen das leichte Auffinden auch einzelner Übungen.

Vorwort zum Teacher's Manual

Die dem LSET beigefügte CD-Extra unterstützt das individuelle Lernen und Üben, indem sie alle Hörtexte der Übungen sowie *Vocab Sheets* (ausfüllbare Arbeitsblätter zum SB-Lernwortschatz einschließlich Kontrollbogen mit Lösungsvorschlägen) zur Verfügung stellt.

Der LSET ist in zwei Ausgaben erhältlich:
- mit CD-Extra ohne Lösungen;
- *with Answer Key:* mit CD-Extra inkl. Lösungen und Lösungsvorschlägen sowie Transkripten der Hörtexte zur Selbstkontrolle.

Website

Webcode: Unter www.context21.de finden sich
- Synopsen der Lehrpläne bzw. Curricula aller Bundesländer;
- die Inhalte der Webcodes zu allen Kapiteln mit weiterführenden aktuellen Materialien und ergänzenden Aufgaben zu den themenbezogenen Links;
- die Lernwortschatzlisten zu den SB-Texten *(Active Vocabulary)*.

Die im Schülerbuch abgedruckten Codes ersparen die Eingabe langer Internetadressen und führen direkt zu den Inhalten.

Interaktive Präsentationen für Whiteboard und Beamer

Mit den interaktiv, multimedial aufbereiteten Präsentationen der Lead-ins stehen L sofort einsetzbare Stundeneinheiten für Whiteboard und Beamer zur Verfügung.

Teacher's Manual mit Vorschlägen zur Leistungsmessung

Das Teacher's Manual bietet abwechslungsreiche Unterrichtsvorschläge, Lösungshinweise zu den Aufgaben bzw. Übungen aller Kapitel sowie umfassende Hintergrundinformationen zu den Inhalten des Schülerbuchs. Übersichten ermöglichen das schnelle Auffinden der Informationen (z.B. Topics, text forms, skills, authors and levels). Das Teacher's Manual enthält

TM-Kapitel Jedes Kapitel des *Teacher's Manual* enthält folgende Elemente:
- ein didaktisches Inhaltsverzeichnis;
- Übersichten mit Informationen zu Quelle, Thema, Textart, Sprachvarietät (z.B. *Irish English*), Länge und Schwierigkeitsgrad *(basic/intermediate/advanced)* eines jeden Textes;
- didaktische Kommentare zu jedem Kapitelteil;
- Lernwortschatz: Zu jedem Text werden ausgewählte Wörter oder Kollokationen angegeben, die die Schülerinnen und Schüler in ihren produktiven Wortschatz integrieren sollen;
- Unterrichtstipps: Hier finden sich u.a. methodische oder praktische Hinweise (z.B. Linktipps) für Zusatzaufgaben wie z.B. Projektarbeit;
- Vorschläge zur Differenzierung mit Arbeitsaufträgen für Leistungsstärkere und -schwächere sowie Zusatzaufgaben für bestimmte Interessen (Kunst, Politik usw.);
- Info bietet englischsprachige Hintergrundinformationen z.B. zu Themen, Autoren oder Begriffen der behandelten Texte;
- Lösungshinweise werden zu allen geschlossenen oder halboffenen Aufgaben gegeben. Sie stellen keinen in jeder Unterrichtssituation zu erreichenden Erwartungshorizont dar, sondern lediglich einen Rahmen für mögliche Schülerformulierungen;

▶ **LSET ex. 1**
- Verweise auf den *Language, Skills and Exam Trainer*.

Kopiervorlagen
- Kopiervorlagen (KV) mit Zusatzaufgaben zur Ergänzung, zur Differenzierung oder zur Vertiefung der SB-Aufgaben;

Topic Vocabulary
- *Topic Vocabulary*-Listen mit dem kapitelrelevantem allgemeinem Themenwortschatz, der jedoch nicht notwendigerweise aus den SB-Texten stammt;

Group Activities
- eine Übersicht über alle in den Kapiteln empfohlenen kooperativen (und anderen) Lernformen;

Vorwort zum Teacher's Manual

DVD-ROM
- eine DVD-ROM mit folgenden Inhalten:
  1. das gesamte *Teacher's Manual* (alle Kapitel, Kopiervorlagen, *Topic Vocabulary* und Übersichten) als PDFs und editierbare Word-Dateien, sodass sie individuell bearbeitet werden können,
  2. *Vocab Sheets* mit dem Lernwortschatz aller SB-Texte (mit Lücken zum Ausfüllen durch die Schülerinnen und Schüler bzw. mit Lösungsvorschlägen),
  3. *Transkripte* aller auf der Audio-CD bzw. Video-DVD befindlichen Hör- und Hör-/Sehtexte inkl. des Bonusmaterials,

Leistungsmessung
  4. sowie *Vorschläge zur Leistungsmessung*.

Die **Vorschläge zur Leistungsmessung** bieten die Möglichkeit, die in *Context 21* vermittelten und trainierten Kompetenzen zu überprüfen. In diesem Aufgabenpaket finden Sie für die Bereiche *reading*, *writing*, *mediating*, *translating*, *listening* und *speaking* Aufgaben, die den Anforderungen entsprechend zusammengestellt werden können. Jedes Aufgabenpaket enthält:
- einen Ausgangstext sowie eine alternative bzw. längere Textversion am Ende des Materials (sofern der Ausgangstext nicht vollständig war),
- mindestens zwei Aufgaben zum Anforderungsbereich I *(comprehension)*,
- zwei Aufgaben zum Anforderungsbereich II *(analysis)*,
- eine „komplexe Aufgabe", in der AFB I und AFB II zusammengefasst sind,
- mindestens drei Aufgaben zum Anforderungsbereich III *(comment/composition/evaluation, etc.)*,
- eine Sprachmittlungsaufgabe *(mediating)*,
- eine Aufgabe zum dialogischen Sprechen,
- Lösungsvorschläge.

Darüber hinaus wird in den meisten Kapiteln eine Aufgabe zum monologischen Sprechen vorgeschlagen.

In den Kapiteln „National Identity and Diversity", „The World of Work and Business" und „Germany in the World" finden Sie Aufgaben zum *listening* sowie jeweils eine weitere zu *mediating* ebenso wie die Transkripte dazu.

Translating aus dem Englischen ins Deutsche ist Bestandteil der Kapitel „National Identity and Diversity", „The UK – Tradition and Change", „India – Past und Present" und „Shakespeare".

Audio-CD
- eine Audio-CD mit allen Hörtexten der *Vorschläge zur Leistungsmessung*.

Symbole

Symbol	Bedeutung
⚠	Dinge, die bei der Organisation des Unterrichts rechtzeitig bedacht werden müssen, oder wichtige Hinweise bzw. Warnhinweise
*column	Wörter mit *Asterisk sind im Glossar erläutert
👥	Partnerarbeit
👥👥	Gruppenarbeit
HA	Hausaufgabe
ZA	Zusatzaufgabe
ALT	Alternative
CD 1.02	Angebot auf der Audio-CD
DVD	Angebot auf der Video-DVD
SB-DVD-ROM	Angebot auf der SB-DVD-ROM
TM-DVD-ROM	Angebot auf der TM-DVD-ROM
Word help	Verweis auf die *Word help* auf der SB-DVD-ROM
Linktipp	Hinweis auf relevante Internetseiten

Abkürzungen

adj	*adjective*	SB	Schülerbuch
n	*noun*	KV	Kopiervorlage
pl	*plural*	LP	*Language Practice*
v	*verb*	SF	*Skills File*
S	Schüler/Schülerinnen	TM	*Teacher's Manual*
L	Lehrkraft		

Vorwort zum Teacher's Manual

**Die „Scheiben"
im Überblick**

SB-DVD-ROM

	Materialien für die Arbeit mit dem Schüler-buch	zusätzliche Materialien
Print-Materialien	Lösungen zu *Language Practice, Skills File, Exam Practice*	
	Transkripte der Hörtexte in *Communicating across Cultures, Language Practice, Skills File* und *Exam Practice*	
	Kopiervorlagen für SB-Aufgaben	
	Active Vocabulary	
	Word help für Audios und Videos	
Audios und Videos	Hörtexte zu *Communicating across Cultures, Language Practice, Skills File* und *Exam Practice*	Hör- und Hör-Sehtexte inkl. Aufgaben, Transkripten und Lösungen
Software		*At the Cutting Edge: Inter-active Introduction to Film Analysis*

Audio-CD

Enthält alle für die Aufgaben im Schülerbuch erforderlichen Hörtexte.

Video-DVD

Enthält alle für die Aufgaben im Schülerbuch erforderlichen audiovisuellen Texte.

LSET-CD-Extra

Enthält:
- *Vocab Sheets* mit Lücken (die Ausgabe *LSET with Answer Key* enthält zusätzlich Lösungsvorschläge)
- Hörtexte zum LSET (die Ausgabe *LSET with Answer Key* enthält zusätzlich die Transkripte dazu)

TM-DVD-ROM

Enthält:
- Vorschläge zur Leistungsmessung inkl. Lösungen
- alle TM-Kapitel
- Kopiervorlagen
- Transkripte aller Hör-/Sehtexte
- *Topic Vocabulary*
- *Vocab Sheets* mit Lücken und Musterlösungen

**Die Wortschatzlisten
im Überblick**

Titel	Inhalt	Wo enthalten
Active Vocabulary	Lernwortschatz aus allen authentischen Texten der Kapitel	SB-DVD-ROM; Website
Vocab Sheets mit Lücken	= *Active Vocabulary*-Listen mit Konzentration auf *memory help* in der mittleren Spalte und von den Schülerinnen und Schülern zu füllen-den Lücken an unterschiedlichen Stellen, sodass sie als Arbeitsblatt zum Üben verwen-det werden können	LSET-CD-Extra; TM-DVD-ROM
Vocab Sheets mit Muster-lösungen	*Vocab Sheets* mit ausgefüllten Lücken zur Selbstkontrolle	LSET-CD-Extra der Ausgabe „*with Answer Key*"; TM-DVD-ROM
Topic Vocabulary	kapitelrelevanter allgemeiner Themenwort-schatz, der nicht ausschließlich aus den Texten der Kapitel stammt	Print-TM; TM-DVD-ROM
Word help	zu Audios und Videos: Erläuterungen unbekann-ter Begriffe aus den Hör- und Hör-/Sehtexten	SB-DVD-ROM

Topics, text forms, skills, authors and levels

Kapitelkürzel:
- GP = Global Perspectives
- IN = India – Past and Present
- IS = The Individual in Society
- ME = The Media
- NI = National Identity and Diversity
- SC = Science, Technology and the Environment
- SH = Shakespeare
- UK = The UK – Tradition and Change
- US = The USA – Dreams and Struggles
- WB = The World of Work and Business
- WE = The World of English

Abkürzungen:
- CaC = Communicating across Cultures
- L-i = Lead-in
- WiC = Words in Context

TOPICS

Adolescence/Youth	**NI** C1; **SC** B2; **US** A1, C3; **WB** B1, B2, B3, B4, B5
Arts and culture	**IS** C2; **NI** B2; **SH** L-i, WiC; **UK** L-i, B1, C1, C2
Australia	**ME** C2; **NI** A1, C1, C4; **WB** CaC; **WE** CaC
Canada	**NI** A1
'Celtic fringe'	**UK** B4, C3, C4
Conflict	**GP** B3, C1; **IS** A3; **SC** B3; **SH** B2, B3
Democratic values	**NI** C4; **UK** B3, B4; **US** Part B, Part C
English as a lingua franca	**WE** L-i, WiC, CaC, C1, C2, C3
Environmental issues	**SC** WiC, B3, C1, C2, C3
Values/Ethics	**GP** A1, A2, A3; **IS** A2, B1; **NI** C3, C4; **SC** B1, B2, B3; **US** D1, D2; **WB** A3, A5
Europe	**GP** C1; **UK** B7
Germany's relationship with the UK/USA	**IS** B2; **NI** A3; **US** CaC
Gender issues	**IN** B3; **IS** B3
Globalization	SB Chapter **Global Perspectives**; **SC** WiC, C1, C2, C3; **WB** A2, B1
India	SB Chapter **India – Past and Present**; **GP** C1; **NI** C2
Intercultural encounters	**IN** CaC; **IS** B2; **NI** CaC, C1, C2, C4; **SH** CaC; **UK** CaC; **US** CaC; **WB** CaC; **WE** B1, CaC
Ireland / Northern Ireland	**UK** B4, C3
Life after school	**WB** B1, B2, B3, B4, B5
Lifestyles (alternative)	**IS** C2
Media/Communication	SB Chapter **The Media**; **SC** A1
Multiculturalism/Diversity	**NI** L-i, WiC, B2, B3, C1, C2, C3, C4; **UK** A3
Personal relations	**NI** C1; **SC** A1, B2; **SH** B1, B3; **US** D3
Politics	**GP** C2, CaC; **NI** A1, C3; **UK** B1, B2, B3, B4, B5, B6, B7; **US** L-i, A3, B2, C1, C2, C4, C5, D1
Regions	SB Chapter **Regions of the UK and the USA**; **UK** WiC, B4, C3, C4; **US** D3
Religion	**UK** B2; **US** Part B
Scotland	**UK** B4, C4
Shakespeare	SB Chapter **Shakespeare**; **UK** B7

Topics, text forms, skills, authors and levels

TOPICS	Stereotypes	**NI** A2, A3
	Society	SB Chapter **The Individual in Society**; **BY** B1; **IN** Part B; **ME** D1; **NI** B3, C3, C4; **SC** A1; **SH** B2; **UK** Part B; **US** A3, B1, C2, C3, C4, C5, D3; **WB** A5
	UK	SB Chapter **The UK – Tradition and Change**; **NI** A1, A2, B1, B2; **RU** L-i, WiC, A1, A2, A3
	USA	SB Chapter **The USA – Dreams and Struggles**; **GW** B1, B2; **NI** WiC, A1, A3, B1, B3, C3, C4; **RU** B1; **UK** B5, B6; **UL** A2, B2, C1, C2; **WB** B3
	Utopia/Dystopia	**IS** A3, C1, C2; **SC** L-I, A2, B1, B2, B3, C2; **US** C3; **WB** A3
	Work, business and the economy	SB Chapter **The World of Work and Business**; **IS** B3; **GP** A1, A2, A3, B1, B2, B3
TEXT FORMS	Adverts	**ME** C1; **UK** B3; **US** C5; **WB** B3
	Fictional texts (extracts)	**GP** B2; **IN** B1, B2, C1, C2; **IS** A3, C2; **NI** C1; **SH** B1, B2, B3; **UK** A3, B3; **US** A1, C3; **WB** A1; **WE** B1, C2
	Music/Songs	**IS** C2; **UK** C2, C3; **US** L-i, A2
	Newspaper and magazine articles (extracts)	**GP** B1; **IN** B3; **IS** A2, B2, B3; **ME** A1, D1; **NI** C2, C4; **SC** A1, C3; **UK** A1, B1, B5; **WB** A2, A3, A5; **WE** C1, C3
	Non-fictional texts (extracts)	**GP** A2, B3, C3; **IN** A1; **ME** D2; **NI** A3, B3, C3; **SC** A2, B3, C2; **SH** C3; **BY** D2; **UK** A2, B2, B4, C4; **US** B1, D2, D3, D4, D5; **WB** B2
	Poems	**GP** L-i, B2; **ME** B3; **NI** B2; **SH** C3; **UK** A3, B7
	Speeches	**GP** C2; **NI** C3
	Statistics/Figures	**GP** A1; **IN** A3; **ME** A1; **NI** B3; **SC** C2, C3; **UK** B7; **UL** WiC; **US** B2, B3; **WB** A2
	Cartoons	**NI** A2, C4; **SC** L-i; **SH** C2; **UK** B7; **US** B1; **WB** A3, A4
	Paintings/Drawings	**NI** B2; **UK** L-i, C1; **US** C4
	Photos	**GP** L-i, B2, B3, C1; **IN** L-i; **IS** A1; **ME** L-i, C1; **NI** L-i; **SC** C1; **SH** L-i; **UK** C4; **US** L-i, D1; **WB** B1; **WE** C2
	Posters	**IS** L-i; **GP** C1; **US** C5; **WB** L-i
Video material		**GP** A3; **IN** CaC, C3, C4; **IS** L-i, C2; **ME** B1, B2, C2; **NI** L-i; **SC** B1, C1; **SH** A1, C1; **UK** B6, C4; **US** A3, C2; **WB** B5, CaC; **WE** B2, CaC
Listening material	Listening only texts	**GP** C2, CaC; **IN** L-i, B4, CaC; **IS** B3, CaC; **ME** A2; **NI** CaC, B1, C4; **SC** A2, B2; **SH** B1, B2, B3; **UK** A4; **UL** A2; **US** A2, CaC, D3; **WB** L-i; **WE** WiC, CaC
	Listening texts in SB *and* on CD	**SH** B1, B2, B3; **US** A2

Topics, text forms, skills, authors and levels

SKILLS AND ACTIVITIES	Analysing poetry	**GP** L-i, B2; **ME** B3; **NI** B2; **SH** C3; **UK** A3, B7
	Creative writing	**GP** B2; **IN** B1, B2; **ME** B3; **SH** C3; **UK** L-i; **US** A1, D1; **WB** A1, A5, C3; **WE** B1
	Discussing/Debating issues	**GP** A2, B3, CaC; **IN** B3; **IS** A1, A2, B2; **NI** A2, C4; **SC** B2, B3; **UK** A3, B6, B7; **US** C1, C2, D1, D5; **WE** L-i
	Doing presentations	**IS** L-i; **SH** A2, B1, B2, B3; **UK** L-i, B4; **US** A3, B1; **WE** B2
	Doing project work	**ME** L-i, B1; **SC** A2F; **UK** B4
	Doing research	**GP** A2, C3; **IN** A1, B2, B3; **IS** B1, C1; **ME** A2; **NI** A1; **SH** A2; **UK** A2, C1; **US** B3, D4; **WB** A3; **WE** B2
	Identifying register	**IS** B3; **NI** WiC, A1, CaC, B3; **UK** CaC
	Information gap exercises	**GP** WiC, B3; **IN** B3; **IS** WiC; **NI** WiC; **SC** WiC; **SH** WiC; **US** WiC, B1; **WB** WiC, B4
	Listening comprehension	**GP** C2; **IN** B4; **ME** A2; **NI** B1; **SC** A2; **UK** C3; **WB** L-i;
	Mediating	**GP** CaC; **IN** CaC; **IS** B2; **ME** CaC; **NI** CaC; **SC** C3; **SH** C3; **UK** CaC, A4, B7; **US** B3, C2; **WE** C3
	Rewriting a text	**GP** A2; **IN** A2; **IS** B2; **US** C3
	Role-plays	**GP** CaC; **ME** D1; **US** CaC; **WB** L-i, B5, C1, CaC
	Viewing comprehension	**GP** A3; **IN** C3, C4; **IS** C2; **ME** B1, B2, C2; **SC** B1; **SH** C1; **UK** B6; **US** C2; **WE** B2, CaC
	Working with pictures (charts, posters, photos, cartoons, etc.)	**GP** L-i, A1, B1, B2, B3, C1; **IN** L-i, B4; **IS** L-i, A1; **ME** L-i, A1, C1; **NI** L-i, A2, B2, C4; **SC** L-i, B1, C1; **SH** C2; **UK** B6, C4; **US** B1, B2, B3, C4, C5, D1; **WB** A3, A4, A5, B1; **WE** L-i, C2

Topics, text forms, skills, authors and levels

AUTHORS

Author	Code	Author	Code
Agard, John	**NI** B2	Layard, Richard	**WB** A5
Alkhazindar, Maha M.	**SC** B3	Legon, Peter	**NI** A2; **WE** L-i
Alterman, Eric	**ME** A1	Livia, Benjamin	**US** D5
Asimov, Isaac	**SC** A2	Lorenz, Kate	**WB** B2
Beaton, Alistair	**UK** B3	McAllister, J.F.O	**UK** B1
Beaufoy, Simon	**IN** C2	McCall Smith, Alexander	**WB** A1
Bingham, Harry	**UK** A1	McCarthy, Cormac	**IS** A3
Breazeal, Cynthia	**SC** A2	McGuire, Stryker	**UK** B5
Bryson, Bill	**US** D3	McKissack, Patricia C.	**US** A1
Clarke, Stephen	**WE** C2	Meeropol, Abel	**US** A2
Conlin, Michelle	**IS** B3	Merriman, Helena	**WB** A2
Danaher, Kevin	**GP** B3	Miliband, David	**GP** C2
Dickey, Christopher	**US** D2	Mistry, Rohinton	**IN** B1
Doctorow, Cory	**US** C3	Parry, Hazel	**ME** D1
Erard, Michael	**WE** C1	Picoult, Jodi	**SC** B2
Eriksen, Thomas Hylland	**GP** B2	Reynolds, Paul	**GP** C3
Faul, Stepahnie	**NI** B3	Rhodes, Bill	**SC** B3
Ford, Martyn	**NI** A2; **WE** L-i	Schiller, Nancy	**SC** B3
Fox, Kate	**UK** B2	Sengupta, Somini	**IN** B3
Friedman, Thomas L.	**GP** B1; **SC** A1; **WB** A3	Shakespeare, William	**SH**; **UK** B7
Fry, Stephen	**US** D4	Sidner, Sara	**IN** A2
Fuhr, Eckhard	**WE** C3	Swarup, Vikas	**IN** C1
Georgiou, Peter	**NI** C4	Tickell, Oliver	**SC** C3
Hasnain, Kazim	**IS** B3	Timmerman, Kelsey	**GP** A2
Huggler, Justin	**IN** B2	Thoman, Elizabeth	**ME** D2
Jacoby, Susan	**US** B1	Wardle, Tim	**UK** A1
Jaffrey, Madhur	**IN** A1	Watterson, Bill	**WB** A4
Kluger, Jeffrey	**IS** A2	Wheatley, Nadia	**NI** C1
Krakauer, Jon	**IS** C2	Zarate, Oscar	**SH** C2
Lahiri, Jhumpa	**NI** C2		

Topics, text forms, skills, authors and levels

Levels of listening, reading and viewing materials

Chapter Part (Media)	Level	Chapter Part (Media)	Level	Chapter Part (Media)	Level
GP A2	Intermediate	ME D2	Advanced	UK B4	Basic
GP A3	Advanced	NI A1	Intermediate	UK B5	Intermediate
GP B1	Advanced	NI A3	Intermediate	UK B6 (DVD)	Intermediate
GP B2	Intermediate	NI B1	Advanced	UK B7	Intermediate
GP B3	Intermediate	NI B2	Advanced	UK C3 (CD)	Intermediate
GP C2	Advanced	NI C1	Intermediate	US A1	Intermediate
GP C3	Advanced	NI C2	Advanced	US A2	Advanced
IN A1	Basic	NI C3	Intermediate	US A3	Advanced
IN A2	Basic	NI C4	Advanced	US B1	Intermediate
IN B1	Intermediate	NI C4 (CD)	Advanced	US C1	Advanced
IN B2	Intermediate	SC A1	Intermediate	US C2	Intermediate
IN B3	Intermediate	SC A2 i	Intermediate	US C3	Advanced
IN B4 (CD 2.21)	Intermediate	SC A2 ii	Intermediate	US D2	Advanced
IN CaC (CD 2.22)	Basic	SC B1	Basic	US D3	Intermediate
		SC B2	Basic	US D4	Intermediate
IN CaC (DVD)	Intermediate	SC B2 (CD)	Intermediate	US D5	Intermediate
IN C1	Intermediate	SC B3	Intermediate	WB Lead-in (CD 3.04)	Intermediate
IN C2	Intermediate	SC C1 (DVD)	Basic		
IN C3 (DVD)	Intermediate	SC C2	Intermediate	WB A2	Advanced
IN C4 (DVD)	Advanced	SC C3	Advanced	WB A3	Intermediate
IS A2	Advanced	SH A1 (DVD)	Intermediate	WB A4	Intermediate
IS A3	Intermediate	SH B1	Intermediate	WB A5	Intermediate
IS B1	Intermediate	SH B2	Advanced	WB B2	Basic
IS B2 i	Basic	SH B3	Advanced	WB B5 (DVD)	Intermediate
IS B3 i	Advanced	SH C1/1 (DVD)	Advanced	WB CaC (DVD)	Basic
IS B3 ii (CD)	Intermediate	SH C1/2 (DVD)	Intermediate	WE Lead-in/1	Basic
IS C2 I (CD)	Intermediate			WE Lead-in/2	Basic
IS C2 ii	Intermediate	SH C2	Intermediate	WE WiC (CD 2.07-10)	Basic
IS C2 iii (DVD)	Basic	SH C3/1	Intermediate		
ME A1	Advanced	UK A1	Basic	WE B1 i	Intermediate
ME A2 (CD)	Advanced	UK A2	Advanced	WE B1 ii	Intermediate
ME B1 (DVD)	Intermediate	UK A3i	Basic	WE B2 (DVD)	Basic
ME B2 (DVD)	Intermediate	UK A3ii	Basic	WE CaC (DVD)	Basic
ME B3	Basic	UK A4 (CD)	Advanced		
ME C2/1 (DVD)	Basic	UK B1	Intermediate	WE C1	Advanced
ME C2/3 (DVD)	Advanced	UK B2	Advanced	WE C2	Intermediate
ME D1	Intermediate	UK B3	Intermediate		

Total: 21 basic, 54 intermediate, 30 advanced texts

1 The UK – Tradition and Change

Dieses Kapitel vermittelt S differenzierte Einsichten in vielfältige Aspekte des Vereinigten Königreichs, das einerseits für die Pflege althergebrachter Traditionen bekannt, andererseits in vielen Bereichen Vorreiter geworden ist. S erwerben landeskundliche Kenntnisse und erweitern ihre interkulturelle, fachmethodische und kommunikative Kompetenz.

Part A – On Being British unternimmt den Versuch, das typisch Britische und die vielfältigen Elemente der britischen Identität herauszuarbeiten.

Part B – Who's in Charge? beleuchtet die politischen Institutionen und die außenpolitische Rolle des Vereinigten Königreichs.

Part C – British Art and Culture eröffnet den Blick auf das kulturelle Schaffen im *United Kingdom* der Vergangenheit und der Gegenwart.

Didaktisches Inhaltsverzeichnis

SB p.	Title	TM p.	Text Form	Topic	Skills and Activities	Language Practice
8	Lead-in	20	Photo	The UK: tradition-bound or forward-looking?	Working with pictures; giving a presentation; creative writing	
10	Words in Context - A Dynamic Country Steeped in Tradition	21	Informative text; maps	UK facts – historical and up-to-date	Using a dictionary; organizing vocabulary	Nationalities; LP 1: collocations with nouns
	Part A – On Being British					
12	A1 Looking for Mr Average Tim Wardle	23	Newspaper article (extract)	The average British person	Reading non-fiction; summarizing; writing a formal letter	Words to describe people; LP 18: Using gerunds and to-infinitives
14	A2 A Humble People Harry Bingham	25	Non-fictional text (extract)	British identity	Reading non-fiction; writing an essay; doing research	Adjectives to describe people and things
	A3 Benjamin Zephaniah on Britain					
16	i) We are the British	26	Non-fictional text (extract)	British ethnic origins	Reading non-fiction; cooperative learning strategy (group puzzle)	
16	ii) Rice and Peas	26	Poem (extract)	Multicultural influences on British food	Reading poetry	
17	A4 Britishness CD 1.14–15	28	Radio report	British national identity	Working with pictures; listening comprehension	
18	Communicating across Cultures CD 1.16	29	Conversations	What do they really mean?	Matching exercise; mediation	LP 22: Using the appropriate register
	Part B – Who's in Charge?					
19	B1 The Queen J.F.O. McAllister	29	Magazine article (extract)	The Queen's functions and duties	Reading non-fiction; analysing style; working with pictures; using a dictionary	Adjectives
20	B2 EXTRA The Church Kate Fox	31	Non-fictional text (extract)	The English attitude towards religion	Summarizing; analysing stylistic devices	
23	B3 The Political Parties Alistair Beaton	33	Drama (extract)	Idealism and realism in politics	Reading drama; devising an ad	
24	B4 EXTRA The National Assemblies	34	Non-fictional text (extract)	The devolution of powers in the UK	Doing research; doing a project; giving a presentation	
25	B5 The USA I Sryker McGuire	36	Magazine article (extract)	The changing relationship between the UK and the USA	Determining the text type; analysing a metaphor; writing an essay	LP 27: Connecting your thoughts
26	B6 The USA II DVD	37	Feature film (extract)	The special relationship between the UK and the USA	Viewing skills; using a dictionary; taking part in a discussion	

19

1 Lead-in

	B7 The European Union					
27	i) Headlines on Britain and the EU	38	Newspaper headlines	The changing British attitude towards the EU	Taking part in a discussion; conducting a poll; giving a presentation	
27	ii) This Sceptr'd Isle William Shakespeare	38	Drama (extract)	The UK as an island nation	Reading drama	
27	iii) International Attitudes to Europe	38	Bar chart	Global attitudes towards the EU	Working with charts	
28	iv) Vision Problems	38	Cartoon	The UK's self-centredness	Working with cartoons	
	Part C – British Art and Culture					
29	C1 Sea Pictures in Oil: Turner	40	Painting	Britain's island status reflected in 19th century art	Working with pictures; doing research	
29	C2 Sea Pictures in Music: Britten CD 1.17–19	41	Opera: interludes (extracts)	Britain's island status reflected in 20th century music	Listening to classical music; describing a sculpture	
30	C3 Popular Culture: Songs Snow Patrol CD 1.20	42	Song	Belfast as a mirror of the Troubles	Listening to popular music; summarizing	
30	C4 Scottish Festivals DVD	43	Advertisements (text; trailers)	The Edinburgh Festival Fringe	Reading non-fiction; viewing a film	

SB S. 8 ## Lead-in

Didaktischer Kommentar
Auf der Basis des Kapiteltitels und eines Fotos schärfen S ihr Bewusstsein für die z.T. widersprüchliche Situation in Großbritannien zwischen Tradition und Erneuerung. Sie reaktivieren dabei ihr Vorwissen über das *United Kingdom* in überwiegend kooperativen Lernformen.

Unterrichtstipps
⚠️ **HA**

4 **EXTRA** S machen sich vorab zuhause oder zu zweit während der Stunde Notizen für mögliche Dialoge.

Differenzierung

2 Durch gezielte Zusammensetzung leistungsheterogener Arbeitsgruppen ist gegenseitige sprachliche Unterstützung möglich. L weist darauf hin, dass jeder in der Lage sein sollte, die Ergebnisse zu präsentieren.

ZA **1** Um die Bildbetrachtung zu vertiefen, vergleichen kunstinteressierte S Gainsboroughs „Mr and Mrs Andrews" mit Hockneys „Mr and Mrs Clark and Percy" (s. *SF 9: Working with pictures*) und bearbeiten dazu die Aufgaben des SF 9. Lösungshinweise: *Individual answers* bzw. s. Info.

> **Info**
>
> *Thomas Gainsborough* (1727–1788) was one of the most important English painters of his time. Roughly half of the more than 500 paintings he made are portraits, often of the aristocracy. 'Mr and Mrs Andrews' (1750) shows the newly-weds Robert Andrews and Frances Carter, members of the landed gentry. The extensive landscape around them can either be seen as a symbol of their wealth and influence (their posture and facial expressions underline this) or as a signal for Gainsborough's dislike of portraiture: the landscape takes up a good half of the painting. The oak in front of which they are posing stands for continuity. One interpretation of the painting sees it as a satire, setting the artificiality of the couple's posture off from the English landscape. What Mrs Andrews was to hold in her lap is unknown; this part of the painting remained unfinished.

Words in Context

> *David Hockney* (born 1937) is an English pop artist living in the USA and one of the most influential British artists. 'Mr and Mrs Clark and Percy' (1970/71) shows the newly-wed fashion designer Ossie Clark, a friend of Hockney's, and his wife Celia Birtwell, a fabric designer. The cat Percy sitting on Clark's crotch is a sign of Clark's infidelity, his sensuality underlined by his foot digging into the soft carpet. Compared to his wife's composed attitude, Clark's posture (laid back, looking disinterested) makes his wife appear the dominant partner. The white lilies, a symbol of purity, are a counterpart to the white cat on his lap.

Lösungshinweise

1a The photo shows two young people in an art gallery looking at an oil painting of a couple in the English countryside (hay, sheep, hills and woods). The lady is sitting on a garden bench, wearing a probably expensive dress and a hat. Standing beside her with his gun and his dog is a man (probably her husband) in hunting clothes. Perhaps the land in the background is owned by them.

1b The contrast between the two couples – their clothes, the time they live in, the way the couple in the painting is posing while the couple looking at the painting is not – shows that the former represent tradition and the latter change.

2–4 Individual answers.

SB S. 10
▶ LSET ex. 1, 2

Words in Context –
A Dynamic Country Steeped in Tradition

Didaktischer Kommentar

S schulen ihr Textverstehen und verbessern ihre Fähigkeit, Dinge zu paraphrasieren. Sie setzen sich mit den Bezeichnungen für Nationalitäten auseinander, wodurch ihr Wortschatz erweitert wird. Durch das Verfassen von mehreren Sätzen, in denen sie die genannten *collocations* verwenden, schulen sie ihre Schreibkompetenz.

SB-DVD-ROM

Lernwortschatz

national region (l. 2), island nation (l. 3), Empire (l. 4), permanent member (l. 7), United Nations Security Council (l. 7), trendsetter (l. 10), time-honoured tradition (l. 12), constitutional monarchy (l. 13), Established Church (l. 13), Church of England (l. 14), monarch (l. 14), Archbishop of Canterbury (l. 14), to reign (l. 16), to rule (l. 16), Government (l. 16), Prime Minister (l. 17), Cabinet (l. 17), Parliament (l. 17), lower house (l. 18), House of Commons (l. 18), upper house (l. 18), House of Lords (l. 19), written constitution (l. 21), devolve legislative power (l. 23), Scottish Parliament (l. 24), national assembly (l. 24), devolution (l. 26), Supreme Court (l. 26), final court of appeals (l. 27), constitutional court (l. 27), constitutional reform (l. 29), school system (l. 32), national curriculum (l. 33), eliminate inequalities (l. 34), political reform (l. 38), classless society (l. 38), social status (l. 39)

Unterrichtstipps

Erläuterung von Zeile 16: *Absolute monarchs reign* and *rule; monarchs in constitutional monarchies merely reign (as the government holds the executive power).*

Differenzierung

3 S umschreiben Kollokationen mit eigenen Worten, die vom Partner oder der Klasse erraten werden.

In arbeitsteiliger Gruppenarbeit sammeln S weitere Informationen zu *Parliament*, *Government* und *Church of England*. Die Präsentation erfolgt in großen Kursen als *jigsaw puzzle* (s. S. 297), in kleineren Kursen als mündliches Referat.

Linktipp: www.parliament.uk/about/how.cfm informiert über das *House of Commons* und das *House of Lords*; www.number10.gov.uk/history-and-tour ist die offizielle Internetseite des Premierministers; www.cofe.anglican.org (die Website der *Church of England*) informiert über alle Aspekte, die mit dem Glauben und der Kirche zusammenhängen.

1 Words in Context – A Dynamic Country Steeped in Tradition

> **Info**
>
> *National Curriculum:* All state schools in England, Wales and Northern Ireland follow the National Curriculum which is divided into four so-called Key Stages. Pupils are tested after each stage: at ages 7, 11 and 14. At 16 they take the General Certificate of Secondary Education (GCSE) in several subjects and at 18 those who have stayed on at school take their A-levels.
>
> *Briton* ['brɪtn]: As there is no singular noun generally used for someone from Britain, an adjective is used instead: 'I'm British.' The noun 'Briton' is used in particular by journalists. 'Brit' (informal) sometimes has a negative connotation.
>
> *Scots (n, adj):* The adjective 'Scottish' is used most often when referring to people or things from Scotland: 'You can hardly tell he's a Scot; his Scots accent is very slight.' 'Scots' is only used to describe the people, law and language of Scotland. 'Scotch' is used in fixed expressions (Scotch whisky) and is considered insulting if used otherwise.

Lösungshinweise

1a 1 national regions; 2 permanent members of the United Nations Security Council; 3 Established Church; 4 Parliament; 5 national assemblies; 6 final court of appeals: Supreme Court; 7 constitutional reform / political reforms; 8 national curriculum; 9 social status

1b
1. somebody who is very fashionable and who others like to copy
2. a way of doing things that has been the same for a very long time
3. the upper house of the British Parliament which is made up of people who acquired their seat through inheritance or merit
4. ministers in charge of different government departments who sit with and advise the Prime Minister
5. past court decisions that are used to help decide new cases
6. a country or community with no differences in social class

2a

Country	People	Person	Language	Adjective
England	the English	Englishman/-woman	English	English
Scotland	the Scots (the Scottish)	Scotsman/-woman	English, Scots, Gaelic (cf. Info)	Scottish, Scots (cf. Info)
Wales	the Welsh	Welshman/-woman	English, Welsh	Welsh
(Northern) Ireland	the Irish	Irishman/-woman	English, Irish, Gaelic	Irish
Great Britain	the British	Briton *(fml)*, Brit *(infml;* cf. Info)	—	British

2b EXTRA Individual answers.

3a 1 national; 2 foreign; 3 run; 4 attend; 5 constitutional; 6 exert

3bc Individual answers.

22

Part A

Part A – On Being British

SB S. 12
▶ LSET ex. 3

A1 Looking for Mr Average — Tim Wardle

Source:	*Daily Mail*, 10 November 2007
	www.dailymail.co.uk/news/article-492872/So-THIS-Britains-Mr-Average.html
Topic:	The average British person
Text form:	Newspaper article (extract)
Language variety:	British English
Number of words:	870
Level:	Basic
Skills/Activities:	Reading non-fiction; summarizing; writing a formal letter

Didaktischer Kommentar

S arbeiten die Kernaussage eines Zeitungsartikels heraus und formulieren sie in eigenen Worten. Sie festigen und erweitern ihren Wortschatz zum Sachgebiet *describing people* und schulen ihre interkulturelle Kompetenz beim Vergleich britischen und deutschen Nationalstolzes.

SB-DVD-ROM

> **Lernwortschatz**
>
> be in debt (l. 2), statistic (l. 4), range from … to … (l. 10), overweight (l. 10), average person (l. 14), to reveal sth. about sb./sth. (l. 17), match many criteria (l. 19), narrow the search (l. 24), specialise in sth. (l. 25), stand out from the rest (l. 47), outskirts (*pl*, l. 49), become apparent (l. 57), virtually (l. 64), recipe (l. 83), contentment (l. 83)

Unterrichtstipps

Einstieg: S beschreiben das Foto zum Text und benennen anschließend, was an dem im Bild Gezeigten durchschnittlich ist.

HA **1c** bietet sich als Hausaufgabe an.

2a S suchen die Gerundien in Partnerarbeit heraus und vergleichen ihre Ergebnisse mit einem anderen Paar.

Differenzierung
ALT

In Lerngruppen, in denen (z. B. wegen der Kürze der Stunden) eine Behandlung des Textes am Stück nicht möglich ist, kann dieser abschnittweise in Gruppen bearbeitet werden:

1. *Read ll. 1–44. Speculate on the 20 questions Tim Wardle formulated to find Mr or Mrs Average and write down at least seven. Then work in groups of five to agree on five questions. Note them down.*
2. *Read ll. 45–65. In your groups, compare whether the criteria Wardle mentions coincide with your speculations.*
3. *Read ll. 66–76 and explain Williamson's philosophy of life. As a group, formulate an aphorism (a short phrase) for this philosophy.*
4. *Read ll. 77–86 and explain Wardle's reaction on Peter as Mr Average.*
5. *Write a comment on ll. 69–72.*

2b In Lesekonferenzen (s. S. 298) wird die beste Beschreibung ermittelt.

3b Der zweite Teil der Aufgabe (Gründe für deutschen Nationalstolz) erfolgt im *think–pair–share*-Verfahren (s. S. 299), bevor im Plenum die häufigsten Gründe für britischen bzw. deutschen Nationalstolz genannt werden.

Part A1 – Looking for Mr Average

ZA HA Im Anschluss verfassen S einen kurzen Text zu der Frage: *Why are you (not) proud to be German?*

> **Info**
>
> *Closed-circuit television (CCTV)* is the use of video cameras to monitor public areas in order to cut down crime. Its widespread use in the UK has sparked a debate about security versus privacy. Its effectiveness in crime prevention is also an issue of debate.

Lösungshinweise

1a *Facts and figures:* The average British male or female drinks three cups of tea a day, believes in God, has a debt of more than £3000, has sex eight times a month, is on CCTV 300 times a day, drives a Ford Fiesta, is overweight, spends one month of his/her life looking for lost socks, says 'sorry' 1.9 million times in his/her life, is married, owns his/her own home, has 1.8 (2) children, knows the words of 'God Save the Queen', goes to the toilet six times a day, considers himself/herself to be working class, is an office worker, has size 10 feet (c. 44 European size), has 14 close friends, is 40 years old

1b Her hobbies were running marathons, skydiving and riding a Harley-Davidson motorcycle – not average hobbies for a 40-year-old woman.

1c The article describes the search for the British Mr Average for a TV documentary. Wardle gathers all the statistics on averageness that he can find and even uses a company specialized in geodemographic profiling to establish that he's most likely to find Mr Average in Essex. But it's not until people begin to hear of Wardle's quest through the newspapers that Michelle Williamson writes to him saying that she thinks her husband answers all Wardle's criteria. And, indeed, Peter Williamson becomes the Mr Average of Wardle's film.

2a collecting (l. 9), running, skydiving, riding (l. 22), profiling (l. 26), having (l. 33), giving up (l. 38)

2b drinks … a day, believes in …, drives a …, is overweight / too thin, Army wife, her/his pastimes include …, fantastic, stands out from the rest, reassuringly average, wearing a …, married father/mother of two, office worker, considers himself/herself working-class; *German Mr/Mrs Average:* Individual answers.

3a EXTRA Individual answers.

3b EXTRA *Williamson might be proud* to be British because he's happy (and thinks that's because of where he lives); because he lives in a monarchy (he knows the words to 'God Save the Queen'); because he has a good office job, a house of his own and a car.

A German might be proud because of Germany's development after 1945, its success at football championships, its achievement in environmental technologies, its democracy, its social achievements.

Part A2 – A Humble People

SB S. 14
▶ LSET ex. 4

A2 A Humble People   Harry Bingham

Source:	*This Little Britain*, 2007
Topic:	British identity
Text form:	Non-fictional text (extract)
Language variety:	British English
Number of words:	404
Level:	Advanced
Skills/Activities:	Analysing style; writing an essay; doing research

Didaktischer Kommentar

Der Text sucht eine Antwort auf die Frage nach der britischen Identität. Dabei arbeiten S den Ton als wirksames Gestaltungsmittel nichtfiktionaler Texte heraus. Indem sie die Adjektive des Textes zur Beschreibung von Dingen und Personen aus dem Text herausfiltern und diese für die eigene Textproduktion verwenden, festigen und erweitern sie ihren Wortschatz sowie ihre Schreibkompetenz.

SB-DVD-ROM

Lernwortschatz

self-assessment (l. 2), inventive (l. 3), irresponsible (l. 5), ill-educated (l. 5), greedy (l. 6), rude (l. 7), self-esteem (l. 12), composite term (l. 18), racial and religious tension (l. 27)

Unterrichtstipps

PRE-READING Vorab wird die Bedeutung von *humble* (demütig, bescheiden) geklärt.
For we British (Zeile 2): Grammatikalisch richtig müsste es „for us British" heißen (Objekt- statt Subjektform des Personalpronomens nach einer Präposition), aber die Wendung wird (umgangssprachlich) auch mit der Subjektform gebraucht, um die Kollokation „we British" unverändert zu zitieren und die Identifikation des Sprechers mit Großbritannien (ironisierend) zu unterstreichen.

ALT

4b Alternativ ergänzen S die Liste, indem sie aus „British" ein *acrostic* bilden, z. B. **B**lack humour; **R**espectful; **I**nnovative; **T**ea connoisseurs; **I**mpartial; **S**tiff upper lip; **H**appy.

Differenzierung

4a S arbeiten in zwei Gruppen und tauschen ihre Argumente anschließend mit einem Partner der jeweils anderen Gruppe aus.

5 EXTRA Die Recherche erfolgt entweder im Unterricht in Partner- oder Gruppenarbeit oder als längerfristig angelegte Hausaufgabe.
Linktipp: www.bbc.co.uk/history bietet eine interaktive *British History Timeline*.

Info

Vikings: Between the 790s and 1066, the Vikings pillaged monasteries and conquered villages in Britain because settlement areas were becoming scarce in Scandinavia. The first recorded attack occurred in 789 in Dorset, where an official came to greet the newcomers and was killed in return.

The 16th century version of a multi-faith society: During the Tudor dynasty (1458–1603), Britain changed faith more than once: Henry VIII (King of England 1509–1547) caused an accelerated growth of Protestantism due to his attempts to divorce Catherine of Aragon. When Mary I ('Bloody Mary') ascended the throne (1553–1558), England returned to Catholicism, with hundreds of Protestants being burned at the stake from 1556 onwards and many going into exile. Under Elizabeth I, the official religion was once again Anglican.

Lösungshinweise

1a *Positive:* inventive, tolerant (l. 2), having a 'national identity, however humble' (l. 13)
Negative: fragmented, degenerate, irresponsible, rude and unfriendly society (l. 4–5); violent kids and ill-educated workers (l. 5); greedy and incompetent managers, bad public services (l. 6); alcoholism (l. 7); high house prices (ll. 7–8); corrupt politicians, crowded roads, bad football team (l. 8)

Part A3 – Benjamin Zephaniah on Britain

1b To the author, multiculturalism in Britain today may occasionally cause tension (although he thinks that this is exaggerated, cf. l. 29), but in the past it caused death and destruction. The examples he gives are the Vikings (who raided Europe between 790 and 1066) and people in the 16th century who wouldn't tolerate those who worshipped differently, burning them alive.

2 *The tone* is set at the beginning with the more personal, informal use of the first person plural (For we British, …') which is meant to draw the reader into the discussion and show that the aim of the text is not scientific precision.
The use of irony emphasises this. The huge list of negative aspects at the start of the extract shows that it's not entirely serious. Lines 9–11 describe a serious process, but in terms that can't be taken seriously – a good example of irony. Lines 12–15 are very ironic in that they claim that showing how bad the Brits think they are proves that they have a national identity.

3a *Adjectives describing people:* inventive, tolerant, ill-educated, greedy, incompetent, sleazy, irresponsible, rude, unfriendly, confused, religious
things: national, fragmented, abysmal, jammed, composite, multicultural, racial
both: difficult, good, bad, degenerate, wrong, crazy, humble, correct, uneasy, new

3b–4 Individual answers.

5 *UK history (ll. 15–20):* Up until 1921 the whole of Ireland was a part of the UK. Since 1921, only the six counties of Ulster have stayed in the UK whereas the other counties formed the Republic of Ireland, an independent country and member state of the EU. Until 1998, when the Good Friday Agreement ended the fighting between Ulster Protestants (who want to remain British citizens) and Ulster Catholics (who want Ulster to be a part of the Republic), the Republic of Ireland claimed Ulster for the Republic. Ireland has now abandoned this claim.
UK history (ll. 30–32): Cf. Info.
Regional attitudes to sport (ll. 21–24): The English cheer the team of any 'home nation' because they feel very much attached to the idea of the UK and see the Welsh and Scottish teams as UK teams. As the English invaded the former independent countries of Wales and Scotland in the Middle Ages, the Welsh and Scots do not see any reason to support the English team. They cheer anyone playing against England as they see England as their common 'enemy' or competitor.

SB S. 16 **A3 Benjamin Zephaniah on Britain**

Source:	*We Are Britain*, 2002
Topic:	Multicultural influences in Britain
Text form:	Non-fictional text (extract); poem (extract)
Language variety:	British English
Number of words:	144; 45
Level:	Basic
Skills/Activities:	Reading non-fiction; reading poetry; cooperative learning strategy (group puzzle)

Didaktischer Kommentar Beide Texte vermitteln einen differenzierten Eindruck der multikulturellen britischen Identität, deren verschiedene Aspekte S in einem Gruppenpuzzle herausarbeiten. Indem sie die Funktion der Gestaltungsmittel Metrum und Reimschema im Gedicht analysieren, schulen S ihre Textkompetenz.

SB-DVD-ROM

Lernwortschatz
adapt (l. 11)

Differenzierung **2a** eignet sich als Hausaufgabe.

Part A3 – Benjamin Zephaniah on Britain

> **Info**
>
> *Benjamin Zephaniah* (born 1958) has been awarded several honorary doctorates in recognition of his literary achievements. In 2003 he publicly refused to accept an OBE (cf. Info **B1**) for his services to literature in objection to the empire and the monarchy that sanctioned the oppression of black people through slavery. He is also an active political and animal rights campaigner.
>
> *Foreign influences: Jamaica* (a British colony from 1655 to 1962): Many Jamaicans fought for Britain even before World War II, and many of these men became the first permanent Jamaican settlers in the UK after World War II. The largest wave of Jamaican migration to the UK followed a major hurricane in 1944, killing many and destroying crops by flooding. Those who left did so also because of the prospect of jobs in the UK (cf. Info 'National Identity and Diversity', **B1**).
>
> *The Celts* were the first immigrants to Britain to leave a linguistic heritage. Some of their descendants in Wales, Scotland and Ireland still speak Celtic languages.
>
> *The 'Great Famine' in Ireland* (1845–55) resulted in massive immigration to mainland Britain (cf. Info 'National Identity and Diversity', **B1**).
>
> *The British Empire* (late 16th century–1997) had colonies all over the world, including Africa and South-East Asia as well as Egypt (British protectorate) and Iraq (British mandate), and many immigrants to the UK came from these countries.
>
> *Indian Independence and Partition* (1947) led to massive immigration from the subcontinent (cf. Fact File before **A1**); Bengalis are people from Bangladesh and India.
>
> *World War II (1939–1945):* the end of the war and the need for labour resulted in the immigration of African Caribbeans and Italians to Britain.
>
> *Africa:* Wars and famine have caused many Africans to immigrate to Britain.

Lösungshinweise

1a *Jajar's parents* are open to all sorts of foods – Jamaican rice and peas, odd vegetables, vegetarian food, English food, Indian food, but they never seem to give him pizza. *Jajar* doesn't want fancy food; like many kids he just likes (Italian) pizza.

1b The message of both texts is that Britain today is a multicultural country in which the races, religions and tastes are all mixed up.

2a Lines 1–5 show that the British enjoy music and dance, food and clothes from around the world. They come from all over the world and so have different eye, skin and hair colours. The British have adopted things from America, Africa, Asia, Ireland, Italy, and Jamaica. They look like Celts, Arabs and Bengalis and wear kilts and saris as well as football shirts, which implies that people in Britain come from all different backgrounds.

2b The *metre* of the poem is fast and bouncy which makes it sound cheerful and light. The regular *rhyme* scheme (a, b, a, b, c, d, e, d) using monosyllabic words emphasises this happy-go-lucky *mood* yet further, so all this helps to convey the *message* that the mix of things is good.

3a *Different foreign influences:* America, Africa, Asia (ll. 2–3), Ireland, Italy, Jamaica (l. 3), Celts, Arabs, Bengals (l. 5), Scotland and India (l. 5). For the *history*, cf. Info.

3b Being British seems to mean being part of an enormous mix of races, religions and customs. Each new arrival is absorbed into the mix, making Britain what it is.

3a Group puzzle (s. *jigsaw puzzle* S. 297) Die Recherche erfolgt im Computerraum oder vorab zuhause. Die Einflüsse werden am Text belegt und stichwortartig an der Tafel / auf einer Folie festgehalten, bevor S in Gruppen eingeteilt werden. S werten in ihrer Gruppe die Informationen aus und halten die Ergebnisse schriftlich fest.

1 Part A4 – Britishness

ZA S mit Interesse an Lyrik schreiben ein eigenes Gedicht zum Thema Multikulturalismus in Deutschland. Unter www.benjaminzephaniah.com/content/tips.php gibt Zephaniah angehenden Dichtern Tipps.

SB S. 17 CD 1.14–15
Transkript s. TM-DVD-ROM

A4 Britishness

Source:	'Britishness', BBC Radio 4, 31 March 2009
Topic:	British national identity
Text form:	Radio report
Language variety:	British English
Length:	Part 1 4:04 min; part 2 2:44 min
Level:	Advanced
Skills/Activities:	Working with pictures; listening comprehension

Didaktischer Kommentar — S lernen anhand des Radioberichts unterschiedliche Ansätze des britischen Selbstverständnisses kennen. Sie kontrastieren diese Definitionsversuche mit ihren eigenen Vorstellungen auch vor dem Hintergrund der in *Part A* gewonnen Erkenntnisse über die britische Identität; dabei festigen und erweitern sie ihre Hörverstehenskompetenz.

Unterrichtstipps

1b S notieren mindestens acht Stichwörter und tauschen sich im *marketplace*-Verfahren (s. S. 298) aus. Die Ergebnisse werden für **3a** auf einer Folie oder an der Tafel gesichert.

1c erfolgt in Partner- oder Gruppenarbeit mit Hilfe von ein- oder zweisprachigen Wörterbüchern.

2 Vor dem Hören machen sich S mit unbekanntem Wortschatz vertraut.

Als Hausaufgabe wählen S ein Bild aus, das sie mit *Britishness* verbinden. Sie beschreiben es und begründen schriftlich ihre Wahl. Die Vorstellung erfolgt in kleineren Gruppen mit anschließender Auswertung im Unterrichtsgespräch.

Differenzierung — Einstieg: In schwächeren Lerngruppen erfolgt zunächst eine Bildbeschreibung.

2 In schwächeren Lerngruppen wird der Hörtext zweimal oder in zwei Abschnitten abgespielt. Nach dem ersten Hören erhalten S Gelegenheit, ihr Grobverständnis mit einem Partner zu vergleichen.

3c wird alternativ zuhause in Form eines Essay erledigt.

Info

Martin Parr (born 1952) is an English photographer considered one of the most influential contemporary photographers worldwide. For him, his photographs reflect everyday situations in an ironical way without being nasty.

Radio 4 is the second most popular British radio station and considered the BBC's flagship, covering all fields except for music and sport. In 1967, Radio 4 replaced the BBC Home Service that became famous during World War II.

Lösungshinweise

1ab Individual answers.

1c

beneficiary: a person who gains as a result of sth. (Nutznießer)
platitude: a boring statement that has been made many times before
end of deference: the end of polite behaviour that shows respect towards sb. / sb.'s opinion

national identity: the qualities and attitudes that a nation has that makes it different from other nations
scone: a small round Scottish bread usually served with tea

Communicating across Cultures

2 To *the presenter*, 'Britishness' means being part of a fair and equitable society. *Various interviewees* name freedom, friendliness, openness, a fair society, queuing, drinking tea, cricket, fair play, democracy, politeness, good manners, 'keep yourself to yourself', stiff upper lip, fish and chips, roast beef on a Sunday, loyalty to the state, tolerance, ability to explore and cross new boundaries, shopping, the Union Jack, eccentricity, the Empire, brutality, colonialism, standards, the monarchy, the hunt, free health care, fat women, slovenliness, lack of respect, being posh, scones

3 Individual answers.

SB S. 18 CD 1.16
▶ LSET ex. 5, 6
Transkript s. TM-DVD-ROM

Communicating across Cultures – What Do They Really Mean?

Didaktischer Kommentar

Im Mittelpunkt stehen interkulturelle Schwierigkeiten in der Kommunikation zwischen Deutschen und Briten. S werden für diese Problematik sensibilisiert und erhalten Strategien um z. B. mit Kritik indirekter und höflicher umzugehen.

Unterrichtstipps
ZA

1a Die irreführenden Signale werden an der Tafel oder auf OH-Folie festgehalten. S schreiben eigene höfliche Sätze, in denen sie diese Signale verwenden und lassen sie von einem Partner in die unhöflichere Variante „übersetzen". Alternativ stellen sie die Dialoge in kurzen Szenen nach.

Differenzierung
⚠ HA

2 Mediation Leistungsschwächere S bereiten vorab zuhause mögliche Antworten vor. Der Hörtext wird abschnittweise vorgespielt. Beim ersten Durchgang sprechen sieben S jeweils eine mögliche Antwort in der dafür vorgesehenen Pause. Anschließend werden verschiedene Vorschläge verglichen.

Lösungshinweise

1a 1d; 2h; 3i; 4b; 5g; 6c; 7j; 8e; 9a; 10f

1bc Misleading signals (= polite sound – blunt or opposite meaning): 1 I'm afraid; 2 not bad at; 3 I wonder; 4 could I trouble you; 5 sometime (a vague date meaning 'never'); 6 know a bit; 7 so sorry; 8 how sweet; 9 that's all right; 10 Oh really?

2 Mediation Cf. transcript on TM-DVD-ROM for suggested answers.

▶ LSET Skills 30, 45

Part B – Who's in Charge?

SB S. 19

B1 The Queen J.F.O. McAllister

Source:	*Time*, 2 April 2005
Topic:	The Queen's function and duties
Text form:	Magazine article (extract)
Language variety:	American English
Number of words:	463
Level:	Intermediate
Skills/Activities:	Reading non-fiction; analysing style; working with pictures; using a dictionary

Didaktischer Kommentar

In seinem Artikel versucht der Autor den Reiz der britischen Monarchie und speziell der Königin zu ergründen. S üben ihre Textkompetenz, indem sie die (positive) Grundeinstellung des Autors herausarbeiten und am Text belegen.

1 Part B1 – The Queen

SB-DVD-ROM

Lernwortschatz

attend a reception (l. 3), stroll (l. 3), be moved (l. 14), sharp (l. 20), exercise power (l. 25), popular consent (l. 31), peculiar (l. 31)

Unterrichtstipps

⚠ HA

PRE-READING S bereiten ihre Beiträge als Hausaufgabe vor, damit zu Beginn der Stunde alles auf einer Folie gesammelt werden kann, die für die Behandlung von **1a** zur Verfügung steht.

ZA (zum Gemälde):
1 Look at the painting and describe what you see (cf. SF 9: Working with pictures).
2 Consider the subject and style of the painting and state whether you think the Queen is represented well.
3 Your opinion: What do you (not) like about the painting?

 ZA S überlegen sich Fragen, die sie Queen Elizabeth II stellen würden, verfassen allein oder zu zweit ein fiktives Interview und tragen es anschließend der Klasse vor. Um möglichst viele S in der Präsentationsphase zu Wort kommen zu lassen, wird nur eine Auswahl der besten Fragen vorgestellt.
1 You are a journalist interviewing the Queen. What would you like to know? Which questions might your readers/listeners be interested in? Alone or with a partner, write down questions and possible answers.
2 Present your interview to the rest of the class.

ZA Interessierte Klassen sehen den Film *The Queen* (97 Minuten), cf. Info.

Differenzierung

PRE-READING Die Aufgabe kann auch als *web quest* im Computerraum erfolgen.
Linktipp: *www.royal.gov.uk/HMTheQueen/HMTheQueen.aspx*

HA **4** eignet sich als Hausaufgabe. *Word cluster* sind mindmapähnliche Darstellungen, in denen hier die Adjektive mit Nomen bzw. Kollokationen verbunden werden.

ZA Um die *conditionals* zu üben und zu festigen beantworten S folgende Frage: *Imagine you were Queen Elizabeth II for a day. What would you like to do?*

Info

Queen Elizabeth II (born 1926) is Head of State of the UK and fifteen other sovereign states. She was born in London as the eldest child of King George VI and Queen Elizabeth. On her father's death in 1952 she acceded to the throne at the age of 25. She is married to Prince Philip, Duke of Edinburgh, and they have four children (Charles, Anne, Andrew and Edward) as well as eight grandchildren.

The Order of the British Empire (OBE, created 1917) is an honorary reward recognizing distinguished service to the arts, sciences, public services outside the civil service and work with charitable and welfare organisations. The motto of the Order is 'For God and the Empire'.

Lucian ['luːsiən] *Freud* was born in Berlin, Germany, in 1922, a grandson of Sigmund Freud. He came to England with his parents in 1931 and became a British citizen eight years later. He began to work full-time as an artist in the mid-forties. Since the early 1950s he has built up a reputation as a figurative painter specializing in portraits and nudes. The portrait of Elizabeth II was painted in 2000–2001 and divided critics. On the one hand the heavily rendered facial features were considered unflattering, on the other hand it was praised for challenging the traditional image of the Queen. Freud decided to show the Queen wearing the Diamond Diadem, the crown rendered in images of the monarch on coins, notes and stamps. The painting was given to the Queen as a gift by the artist.

Part B2 – The Church

> *The Queen* (Great Britain, 2006; director: Stephen Frears; screenplay: Peter Morgan) deals with Lady Diana's death in 1997. The recently elected Tony Blair commemorates Diana in a speech, while the Queen (Helen Mirren) refuses a public statement, no longer considering Diana as royalty because of her divorce from Charles a year earlier. Blair tries to convince the Queen to pay her last respects. Finally, she gives in and regains her popularity.

Lösungshinweise

1a *Duties:* conferring awards (OBE to cricketers, l. 6), acting as a symbol of the country (l. 24), also opening Parliament, appointing the PM, consulting with the PM regularly, serving as head of the Church of England (cf. also Fact File before **B3** in 'The UK – Tradition and Change').

1b Without being elected, the Queen receives support for working hard and being visible while doing so (ll. 31, 36).

2a *Rhetorical questions:* 'Really? That grandmotherly figure who always carries a handbag and never says anything controversial?' (ll. 17–19); 'How can one person … respect is way too small a word?' (ll. 23–24). Both questions sound slightly sarcastic and sceptical, thus setting the tone for the whole text.

2b EXTRA The sarcasm of the rhetorical questions (cf. **2a**) and other statements ('the enduring enigma of royalty', l. 22; 'the idea of monarchy is self-evidently nonsensical', l. 23) make the reader think the writer is going to be particularly critical of the Queen and/or the institution of the monarchy. So by quoting only people who praise the Queen and using positive descriptions of her and her work, he influences the reader very subtly: 'the star of the show' (l. 8); 'a really dazzling smile' (l. 11); 'not for the Queen a quiet retirement' (l. 36–37).

3 Individual answers; cf. Info.

4a *Adjectives and the nouns they modify:* virtual demigods (l. 1), last summer (l. 2), new status (l. 5), proud families (l. 7), studied placidity (l. 10), dazzling smile (l. 11), Ashley Giles […] starstruck (l. 12), top-level sports (l. 13), [Ashley Giles] was moved (l. 14), incredible honor (l. 15), memorable days (l. 17), grandmotherly figure (l. 18), anything controversial (l. 18), living link (l. 19), important – modifies 'which', which in turn refers to the previous clause (l. 19), [the Queen is] sharp (l. 20), fantastic job (l. 20), beautiful woman (l. 21)

4b Individual answers. The most (unknown) useful seven adjectives might be *virtual, dazzling, moved, incredible, memorable, sharp* and *fantastic*.

SB S. 20   **B2** EXTRA **The Church**   Kate Fox

Source:	*Watching the English*, 2004
Topic:	The English attitude towards religion
Text form:	Non-fictional text (extract)
Language variety:	British English
Number of words:	494
Level:	Advanced
Skills/Activities:	Summarizing; analysing stylistic devices

Didaktischer Kommentar

Kate Fox bezeichnet die Einstellung der Engländer zur Religion und zur *Church of England* als „wohlwollende Gleichgültigkeit". S arbeiten diese Einstellung heraus und vergleichen sie mit der Situation in Deutschland; dadurch schulen sie ihre interkulturelle Kompetenz.

1 Part B2 – The Church

SB-DVD-ROM

Lernwortschatz

ignore sb./sth. (l. 3), irrelevant (l. 6), imply (l. 11), a degree of (l. 11), reject sb./sth. (l. 12), opinion poll (l. 13), take sth. at face value (l. 14), be indifferent to sb./sth. (l. 24), objection to sb./sth. (l. 26), refrain from doing sth. (l. 33), tedious (l. 34), suspicious of/about sb./sth. (l. 38)

Unterrichtstipps

PRE-READING Die Begriffe *social anthropologist (a scientist who studies how human beings behave in groups)* und *benign indifference (well-meaning lack of interest or concern)* werden vorab geklärt. Beiträge werden an der Tafel bzw. auf einer Folie gesichert, damit sie für **1c** zur Verfügung stehen.

1c Der Abgleich erfolgt im Plenum, wobei S ihre Antwort anhand von Textstellen belegen.

2a wird als Hausaufgabe bearbeitet und in Kleingruppen ausgewertet.

2b erfolgt in Partner- oder Gruppenarbeit.

2c S ergänzen ihre im *Lead-in* angelegte Mindmap als Hausaufgabe.

Differenzierung

2a Um die von Fox geäußerte These zu belegen oder zu widerlegen, stellen interessierte S zusätzlich einen Vergleich mit den USA an. Dazu können sie u.a. die Informationen aus Part B des Kapitels „The USA – Dreams and Struggles" nutzen.

Info

Church of England: In 1529 King Henry VIII, angry at the refusal of Pope Clement VII to annul his marriage to Catherine of Aragon, asked Parliament to pass a series of laws denying the pope power or jurisdiction over the Church of England. To ensure his wishes he gave himself the position of Supreme Governor of the Church of England, a position English and British monarchs have continued to hold. The spiritual leader (the Archbishop of Canterbury) is selected by the monarch on advice of the Prime Minister and a committee appointed by the Church.

Dr George Carey (born 1935) was Archbishop of Canterbury from 1991–2002. During this time, the Church of England permitted the ordination of women priests and started a controversial debate about homosexuality.

Lösungshinweise

1a Carey's comment in ll. 3–4 sounds as if he had given up: he doesn't approve of the British attitude to religion, but feels there is nothing he can do about it.

1b Fox agrees with Carey's comment and sees the British as indifferent to religion. Although she claims that many are reluctant to deny the fact that there is or might be a God, it is bad form to mention faith at all. This, according to Fox, is the only instance in which the British stop being indifferent: when someone else displays his faith, the British become very uncomfortable.

1c Individual answers.

2a In contrast to the UK, Germans are more open about their beliefs, but less so than Americans (ll. 28–31). Germany has political parties that carry the word 'Christian' in their names. In some German *Bundesländer*, crosses appear in places they would be unthinkable in Britain, e.g. in classrooms and courtrooms. And Germany has a 'church tax', which is unheard of in Britain.

2b Individual answers.

2c Comparing the Church to an 'elderly lady' is clearly saying that it is tradition-bound; the fact that most people ignore this old lady might be taken to show that things have changed and may possibly even be setting a new trend away from established religion.

Part B3 – The Political Parties

SB S. 22 **Fact File**

Differenzierung ZA

Politisch interessierte S ergänzen die Tabelle um Informationen zum US-amerikanischen Regierungssystem.

> **Info**
>
> *Constituencies in the UK (l. 26):* General elections are held to elect the Members of Parliament (MPs) forming the House of Commons (cf. 'The British System of Government', p. 350). In the general election on 6 May 2010, the boundaries of the constituencies (electoral districts) were altered, causing the number of seats to rise from 646 to 650.

Lösungshinweis

	UK	**Germany (common translations)**
head of state	Queen/King	Bundespräsident/in ([Federal] President)
legislature (lower and upper house)	Parliament (House of Commons and House of Lords)	Bundestag (Federal Assembly = national parliament) Bundesrat (Federal Council = assembly of the federal states)
head of government	Prime Minister	Bundeskanzler/in ([Federal] Chancellor)
constitutional court	Supreme Court	Bundesverfassungsgericht (Federal Constitutional Court)
important ministers (finance, foreign and internal affairs)	Chancellor of the Exchequer Foreign Secretary Home Secretary	Finanzminister/in (Finance Minister) Außenminister/in (Foreign Minister) Innenminister/in (Minister of the Interior)

SB S. 23 **B3 The Political Parties** Alistair Beaton

> Source: *Feelgood*, 2001
> Topic: Idealism and realism in politics
> Text form: Drama (extract)
> Language variety: British English
> Number of words: 302
> Level: Intermediate
> Skills/Activities: Reading drama; devising an ad

Didaktischer Kommentar

An diesem Text schulen S ihre Textkompetenz bzgl. der Analyse dramatischer Texte und der handelnden Figuren. Inhaltlich setzen sie sich mit einem für sie als Jungwähler aktuellen Thema auseinander, indem sie in Gruppenarbeit Werbematerial gegen Politikverdrossenheit entwerfen.

SB-DVD-ROM

> **Lernwortschatz**
>
> credible (l. 5), agenda (l. 8), govern (l. 13), appointment (l. 21), desperate to do sth. (l. 25)

Unterrichtstipps

Einstieg: *In class, discuss what you think about politics in general and politicians in particular. Do you trust politicians? Why or why not?*

⚠ **3** S bringen von zuhause Material für Poster mit und arbeiten in Gruppen von 3–4 S. Die Auswertung der Poster erfolgt als *gallery walk* (s. S. 297), die Fernseh- und Radiospots werden präsentiert.

ZA *Eddie is reflecting on his talk with Liz. Write a dialogue between him and the prime minister. Alternatively, write a journal entry in which he discusses Liz' arguments.*

Part B4 – The National Assemblies

Differenzierung

2 wird in arbeitsteiliger Partnerarbeit erledigt. Schnelle S überlegen sich anschließend die ideale Besetzung für die Rollen: *Which actor/actress would you cast as Eddie/Liz? Which characteristics should they embody?*

> **Info**
>
> *Alistair Beaton* (born 1947 in Glasgow) is a left-wing political satirist, journalist, novelist and BBC Radio4 presenter. He studied Russian and German and worked as a speechwriter for Gordon Brown, British Prime Minister from 2007–2010.

Lösungshinweise

1a *Liz:* Politicians are only interested in getting elected, not in improving things in the country. They are making a mess of the democratic process and voters are getting angry.
Eddie: People who criticize politicians are not being realistic and don't want to understand that real change takes time and can only be done bit by bit. It is important to get voters on board.

1b The 'feelgood factor', according to Liz, is politicians wanting voters to be happy so that they will vote for them. She sees this as the driving force in politics.

1c Liz believes that people are getting fed up with politics because the politicians are not interested in changing or improving things, but only in being re-elected. Since all politicians want happy voters, there won't be any difference between the parties and no one will care who's in office. People wouldn't vote any more, thus 'fucking' up democracy.

2a *Liz is idealistic* because she expects politicians to make radical changes ('redistribution of wealth', l. 7) in the people's interest. She expects them to embrace conflict in order to achieve 'real politics' (l. 9). *Liz is naive* for the same reasons: she expects politicians to behave altruistically, which is unrealistic.
Eddie is a realist. He may have wanted to change society and make it more fair, but now sees that radical change cannot be achieved all at once. He believes in 'incremental change' (l. 19) and wants to convince people before changing anything. *Eddie is a cynic.* He has given up any ideals he may once have had for the sake of his party. He doesn't work for the benefit of society, but to make his party 'electable' (l. 5). He doesn't defend a position but uses empty phrases like 'getting beyond the old politics of left and right' (l. 11). And most cynical of all, he doesn't seem to mind that 'people are getting hacked off'; his only concern is that they should still vote for his party.

3 Individual answers.

SB S. 24

B4 EXTRA **The National Assemblies**

Source:	The website of Directgov, 8 October 2009; www.direct.gov.uk
Topic:	The devolution of powers in the UK
Text form:	Non-fictional text (extract)
Language variety:	British English
Number of words:	108
Level:	Basic
Skills/Activities:	Doing research; doing a project; giving a presentation

Didaktischer Kommentar

In arbeitsteiliger Projektarbeit erarbeiten S eine der grundlegendsten Änderungen, die das politische System des Vereinigten Königreichs seit Beginn der 90er Jahre erfahren hat. Die Dezentralisierung *(devolution)* bedeutet ein Ende der Bevormundung von Wales, Nordirland und Schottland durch Westminster und mehr Autonomie in Bereichen wie Kultur, Sprache, Bildung und Erziehung.

Part B4 – The National Assemblies

SB-DVD-ROM

Lernwortschatz

government policies (l. 1), public services (l. 1), devolved government (l. 3), referendum (l. 6), transfer sth./sb. to sb./sth. (l. 7), range (l. 7), administrative (l. 11)

Unterrichtstipps

Einstieg: S besprechen die Regionen des Vereinigten Königreich (s. Abbildungen *Words in Context*) und nennen Assoziationen zu den einzelnen Teilen (Reaktivierung von Vorwissen) bzw. berichten von Reisen dorthin.

ZA

S mit Auslandserfahrung bringen für sie typische Bilder verschiedener Regionen des Vereinigten Königreichs mit. Die übrigen S beschreiben die Bilder und ordnen sie einer bestimmten Region zu.

Differenzierung

2a–d Die Lerngruppe wird in sechs Arbeitsgruppen eingeteilt, die jeweils einen der durch Spiegelstriche markierten Aspekte bearbeitet:
- Leistungsschwächere: „the sorts of powers that are (not) devolved" und „England: why there is no devolved government and whether there are movements in favour of devolution"
- Leistungsstärkere: „devolution in Northern Ireland: historical background"
- L teilt die verbliebenen drei Themen unter den übrigen S auf.

Während der Präsentationen nutzen S **KV 1** für die spätere Auswertung. Der Webcode bietet URLs mit Hintergrundinformationen zu den Themen in **2a**.

Info

Devolution is the transfer of powers from the British Government to the UK's nations and regions in areas like education and health. The scope of those powers differs between each political institution. Scotland has the most power followed by Northern Ireland, Wales, London and the planned English regional assemblies. Backers say democracy is improved by devolution as people gain more control of their own affairs, but critics say it is costly and divisive. During the election campaign of 1997, Tony Blair's Labour party committed itself to decentralising governmental power with the establishment of a parliament in Scotland and an assembly in Wales.

Lösungshinweise

1 Devolution is the transfer of power from a central authority to local authorities.

2ab Possible subtopics for each of the six topics:
- *Devolved powers:* education, law, health. *Not devolved:* defence, international relations, economic policy
- *Devolution in Scotland:* the Scottish Parliament (and its controversial construction), Scottish Government; possibly also historical background, Scottish national identity, the political parties (SNP)
- *Devolution in Wales:* the National Assembly for Wales, the Welsh Assembly Government and possibly also historical background, Welsh national identity, the political parties (Plaid Cymru, etc.)
- *Devolution in Northern Ireland (historical background):* British occupation, Home Rule, the Troubles (cf. Info C3), the Good Friday Agreement (1998)
- *Devolution in Northern Ireland:* the Northern Ireland Assembly and Northern Ireland Executive; possibly the many political parties and reasons for them
- *England:* public opinion and referendum, regional disparities (north and south), Westminster

2cd Individual answers; cf. **KV 1**.

Part B5 – The USA I

2e The UK consists of four *national regions* (England, Northern Ireland, Scotland, Wales) whereas Germany has got 16 *federal states* ('Länder'). Each federal state in Germany has got a *state parliament* and a first minister ('Ministerpräsident'), unlike the UK, where England does not have a regional assembly. The 'Länder' are responsible for their own police forces, their cultural politics, their school system and some taxes, though they cannot create new tax laws or alter existing tax laws. The 'Länder' have an important say in the national *law-making process*: after passing the national parliament ('Bundestag'), each national law must be approved by the assembly of the federal states ('Bundesrat'). If they block a law, the federal states and the national government must negotiate a *compromise*. This feature is unknown in the UK. Each federal state has got a kind of *commissioner* (members of the 'Landesregierung') in Berlin who makes sure that the interests of their state are well heard by the national government. This does not exist in the UK. Some German federal states have opened representative offices in Brussels to be close to European Union institutions. UK regions are not entitled to do this as they are represented by the central government.

SB S. 25
▶ LSET ex. 7, 8, 10

B5 The USA I Stryker McGuire

Source:	*Newsweek*, 23 February 2009
Topic:	The changing relationship between the UK and the USA
Text form:	Magazine article (extract)
Language variety:	American English
Number of words:	325
Level:	Intermediate
Skills/Activities:	Determining the text type; analysing a metaphor; writing an essay

Didaktischer Kommentar

Der Zeitschriftenkommentar eröffnet eine neue Sicht auf das Verhältnis zwischen Großbritannien und den USA. S setzen sich mit dieser Sichtweise auseinander und festigen ihre Textkompetenz, indem sie den Texttyp bestimmen und eine Metapher analysieren, die diese neue Sichtweise bildlich darstellt.

SB-DVD-ROM

Lernwortschatz

increasing (l. 7), be bound to do sth. (l. 8), it's no accident that ... (l. 13), see the need for sb. to do sth. (l. 15), be confident of sb./sth. (l. 16), be in short supply (l. 21), launch a campaign (l. 22), dignity (l. 27)

Unterrichtstipps PRE-READING kann im *think–pair–share*-Verfahren (s. S. 299) erfolgen.

⚠ HA **1a** S lesen den Text, notieren sich die Gründe und fassen sie entweder schriftlich zusammen oder bereiten eine mündliche Zusammenfassung vor.

2b S machen sich Notizen, auf deren Grundlage die Auswertung im Unterrichtsgespräch erfolgt.

3 In Vorbereitung auf den Essay erhalten S folgende Aufgabe: *What does 'Germany's relationship with the USA' make you think of? Brainstorm ideas in groups of three. Collect metaphors and similes. Then choose the image that best illustrates the relationship and use it for your essay.*

Differenzierung **1b** In schwächeren Kursen wird zunächst das *British Empire* (zeitliche und geografische Ausdehnung; s. Info **A3**) besprochen.

Leistungsstärkere klären, für welche Leserschaft der Text geschrieben wurde.

Part B6 – The USA II

> **Info**
>
> *Stryker McGuire* (born 1947 in New York) is a journalist; he was the London bureau chief of the American magazine *Newsweek* from 1996–2008.

Lösungshinweise

1a The USA has a larger Hispanic population than before, so the UK plays an ever smaller role. Economically, the USA is tied to Asia, and countries like Japan and China (because they hold American debt), Saudi Arabia (which has oil to offer) or Mexico (where immigrants come from), are now more significant. America has friends all over the world.

1b 'Post-Empire malaise' describes the somewhat depressed feeling the British have due to the fact that their country has lost much of its significance along with its Empire.

1c 'Moving on' here refers to a change in mentality: instead of being nostalgic about the Empire that was, the British should start looking forward and see what's good about their country today.

2a When you look through the smaller end of a telescope, everything you see through it looks bigger; if you look through the bigger end, everything you see is reduced in size. The idea is that the UK, as the smaller country, is looking through the smaller end and seeing the USA as very big and important, while the USA is looking through the big end and seeing the UK as even smaller than it is, reduced almost to the point of insignificance. At the beginning of the extract, the metaphor establishes that the text will be about perspectives and perceptions, expressing the relative importance the special relationship has for each of the two countries.

2b The text is clearly a comment. The writer is not informing his readers of a particular event, even though he mentions some. Instead, he analyses the situation, giving his interpretation (ll. 1–3: cf. **2a**; l. 13: 'it's no accident'; l. 16: 'And why not?'; l. 20: 'there's no reason') and even advising Britain that it 'move on' (l. 28).

3 EXTRA Individual answers.

SB S. 26 DVD
Transkript s. TM-DVD-ROM

B6 The USA II

Source:	*Love Actually*, Great Britain, 2003
Topic:	The 'special relationship' between the UK and the USA
Text form:	Feature film (extract)
Language variety:	British English; American English
Length:	*Scene* 1 0:41; scene 2 3:58
Level:	Intermediate
Skills/Activities:	Viewing skills; using a dictionary; taking part in a discussion

Didaktischer Kommentar

Am Beispiel zweier Filmsequenzen schulen S ihr Hör-Seh-Verstehen und setzen sich kritisch mit den Aussagen des (fiktiven) Premierministers darüber auseinander, worauf Großbritannien stolz sein kann. Sie reflektieren die möglichen Konsequenzen dieser Aussagen in der realen politischen Welt.

Unterrichtstipps

1b erfolgt mit Hilfe von ein- oder zweisprachigen Wörterbüchern in Partnerarbeit; alternativ als vorbereitende Hausaufgabe.

2 Sollte S der Film unbekannt sein, können beide Szenen zunächst ohne Ton präsentiert werden. S spekulieren über das in den Szenen Gesagte, bevor sie den Film mit Ton sehen und ihre Spekulationen überprüfen.

Differenzierung

2 Leistungsstärkere S schulen ihre Schreibkompetenz, indem sie ihre Spekulationen über den Inhalt der Rede des Premierministers (s. Unterrichtstipps zu **2**) in einer eigenen Rede festhalten. Einige S tragen ihre Reden vor, bevor der Abgleich mit dem Original erfolgt.

Part B7 – The European Union

3a Um die Zusammenfassung der beiden Handlungsstränge gerade in leistungsschwächeren Gruppen zu erleichtern, erstellen S nach dem zweiten Sehen ein *viewing log* (s. *SF 20: Viewing a film*), das während des Films ausgefüllt wird. Ggf. erfolgt anschließend ein Austausch in Partnerarbeit.

4 Vor der Diskussion halten S ihre Gedanken stichwortartig fest. Um den Sprechanteil Einzelner zu erhöhen, wird die Lerngruppe in Kleingruppen eingeteilt.

> **Info**
>
> *Love Actually* (2003; director and screenplay: Richard Curtis) is a British romantic comedy telling different 'love stories', among them that of the recently elected British Prime Minister (Hugh Grant) and Natalie (Martine McCutcheon), a new member of the household staff at 10 Downing Street.

Lösungshinweise

1a The first photo shows a Cabinet meeting, where the Prime Minister discusses policy with other ministers, or a business meeting. The second photo shows a press conference involving statements by a UK and a US official which are usually followed by questions from the press.

1b

take a stand (on sth.): have an opinion on sth.;
petulant child: bad-tempered, unreasonable child (trotzig);

screw sb. (taboo, sl): have sex with sb.;
pathetic (infml): weak, absurd;
all manner of sb./sth.: many different types of people/things (alles Mögliche)

2 *Storyline 1* (political) involves the UK Prime Minister and the US President, *storyline 2* (love-related) involves the PM and a member of his staff.

3a *Storyline 1:* The PM explains that he is not going to take a stand and appear too firm. *Storyline 2* gives impressions of the US President's visit and of his firmness. The PM leaves the President for a minute and when he returns, he catches the President coming on to Natalie, who the PM is in love with. In the press conference the next day, the President states his stay was satisfactory, while the PM vows to take a stand and be stronger in the future.

3b Shakespeare and Churchill were truly great men with tremendous influence, one on literature worldwide, the other on the fate of Britain and the world; a politician could be expected to name them. This is not the case for 'The Beatles' and Sean Connery, even though a hugely successful music group that influenced a whole generation and a world-famous actor are things to be proud of. Harry Potter and David Beckham's feet, however, do not normally appear on such lists, as can be seen by the reaction (laughter) of the members of the press.

4 Individual answers.

SB S. 27 **B7 The European Union** William Shakespeare
ii)

Source:	*King Richard II, act II, scene i, ll. 40–47*
Topic:	The relationship between the UK and the EU
Text form:	Headlines (i), drama (ii), bar chart (iii), cartoon (iv)
Language variety:	British English
Number of words:	51
Level:	Intermediate
Skills/Activities:	Reading drama; working with charts; working with cartoons; taking part in a discussion; conducting a poll; giving a presentation

Part B7 – The European Union

Didaktischer Kommentar

Das delikate und zum Teil widersprüchliche Verhältnis Großbritanniens zur EU steht im Mittelpunkt. Mithilfe verschiedener Materialien arbeiten S die Einstellung der Briten zur EU heraus und bewerten die gewonnenen Erkenntnisse.

SB-DVD-ROM

Lernwortschatz

cautious (i), headline 1), frontier (i), headline 2)

Unterrichtstipps

1 S bilden nach Neigung vier Gruppen, die i), ii), iii) oder iv) samt Aufgabe (**1a, 1b, 1c** oder **1d**) in Einzelarbeit bearbeiten, bevor sie sich in ihrer Gruppe darüber austauschen. Die Auswertung erfolgt im Unterrichtsgespräch.

Differenzierung

1 In schnell und selbstständig arbeitenden Gruppen werden Vierergruppen gebildet, die zusammen die vier Teilaufgaben beantworten und ihre Ergebnisse stichwortartig festhalten.

2 S notieren stichwortartig ihre Meinung, bevor sie sich im Marktplatzverfahren (s. S. 298) darüber austauschen.

3 S machen sich vorab Notizen. In großen Lerngruppen ist die Bildung kleiner Diskussionsgruppen sinnvoll, um möglichst viele S zu beteiligen.

Info

The UK and the EU: The UK did not join the European Community when first established in the 1950s. It was thought that membership might weaken Britain's strong trade links with Commonwealth countries and its political ties with the USA or create a loss of sovereignty by conceding power to 'mainland Europe'. The UK was initially more interested in creating a European free trade area involving no sacrifice of national sovereignty. As a result, the European Free Trade Association (EFTA) was created in 1959 by Britain, Norway, Sweden, Denmark, Austria, Portugal, Iceland, Switzerland and Finland. However, Britain soon realised that it risked economic and political isolation if it remained outside the Community. Still, it was not until 1973 that Britain actually achieved membership after a referendum. But Britain remained a rather Euro-sceptic country and consequently has not joined the Schengen agreement or the monetary union.

Lösungshinweise

1a *Headline 1* indicates that the feeling was one of apprehension and healthy scepticism. The UK was just entering the European Community, so people were nervous about what the step might bring.
Headline 2 is characterized by fear. This was after the Schengen agreement was signed (1985) which allowed free movement within the EU.
Headline 3 is marked by defiance. It refers to the discussion of a new uniform currency for Europe which was introduced in 2002.
Headline 4: The feeling in 2006 – after ten new eastern and southern European countries joined the EU in 2004, causing a huge wave of immigration to Britain and Ireland – was one of renewed scepticism.
Headline 5: The feeling is one of increased openness towards the EU, probably brought about by the financial crisis (2007) and the need for more cooperation among the states of Europe.

1b The extract from *Richard II* shows huge affection for the country ('This other Eden, demi-paradise'; l. 3; 'precious stone', l. 7) which gives its population great happiness (l. 6). It also shows that the British are grateful for the safety their island status affords them ('this fortress built by nature for herself', l. 4; 'the silver sea / Which serves it in the office of a wall', ll. 7–8) – safety both from disease and military attack (l. 5). It is inhabited by people willing to defend their country ('this seat of Mars', l. 2).

1c Britain is in the yellow section of the table, a placement that is roughly two-thirds down the table: nearly two thirds of the populations surveyed had a more positive attitude than the British. Of the countries represented, Britain has the lowest opinion of any European country; only the countries of the Muslim world, two Latin American nations, traditional rival China and the former colony India (along with Pakistan, a Muslim country) have a lower opinion of the EU.

1d The cartoon shows a patient at the optician's, taking an eye test. The doctor is pointing glumly to a chart full of different-sized Euro symbols, but all the patient can see are pound symbols. The cartoonist is obviously implying that the British are blind to certain developments around them and so self-centred that all they see is what they want to see and are used to.

2–4 Individual answers.

▶ LSET ex. 10; Skills 18, 19

Part C – British Art and Culture

SB S. 29
▶ LSET Skills 9, 39

C1 Sea Pictures in Oil: Turner

Didaktischer Kommentar

Am Beispiel von Turners „The Fighting Temeraire" festigen S ihre Kompetenz im Umgang mit visuellen Materialien. Gleichzeitig schulen sie ihre interkulturelle Kompetenz, wenn sie das Gemälde in seinen (kultur)historischen Kontext einordnen.

Unterrichtstipps
ZA

S sammeln an der Tafel, was für sie alles unter Kunst und Kultur fällt. Dabei entsteht im Verlauf der Stunde eine Art Mindmap, die im Anschluss an *Part C* durch Namen von Künstlern, Gattungen usw. ergänzt wird.

1 S notieren ihre Beschreibung, bevor sie ihre Eindrücke mit einem Partner austauschen.

⚠ HA **2b** EXTRA Diese Aufgabe sollte in Gruppenarbeit erfolgen, wobei die notwendigen Informationen als vorbereitende Hausarbeit gesammelt werden. Im Unterricht erfolgt die Auswertung sowie die Organisation der gesammelten Informationen und Gestaltung des Posters. Die Vorstellung und Evaluation der Poster erfolgt im *gallery walk* (s. S. 297).

Differenzierung
ZA

Kunstgeschichtlich interessierte S recherchieren die Geschichte des Kriegsschiffs und schreiben eine Bildanalyse und -interpretation (s. *SF 9: Working with pictures*): *In what battle did the ship fight? Which period in the ship's life did Turner capture in his painting (cf. its full title)? What happened to the ship afterwards?* Lösungshinweise: s. Info.

> **Info**
>
> *The Temeraire* fought alongside the Victory (Nelson's ship) against the French fleet at the Battle of Trafalgar in October 1805. 'The Fighting Temeraire tugged to her last Berth to be broken up, 1838' (the full title of the 1839 painting) shows the ship being towed up the Thames to be broken up (taken apart to reuse the material) at a harbour in East London.
>
> *Impressionism* in painting arose in the second half of the 19th century. The impressionists' primary object was a spontaneous, undetailed rendering of the world through careful representation of the effect of natural light on objects.

Lösungshinweise

1 *The style:* The painting is not abstract – the steamboat and the sailing ship are painted in some detail – but the sky and the setting sun are impressionistic.

Part C2 – Sea Pictures in Music: Britten

The subject: On the left are boats in a harbour or on a river (the water is very calm, so it's probably not the open sea). In the foreground is a small steamboat with a funnel sending smoke up into the air. Behind this, bathed in the light of the setting sun, is the Temeraire, which the little steamboat seems to be pulling. The Temeraire seems to be a large sailing ship, a warship (cf. title). On the right almost all the picture is taken up with the setting sun and its reflection in the water, but there is also land on the right edge of the painting and something sticking out of the water. *The light* floods the whole picture and colours the clouds.

2a The subject of the painting is an old-fashioned, traditional sailing ship. But black and dirty and quite dominant in the painting is a steamboat, relatively new and modern at the time. In terms of painting technique, the left side of the painting looks more traditional, whereas the right side looks very modern. As an influence on Impressionist painters in France, Turner must be considered a trendsetter.

2b EXTRA Individual answers.

SB S. 29 CD 1.17–19
Transkript s. TM-DVD-ROM

C2 Sea Pictures in Music: Britten

Source:	*Peter Grimes*, 1945
Topic:	Britain's island status reflected in 20th century music
Text form:	Opera: Interludes (extracts)
Length:	*Extract 1* 0:46 min; *extract 2* 0:38 min; *extract 3* 0:44 min
Skills/Activities:	Listening to classical music; describing a sculpture

Didaktischer Kommentar

Benjamin Brittens Oper thematisiert wie kaum ein anderes Musikstück den Aspekt der Inselnation, der für Großbritannien prägend ist. In einem ganzheitlichen Ansatz setzen sich S mit der Musik auseinander, die Ausgangspunkt ist für die Beschäftigung mit verschiedenen Aspekten des Lebens und dessen Einflüssen auf die Kultur der Inselnation. Dadurch erwerben S soziokulturelles Wissen und festigen und erweitern ihre interkulturelle Kompetenz.

Unterrichtstipps

1 S hören die Musikbeispiele, machen sich Notizen (unter Einsatz von **KV 2**) und begründen ihre Wahl.

Differenzierung

1 (Musik-)Interessierte S recherchieren Handlung und Hintergründe der Oper. Lösungshinweise: s. Info.

2 S überlegen, welche Kriterien für ein Denkmal wie das *Britten memorial* und dessen Eignung eine Rolle spielen: *What is shown? How does this relate to the artist in question? Does the style of the memorial reflect the artist's adherence to tradition or innovative ideas?*

Info

Peter Grimes (1945) is an opera in a prologue and three acts set on England's east coast in the 1830s. Benjamin Britten wrote it to give a voice to those who live off the sea and to express the struggle of the individual against the masses. When Peter Grimes' apprentice dies, Grimes is suspected of murder, but acquitted. The opera tells the tale of Grimes' effort to procure another apprentice despite the villagers' disapproval. When the second apprentice dies after falling off a cliff, Grimes's sanity is at stake. A special feature are the opera's six sea interludes, four of which Britten released later under the title *Four Sea Interludes*: I: 'On the beach (Dawn)', II: 'The Storm', III: 'Sunday morning by the beach', IV: '(Passacaglia)', V: Evening, VI: 'Fog'. The libretto was written by Montagu Slater after the poem 'The Borough' by George Crabbe.

The Britten memorial ('Scallop', 2003) was designed at a cost of £70,000 by Suffolk-based artist Maggi Hambling. The solid-steel structure is located on the beach at Aldeburgh which Britten is said to have visited daily.

1 Part C3 – Popular Culture: Songs

Lösungshinweise

1 *Extract 1:* 'Dawn': violin and flute (trill), very high and clear, slower at first, then more strings and some brass, building up as the sun gains more strength.
Extract 2: 'The Storm': percussion and strings, excited, crescendo
Extract 3: 'Fog': drum roll, a single flute, slow at first, then more excited, then slower again, string-plucking

2 The memorial shows sea/scallop shells, standing – broken open – on a beach. Since Benjamin Britten was inspired by the sea, the image of the shell seems appropriate. The fact that it's broken could represent the fact that his life is over or that his soul (the animal inside) has been released.

3 Individual answers.

SB S. 30 CD 1.20
Transkript s. TM-DVD-ROM
▶ LSET ex. 10

C3 Popular Culture: Songs   Snow Patrol

Source:	*A Hundred Million Suns*, 2008
Topic:	Belfast as a mirror of the Troubles
Text form:	Song
Language variety:	Irish English
Length:	4:48 min
Level:	Intermediate
Skills/Activities:	Listening to popular music; summarizing

Didaktischer Kommentar

Die Materialien eröffnen den Blick auf die Art und Weise, wie Probleme und Konflikte (hier der Nordirlandkonflikt) als Teil der Popkultur aufgegriffen und thematisiert werden. Durch die Analyse des Liedtextes und der musikalischen sowie visuellen Gestaltungsmittel erweitern S ihre *media literacy* und ihr soziokulturelles Wissen.

Unterrichtstipps
⚠ HA

Einstieg: S bereiten sich vorab zuhause vor, z. B. indem sie online recherchieren (s. Linktipp unter Info), und tragen im Unterricht vor, was sie über den Nordirlandkonflikt wissen.

a S nutzen **KV 3** um ihre Reaktionen festzuhalten, bevor sie sich in einer Blitzlichtrunde (pro S ein Stichwort) untereinander austauschen.

b erfolgt im Plenum.

HA **d** eignet sich als Hausaufgabe.

Differenzierung

In leistungsschwächeren oder musikinteressierten Lerngruppen wird **KV 3** eingesetzt: **1–3** werden im Unterricht, **4** zuhause bearbeitet. So kann der Videoclip beliebig oft angesehen werden. L kann S für **2** und **4d** das Transkript zur Verfügung stellen. Lösungshinweise:

1 1G; 2H; 3A; 4F; 5C; 6D; 7B; 8E

2 *Chorus 1* (ll. 1–4): sung twice; *chorus 2* (ll. 17–25): sung twice; *chorus 3* (ll. 26–33): sung three times

3–4d Individual answers.

4e Examples: *Cradled and crushed* are complete opposites. Where one represents a loving relationship, the other depicts a destructive, hate-filled relationship. The contrast confronts us with an image of being destroyed by those who love us.
It's a mess / It's a start: When confronted with a mess we tend to be frustrated, helpless or hopeless. Surprisingly, this mess is presented in a more positive light, celebrating the imperfection and potential that Belfast has to offer.

ZA TM-DVD-ROM   L erstellt aus dem Transkript einen Lückentext und verteilt ihn mit der Aufgabe, beim ersten Hören die Lücken entsprechend auszufüllen.

ALT   Alternativ erhalten S den Liedtext in ungeordneter Reihenfolge und bringen die Teile beim Hören in die richtige Reihenfolge.

Part C4 – Scottish Festivals

ZA Interessierte Lerngruppen behandeln weitere Lieder zum Nordirlandkonflikt und kontrastieren sie mit **C3**, z. B. „Give Ireland Back to the Irish" (Paul McCartney, 1972), „The Town I Loved So Well" (Phil Coulter, 1973), „Ninety Miles From Dublin" (Christy Moore, 1978), „Sunday Bloody Sunday" (U2, 1983), „Barbed Wire Love" (Stiff Little Fingers, 1988), „Belfast Child" (Simple Minds, 1989), „Zombie" (The Cranberries, 1994), „Belfast" (Elton John, 1995).

> **Info**
>
> *The Troubles* was the period of violent conflict in Northern Ireland which began in the late 1960s with the Catholic civil rights marches and ended with the 1998 Good Friday Agreement. In 1969, British troops were deployed to restore peace in Belfast and Londonderry. Sectarian violence involving protesters, troops and police were widespread and terrorist attacks from both loyalist and republican paramilitaries led to the deaths of more than 3600 people during the Troubles.
> **Linktipp:** *www.bbc.co.uk/history/recent/troubles*
>
> *The Saville Report* (published 2010) investigated the deaths of 14 civil rights marchers at the hands of the British army in 1972 on what has become known as 'Bloody Sunday'. The report condemned the action of the army as wrong, and as a result Prime Minister David Cameron apologized on behalf of the British Government. It is hoped that the report will be finally allow people to put the events of the Troubles behind them once and for all.
>
> *The photo* shows Belfast City Hall with a Ferris wheel in the background.

Lösungshinweise

a Individual answers.

b *Message:* Belfast has a lot of potential. Although far from perfect, it belongs to the people to make of what they can ('your call'). It captures the flavour of the song in that the whole song is about contrasts – bad things in the past and good things to come ('a start').

c The song expresses Lightbody's love for Belfast, yet he acknowledges the dual role the city plays: on the one hand it nurtures and comforts its inhabitants like a parent ('cradled'), on the other it destroys them ('crushed'). This destruction is clear in the cracks and the craters mentioned in the song, but Lightboy's love is unconditional ('We're all gluttons for it') and can see past it to a promising future.

d Lightbody clearly depicts the Troubles as a past event. However, the past still has a negative influence on the present: 'All these years later and it's killing me'. The numerous victims of the Troubles are perhaps represented by the craters and cracks, but he chooses not to focus on this but rather on how they are to go on from this. The people of Belfast are confronted by a 'mess' of a building site on which they have to build a future for themselves. Part of the charm and appeal of the city is the tension and danger just below the surface. This is represented by the image of the city 'baring its teeth'.

SB S. 30 DVD
Transkript s. TM-DVD-ROM
▶ LSET ex. 12

C4 Scottish Festivals

Source:	The Official Edinburgh Festivals TV Channel, 2009
Topic:	The Edinburgh Festival Fringe
Text form:	Advertisements (text; trailers)
Language variety:	British English
Number of words:	175
Level:	Basic
Skills/Activities:	Reading non-fiction; viewing a film

1 Part C4 – Scottish Festivals

Didaktischer Kommentar Ausgehend von einem Werbetext setzen sich S mit drei Werbefilmclips auseinander. Ziel der *Context Task* ist die Umsetzung der Erkenntnisse und Einsichten aus dem Kapitel in einem kreativen, produktorientierten Lernarrangement. Dabei schulen S ihre Kompetenz, Informationen angemessen zu recherchieren, zu organisieren und zu präsentieren.

Unterrichtstipps

⚠ HA ● Word help

2 Vor dem ersten Sehen des Videoclips machen sich S mit unbekanntem Wortschatz vertraut.

⚠ 👥 HA

CONTEXT TASK b erfolgt in Kleingruppen, wobei die Informationen als vorbereitende Hausaufgabe gesammelt werden sollen. Die Auswahl, Verarbeitung und Organisation erfolgt im Unterricht.

Differenzierung

2c Interessierte S sehen sich Werbefilme für Aufführungen des EIF 2010 an und stellen den direkten Vergleich an: *http://eif.co.uk/multimedia*. Sie arbeiten die werblichen Eigenschaften heraus und beurteilen die Effektivität der Filme als Werbefilme.

👥 ZA

Select a German or British festival, stating its aims and how well it fulfils them. In groups of three, vote for the most interesting festival, prepare a presentation and present it to the class.

👥 ZA

1 Have you ever been to or participated in a festival? What made you go (advertisement/friends/…)? State whether you would go again, giving reasons.
2 Imagine you were organizing a festival. How would you try to attract people? Assess the suitability of the video clips you watched in 2a and state what you would change, if anything.

Info

Bankside Power Station generated electricity from 1952 to 1981. By 1990 the Tate Collection had outgrown the original Tate Gallery on Millbank and was looking for a new building. Architects Herzog & de Meuron converted the power station into an art gallery in 2000: the turbine hall became the entrance area as well as a display space for very large sculptural projects, the boiler house became the galleries. Above the original roofline of the power station a two-storey glass penthouse was added and the chimney was capped by a coloured light feature.

The photo shows members of the Scots band 'Albannach' entertaining crowds outside the Royal Scottish Academy at the Edinburgh Festival Fringe.

DVD

Luke Perry: American actor starring in *Beverly Hills 90210*; *Eric Bana:* Australian actor starring in *Hulk*; *Melanie Griffith:* American actress; *Heather Locklear:* American actress starring as Amanda Woodward in *Melrose Place*, a US TV series (1992).

Lösungshinweise

1 In contrast to the EIF, the Festival Fringe is not only for top-class performers, but for any unknown busker interested. Since eight theatre groups came uninvited to the first EIF in 1947, this unofficial festival was institutionalized in 1958 by founding the Festival Fringe Society, publishing a programme and opening a central box office. It is now bigger than the EIF.

2a 'Raw' is a dance performance, 'List Operators' a comedy, 'Power Plant' an installation / a 'sound and light' event.

2bc Individual answers.

Kopiervorlage 1: Evaluating a Presentation

Topic: Date: Speaker/Group:

Fill in the copymaster after listening to the presentation. Use your notes to give your classmates constructive feedback or assess your own presentation.

	Excellent	Good	Average	Fair	Poor
The presentation …					
… was informative.					
… had a clear focus.					
… was well researched.					
… was easy to follow.					
… had effective visual aids.					
The speaker(s) …					
… maintained eye contact with the audience.					
… spoke adequately without reading out the notes.					
… responded to questions.					
For group presentations: Did everyone participate? Were the roles clear?					
The overall impression of the presentation					

	Other observations
Speaker/Group 1	
Speaker/Group 2	
Speaker/Group 3	
Speaker/Group 4	
Speaker/Group 5	
Speaker/Group 6	

Kopiervorlage 2: Listening to Music

1 Topic vocabulary
Read the vocabulary relevant to the music you are going to listen to.

Instruments (classical and popular)
brass [brɑːs ☆ bræs]: French horn *(Waldhorn)*, trombone *(Posaune)*, trumpet, tuba
percussion: bass drum, chimes *(Glockenspiel)*, cymbals *(Becken)*, drum, snare drum, xylophone
piano-like instruments: harpsichord *(Cembalo)*, keyboard, organ *(Orgel)*, piano
strings: (double) bass [beɪs], cello [ˈtʃeləʊ ☆ -loʊ], harp *(Harfe)*, viola *(Violine)*, violin *(Geige)*   Example: String instruments can be plucked (with fingers) or bowed (with a bow [baʊ ☆ boʊ]).   lead guitar, bass guitar, rhythm guitar
woodwind: bassoon *(Fagott)*, clarinet, flute *(Querflöte)*, oboe, saxophone

Classical music	Popular music
pitch: soprano, alto, tenor, baritone, bass (for singing voice and instruments)	lead vocals / lead singer, backing vocals

Other terms	Other terms
composer	songwriter
libretto *(Text einer Oper)*	lyrics *(Liedtext)*, libretto *(Text eines Musicals)*
(chamber) orchestra	band/group
solo, accompaniment	solo, accompaniment
crescendo, diminuendo, tremolo/trill Example: The instruments rose in a crescendo. / The piece ends with a diminuendo.	bridge, chorus/refrain
chamber music, concerto, opera, symphony	alternative, country, grunge, heavy metal, jazz, pop, rap, rhythm and blues (R&B), rock, soul
melody, harmony	melody, harmony

2 Listening log

a Before listening, fill in the five W's: who (name of group/composer), what (song, opera, instrumental, etc. and title), when (date of composition), where and why it was written (e. g. for a wedding/funeral):

Who	What	When	Where	Why

b Then describe the music. The topic vocabulary (cf. **1**) and the words below may help you.

Instruments/Voices	
Intensity of the sound	sing at the top of one's voice – sing very softly/sweetly; become louder (rise in a crescendo) – become softer (there is a diminuendo)
Music	aggressive – peaceful; emotional – unemotional; boring – exciting; fast – slow; heavy – light; loud – soft; melancholic; monotonous – varied; moving/stirring; sad – happy; sentimental, sombre
Melody/Tune	simple, regular, irregular
Rhythm	fast – slow; regular; irregular; a constant change from slow to fast
Other observations	

Kopiervorlage 3: Take Back the City   Snow Patrol

1 Before listening

Match the words and phrases on the left to their explanations on the right.

1	put one's life into sb. else's hands	A	suggest that sb. has said sth. when they haven't really
2	make demands on sb.	B	do sth. till you can't do it anymore because you are too weak
3	put words into sb. else's mouth	C	a person who enjoys doing difficult or unpleasant tasks
4	epitaph	D	promises not kept
5	a glutton for work/punishment	E	a decision
6	broken words	F	words said or written about sb., esp. on a tombstone
7	do sth. till you drop *(infml)*	G	trust sb. at the risk of your own life
8	a call *(infml)*	H	expect that sb. does sth., esp. sth. that is difficult or challenging

2 Listening to the song

a   Form three groups. Each pays particular attention to one part of the chorus (chorus 1, 2 or 3). Note down whether 'your' chorus has positive or negative connotations and how often it is sung.

b   What conclusions can you draw from **2a** and **2b** regarding the atmosphere of the song?

3 After listening

a   Classify the following descriptions of songs as positive or negative according to your taste:

> catchy tune • poetic • melancholic • aggressive • cheerful • loud • nonsensical • monotonous • funny • hollow • fast • boring • interesting • makes me want to sing along • soft • thought-provoking • makes me want to dance along • doesn't touch me • sophisticated rhymes • simple • gives me a headache • emotional • clichéd

b   Describe the music and the lyrics using at least three of the above descriptions.

4 Watching the video clip

a   Before watching, speculate what the video clip might show. Then watch it:
www.snowpatrol.com/player/default.aspx?meid=3067

b   Classify the following descriptions as positive or negative according to your taste:

> original • goes well with the text/music • doesn't go well with the text/music • tells a story • fast cuts • modern • dated • incomprehensible • weird • funny • thought-provoking • boring • sentimental • cheap • many special effects • neutral • grim • happy • depressing • melancholic • romantic • cold • aggressive • sad • realistic

c   Then describe (the atmosphere of) the video clip using at least three of the descriptions.

d   Do your answers to **3** and **4ab** overlap? If so, explain how the video underlines the lyrics.

e   Identify some of the contrasts in the song and choose two to analyse. Explain why they are surprising.

Context 21 Politics: Topic Vocabulary

Word/Phrase	Memory Aid	German
the executive [ɪgˈzekjətɪv] *(fml)*	*definition:* the branch of government that has sole authority and responsibility for the daily administration of the state.	Exekutive, ausführende Gewalt, vollziehende Gewalt
legislature [ˈledʒɪsleɪtʃə]	*definition:* assembly with the power to pass, amend, and repeal laws (also called a legislative assembly)	Legislative
(to) **abolish** sth.	*word family:* (to) abolish sth. – abolition – abolished (adj)	etwas abschaffen
(to) **adopt a policy**	*other collocations with* **policy**: (to) develop / (to) implement / (to) pursue a policy	eine politische Richtung einschlagen
democracy	*definition:* a political system where the government is chosen by the people in a vote	Demokratie
republic	*example sentence:* South Africa became a ~ in 1961.	Republik
constitutional court	*definition:* a court which decides whether laws that are questioned are constitutional or not	Verfassungsgericht
head of government	*example sentence:* Britain had Tony Blair as its ~ **of government** for 10 years.	Regierungsführer
head of state	*definition:* the official leader of a country	Staatsoberhaupt
(to) **hold a referendum**	*definition:* to give all the people in a country the opportunity to vote on an important issue	eine Volksabstimmung durchführen
(to) **hold elections**	*other collocations with* **election**: (to) win/lose an / vote in an / stand for election	Wahlen abhalten
minister	*definition:* a person in a high position in government	Minister/in
(to) **pass a law**	*other collocations with* **law**: (to) be against the / (to) become a / (to) break the / (to) be within the law	ein Gesetz verabschieden
political party	*example sentence:* The two largest ~ **parties** in Britain are the Conservative Party and the Labour Party.	politische Partei
proportional representation	*definition:* a system which gives each party a number of seats in parliament based on how many votes they receive in an election	Verhältniswahlsystem
(to) **sign a petition**	*example sentence:* Thousands of people ~**ed a petition** against the sale of meat from cloned animals in supermarkets.	eine Petition unterzeichnen

Context 21 Politics: Topic Vocabulary

Word/Phrase	Memory Aid	German
(to) **win a seat**	*example sentence:* The party got very few votes in the election and therefore didn't ~ any **seats** in parliament.	einen Sitz gewinnen

GERMANY

Word/Phrase	Memory Aid	German
(to) **be divided into two states**	*example sentence:* Germany was ~ **into two states** in 1961.	in zwei Staaten geteilt sein
(Federal) Chancellor	*example sentence:* Angela Merkel was elected as the ~ of the grand coalition in Germany in 2005.	(Bundes-)Kanzler/in
(Federal) President	*word family:* (to) preside at/over sth. – president – presidential	(Bundes-)Präsident/in
federal state	*definition:* an administrative territory into which a country is divided which controls its own affairs but is ruled by central government	Bundesland
First Minister	*other collocations with* **Minister**: Finance / Foreign / Prime Minister	Ministerpräsident
reunification	*word family:* (to) reunify – reunification – reunified *(adj)*	Wiedervereinigung

THE UK

Word/Phrase	Memory Aid	German
(constitutional) monarchy	*word family:* monarchy – monarch – monarchist – monarchical	(konstitutionelle) Monarchie
constituency	*example sentence:* His ~ is known for voting Labour.	Wahlkreis
first-past-the-post	*definition:* a system where only the party with the most votes is elected to government	Mehrheitswahlrecht
House of Commons	*definition:* the lower house of the British parliament, composed of representatives voted for by the public, including the Prime Minister	Britisches Unterhaus
House of Lords	*definition:* the upper house of the British parliament, composed of the leading clergy and nobles	Britisches Oberhaus
Member of Parliament (MP)	*example sentence:* The ~s of ~ were outraged when the Prime Minister told them their budget had been cut.	Parlamentsmitglied
monarch ['mɒnək]	*synonym:* king – queen	Monarch/in
Prime Minister	*definition:* the head of the government and head of the executive branch	Premierminister/in

Context 21 Politics: Topic Vocabulary

Word/Phrase	Memory Aid	German
THE USA		
Congress	*definition:* the legislative branch of the US government comprising the Senate and the House of Representatives	Kongress
House of Representatives	*definition:* one of the two houses of the US legislature consisting of representatives from each state, whose number is determined according to the population of the state	Repräsentantenhaus
Senate	*definition:* one of the two houses of the US legislature consisting of two senators from each state	Senat
Democrat	*definition:* person belonging to the Democratic Party, a centre-left US political party	Demokrat/in
Republican	*definition:* person belonging to the Republican Party, a centre-right US political party	Republikaner/in
Amendment (to the Constitution)	*word family:* (to) amend – <u>amendment</u> – amended (adj)	Verfassungszusatz (zur amerikanischen Verfassung)
caucus	*definition:* a meeting of the members of a political party held to choose candidates or make decisions	Fraktionssitzung
checks and balances	*example sentence:* The system of **~ and balances** ensures that no one branch of government becomes too powerful.	politische Kontrollmechanismen
(to) **found** sth.	*synonyms:* (to) establish / (to) start sth.	etwas gründen
governor	*definition:* the chief executive officer in a US state	Gouverneur/in
primary (election)	*example sentence:* It was clear from the **~** results that he was the most popular candidate in the party.	Vorwahl
(to) **run for president**	*example sentence:* Barack Obama was the first black person to successfully **run for ~** in the USA.	als Präsident/in kandidieren
Supreme Court	*definition:* the highest court in a country or state	Oberster Gerichtshof
two-party system	*definition:* a system of government where just two political parties dominate all elections	Zweiparteiensystem

2 The USA – Dreams and Struggles

Das Kapitel beleuchtet den Amerikanischen Traum sowohl im Hinblick auf wesentliche Aspekte der US-amerikanischen Geschichte und des aktuellen politischen Lebens als auch im Hinblick auf individuelle Einstellungen zu Land und Leuten in den USA.

Part A – Dreaming of Equality ermöglicht eine differenzierte Auseinandersetzung mit den Bedingungen für die Gleichberechtigung von Schwarz und Weiß in den USA.

Part B – Dreaming of 'God's Own Country' beleuchtet die Bedeutung von Religion in den USA.

Part C – Dreaming of Rights and Freedoms diskutiert wesentliche Aspekte der Verfassung und ihrer *Amendments*.

Part D – Different Dreams gibt Einblicke in unterschiedliche Sichtweisen der USA von Menschen innerhalb und außerhalb des Landes.

Didaktisches Inhaltsverzeichnis

SB p.	Title	TM p.	Text Form	Topic	Skills and Activities	Language Practice
32	Lead-in CD 2.01	52	Photos; song	Different aspects and views of the USA	Cooperative learning strategies (think-pair-share, gallery walk); working with pictures; listening comprehension; giving an oral summary	
34	Words in Context – The American Dream	53	Informative text	The American Dream	Paraphrasing; word building; activating passive vocabulary	LP 1: Collocations with nouns
	Part A – Dreaming of Equality					
36	A1 What Are They Scared of? Patricia C. McKissack	55	Novel (extract)	A slave girl secretly learning to read and write	Reading fiction; writing a diary entry	
38	A2 Strange Fruit Abel Meeropol CD 2.02	56	Song	Lynching of Blacks in the South	Listening comprehension; reading poetry; analysing stylistic devices	
39	A3 Civil Rights DVD	58	Documentary film (extract)	Martin Luther King's dream of equality	Viewing comprehension; working with a cartoon; doing research (online); writing a comment; giving a presentation	
	Part B – Dreaming of 'God's Own Country'					
40	B1 Fundamentalism in America Susan Jacoby	60	Non-fictional text (extract)	Fundamentalism in American society	Reading non-fiction; working with cartoons	LP 2: Prepositions
42	B2 How Religious Are Young Americans?	63	Questionnaire; chart; diagram	Young Americans' attitude to religion	Doing a survey; working with charts and diagrams; comparing results; giving a presentation	
44	B3 Americans' Religious Affiliations	64	Chart	Religious affiliation in the USA	Working with charts and diagrams; doing research; mediating	
	Part C – Dreaming of Rights and Freedoms					
45	C1 The First Amendment	65	Non-fictional text	Freedom of religion, speech, assembly	Rewriting a text; taking part in a discussion	False friends
46	C2 Dissent is Patriotic DVD	65	Documentary film (extract)	ACLU defending First Amendment rights	Viewing a film; mediating; debating	
47	C3 A Social Studies Lesson Cory Doctorow	68	Novel (extract)	Questioning the right to suspend the Bill of Rights in a crisis	Dealing with narrative texts: point of view	*-ing* forms

2 Lead-in

SB p.	Title	TM p.	Text Form	Topic	Skills and Activities	Language Practice
50	C4 Freedom of Speech Norman Rockwell	70	Painting	Speaking up at an assembly	Working with pictures: analysing a painting	
50	C5 The Gun Control Debate – A Group Puzzle	71	Posters	Different attitudes toward gun control	Working with pictures: creating a slogan; using a dictionary; group puzzle	
52	Communicating across Cultures CD 2.03–04	72	Conversations	Talking to somebody about their country	Making and taking notes; listening comprehension; analysing conversations; doing a role-play	
	Part D – Different Dreams					
53	D1 Global Americans	72	Photos	Americans in different functions abroad	Working with photos; writing letters and emails	Reported speech
54	D2 EXTRA American Patriots Christopher Dickey	73	Magazine article (extract)	Patriotism vs. nationalism	Reading non-fiction; determining text types; writing a comment	
55	D3 Smalltown Americans Bill Bryson CD 2.05–06	74	Non-fictional text (extract); interview	The friendliness of smalltown Americans	Listening comprehension; reading non-fiction; paraphrasing; analysing humour	
57	D4 Contradictory Americans Stephen Fry	76	Speech (extract)	Contradictory aspects of what is typical of Americans	Analysing stylistic techniques	
58	D5 What America Means to Me Benjamin Livian	77	Essay (extract)	Loving America	Analysing an essay; commenting; writing an essay	

SB S. 32 CD 2.01
Transkript s. TM-DVD-ROM

Lead-in

Didaktischer Kommentar Die Materialien dieser Doppelseite erlauben S zu Beginn des Kapitels ihr Wissen und ihre Einstellung zu den vielfältigen Aspekten der USA zu äußern. Übungs- und Medienauswahl bereiten sie auf die methodisch-mediale Vielfalt des Kapitels vor.

SB-DVD-ROM

Lernwortschatz

insight (task 2c)

Unterrichtstipps **1** Die *language help* der Aufgabe **2** wird auch für die Bearbeitung der *think-pair-share*-Aufgabe verwendet.

2b L sollte darauf bestehen, dass jeder S mindestens ein aus seiner Sicht aussagekräftiges Foto aufhängt. Wenn dasselbe Bild mehrfach auftaucht, wird es nur einmal aufgehängt, der Umstand sollte jedoch in der Diskussion eine Rolle spielen.

Zuerst haben alle S die Möglichkeit, sich alle Fotos anzusehen. Dann erst erfolgen die Gruppenaufteilung und der erneute Halbrundgang mit der Auflage, Notizen für die anschließende Präsentation zu machen. Für diesen Rundgang empfiehlt sich die Aufteilung in Untergruppen von 2–3 S (je nach Kursgröße), um die nachfolgende Präsentation zu vereinfachen.

2c Die Gruppenzusammensetzung sollte für diese Diskussion geändert werden, sodass sie zur Hälfte jeweils aus A- und B-Gruppenmitgliedern besteht.

Differenzierung **1c** Leistungsstärkere S können durch das Kapitel blättern, um Zuordnungen der Bilder zu den Themen der Parts vorzunehmen.

Words in Context

> **Info**
>
> 'Proud to Be an American' (1984, by Lee Greenwood) was a song originally known as 'God Bless the USA'. Beyoncé Knowles [nəʊlz], born 1981 in Houston, Texas, is a successful American R&B singer and actress. She sang her version of 'Proud to Be an American' during the 'We Are One: The Obama Inaugural Celebration at the Lincoln Memorial' on 19 January 2009.

Lösungshinweise

1–2 Individual answers.

3 *The song in one sentence:* The message of the song seems to be that the singer is not only proud to be an American, but also values the freedom America gives its people and would never want to live anywhere else.
Possible answers: All photos illustrate freedom or reasons for pride in the USA:
- A because you're free to follow any religion and it shows a nice photo of people going to their church.
- B because there are many countries where, if you protest, you are put in prison or killed but in America that is not the case: people are free to march or protest.
- C because it shows how Americans celebrate their independence and their country every year and are proud to decorate their houses with their flag.
- D because the USA has always been technologically very advanced and they were very proud when they sent the first man to the moon.
- E because in a country where many people are white, people decided to vote for an African American President for the first time.
- F because the singer seems proud of American soldiers who fight for freedom and help to keep the peace in other countries.

SB S. 34
▶ LSET ex. 1, 2; Skill 44

Words in Context – The American Dream

Didaktischer Kommentar

Der Text beleuchtet Eckpunkte des *American Dream* von seiner Genese über wichtige Bestandteile bis hin zu möglichen kritischen und bewundernden Einstellungen dazu. Er dient der kontextuell sinnvollen Einführung des Basis-Lernwortschatzes des Kapitels unter besonderer Berücksichtigung grundlegender Begriffe zur Entstehung und Definition des *American Dream*.

SB-DVD-ROM

> **Lernwortschatz**
>
> American Dream (l. 1), hard work (l. 3), from rags to riches (l. 4), Founding Fathers (l. 6), personal liberty (l. 8), individual rights (l. 8), Declaration of Independence (l. 9), inalienable rights (l. 10), liberty (l. 10), pursuit of happiness (l. 10), US Constitution (l. 12), separate and independent branches (l. 13), system of checks and balances (l. 14), abuse one's power (l. 16), Bill of Rights (l. 19), freedom (l. 20), citizen (l. 20), limit the power of the government (l. 20), the separation of church and state (l. 22), achieve full legal equality (l. 27), Civil Rights Movement (l. 27), post-racial society (l. 29), election (l. 29), discrimination (l. 30), sole remaining superpower (l. 32), anti-American sentiment (l. 34), American way of life (l. 36)

Unterrichtstipps
HA

S lesen den Text (ggf. als Hausaufgabe) und vergewissern sich, dass sie alle markierten Begriffe erläutern, ggf. auch übersetzen können. Im Anschluss können **1a** und **1b** durchgeführt werden.

1ab S kontrollieren sich gegenseitig zu zweit oder in Dreiergruppen.

2ab kann ggf. arbeitsteilig in Partnerarbeit durchgeführt und anschließend gegenseitig ergänzt werden.

3 EXTRA Die gesuchten Ausdrücke sind hier bewusst nicht die im Text markierten, sondern stehen jeweils im Kontext solcher markierten Begriffe.

Part A

Lösungshinweise

1a
1. becoming rich
2. the men who wrote the Declaration of Independence and the US Constitution, thus creating the USA
3. system which tries to keep any one of a number of different groups from becoming too powerful by allowing each group to watch and limit the powers of the others
4. overstep the limits of one's power or use it to do bad things
5. basic freedoms that all people have or should have
6. country that can extend its military or economic power to anywhere on earth

1b
1. Americans are proud of the <u>Founding Fathers</u>, who risked their lives to fight for <u>independence</u> from Britain and establish a new country.
2. Many of the Framers of the <u>Constitution</u> were afraid of giving any one person or <u>branch</u> of government too much power.
3. … anyone born in America would automatically become a <u>citizen</u>.
4. Despite the <u>separation</u> of church and state, Americans are more religious …
5. Most experts agree that the USA is the only <u>superpower</u> left …

2a
discriminate; economy; elect; equal; govern; depend; move; person; power; race; separate

2b
Individual answers.

3 EXTRA
1. Most Americans are very optimistic and believe that anything is possible, <u>no matter</u> how difficult the task may be.
2. The three branches of government <u>watch over one another</u>.
3. The system of checks and balances <u>is supposed to</u> prevent the president, for example, from becoming too powerful.
4. Discrimination is a <u>fact of life</u> for many Americans.
5. The USA didn't only become a superpower because of its military strength, but also <u>by other means</u>.
6. The United States <u>is much admired</u> in many countries of the world.

Part A – Dreaming of Equality

Timeline of African American History

Since 1640	Slavery an essential part of cotton and tobacco-growing industries in the South
1775	American War of Independence between Britain and its American colonies begins
1776	Declaration of Independence adopted
1783	American colonies win the War of Independence against Britain
1860	President Abraham Lincoln tries to abolish slavery; Southern States of America try to leave the Union in protest
1861	Northern States of America march on the South to prevent the break-up of the USA; the American Civil War begins
1863	Emancipation Proclamation signed by Abraham Lincoln, freeing all slaves
1865	American Civil War ends with a victory of the Northern States; 13th Amendment to the Constitution makes slavery illegal in the USA; the Ku Klux Klan is founded, resulting in lynching of and discrimination against Blacks well into the 20th century

Part A1 – What Are They Scared of?

1870	15th Amendment to the Constitution gives all men the right to vote, regardless of race, but Jim Crow Laws make this difficult in reality and segregation of Blacks is still the norm in American society
1950s and 1960s	Civil Rights Movement in America, led by Dr Martin Luther King Jr.
1955	Rosa Parks refuses to give up her seat on a bus – Montgomery Bus Boycott begins
1956	Montgomery Bus Boycott ends – buses are no longer segregated
1957	Little Rock Nine escorted into Little Rock High School by federal troopers, signalling the end of segregated education
1963	Martin Luther King leads a march on Washington and delivers the speech 'I Have a Dream'
1964	Civil Rights Act passed; last of the Jim Crow Laws regarding segregation of Blacks are abolished
1968	Martin Luther King assassinated
2008	Barack Obama elected as President of the USA

SB S. 36
▶ LSET ex. 3

A1 What Are They Scared of?   Patricia C. McKissack

Source:	*Slave Girl*, 1997
Topic:	A slave girl secretly learning to read and write
Text form:	Novel (extract)
Language variety:	American English, non-standard
Number of words:	377
Level:	Intermediate
Skills/Activities:	Reading fiction; writing a journal entry

Didaktischer Kommentar   Dieser literarische Text bietet S einen Einblick in die Lebensumstände einer jungen Sklavin und ermöglicht ihnen, auf der Basis der von ihr gestellten Frage nach den Hintergründen des Lernverbots für Sklaven eine Auseinandersetzung mit der Bedeutung von Wissen im Machtgefüge *master/slave*. Die Auseinandersetzung mit der *slave vernacular* der Ich-Erzählerin schärft den Blick der S für heutige Standardsprache und Idiomatik.

SB-DVD-ROM

> **Lernwortschatz**
>
> be fine with sb. (l. 2), season (l. 4), wrap sth. (in sth., l. 16), aim to do sth. (l. 18), have the law on one's side (l. 23), be determined to do sth. (l. 25), keep sb. from sth. (l. 25)

Unterrichtstipps   Der Text sollte wenigstens in Teilen laut gelesen werden, entweder von L oder von ausgewählten S; ansonsten Lesen in Stillarbeit oder als Hausaufgabe möglich.

1 S beantworten die Fragen in Partnerarbeit. Eine Kontrolle durch L erübrigt sich.

2 eignet sich entweder als schriftliche Hausaufgabe oder als Partnerarbeit.

3a kann in Kleingruppen (2–3 S) diskutiert werden.

3b bietet sich als schriftliche Hausaufgabe an, die anschließend exemplarisch im Plenum präsentiert und diskutiert wird.

Differenzierung   L bittet S mit amerikanischer Aussprache, einen Absatz des Textes zum möglichst authentischen Vorlesen vorzubereiten.

Part A2 – Strange Fruit

1–2 Für leistungsschwächere S werden nach der Bearbeitung in Partner- oder Gruppenarbeit die Antworten vorgetragen und ggf. auf Folie oder an der Tafel festgehalten.

Lösungshinweise

1a They are Master William and Miss Lilly, the children of Clotee's owner, Master Henley. Her job is to fan the children during the hot summer while they do their school work.

1b While Clotee is fanning the children she looks at the books on their desks and silently learns the things they learn. This is how she teaches herself to read; it is dangerous because slaves can be beaten for learning to read and write.

2a
the heat's come early = summer's early
stirs the thick air = moves the air around
I come to know my ABCs = I've learned the alphabet
fall down in a fit = faint
It don't matter to me = I'm not bothered
I got to be real particular = I have to be really careful
fall under the whip = be beaten

2b It may seem like a silly job. But I'm not bothered, because while William's learning, I am too. Standing there fanning – up and down, up and down – I've been able to learn the alphabet and the sounds the letters make. I have taught myself how to read. Now, I can understand things – like newspapers that have been thrown away, letters in the trash can and books that I take off Master Henley's shelf. Sometimes it scares me to know what I know. Slaves aren't supposed to know how to read and write, but I do.

3a Clotee wrote her diary just before the Civil War, a time in which white slave owners were very worried about their slaves wanting to be free. The more education the slaves had, the more they could find out about what was going on and the more likely they were to want to lead independent lives free from slavery.

3b Without being able to put it into words, Clotee is already dreaming of equality. She is at least trying to learn the same things her white master's children are learning – a major step in that direction.

4 Individual answers.

SB S. 38 CD 2.02
▶ LSET ex. 4

A2 Strange Fruit   Abel Meeropol

Source:	'Strange Fruit', 1939
Topic:	Lynchings of Blacks in the South
Text form:	Song
Language variety:	American English
Length/Number of words:	2:33 min / 90 words
Level:	Intermediate
Skills/Activities:	Listening comprehension; reading poetry; analysing stylistic devices

Didaktischer Kommentar

Durch die intensive Auseinandersetzung mit diesem historischen Text- und Musikdokument werden S auf die Zwiespältigkeit jener Zeit hingewiesen. Die Analyse des Liedtextes und der Bildsprache hilft S, ihre Gefühle und deren Entstehen zu verstehen und auszudrücken.

SB-DVD-ROM

Lernwortschatz

bear sth. (l. 1), root (l. 2), twisted (l. 6), flesh (l. 8), crop (l. 12)

Part A2 – Strange Fruit

Unterrichtstipps — Einstieg: SB geschlossen. S hören das Lied und sprechen kurz über ihre Eindrücke. Anschließend gründliches Lesen des Textes mithilfe der Annotationen, um das zweite Hören vorzubereiten.

1 S besprechen ihre eigenen Gefühle erst mit einem Partner. Hierbei sollten sie auch auf den Unterschied zwischen ihrem Eindruck vor und nach der Textlektüre eingehen. Als Vorbereitung auf die Analyse der Bildsprache werden einige Reaktionen im Plenum diskutiert und festgehalten.

Differenzierung — **1** Leistungsschwächere S nutzen folgende *Language help* für die Formulierung ihrer Reaktionen:

> I found the way the singer stressed … disturbing – I feel shocked after listening – I felt melancholy while listening – listening to the song upset me because … – the way she sang sometimes seemed threatening

Leistungsstärkere S bearbeiten **KV 4** mit einem Auszug aus der Kurzgeschichte „Saturday Afternoon" von Erskine Caldwell. Lösungshinweise:

1 The white men are jealous of Will Maxie because he is a better farmer than they are and makes more money than they do.

2 The scene is dominated by the excitement of the lynching, which is described in a strangely festive mood: it appears more like a sports event with drinks being offered to the spectators. What's more, the cooling of the drinks seems just as important as the preparations for the actual lynching. We learn that the man who is being lynched leads a peaceful life as a good husband, father and farmer – and is surprisingly seen as a good Negro even by those who are about to kill him. The hate the lynch mob feels for him is contrasted with his goodness. The mood of the scene is thus one of excitement on the one hand and eerie matter-of-factness on the other.

3 The mood is created in a similar way: the body of the lynched man is compared to fruit hanging on a tree as if that were a natural thing. In the story, lynching Will Maxie appears to be a normal way to spend a few hours on a Saturday afternoon.

4 By juxtaposing everyday matter-of-factness and the wilful killing of a man, the author is criticizing the attitude of white Southerners of his time.

Linktipp: *www.nbu.bg/webs/amb/american/4/caldwell/afternoon.htm* Interessierte S lesen hier die vollständige Kurzgeschichte.

Info

'Strange Fruit' (released 1939) is the best-known song of protest against the lynching of Blacks in the South. The expression 'strange fruit' became symbolic for lynchings – common in the American South until well into the 1930s.

Abel Meeropol (1903–1986) (who used the pseudonym Lewis Allen) was an American Jewish teacher and writer. He wrote the poem 'Strange Fruit' which he later put to music.

Billie Holiday (1915–1959), whose birth name was Eleanora Fagan, was an American jazz singer and songwriter. 'Strange Fruit' was one of her most memorable performances.

Lynching of Blacks: Black slaves could be spontaneously executed without trial by a mob without the executioners ever being called to justice. After the slaves were freed, many Whites in the South felt the need to uphold white supremacy by keeping Blacks in their place: a result of this was the founding of the Ku Klux Klan in 1865 and the introduction of the so-called *Jim Crow laws* (cf. Info A3). The term 'lynching' for these executions probably comes from the name of Charles Lynch (1736–1796), a fierce Justice of the Peace who ruled in Virginia.

Part A3 – Civil Rights

Lösungshinweise

1 Individual answers.

2a The image refers to black men hanging from trees like pieces of fruit. The writer emphasizes the image in the last stanza: from l.9 on there is a series of images which most naturally apply to fruit, rather than a man – birds picking at it, rain collecting on it, the wind blowing it, the sun rotting it until it finally falls to the ground as a bitter crop: not a fruit, but a dead body.

2b The scent of a flowering tree is very pleasant. The contrast between the flowers' scent and the horrible smell is meant to shock: it works by first creating a very idyllic image and then suddenly destroying it.

2c EXTRA The tone is serene and calm to conjure up images of the beautiful houses and gardens of the old south. The intention is to lull the reader/listener into a false sense of calm and to give a hint of irony through the use of the word 'gallant' (a literary term meaning 'brave, noble, polite' and often used in descriptions of the South).

3a The death penalty can be imposed on somebody by a judge after a trial in court (and only in states where the law allows such a punishment). As a rule, a certain amount of time passes between the pronouncement of the death sentence and the actual execution. In contrast, a lynching is an informal execution by an angry mob without trial.

3b African-American dreams at the end of the 1930s were probably mainly to do with being given full civil rights and being treated as equal citizens, and not to have to fear death with no justice.

SB S. 39 DVD
Transkript s. TM-DVD-ROM
▶ LSET Skill 27

A3 Civil Rights

Source:	SoundWorks, 2004
Topic:	The March on Washington 1963 and Martin Luther King's dream of equality
Text form:	Documentary film (extract)
Language variety:	American English
Length:	7:40 min
Level:	Advanced
Skills/Activities:	Viewing comprehension; working with cartoons; doing research (online); writing a comment; giving a presentation

Didaktischer Kommentar

S lernen mit der berühmten Rede Martin Luther Kings ein klassisches Dokument der Bürgerrechtsbewegung kennen. Die Auseinandersetzung mit dem Dokumentarfilm ermöglicht S, ihr Wissen über diese wichtige Epoche der amerikanischen Geschichte zu erweitern und differenzierte Aussagen darüber zu machen. Durch das Medium Film wird die Fertigkeit, eine authentische Rede zu verstehen, geschult.

Unterrichtstipps
⚠ HA ● Word help

Vor der Betrachtung des Films machen sich S mit unbekanntem Wortschatz vertraut. Es bietet sich an, vorab im Plenum über Inhalte zu spekulieren.

Differenzierung

Leistungsstärkere S achten beim erneuten Betrachten auf die Rhetorik Martin Luther Kings (z. B. den Gebrauch von Gegensätzen oder Bildsprache).

⚠ **1b** Leistungsschwächere S erhalten das Transkript (oder zumindest einen Abschnitt wie z. B. den berühmten Schlussteil) zur Vorbereitung (s. TM-DVD-ROM).

Part A3 – Civil Rights

> **Info**
>
> *The Ku Klux Klan* (founded in 1865) is a racist hate group formed in the USA with the aim of securing and upholding white supremacy in the USA after the abolition of the slave trade. The Klan was revived again post-World War I and once more during the Civil Rights Movement in the 1950s and 60s. Over the decades, the Ku Klux Klan has carried out numerous hate crimes, acts of terrorism and intimidation against Blacks such as lynching, murder and house-burning. Their distinctive costumes (white robes, masks and conical hats) were intended to scare people and to prevent Klan members from being recognized. Independent Ku Klux Klan groups still exist alongside other white supremacist groups across the USA today.
>
> *The Little Rock Nine* were a group of nine black students who enrolled at the all-white Little Rock Central High School, Arkansas, in 1957. Despite the fact that racial segregation in schools had been declared illegal in 1954, the students were initially physically prevented from entering the school by soldiers and outraged members of the community. This act made national news and eventually the Little Rock Nine had to be escorted into their new school by federal troopers. They experienced much racism and abuse at the hands of their fellow white students.
>
> *Jim Crow* refers to the laws in place in the USA between 1876 and 1965 which enforced the segregation of Blacks and Whites and ensured that Blacks did not have equal rights regarding voting, employment etc. The name probably comes from a popular song performed in 1828 by T.D. Rice called 'Jump Jim Crow' which caricatures African Americans.
>
> *Abolitionism* was a movement to end the slave trade and emancipate slaves in Western Europe and the Americas. In 1808 the USA banned the importation of African slaves, but this did not prevent the continued mistreatment and sale of slaves already in the country. In 1863 Abraham Lincoln signed the Emancipation Proclamation and most slaves were freed as a result. Only after the 13th Amendment was passed in 1865 did slavery finally become completely illegal in the USA.
>
> *Rosa Parks* (1913–2005) was a black woman who, on 1 December 1955, refused to give up her seat on the bus to a white man in Montgomery, Alabama. Her subsequent arrest lead to the Montgomery Bus Boycott – a protest headed by Martin Luther King in which no black person used the bus system in the city for 381 days. Instead, they organised other means of getting around such as car-sharing, cycling or walking. The boycott put the city under tremendous financial pressure. In 1956, using Rosa Parks's case as an example, the courts ruled that the segregation of Blacks and Whites on public transport was unconstitutional and must end.
>
> *Martin Luther King* (1928–1968) was the leader of the Civil Rights Movement in the USA during the 1950s and 60s. King was an excellent orator and a great advocate of non-violent protest. He helped to secure the advancement of equal rights for black people in the USA. His most famous speech, 'I Have a Dream', was given at Washington in 1963 and called for racial harmony throughout the world. This speech is often credited with helping to pass the Civil Rights Act of 1964.
>
> *The assassination of Martin Luther King* took place on 4 April 1968 while he was standing on the balcony of the Loraine Motel in Memphis, Tennessee. His assassination caused a wave of riots in more than 100 cities across the USA, causing American leaders to ask people to uphold King's legacy of non-violence. James Earl Ray was later arrested in London and admitted to the assassination.

2 Part B

Lösungshinweise

1a Individual answers.

1b Martin Luther King's dream was that one day black Americans would have all the same rights and opportunities as white Americans, that they would not be economically disadvantaged and that, in every state in America they would be able to live side by side with white Americans without any problems. He hoped that a day would come when all Americans would be judged by their character, not their colour.

2 *Left page:*
- A slave in chains (cf. A1, fact file)
- An ad for a slave auction
- The body of a lynched black man hanging from a tree
- Jim Crow: a caricature of a black man – symbol of laws that segregated Blacks and Whites
- A sign pointing coloured people (African Americans) towards segregated facilities
- A hooded member of the Ku Klux Klan with a burning cross

Right page:
- One of The Little Rock Nine students, trying to enter a previously all-white high school in 1957
- A drawing of Barack Obama bursting through the pages of the history book
- A black man drinking at a segregated drinking fountain
- Rosa Parks sitting in a 'Whites only' seat on a bus in Montgomery, Alabama, 1955
- White US police grappling with Blacks
- Dr Martin Luther King, US Civil Rights leader
- Martin Luther King's supporters shortly after his assassination

The cartoon shows the long way from slavery to freedom, beginning with how black slaves were brought from Africa in chains and sold like animals at slave auctions. It depicts their oppression (lynching, the Ku Klux Klan, segregated facilities), their determination to get equal rights (the Little Rock Nine going to a previously white school, Rosa Park's refusing to give up her seat, Martin Luther King and the Civil Rights Movement). Although MLK was assassinated, his dream for Blacks and Whites has come a long way: in 2008 Barack Obama, son of a white mother and a black African father, was elected president of the USA.

3–4 Individual answers.

Part B – Dreaming of 'God's Own Country'

SB S. 40
▶ LSET ex. 5, 6

B1 Fundamentalism in America   Susan Jacoby

Source:	*The Age of American Unreason*, 2008
Topic:	Fundamentalism in American society
Text form:	Non-fictional text (extract)
Language variety:	American English
Number of words:	384
Level:	Intermediate
Skills/activities:	Reading non-fiction; working with a cartoon

Didaktischer Kommentar

Als Einstieg in das Teil-Kapitel dient ein provokativer Auszug aus einem amerikanischen Sachbuch zum Thema „Fundamentalismus in den USA". Eine satirische Weiterverarbeitung des Themas in einem Cartoon folgt in Aufgabe 4. Gerade die einseitige und provozierende Darstellung des Kreationismus im Rahmen der evangelikalen Bewegung Amerikas fordert die kritische Auseinandersetzung der S heraus und soll sie zu begründeten Stellungnahmen anregen. Das *Fact File* ergänzt Sachinformationen über die Kontroverse um den Kreationismus.

Part B1 – Fundamentalism in America

SB-DVD-ROM

> **Lernwortschatz**
>
> do harm (l. 1), sin (l. 2), against all evidence (l. 5), follow a course (l. 7), deny sth. (l. 11), contemporary (*n*, l. 14), mainstream (l. 29), creator (l. 32)

Unterrichtstipps

PRE-VIEWING S klären ihr Vorwissen über religiösen und politischen Fundamentalismus ggf. mithilfe von Wörterbüchern bzw. Lexika.

4c L teilt die Klasse in zwei Gruppen auf. Die Gruppen bereiten entsprechend Argumente pro und contra Kreationismus-Lehre an Schulen vor. L fungiert als Moderator der Diskussion, ein S wird zum Festhalten der Argumente an der Tafel / auf Folie bestimmt.

Ergänzend zum *Fact File* recherchieren S im deutschen Grundgesetz, ob dort ein ähnliches Verbot des Unterrichtens von religiösen Ansichten an öffentlichen Schulen verankert ist. Dies kann in Partnerarbeit oder als Hausaufgabe erfolgen.

Linktipp: *www.bundestag.de/dokumente/rechtsgrundlagen/grundgesetz/index.html*
Auf der Seite des Deutschen Bundestages steht S das Grundgesetz als HTML-Dokument zur Verfügung.

Als Gegenüberstellung zum Artikel von Susan Jacoby als bekennender Atheistin kann **KV 5** mit einem Interview des Evangelikalen Leith Anderson bearbeitet werden. Lösungshinweise:

1 Anderson argues that the evangelical movement is a broad one which comprises many different social and political positions. The only things that unite evangelicals are their belief in the Bible and in their personal relationship with Jesus. He uses examples from the world of politics (evangelicals vote for both Republicans and Democrats) and ecology (many evangelicals care about the environment).

2 Anderson believes that intelligent design should be taught in schools. While he himself believes in intelligent design ('a correct understanding of reality', l. 72), he is careful to say he is not an expert on the matter. He claims not to care under which subject it is taught, arguing that it is important for educated people to know what other people believe.

3 Possible answers:
- Anderson knows intelligent design has often been banned from classrooms as it is not science, so he would be happy if it finds some place in the classroom. His indifference to which subject it is taught under could be masking his desire to ensure it gets taught, no matter how.
- Anderson is right that education should give students information about different opinions.
- One should consider if the creation stories of all cultures should be included in the education system.
- If the 'intelligent design' theory is correct, then it should one day oust evolution from the classroom.

Differenzierung

2 Leistungsstärkere S fassen vorab die Hauptaussagen des Textes zusammen.

4b Interessierte und künstlerisch begabte S fertigen einen Cartoon an, der ihre Meinung und/oder Erfahrungen zum Thema darstellt. Möglich ist auch eine Art „Gegendarstellung" des Cartoons, in der z. B. ein anderes Land witzig oder kritisch dargestellt wird. Die Cartoons können z. B. in der Schülerzeitung abgedruckt und als weitere Grundlage für die Diskussion genutzt werden.

4c In leistungsstärkeren Lerngruppen lässt sich die Diskussion auch als *zigzag debate* (s. TM S. 299) führen, die eine genaue Vorbereitung und mehr Argumente (ein Argument pro S) erfordert.

Part B1 – Fundamentalism in America

> **Info**
>
> *The Creation of Adam* is part of a larger fresco by Michelangelo (1475–1564) depicting the scenes of Genesis on the ceiling of the Sistine Chapel in Rome. The fresco was commissioned by Pope Julius II and took four years to complete. The scene which portrays God giving life to Adam was completed in c. 1511.
>
> *Susan Jacoby* (born 1946) is an award-winning American author, essayist and the director of the Center of Inquiry – a non-profit educational organization – in New York. As an outspoken secularist and atheist she often picks up on religious anti-intellectualism in her works which include Freethinkers: *A History of American Secularism* (2004) *and The Age of American Unreason* (2008)
>
> *Evangelicalism* is a religious stream that has emerged from Protestantism. It is based on four concepts: conversionism (the belief of being born again), activism (sharing the gospel), biblicism (conviction of biblical authority) and crucicentrism (the belief in Jesus's death and resurrection). Approximately a quarter of the US population claim to be evangelicals, belonging to various churches. There are several forms of evangelicalism, ranging from rather liberal to more conservative types. The latter are often confused with fundamentalism. Fundamentalists believe that the Bible is literally true, so they believe that the world and humanity were created exactly as described in the Bible.
>
> *The National Association of Evangelicals (NAE)* is an American organization linking Christian groups, churches and individuals with the principle aim of spreading Christian messages. Its various initiatives cover the media industry, world relief and national projects focusing on specific Christian concerns, e.g. religious teaching in schools and reducing the number of abortions in the USA. One key belief of the NAE is that government is a gift from God for the common good. In 2004 they adopted 'For the Health of the Nation', a strategic framework for engagement in political activity. Since then, the association has been outspoken on a variety of issues, from the interrogation methods for terror suspects in Guantanamo Bay to the possibility of nuclear disarmament in America.

Lösungshinweise

1a It wasn't a problem if people in the 19th century thought that death and disease were God's punishment for sinning and had to be accepted. Science and medicine had practically nothing else to offer.

1b Jacoby says that fundamentalists make false claims about the role of condoms in fighting AIDS and that, by championing abstinence, which most people won't adhere to, they are partly responsible for the spread of this deadly disease. She says that, by insisting on the teaching of creationism as an alternative to evolution in American schools, fundamentalists are making Americans stupider and less competitive in the sciences.

1c According to Jacoby, an evangelical is anyone who has a deep personal relationship with God. This includes fundamentalists who, in contrast to most evangelicals, believe that everything in the Bible is absolutely true. (cf. also Info on 'evangelicalism')

2 She makes a comparison between 19th century beliefs and modern beliefs (ll. 1–14), thereby linking superstition of another age to this age. She brings in various topics (like AIDS and evolution), and uses them to display the ignorance of all churches. She makes a close link between fundamentalism and education, implying that fundamentalists are not well-educated. There are, however, fundamentalists who are well-educated. In the final paragraph one can see how she uses words to put down fundamentalists: There is a 'powerful' correlation which is 'unquestionable'; she refers to their beliefs derogatively as 'that old-time faith'.

Part B2 – How Religious Are Young Americans?

3

1 The percentage <u>of</u> people who believe <u>in</u> a literal interpretation <u>of</u> the Bible is highest <u>among</u> those who have only attended high school.
2 There is a strong relationship <u>between</u> a lack <u>of</u> proper information <u>about/on</u> AIDS and other diseases and the spread <u>of</u> those diseases.
3 Large numbers <u>of</u> people <u>in</u> Africa are infected <u>with</u> HIV, but fundamentalists are still <u>against</u> the use <u>of</u> condoms. Some critics argue that this makes the fundamentalists at least partly responsible <u>for</u> the continuing epidemic.
4 The writer has obviously done quite a bit <u>of</u> research <u>into</u> fundamentalist beliefs and practices. There is no real alternative <u>to</u> that sort <u>of</u> approach in scientific writing.

4a *The cartoon* shows a world map as the cartoonist imagines it in the year 2050. The five countries labelled have been renamed: Canada is called 'Canadian Environmental Provinces', the USA is called 'United States of Creationism', Europe is called 'European Scientific Union', China 'Modern China', and India 'Research Centers of India'. There is a speech bubble for every renamed country talking of advances in medicine, science and technology – only the USA merely says, 'At least we're not descended from monkeys'.
The message seems to be twofold: the denial of evolution is holding the country back in the areas of science and technology, and it can even be seen as a warning to Americans that they must wake up to reality or lose their place as a superpower.

4b *Comparison:* While Jacoby states that American students are currently trailing their peers in their knowledge of science, the cartoon looks to the future, saying that the USA will fall behind the rest of the world. The writer and the cartoonist would probably agree on both points.
Effectiveness: Individual answers.

4c Individual answers.

SB S. 42
▶ **LSET ex. 7**

B2 How Religious Are Young Americans?

Source:	National Institute of Child Health and Human Development, 2005
Topic:	Young Americans' attitude to religion
Text form:	Questionnaire; chart; diagram
Language variety:	American English
Number of words:	134
Level:	Basic
Skills/Activities:	Doing a survey; working with charts and diagrams; comparing results; giving a presentation

Didaktischer Kommentar

Sofern es die Konstellation der Lerngruppe erlaubt (s. a. Unterrichtstipps) und unter Wahrung der Privatsphäre erheben S zunächst die Daten zur religiösen Bindung innerhalb ihrer eigenen Kursgruppe, bevor sie sich mit den Ergebnissen der amerikanischen Untersuchung beschäftigen. Anschließend wird beides verglichen. Sie erwerben Kompetenzen in der Beschreibung grafischer Auswertungen von Befragungen in englischer Sprache.

SB-DVD-ROM

Lernwortschatz

questionnaire (introductory text), religious service (l. 5), somewhat (l. 15), major (l. 17)

2 Part B3 – Americans' Religious Affiliations

Unterrichtstipps ⚠ L achtet darauf, dass S den Fragebogen anonym ausfüllen, sodass ihre Privatsphäre gewahrt bleibt. L weist S zudem darauf hin, dass es ihnen freigestellt ist, ob sie alle Angaben machen. In Klassen, in denen L das Thema aufgrund der Klassenkonstellation als zu sensibel erachtet, werden lediglich die amerikanischen Ergebnisse in Aufgabe 2 analysiert.

1 Die Ergebnisse für Frage 2 sollten am besten als Kreisdiagramm, die restlichen als Balkendiagramme dargestellt werden.

Lösungshinweise **1–2** Individual answers.

SB S. 44 ## B3 Americans' Religious Affiliations

Didaktischer Kommentar S üben sich in der Auswertung von und Auseinandersetzung mit statistischen Erhebungen und deren angemessener Präsentation. Sie erwerben sowohl differenzierteres Wissen als auch die Fähigkeit, darüber zunehmend differenziert in englischer Sprache zu berichten. Im Sinne interkultureller Studien vergleichen S Ergebnisse mit relevanten Verhältnissen in Deutschland.

SB-DVD-ROM

> **Lernwortschatz**
> Orthodox (chart, l. 4)

Unterrichtstipps **3** S werden darauf hingewiesen, dass es sich nicht um eine wörtliche Übersetzung, sondern eine Zusammenfassung für den amerikanischen Adressaten handelt.

Lösungshinweise **1a** *Christian groups:* Evangelical Protestant Churches, Mainline Protestant Churches, Historically Black Churches, Catholic, Mormon, Jehovah's Witnesses, Orthodox, Other Christian.
Other religions: Judaism (Jewish), Buddhism (Buddhist), Islam (Muslim), Hinduism (Hindu), Other World Religions, Other Faiths
No religion: Unaffiliated (it is difficult to classify 'Don't Know / Refused').

1b *Percentages:*
Christian: 78.5 %
Other religions: 4.6 %
Unaffiliated: 16.1 %
Don't Know / Refused: 0.8 %
Conclusion: American society is dominated by people who consider themselves Christians. There is, however, a sizable group that is not affiliated with any church. Other religions play no role, statistically speaking.

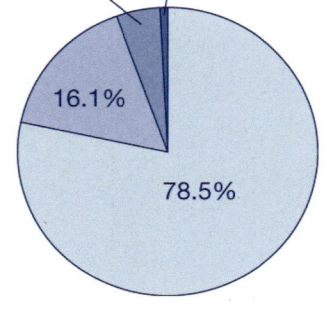

2 **EXTRA** *Percentages in Germany (from: http://fowid.de/fileadmin/datenarchiv/Religionszugehoerigkeit_Bevoelkerung__1950-2008.pdf):*
Christian: 59 %
Other religions: 7 %
Unaffiliated: 34 %

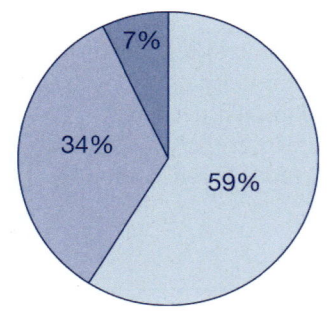

3 **Mediation**:
- Muslims and Jews should have been invited to take part in the religious service
- Muslims and Jews weren't even asked to help plan it
- such a celebration should include everyone living in Germany; all religions or none
- if Germans want Muslims to state their agreement with the constitution (which they do), they should include them in the celebrations of the constitution

Part C – Dreaming of Rights and Freedoms

SB S. 45 ## C1 The First Amendment

Source:	The Bill of Rights, 1791
Topic:	Freedom of religion, speech, assembly
Text form:	Non-fictional text
Language variety:	American English
Number of words:	45
Level:	Advanced
Skills/Activities:	Rewriting a text; taking part in a discussion

Didaktischer Kommentar

Die intensive Arbeit mit dem *First Amendment* hilft S, seine große Bedeutung in der US-amerikanischen Gesellschaft zu verstehen und sich über die dargestellten Einzelfälle differenziert zu äußern.

SB-DVD-ROM

Lernwortschatz

controversy (introductory text), prohibit sth. (l. 3)

Unterrichtstipps

2 Die einzelnen Fälle können ggf. arbeitsteilig in Partner- oder Gruppenarbeit besprochen werden, um den Zusammenhang mit dem *First Amendment* zu klären. Dieser sollte dann im Plenum benannt werden.

3a Die Gruppen sollten sich anders als zu **2** zusammensetzen, um S andere Perspektiven zu ermöglichen.

Lösungshinweise

1 Congress is not allowed to make a law which would establish an official church, and it cannot prohibit anyone from practising their religion. It cannot limit the freedom of speech or of the press in any way. It cannot prevent people from getting together in a peaceful way, and it cannot stop people from petitioning the government to correct things they think are unfair.

2
1. Hanging a cross in the school promotes a particular religion which is prohibited in a public school, an institution of the state, by the First Amendment. So this is clearly a First Amendment issue.
2. Praying at a school function sends the message that the school endorses religion, which the First Amendment clearly does not allow.
3. Here the school may have violated the student's freedom of speech in which case the First Amendment applies.
4. The First Amendment clearly states that people have the right to *peaceably assemble* and to express their opinions. By refusing to give them a permit for their march, the police may have violated the Neo-Nazis' right.
5. The case relates to the First Amendment insofar as it involves the professor's right to free expression.

3 Individual answers.

SB S. 46 DVD
Transkript s. TM-DVD-ROM

C2 Dissent Is Patriotic

Source:	Sundance Channel / Sundance Institute, 2005
Topic:	Defending First Amendment rights
Text form:	Documentary film (extract)
Language variety:	American English
Length:	7:51 min
Level:	Intermediate
Skills/Activities:	Viewing a film; mediating; debating

2 Part C2 – Dissent Is Patriotic

Didaktischer Kommentar

Der Dokumentarfilm knüpft an die in **C1** studierten Aussagen zum *First Amendment* an und verlangt von S eine intensive Auseinandersetzung mit dem Thema. S beschäftigen sich mit der Struktur des Dokumentarfilms und üben ihre medienkritischen Hör-/Sehkompetenzen.

Unterrichtstipps
⚠ HA ● Word help

Vor dem Sehen des Dokumentarfilms machen sich S mit unbekanntem Wortschatz vertraut.

Vor Betrachten des Films empfiehlt sich die Besprechung des *First Amendment* wie in **C1** vorgesehen. Der Wortlaut sollte S bekannt sein.

2 Für die Bearbeitung dieser Aufgaben empfiehlt sich ein zweites Sehen. Dazu könnte sich jeweils ein Drittel des Kurses auf **a**, **b** und **c** konzentrieren. Anschließend Besprechung im Plenum.

3 Für eine gründliche Analyse empfiehlt sich ein drittes, auf formale Elemente konzentriertes, Sehen. Expertengruppen können sich auf die einzelnen Punkte konzentrieren und anschließend ihre Ergebnisse mithilfe der *Language help* 2 im Plenum vorstellen. Zusätzlich bietet es sich an, die Struktur der Bilderfolge (*images, cuts*) und ihre Wirkung auf den Zuschauer untersuchen zu lassen. Die Schlussfolgerung über die Neutralität des Filmemachers erfolgt im Plenum.

HA **4** ist als Hausaufgabe geeignet. S sehen sich das gewünschte Format zunächst in einer Zeitung an.

5 Vor der Debatte wird *SF 25: Debating* bearbeitet.

Info

The 2004 Republican National Convention, at which the Republican Party of the USA nominated their presidential candidate George W. Bush, took place from 30 August to 2 September at Madison Square Garden in New York City, and faced more protests than any other convention before or since.
Background to the film:
- The original title of the film was *Some Assembly Required*. This is a reference to a common disclaimer on American products, warning that the contents are not pre-assembled but require a certain amount of putting together. It is also, of course, a play on words of the other meaning of 'assembly' as it is used in the First Amendment.
- At the beginning protesters are seen on bikes riding through the streets ringing bells and calling out 'The Republicans are coming' and 'New Yorkers, defend your city'. Some are even wearing three-cornered hats, which is a humorous reference to popular US mythology, when Paul Revere (cf. Longfellow's 'Midnight Ride of Paul Revere') rode on horseback through the streets of Lexington and Concord warning that 'The Redcoats [= British soldiers] are coming!'
- At one point a man is seen carrying a sign that reads 'Have another pretzel'. This is a reference to then-President George W. Bush, who nearly choked to death on a pretzel in January 2002.
- PATH Station (Port Authority Trans-Hudson) is one of the New York train systems, running between Manhattan and Newark, New Jersey.

Lösungshinweise

1 Individual answers.

2a *Protesters in the film say:*
- 'Everybody has a right to be speaking out no matter whether they're accusing the protesters of being unpatriotic … Dissent is patriotic.' (N. Parish)
- 'People tend to think that dissent is usually bad. But we should tolerate it because that's part of the price of freedom. What we probably neglect is that the idea of free speech protects society as a whole even more than it protects individual speakers.' (Cass Sunstein)

Part C2 – Dissent Is Patriotic

- 'You can get a great deal of order if you suppress freedom and protest, but that order is at the expense of law.' (Cass Sunstein)

2b The police violated the protesters' rights in several ways: during the anti-Iraq war demonstration they didn't allow people to move freely through the streets to get to the demonstration in the first place. When the protesters were at the march, the police attacked them with mounted units, knocked them down and pepper-sprayed them even though they weren't doing anything illegal. They also used barricades and arrested hundreds of people.

2c Those who say it is not legitimate to criticize the government after 9/11 claim that to do so is 'unpatriotic' and endangers national security.
Those who feel criticism is in order say that dissent is patriotic, that it helps to protect society as a whole by pointing out when the country is on the wrong course. They say protest is very much a part of the American tradition and that the First Amendment not only allows but also encourages it.

3 *Choice of interviewees:* He probably chose a church organist because even the most conservative of viewers would think of her as 'good' and not likely to be unpatriotic or radical. Parish is made even less suspect by the fact that she was brought up to 'not make waves'. This is a clever choice if the purpose of the film is to convince conservative viewers of the legitimacy of the protesters' arguments.
The choice of Alex Vitale must have to do with his briefing paper after his upsetting experiences during a demonstration, giving the director the chance to show police intervention as well as one example of a demonstrator's reasonable reaction to it.
Cass Sunstein was chosen to provide the patriotic theory behind dissent, in order to convince sceptics not only on the basis of experience and patriotic feeling, but also on grounds of rational thought.

Choice of music: The classical music used for most of the film has a soothing effect which provides a nice contrast to some of the scenes at the protest marches. It also reminds us of the role of Nancy Parish, the church organist, who plays these pieces in one of the scenes.
The percussion music which is playing during the planning meeting for the convention protests helps to build tension in a section of the film that might otherwise have become a bit dull. It signals that what is coming might be action-packed.

During the march we hear the classic protest song *When the saints go marching in*, which is probably what they were actually marching to.

Camerawork: There are shots taken from different ranges and angles of the various marches and demonstrations to focus on different aspects: long and medium long (full) shots for overviews of scenes, or to show police and demonstrators interacting; close-ups are used to focus on individual interviewees. In two scenes the camera tracks the interviewees Nancy Parish and Alex Vitale to give more 'life' to the documentary. There are a few surprising close-ups, i.e. of Nancy Parish's hands on a piano keyboard or of Nancy Parish's dog. Such images help the audience to see the protesters as normal people and not militants.

Range of images/cuts: The film makes use of several techniques to give the film its pace without making it too fast for a serious message. Scenes with action alternate with static interview scenes.

The documentary starts with a seemingly chaotic sequence of people shouting into their cell-phones, letters and words appearing, dissolving and falling into place to make up the wording of the First Amendment. The words *SOME ASSEMBLY REQUIRED* are created through a cross-fade of people walking through the station, whose image gradually turns into elements of the letters that eventually make up the three words.

Part C3 – A Social Studies Lesson

The sequence showing protesters in 'Paul Revere mode' has elements of comedy and satire (horse head on cyclist's handlebars, 18th-century hats).
In several sequences there are flashback images, i.e. of the Twin Towers in black and white. The chamber music session with Nancy Parish is given an extraordinary amount of individual attention.
Film-maker's point of view: It seems clear that the film-maker is on the side of the ACLU and the protesters, as he shows everything from their perspective throughout the film. The ACLU representatives and the protesters are portrayed as reasonable people whereas police are shown as sometimes taking extreme actions against the protesters.

4 Mediation Dissens ist patriotisch – so der programmatische Titel eines kurzen Dokumentarfilms über Amerikaner, die auch nach den Terrorakten des 11. September 2001 ihr Recht auf Demonstrationen gegen die Regierung verteidigen. Menschen laufen durch eine U-Bahn-Station in New York, zitieren dabei Passagen über Rede- und Versammlungsfreiheit aus der Verfassung in ihre Mobiltelefone; ein Fahrradkorso warnt vor den Republikanern wie im 18. Jahrhundert Paul Revere vor den britischen Soldaten. Brave Kirchenmusiker und Professoren – alle stehen zu ihrem Recht auf Protest und erklären, warum er wichtig ist auch in Zeiten nationaler Krisenstimmung. (88 words)

SB S. 47
▶ LSET ex. 8, 9, 10, 11

C3 A Social Studies Lesson Cory Doctorow

Source:	*Little Brother*, 2008
Topic:	Questioning the right to suspend the Bill of Rights in a crisis
Text form:	Novel (extract)
Language variety:	American English
Number of words:	1329
Level:	Advanced
Skills/Activities:	Dealing with narrative texts: point of view

Didaktischer Kommentar

Die Lektüre und Interpretation dieses Auszugs eröffnet S Einblicke in ein kontroverses gesellschaftspolitisches Thema: Krisenmanagement durch Beschränkung von Rechten. Sie lernen eigene Assoziationen mit realen Ereignissen in ihre Interpretation des Romanauszugs einzubeziehen sowie Argumente in der Diskussion zu durchschauen, einzuordnen und zu bewerten.
Die Auseinandersetzung mit der Erzählperspektive eröffnet weitere Differenzierungsmöglichkeiten bei der Interpretation.

SB-DVD-ROM

Lernwortschatz

circumstance (l. 8), conduct a search (l. 14), endanger sb./sth. (l. 26), optional (l. 36), policy (l. 45), secure sth. (l. 65), threaten sb./sth. (l. 79), claim to do sth. (l. 112)

Unterrichtstipps

Einstieg: Vor dem ersten Lesen empfiehlt sich eine Zusammenfassung von Ergebnissen der Diskussionen über das First *Amendment* (**C1**) und den öffentlichen Protest (**C2**).

HA **1** eignet sich als Hausaufgabe.

Direkt im Anschluss an die Lektüre können S kurz Situation und Stimmung im Klassenzimmer beschreiben und kommentieren, bevor sie sich inhaltlich mit der Diskussion auseinandersetzen.

Differenzierung
ZA

Zur schriftlichen Übung können S arbeitsteilig ein *character profile* von Mrs. Andersen, Charles oder Marcus erstellen.

Part C3 – A Social Studies Lesson

> **Info**
>
> *Miss/Mrs./Ms.:* Instead of the traditional forms 'Miss' for unmarried women and 'Mrs.' for married ones, many women choose to call themselves or to be addressed as 'Ms.' in order to prevent their marital status from being revealed. In modern-day USA, it has become common for professional women to use 'Ms.' regardless of their marital status.

Lösungshinweise

1 Mrs. Andersen believes that basic rights can be suspended to protect individuals in society or to protect society as a whole, i.e. in the name of national security. She sees the right to life as more important than other rights, such as liberty and the pursuit of happiness which *might* come later.

Marcus believes that rights are absolute and can neither be taken away nor given up. There are no priorities – all rights are of equal value and importance. He wants to be part of a country which he is convinced the Founders wanted, i.e. one of 'dissidents and fighters and university dropouts and free speech people'. (ll. 103–104).

2a He is proud because his fellow students are standing up for what they believe. They are expressing unpopular beliefs in the face of an authority figure who clearly thinks otherwise.

2b Marcus stands for those who do not accept their rights being compromised in the name of national security and who believe that these rights are 'inalienable'.

Mrs. Andersen stands for all those in the USA who feel that being safe from terrorism is more important than other rights.

2c

Passage from the text	How it characterizes Marcus
'set off alarm bells' (l. 3)	sensitive to subtleties of language
'prepared to overlook it' (l. 5)	generous, willing to give someone the benefit of the doubt
'not waiting to be called on' (l. 11) 'I shook my head' (l. 44)	has strong opinions and isn't afraid to express them
'I was feeling sick. This was not what I'd learned or believed about my country.' (l. 33)	has opinions so strong that he can feel physically sick when his beliefs are violated
'giving me a fake smile' (l. 38) 'She shook her head at us like we were being very stupid.' (l. 77)	sensitive to others' body language
'I was so proud of my fellow students' (l. 75)	feels an almost fatherly relationship towards his fellow students; perhaps he has been acting as a 'missionary'
'I tried hard not to stiffen.' (l. 80)	afraid that he might inadvertently show his thoughts
'I shouted. God, she had me so steamed.' (l. 86) 'I boiled.' (l. 90)	prone to anger when deeply felt beliefs are attacked
'I didn't try. I was running away.' (l. 108)	prone to feelings of guilt when he doesn't act according to his beliefs

2d The use of first-person narration makes the incident in the classroom seem more immediate and relevant. We can see how it directly affects Marcus.

3a–b Individual answers.

Part C4 – Freedom of Speech

4a Both forms are present participles.
- *ll. 9–10:* '… she said, <u>turning</u> to the blackboard and <u>writing</u> down a row of numbers'
  = she said as she turned to the blackboard. Then she started writing a row of numbers.
- *l. 11:* '… I said, not <u>waiting</u> to be called on.'
  = I said without waiting to be called on. / I didn't wait to be called on and simply said …

4b EXTRA
- *l. 29:* '… Charles said, not waiting for her to call on him again.'
  = Charles wartete nicht darauf, von ihr aufgerufen zu werden / bis er aufgerufen wurde, und sagte: …
- *l. 38:* ‚… she said, giving me a fake smile.'
  = … sagte sie und schenkte mir ein aufgesetztes Lächeln.

5 EXTRA *Events in the novel and in US history:* The bombing of the Bay Bridge in the novel is a parallel to the terrorist attacks on the World Trade Center in 2001.
Mrs. Andersen's beliefs stand for the conservative backlash which pitted national security against civil rights after 9/11.
The arrest of apparently peaceful people in the park is similar to police behaviour at various demonstrations, e.g. those shown in the DVD in **C2**.

SB S. 50

C4 Freedom of Speech

Didaktischer Kommentar

In der Auseinandersetzung mit Norman Rockwells Gemälde ‚Freedom of Speech' üben S die wichtige Fertigkeit, eine Bildaussage in zielsprachliche Worte zu fassen.

Differenzierung
ZA

Interessierte S können im Internet oder in Bildbänden weitere Bilder von Norman Rockwell recherchieren und eines davon zur zusätzlichen Übung, wie in **1a** beschreiben, analysieren und im Kurs präsentieren.

> **Info**
>
> *Norman Rockwell:* Norman Rockwell (1894–1978) was a highly prolific and popular commercial American painter and illustrator active throughout the greater part of the 20th century. He is famous for his magazine cover illustrations, which would typically depict everyday life scenarios, but is best-known for 'The Four Freedoms', a series of four oil paintings which were inspired by a speech given by the then US President Franklin Roosevelt in 1941. In his speech, Roosevelt outlined four essential human rights that should be protected at all costs and that should serve as a reminder of America's reasons for participating in World War Two. The four freedoms named by Roosevelt were: the Freedom of Speech, the Freedom to Worship, the Freedom from Want, and the Freedom from Fear. Rockwell's series depicted each of these freedoms individually on the cover of the *Saturday Evening Post*.

Lösungshinweise

1a 'Freedom of Speech' by Norman Rockwell is a realistic painting of people at a public meeting of some sort. The setting might be a school as there is a blackboard in the background. All of the people in the painting are male (except perhaps for the partially covered face on the left-hand side, which might be female). The men are seated, they are wearing suits and ties. Only the man in the centre of the picture is standing and speaking. In contrast to the others, he is wearing a simple checked blue shirt and jacket. Everyone is looking at him, apparently listening to what he has to say.

1b The man's checked shirt and rough leather jacket indicate that he is a worker or farmer. The other men are dressed in white shirts, suits and ties, indicating that they work in offices and have a higher social and educational level. The speaker has the same right to speak as the other men, despite their different backgrounds. Rockwell is showing that classless freedom is an essential part of American society.

Part C5 – The Gun Control Debate – A Group Puzzle

2a As the painting was created in 1943, i.e. the middle of World War II, one purpose might have been to show Americans what they were fighting for.

2b EXTRA Individual answers.

SB S. 50
▶ LSET Skills 18, 19

C5 The Gun Control Debate – A Group Puzzle

Didaktischer Kommentar

S setzen sich in wechselnder Gruppenarbeit mit pointierten Aussagen zum kontrovers diskutierten Bereich der *gun control* auseinander. Sie gewinnen vertiefte Erkenntnisse über den Gegenstand der Kontroverse, lernen provokant-pointierte Slogans zu entschlüsseln und selbst anzuwenden. Sie üben sich im Weitergeben, Erhalten und Verwerten von Informationen in Kleingruppenarbeit.

SB-DVD-ROM

Lernwortschatz

control (*n*, bumper sticker), law-abiding (bumper sticker), be in place (T-shirt slogan), ignore sth. (T-shirt slogan),

Unterrichtstipps

Sollte die Kursgröße es nahelegen, kann das Gruppenpuzzle auch mit acht Gruppen durchgeführt werden.
Innerhalb der Gruppen erhält jeder S eine eigene Nummer: bei acht Gruppen empfiehlt sich eine weiterlaufende Nummerierung (zwei Themengruppen A, S 1–8), um arbeitsfähige Kleingruppen für die Umverteilung (**1b**) zu behalten.

1a Ggf. empfiehlt sich vor Beginn der Gruppenarbeit eine Wiederholung der Begriffe *explicit*, *implicit* und *tone*, damit alle Gruppen auf demselben Niveau arbeiten können.

HA **3ab** Für die Erläuterung des Begriffs wird ein einsprachiges, für die anschließende Übersetzung ein zweisprachiges Wörterbuch benötigt. Die Aufgabe kann als Hausaufgabe erledigt werden. Besprechung im Plenum.

Info

Adolf Hitler: fascist dictator of Germany (1933–1945)
Fidel Castro: premier, then president of Cuba (1959–2008)
Muammar al-Qaddafi: leader of Libya (since 1970)
Joseph Stalin: General Secretary of the Communist Party of the USSR (1922–1953)
Idi Amin: military dictator of Uganda (1971–1979)
Mao Tse Tung (also: Mao Zedong): communist chairman of the People's Republic of China (1949–1959)
Pol Pot: totalitarian leader of Cambodia (1975–1979)
Kim Jong-il: ruler of North Korea (since 1994)

Lösungshinweise

1a
A: Guns are needed for protection, as there isn't always a policeman around to help.
B: If people weren't allowed guns, only criminals would have them; they would kill off law-abiding citizens one at a time.
C: Guns provide the means to rebel against the government in case it becomes oppressive.
D: Gun control is a measure that allows dictators to come into power, who then prohibit others from having them.

1b–c Individual answers.

2 Individual answers.

2 Communicating across Cultures

3a *Waffenkontrolle* either means checking whether someone has a weapon or checking if weapons are in proper order.
Gun control, on the other hand, means an attempt to limit the number of guns in a society or to regulate who may own them.

3b Individual answers.

SB S. 52 CD 2.03–04
Transkript s. TM-DVD-ROM
► LSET Skill 24

Communicating across Cultures – Talking to Somebody about Their Country

Didaktischer Kommentar S üben interkulturelle Kommunikation, indem sie für kulturell bedingte Missverständnisse sensibilisiert werden und lernen, diese im Gespräch zu vermeiden.

Lösungshinweise **1a** The first conversation ended badly, the second well. That's because in the first conversation Tobias was too direct. He didn't try to be tactful or to find nice things to say about the USA to balance his criticism. The fact that he was so prejudiced annoyed Linda, which made her express some prejudices about Germany. In the second conversation Anne was able to be tactful and positive without ruling out that there probably were some things she didn't like about the USA. She was also careful to point out that since she hadn't been to America, she was relying on what other people had told her.

1b *What went wrong:*
- Tobias was rude right at the start, criticizing the Americans for not speaking other languages.
- Tobias was very critical about Linda's defence. He began one sentence with 'You Americans …' which is a gross generalization and thus insulting.
- He bases his general prejudices on Mallorca which leads Linda to retaliate.
- He's arrogant about Munich having the best discos in Europe which provokes a similar response from Linda about New York.

Useful phrases:
It's a good thing you speak … because I don't speak …
- There might be some things I wouldn't like about …, but I hope I can go there one day and see for myself.
- I've often read that …
- I really admire that …
- In school we learned that you … I really think that's not good. It would be nice if that could stop.
- I'm proud to be …, and I think we have lots of good points but … is not one of them.
- So tell me, I'm really interested, what are the things that make you proud to be …?
- … it's not perfect, but …
- You're a very good advertisement for …

1c–2 Individual answers.

Part D – Different Dreams

SB S. 53   **D1 Global Americans**

Didaktischer Kommentar Die Fotos machen S auf sehr unterschiedliche Auftritte US-amerikanischer Bürger in der Welt aufmerksam und regen zur Diskussion über deren globale Rolle an. S üben hier intensiv das Versprachlichen von und die Auseinandersetzung mit Bildern.

Unterrichtstipps **2** Die *Language Help*-Box enthält nicht nur Formulierungs-, sondern auch inhaltliche Diskussionshilfen, von der S regen Gebrauch machen sollten.

Part D2 – American Patriots

Differenzierung Sollte die Zahl der Kursteilnehmer nicht nur Vierergruppen zulassen, empfiehlt sich die Zuteilung einzelner lernschwächerer S zu einem jeweils lernstärkeren S zur gemeinsamen Auseinandersetzung mit einem der Fotos.

Lösungshinweise **1** *Photo 1:* A white woman is talking to a group of black boys. She is holding up a book or a picture. They are in a classroom: there is a blackboard in the background and the boys are sitting at school desks. The woman could be a teacher or volunteer worker teaching English at an African school. She has one hand in her pocket, so she is probably relaxed and feels comfortable in her surroundings.
Photo 2: Two American soldiers; they could be in Iraq or Afghanistan as the scenery looks like the desert. They would be there as part of the Western alliance troops trying to keep or restore the peace. Both look as if they were worried or watching something very carefully.
Photo 3: Two American and two Asian businessmen facing one another at a conference table. One pair is bowing, the other is shaking hands. They seem to be closing a deal and look pleased.
Photo 4: Two girls whose backs are all we can see. They are tourists taking pictures of the Taj Mahal.

2–3 Individual answers.

SB S. 54 **D2 EXTRA American Patriots** Christopher Dickey

Source:	*Newsweek*, 6 July 2006
Topic:	Patriotism versus nationalism
Text form:	Magazine article (extract)
Language variety:	American English
Number of words:	367
Level:	Advanced
Skills/Activities:	Reading non-fiction; determining text types; writing a comment

Didaktischer Kommentar Indem S sich mit dem Begriffspaar „nationalism" und „patriotism" auseinandersetzen, lernen sie eine wichtige Unterscheidung zu formulieren.

SB-DVD-ROM

> **Lernwortschatz**
>
> patriot (heading), nationalism (l. 1), live up to sth. (l. 14), essentially (l. 22), principle (l. 26)

Unterrichtstipps **1** S sollten für das Lösen der Aufgabe sowohl die einschlägigen Wörterbuchdefinitionen als auch die im Text verwerteten Orwell-Zitate kennen. Als möglichen Zwischenschritt können S zunächst die entscheidenden deutschen Schlüsselwörter aufschreiben und übersetzen, bevor sie ihre englische Definition notieren.

> **Info**
>
> *George Orwell* (1903–1950), whose real name was Eric Arthur Blair, was an English author. He is best-known for his satirical novella *Animal Farm* (1945) and his dystopian novel *Nineteen Eighty-Four* (1949). His writings reveal a passionate commitment to democracy and socialism.

Lösungshinweise **1** Patriotism is the feeling of belonging somewhere, of being proud of that place and feeling affection towards it. Nationalism is more a political feeling, that is often tinged with aggression toward other nations, specifically the feeling that your own nation is better than any other.

2 It is an argumentative text in which the quotations are used to back up the arguments the writer puts forward. Since these are from an author known for his political writings, they also serve to give special credibility to the arguments.

Part D3 – Smalltown Americans

3a Individual answers.

3b Some people may seek happiness in quite different ways to Americans. So Americans should not force their idea of happiness on anyone who doesn't share it.
The picture of the white teacher can be seen as that of an American generously volunteering to give a good education to the less fortunate. It can, however, also be interpreted as an American imposing typical American ideas of civilization and culture on other people.
The picture of the soldiers could be used as an argument that Americans try to share their dream of democracy and freedom with the world, but it could alternatively be perceived as evidence that they believe they can impose their views on the world by using their military.
The picture of the businessmen might make one think of the USA's huge financial power and that this power is often used to help nations in need, but it is also used to 'buy' support.
The picture of the tourists could be seen as Americans trying to discover other cultures and share their own with others, or as tourists merely taking a superficial view of what other cultures have to offer (e.g. a few attractive sights) and nothing more; they may even be expecting that the host country offers them the lifestyle they are used to.

3c Individual answers.

SB S. 55 CD 2.05–06
Transkript s. TM-DVD-ROM

D3 Smalltown Americans Bill Bryson

Source:	*I'm a Stranger Here Myself*, 2000
Topic:	The friendliness of smalltown Americans
Text form:	Non-fictional text (extract)
Language variety:	American English
Number of words:	480
Level:	Intermediate

Source:	Minnesota Public Radio, 2004
Topic:	Returning to one's own country after a long absence
Text form:	Interview (extract)
Language variety:	American English
Length:	6:45 min
Level:	Intermediate

Skills/Activities:	Listening comprehension; reading non-fiction; paraphrasing; analysing humour

Didaktischer Kommentar In diesem Auszug lernen S die Gastfreundschaft und Hilfsbereitschaft der US-Amerikaner kennen. Durch die Analyse des Textes lernen sie, zwischen den Zeilen zu lesen und Stilmerkmale von Humor zu erkennen.

SB-DVD-ROM

Lernwortschatz

leap (l. 3), insist (on sth.) (l. 11), evident (l. 14), essentials (l. 20), go to waste (l. 35)

Unterrichtstipps
⚠ HA ● Word help

PRE-LISTENING b Vor dem Hören des Interviews machen sich S mit unbekanntem Wortschatz vertraut.

👥 👥👥 HA   Nach gemeinsamer Bearbeitung des Interviews im Unterricht können Textlektüre und Aufgabe 1 als Hausaufgabe erledigt werden. Ergebniskontrolle in PA oder Kleingruppen im Unterricht.

Part D3 – Smalltown Americans

Differenzierung
ZA

Im Anschluss an Aufgabe 3 können lernstärkere S sich intensiver mit Brysons Humor im Text auseinandersetzen:
Look at ll. 2–3, 5–8, 13–16, and explain how Bryson achieves a humorous effect.
Lösungshinweise:
In ll. 2–3 Bryson starts a small list of wonderful things about America. After naming two sacred concepts on which the country is built, he gives 'free refills' (of coffee in a restaurant) as the third item on his list, which is both unexpected and irreverent. In ll. 5–8 (cf. 3a, no.1) he exaggerates about his new neighbours' happiness to see him and his family ('the one thing'). When (in ll. 13–16) he says that their furniture is travelling around the world to exotic ports, this is of course an exaggeration. Besides exaggeration, he uses understatement ('the most trifling', l. 12), which contrasts with the normality of the situation. The unexpectedness of such comments makes the text funny.

Info

Bill Bryson (born 1951 in Des Moines, Iowa) is a best-selling American author. He is famous for his humorous travel books on Britain (*Notes from a Small Island*, 1995), America (*I'm a Stranger Here Myself*, 1999), Australia (*Down Under In a Sunburned Country*, 2000) and mainland Europe (*Neither Here Nor There*: *Travels in Europe*, 1991). More recently he has written books on the English language, Shakespeare and general science (*Bryson's Dictionary of Troublesome Words*, 2002; *A Short History of Nearly Everything*, 2003). His writing style is characterized by his wry humour, which has probably contributed substantially to his popularity and accessibility as a writer. Bryson currently lives in Britain with his wife and children, having returned from the USA after eight years in New Hampshire.

Lösungshinweise

PRE-LISTENING **a** It means that although he is technically an American, he feels just as foreign in the USA as any foreigner would.

1 1 b; 2 b, d; 3 a, d

2 *Characteristics described by Bill Bryson:* He describes outstanding friendliness (l. 3), generosity and kindness (people bring things, ll. 7–8), hospitality (invitation, ll. 9–12); thoughtfulness (welcome on return from UK, ll. 21–23); all of these things are illustrated in the anecdote about the tickets to the basketball game.

3a
1 People were very happy to see us and acted as if they had missed us in their lives up until now.
2 so little trouble as to be insignificant
3 the first answer I thought of
4 He gave me the tickets quickly and forcefully.
5 which was due to the fact that I usually don't understand people's intentions very well

3b The paraphrases are less formal than Bryson's sentences, using expressions and grammatical constructions from everyday language. His use of both complex language and grammatical constructions to describe everyday situations are part of what makes the piece funny because they reveal unexpectedly simple things.

3c **EXTRA** Individual answers.

2 Part D4 – Contradictory Americans

SB S. 57 **D4 Contradictory Americans** Stephen Fry

Source:	Spectator Lecture, 2009
Topic:	Contradictory aspects of what is typical of Americans
Text form:	Speech (extract)
Language variety:	British English
Number of words:	102
Level:	Intermediate
Skills/Activities:	Analysing stylistic techniques

Didaktischer Kommentar

In der Auseinandersetzung mit dem Auszug wird S deutlich, dass es unmöglich ist, einen Volkscharakter zu verallgemeinern, weil immer auch das Gegenteil richtig ist. Dies ist eine sehr wichtige interkulturelle Erkenntnis für S.

SB-DVD-ROM

Lernwortschatz

contradictory (heading), reverse (n, l. 8)

Unterrichtstipps

Zur Vorentlastung von **1a** können S den Text zuhause lesen und die genannten Namen und Gegensatzpaare recherchieren.

1b kann in Partnerarbeit vorüberlegt und im Plenum diskutiert werden.

Info

'As American as apple pie' is an expression meaning 'typically American'

Apple Inc. is an American corporation that makes and sells computers and other electronic devices.

Wal-Mart Stores Inc. is the name of the corporation that runs Walmart discount stores worldwide.

Wall Street is a street in Manhattan, NYC, that stands for the New York Financial District since 1792.

Trump Towers: a) Trump World Tower in Manhattan: one of the most luxurious residential towers in the world; b) chain of luxury hotels.

Twin Towers: the two towers of the World Trade Center in Manhattan that were destroyed by terrorists in the attack on 11 September 2001.

Jimi Hendrix (1942–1970): American rock guitarist, singer and songwriter.

Jimmy Stewart (1908–1997): American film and stage actor who played in a variety of film genres.

Lösungshinweise

1a
- Wal-Mart / Wall street = low-paid jobs / high-paid jobs
- Trump Tower / Twin Towers = symbol of progress and glitz / symbol of modernity and destruction
- Jimi Hendrix / Jimmy Stewart = hard-edged pop culture, innovative icon / tough western icon, old-fashioned romance
- blue collar / red neck = factory work / farm work
- opportunity / opportunism = given a chance / ruthlessly taking what you can

1bc Individual answers.

2a *Techniques:*
- contrasts, e.g. 'white supremacy or black power'
- wordplay, e.g. Wal-Mart / Wall Street
- starting a pair with the same stem or word, but ending in a contrast, e.g. 'opportunity or opportunism', 'small-town courtesy or small-minded bigotry'

Part D5 – What America Means to Me

Effectiveness: The effectiveness of his techniques lies mainly in the surprise generated by the contrasts, and the better known they are, the more effective they are.

2b Individual answers.

SB S. 58

D5 What America Means to Me Benjamin Livian

Source:	Thirteen Ed Online, 2001
Topic:	Loving America
Text form:	Essay (extract)
Language variety:	American English
Number of words:	501
Level:	Basic
Skills/Activities:	Analysing an essay; commenting; writing an essay

Didaktischer Kommentar

Mit diesem Essay wird S zum Abschluss des Kapitels die patriotische Haltung eines Altersgenossen vorgeführt. Es dient ihnen als Impuls für ihr eigenes Abschluss-Essay, wonach sie der positiven Vorlage folgen, sich aber auch kritisch mit ihr auseinandersetzen können.

SB-DVD-ROM

Lernwortschatz

tremendous (l. 3), vast (l. 3), widespread (l. 10), attorney (l. 24), miracle (l. 41)

Unterrichtstipps

Das Essay sollte zuhause gelesen werden und anschließend Aufgabe 1 in Form eines schriftlichen Statements oder in Stichpunkten notiert werden.

2ab kann mit gegenseitiger Kontrolle in Partnerarbeit durchgeführt werden.

3 kann in Partnerarbeit oder als Hausaufgabe erledigt werden. Besprechung im Plenum.

5ab eignet sich als Partner- oder Kleingruppenarbeit (3 S). Für die Begründung (**b**) bietet sich eine kurze Internetrecherche an.

5c sollte nach gründlicher Vorbereitung aller S im Plenum diskutiert und das abschließende Ergebnis als gemeinsames Statement festgehalten werden.

ZA Für die Kurse, die sich mit „A Social Studies Lesson" (C3) beschäftigt haben, bietet sich ein Perspektivenwechsel an:
What would Marcus tell Benjamin Livian about American freedoms after Mrs Anderson's Social Studies lesson? Write a comment from his point of view.

CONTEXT TASK L weist S auf die besondere Bedeutung von „Stage 3: Revising Your Draft" hin. Für die gesamte Aufgabe sollte S eine Woche Zeit gegeben werden, damit alle Schritte durchgeführt werden können.

KV 6 kann für beide Themen („What America/Germany means to me") herangezogen werden: entweder als weitere Grundlage oder als Vergleich mit den Verhältnissen in Deutschland.

Lösungshinweise

1 Individual answers.

Part D5 – What America Means to Me

2a *Positive characteristics of the USA in the essay:*
- a world leader (l. 2)
- the most advanced nation in the world (l. 5)
  - tremendous military strength (l. 3)
  - vast technology (l. 3)
  - high standard of living (l. 4)
- freedom (l. 7)
- opportunity (l. 7)
- diversity (l. 7)
- rights only dreamed of by others around the world (ll. 12–25)
  - freedom of speech, press, religion, assembly and petition
  - democracy
  - innocent until proven guilty
  - right to a fair trial and to an attorney
- everyone is guaranteed specific liberties (l. 25)
- a sense of equality (l. 26)
- 'from rags to riches' – the American Dream (ll. 27–30)
- harmony in the 'melting pot' (ll. 31–35)

2b Individual answers.

3 The first paragraph begins with Livian's thesis that the USA is the world's only superpower, offering military strength, technology and a high standard of living as arguments for his thesis. The paragraph continues with the ideals of freedom, opportunity, and diversity – all that the US flag stands for in the view of the writer.
The next paragraph deals with the rights every American has, including the freedoms mentioned in the First Amendment, the freedom to protest, to hold democratic elections, and the freedom of the justice system.
In the next paragraph, the topic Livian deals with is the American Dream and how everyone has the chance to climb the social ladder. He calls the American Dream a 'beautiful thing'.
The idea of the American melting pot, in which all elements exist together in harmony, is the topic of the fourth paragraph.
The concluding paragraph is a summary of the ideas and key terms already mentioned.
The structure shows how in America all the good things hang together, one element leads to the mentioning of another, and the subjective first and last paragraphs emphasize the fact that the American nation is inherently welcoming to and good for all who want to live there.

4 Individual answers.

5a They compare very well as the German constitution guarantees them in the same way as the American constitution does. In Germany there is freedom of speech, freedom of press, freedom of religion, freedom of assembly and petition. There are democratic elections and the German justice system offers the same rights and freedoms as the US system does.

5b Criticism might include slavery, segregation, Guantánamo Bay, Abu Ghraib, the Homeland Security Act, etc.

5c It defines the American Dream well because Livian doesn't only list ideas but mentions a personal example: His father came to the USA with nothing but the dream of a better life, and he was able to achieve it.

CONTEXT TASK Individual answers.

Kopiervorlage 4: Lynching Will Maxie

Will Maxie, an African American, is supposed to have 'said something' to the daughter of a white citizen, and now all the men in the small farming town are out to 'get him'.

They had a place already picked out at the creek. There was a clearing in the woods by the road and there was just enough room to do the job like it should be done. Plenty of dry brushwood nearby and a good-sized sweet-gum tree in the middle of the clearing. The automobiles stopped and the men jumped out in a hurry. Some others had gone for Will Maxie. Will was the gingerbread Negro. They would probably find him at home laying his cotton by. Will could grow good cotton. He cut out all the grass first, and then he banked his rows with earth. Everybody else laid his cotton by without going to the trouble of taking out the grass. But Will was a pretty smart Negro. And he could raise a lot of corn too, to the acre. He always cut out the grass before he laid his corn by. But nobody liked Will. He made too much money by taking out the grass before laying by his cotton and corn. He made more money than Tom and Jim made in the butcher shop selling people meat.

Doc Cromer had sent his boy down from the drugstore with half a dozen cases of Coca-Cola and a piece of ice in a wash tub. The tub had some muddy water put in it from the creek, then the chunk of ice, and then three cases of Coca-Cola. When they were gone the boy would put the other three cases in the tub and give the dopes a chance to cool. Everybody likes to drink a lot of dopes when they are nice and cold.

Tom went out in the woods to take a drink of corn with Jim and Hubert Wells. Hubert always carried a jug of corn with him wherever he happened to be going. He made the whisky himself at his own still and got a fairly good living by selling it around the courthouse and the barbershop. Hubert made the best corn in the county.

Will Maxie was coming up the big road in a hurry. A couple of dozen men were behind him poking him with sticks. Will was getting old. He had a wife and three grown daughters, all married and settled. Will was a pretty good Negro too, minding his own business, stepping out of the road when he met a white man, and otherwise behaving himself. But nobody liked Will. He made too much money by taking the grass out of his cotton before it was laid by.

Will came running up the road and the men steered him into the clearing. It was all fixed. There was a big pile of brushwood and a trace chain for his neck and one for his feet. That would hold him. There were two or three cans of gasoline, too.

Doc Cromer's boy was doing a good business with his Coca-Colas. Only five or six bottles of the first three cases were left in the wash tub. He was getting ready to put the other cases in now and give the dopes a chance to get nice and cool. Everybody likes to have a dope every once in a while.

[…]

Will Maxie did not drink Coca-Cola. Will never spent his money on anything like that. That was what was wrong with him. He was too damn good for a Negro. He did not drink corn whisky, nor make it; he did not carry a knife, nor a razor; he bared his head when he met a white man, and he lived with his own wife. But they had him now! God damn his gingerbread hide to hell! They had him where he could not take any more grass out of his cotton before laying it by. They had him tied to a sweet-gum tree in the clearing at the creek with a trace chain around his neck and another around his knees. Yes, sir, they had Will Maxie now, the yellow-face coon! He would not take any more grass out of his cotton before laying it by!

Tom was feeling good. Hubert gave him another drink in the woods. Hubert was all right. He made good corn whisky. Tom liked him for that. And Hubert always took his wife a big piece of meat Saturday night to use over Sunday. Nice meat, too. Tom cut off the meat and Hubert took it home and made a present of it to his wife.

Will Maxie was going up in smoke. When he was just about gone they gave him the lead. Tom stood back and took good aim and fired away at Will with his shotgun as fast as he could breech it and put in a new load. About forty or more of the other men had shotguns too. They filled him so full of lead that his body sagged from his neck where the trace chain held him up.

The Cromer boy had sold completely out. All of his ice and dopes were gone. Doc Cromer

---

4 **brushwood** small broken or dead branches of trees
10 **lay (a crop) by** *(AE Southern)* care for the crop for the last time before the harvest
23 **drugstore** *(AE)* shop that sells medicine (drugs) as well as soft drinks, etc.
29 **dope** *(AE Southern)* a Cola drink
50 **trace chain** chain with which an animal pulls a wagon
75 **coon** *(taboo, sl)* black person
91 **lead** [led] Blei
sag hang heavily

would feel pretty good when his boy brought back all that money. Six whole cases he sold, at a dime a bottle. If he had brought along another case or two he could have sold them easily enough. Everybody likes Coca-Cola. There is nothing better to drink on a hot day, if the dopes are nice and cool.

After a while the men got ready to draw the body up in the tree and tie it to a limb so it could hang there, but Tom and Jim could not wait and they went back to town the first chance they got to ride.

From: Erskine Caldwell, 'Saturday Afternoon', in: *American Earth*, New York: Scribner, 1931

Tasks:
1. Explain why the men want to kill Will Maxie.
2. Analyse how the particular mood is created through contrasts.
3. Compare the mood created in the story with that created by the song 'Strange Fruit' (**A2**).
4. What point is the author making by writing such a story? Write a comment.

Kopiervorlage 5: Issues in Evangelicalism

In 2006 Leith Anderson, president of the National Association of Evangelicals, was interviewed by Fred De Sam Lazaro for the American broadcaster PBS.

Q: What do you think are some of the most misunderstood things about evangelicals in the broader media and in the general public?

A: In the media I think there has been a growing understanding over the last ten years, at least in my experience with the press, in the broad diversity among evangelicals. I think in the past there has been a misperception that the group is something of a monolith in terms of race and politics and a multitude of other areas where individuals have been perceived as the spokepersons for many, when in fact they may be the spokespersons only for some. The integrating motif of evangelicals is a belief in the Bible and the expectation of having a personal relationship with God through Jesus Christ, so those are spiritual values, and beyond that the diversity comes in race and background and politics and a whole array of differences.

Q: Have 'evangelical' and 'Christian right' come to be synonymous in America today?

A: I think that is the misperception of some, and perhaps that's because those voices have been largely heard. I don't know whether this is a correct statistic or not, but following the last general election one of the numbers that I read in the press was an estimate that one third of evangelicals voted as Democrats and two thirds voted as independents or Republicans. If that number is correct, that would show a two-to-one diversity at least in terms of blue and red. There are certainly many evangelicals who hold conservative right politics, but there are many who do not. […]

Q: Are you politically involved, and do you intend to be outspoken on social issues that have been important to evangelical Christians?

A: There are some political issues on which I have and will speak, although I do not see myself as someone who succumbs to Potomac fever or largely engages in that. I'm the pastor of a local church, and in our local church people in the congregation have run for office and been elected, but we don't talk about that within the life of the congregation.

Q: What are the issues that most concern you, that you think evangelicals ought to be involved with?

A: I can tell you issues that I'm personally concerned about, and of course I would extend that to other evangelicals and wish that they would share those concerns. I'm concerned for the poor. I'm concerned for justice for the disenfranchised. I have a great concern and the church of which I am a part is deeply involved in the HIV/AIDS issues in Africa and concerned that we be responsible in providing aid and sustenance and encouragement and everything that we can possibly do. I do share certain aspects of the social agenda in terms of being pro-life, and while not all evangelicals would share that, that would be pretty broad-based within the evangelical community – a desire to be a protector of the unborn.

Q: How do you come down on the teaching of intelligent design?

A: Well, I'm not an expert on that, so as a layperson I certainly am aware of intelligent design, and because I am a believer in God and believe that God is ultimately behind all that exists, of course I believe in intelligent design, and therefore I think it's a correct understanding of reality.

Q: So you think it ought to be taught alongside evolution in our schools?

A: It's always a difficult question of what should be taught in schools. There are some ways in which you would prefer that neither be taught in schools and that the choices be made within the church and other communities in terms of what is taught. I am certainly wide open to diverse opinions being taught within appropriate classrooms in schools and therefore think that there is a place for the teaching of intelligent design.

Q: Alongside evolution in the science class?

A: I certainly do think that an educated person today needs to understand what all the arguments are for evolution, so it is appropriate within education that evolution be taught as one alternative to a diverse opinion of many people of how reality has come to be.

Q: Is it your position that this should be taught within a science curriculum or in a broader philosophical context?

A: It's interesting that you say, should this be taught in the science class and should this be taught in the philosophy class, because I reflect back on my own education in public schools, and I don't always recall who is my science teacher and who is my history teacher, so where it's taught probably is dicing it down to a fine line, and if it is an acceptable alternative that it be taught in a different classroom, I'm OK with that. […]

Kopiervorlage 5: Issues in Evangelicalism

Q: You gained some notoriety coming out in favor of an evangelical environmental initiative, acknowledging that we face global warming. Is that one of those issues which is potentially a fracturing issue?

A: The evangelical climate initiative, which had 86 signatories (in alphabetical order, so with Anderson I was at the top of the list), had as a priority to put climate concerns, or as we would sometimes say 'creation care issues', on the evangelical agenda. I think that effort was highly successful, so it has significantly come into evangelical conversation – not that it hasn't been there for a long time, but it became broader and better understood, and I think clearly the direction is that evangelicals are engaging in this issue. A recent Newsweek poll reported that a high percentage of evangelicals are significantly concerned about climate care and related matters, and it makes sense, because as evangelicals we say that we believe the Bible, we take the Bible seriously, the Bible is our guide for faith and practice, and the Bible says that God is the creator of the universe and that we are to be stewards of that which we have on his behalf. So of course we would be concerned about the climate.

From the website of PBS, 12 November 2006;
www.pbs.org/wnet/religionandethics/week1013/interview.html

- 8 **misperception** falsche Wahrnehmung
- 19 **array** a large group of different things
- 31 **blue** *(here)* Democrat
- 31 **red** *(here)* Republican
- 41 **succumb to Potomac fever** have a strong desire to get involved in politics and government
- 54 **disenfranchised** [ˌdɪsɪnˈfræntʃaɪzd] having no say in politics
- 58 **sustenance** ['- - -] act of giving food and drink to people who need it
- 63 **broad-based** *(here)* supported by a wide variety of people
- 65 **come down on sth.** *(infml)* have an opinion about sth.
- 100 **dice sth. down to a fine line** *(here)* give too detailed an opinion on sth.
- 110 **signatory** [ˈsɪɡnətri] person who signs a petition or letter
- 127 **steward** Verwalter/in

Tasks:

1 State what Anderson is trying to say about the evangelical movement in the USA.

2 Analyse Anderson's position on the role of 'intelligent design' in education.

3 Comment on what you think of his position.

Kopiervorlage 6: Ignorant Citizens

Immigrants seeking to become U.S. citizens have to pass a test [...]. That's more than you can say for a group of Arizona high school students who were surveyed recently on their knowledge of
5 U.S. history and civics.

Just in time for Independence Day, the Goldwater Institute, a non-profit research organization in Phoenix, found that just 3.5% of surveyed students could answer enough questions cor-
10 rectly to pass the citizenship test. Just 25%, for example, correctly identified Thomas Jefferson as the author of the Declaration of Independence.

Other questions, all culled from the test, included: Who is in charge of the executive
15 branch? (The president.) What is the supreme law of the land? (The Constitution.) How many justices are on the Supreme court? (Nine.) The vast majority of students flubbed them all.

Unfortunately, and unsurprisingly, this was no
20 aberration. A survey done last year found about half of 17-year-olds didn't know that the controversy surrounding Sen. Joseph McCarthy in the 1950s concerned his witch hunt into communist activity. In 2006, a national assessment test given
25 to U.S. 12th-graders found that a third lacked basic knowledge about civics.

Instead of worrying about how immigrants might change America, this weekend was a good time to wonder whether the ignorance of citizens
30 about the roots of their own cherished freedoms is the greater threat. Simply put, democracy requires knowledge.

Totalitarian governments do best when they can keep their citizens in the dark. So do dema-
35 gogues who stoke anger to steal power. Without knowing the lessons of history, how can people elect intelligent leaders and know when freedoms are threatened?

The big challenge is finding better ways to
40 educated young people about history and civics. Meantime, we've got a suggestion. Why not make the 100-question citizenship test part of the high school curriculum, and passage a graduation requirement?

45 All U.S. citizens, not just the newest ones, should know there's more to Independence Day than fireworks.

From: Steve Marshall, 'Independence Day', *USA Today*, 2 July 2009

13 **cull sth.,** *here* take sth.
17 **justice,** *here* judge
18 **flub sth.** *(AE)* do sth. badly

20 **aberration** unusual behaviour
26 **civics** Staatsbürgerkunde
30 **cherished** beloved

Tasks:

1 Sum up the problem the article deals with in one or two sentences.

2 In a small group, discuss whether the problem exists in Germany as well. Decide on a few history and civics questions you could ask other students to find out.

3 Discuss whether the suggestion made by the newspaper to overcome the problem (ll. 42–45) would be helpful or not, either in Germany or in the USA. Write a comment.

Context 21 Religion: Topic Vocabulary

Word/Phrase	Memory Aid	German
(UN-)BELIEVERS AND BELIEFS		
Buddhist ['bʊdɪst]	Buddhism – Buddhist (*adj*) – <u>Buddhist</u> (person)	Buddhist/in
Christian	Christianity – Christian (*adj*) – <u>Christian</u> (person)	Christ/in
Hindu	Hinduism – Hindu (*adj*) – <u>Hindu</u> (person)	Hindu
Jew	*word family:* Judaism ['dʒuːdeɪɪzəm ☆ -dəɪzəm] – Jewish (*adj*) – <u>Jew</u> (person)	Jude/Jüdin
Muslim	Islam - Muslim (*adj*) – <u>Muslim</u> (person)	Muslim/in
Sikh	Sikhism – Sikh (*adj*) – <u>Sikh</u> (person)	Sikh
faith	*synonyms:* (strong) belief / creed / religion	Glaube
fundamentalist (*adj*)	*definition:* following religious teachings very strictly	fundamentalistisch
heaven	*definition:* according to Christian belief, the place where good people go after death	Himmel
hell	*example sentence:* Buddhists believe in reincarnation after death, rather than the idea of heaven and ~.	Hölle
orthodox (*adj*)	*definition:* following the traditional practices of a religion very closely	orthodox
pagan **(paganism)**	*synonyms:* heathen/unbeliever	Heide (Heidentum)
pope (also: **the Pope**)	*definition:* the head of the Roman Catholic Church	Papst
priest	*synonyms:* clergyman/minister/vicar	Priester/in, Pfarrer/in
reincarnation	*example sentence:* The concept of ~ – of the soul being reborn as a different person, animal or thing – was a mystery to Ben.	Wiedergeburt
soul	*opposite:* body	Seele

Context 21 Religion: Topic Vocabulary

Word/Phrase	Memory Aid	German
RELIGIOUS TEXTS AND PRACTICES		
the **Bible**	*word family:* the Bible – biblical	die Bibel
the **Koran**	*example sentence:* Muslims believe God used the Prophet Mohammed to write the ~ in 610 AD.	der Koran
the **Torah**	*definition:* the first and most important part of the holy book of the Jewish religion	die Thora
circumcision [ˌsɜːkəmˈsɪʒn]	*word family:* (to) circumcise – circumcision – circumcised *(adj)*	Beschneidung
(to) **commit a sin**	*other collocations:* (to) confess / (to) forgive a sin	eine Sünde begehen
(**Holy**) **Communion**	*definition:* a ceremony in the Christian Church during which people eat bread and drink wine in memory of Jesus's Last Supper	Abendmahl
(to) **do missionary work**	*example sentence:* Liz went to Nigeria last year to **do ~ work**.	missionieren
(to) **do penance**	*word family:* (to) do penance – penitent *(n, adj)*	Buße tun
gospel	*collocations:* (to) preach / proclaim / spread the ~	Evangelium
Islamic Law	*example sentence:* According to **Islamic ~**, people should not drink alcohol or eat pork.	Islamisches Gesetz
jihad	*definition:* 1. a struggle in yourself to remain faithful to Muslim beliefs and morals 2. a holy war fought by Muslims to defend Islam	Dschihad
(to) **obey the Ten Commandments**	*opposite:* (to) break the Ten Commandments	die Zehn Gebote halten
pilgrimage	*word family:* (to) go on a pilgrimage – pilgrim	Wallfahrt, Pilgerfahrt

(PLACES OF) WORSHIP		
church	*collocations:* churchgoer / ~ service / ~ bell	Kirche
mosque	*example sentence:* The largest ~ in the world is located in the city of Mecca.	Moschee
synagogue [ˈsɪnəgɒg ☆ -gɑːg]	*example sentence:* The Jewish family went to the ~ to celebrate their son's bar mitzvah.	Synagoge

Context 21 Religion: Topic Vocabulary

Word/Phrase	Memory Aid	German
(PLACES OF) WORSHIP		
temple	*definition:* the religious building used by Buddhists, Sikhs or Hindus	Tempel
(to) **answer a prayer**	*other collocation:* (to) say a prayer	ein Gebet erhören
(to) **attend a service**	*synonyms:* (to) worship / (to) go to (morning) worship	einen Gottesdienst besuchen
(to) **believe in God/Jesus/Allah**	*opposite:* (to) be an atheist/unbeliever	an Gott/Jesus/Allah glauben
(to) **convert to a faith**	*example sentence:* Michael ~ed to Judaism when he was 20.	zu einem Glauben konvertieren
hymn	*collocations:* (to) play/sing a ~ / ~book	Hymne
(to) **practise** *(BE)* / **practice** *(AE)* **a religion**	*other collocations:* (to) belong to a / (to) follow a / (to) reject a ~	eine Religion ausüben
(to) **pray**	*word family:* (to) pray – prayer	beten
(to) **repeat a mantra**	*definition:* to repeat a word, phrase or sound again and again in prayer or meditation	ein Mantra wiederholen
CELEBRATIONS AND RITUALS		
(to) **break a fast**	*opposite:* observe a fast	fasten brechen
(to) **celebrate Easter/Passover**	*other collocations:* (to) celebrate a birthday / an anniversary / New Year's Day	Ostern / das Passahfest feiern
Lent	*example sentence:* I have given up sweets and chocolates for ~.	Fastenzeit
Ramadan	*definition:* a period of fasting and prayer during the ninth month in the Islamic calendar	Ramadan
the Hajj	*example sentence:* It is important for Muslims to go on the ~ to Mecca at least once in their lives.	Wallfahrt nach Mekka
(the) Sabbath ['--]	*definition:* the holy day of the week for Christians (Sunday) and Jews (Saturday), used for worshipping God and resting	Sabbat

3 The Individual in Society

S erarbeiten sich den Titel des Kapitels, um das Thema sowie ihren eigenen alltäglichen Spagat als Individuum in der Gesellschaft zu verstehen sowie Schlüsse für eigene Handlungsweisen ziehen zu können. Die Text- und Methodenvielfalt des Kapitels verlangt von S ein hohes Maß an (Selbst-)Reflexion, Aktivität und zielsprachlicher Kommunikation.

Part A – People are People analysiert, welche Faktoren das Zusammenleben von Individuen in der Gesellschaft beeinflussen.

Part B – Equal in Dignity and Rights? greift die Themen Menschenrechte und Menschenwürde anhand verschiedener Beispiele auf: der UN-Menschenrechtscharta sowie Hör- und Lesetexten zu Ausländerfeindlichkeit und Geschlechterrollen.

Part C – Different Ideas about Life thematisiert das Engagement von Hilfsorganisationen und stellt alternative Lebensentwürfe zur Diskussion, die mit der *Context Task* über den Platz eines jeden in der Gesellschaft abgerundet wird.

Didaktisches Inhaltsverzeichnis

SB p.	Title	TM p.	Text Form	Topic	Skills and Activities	Language Practice
60	Lead-in DVD	88	Posters; screenshots; animated film	The individual's role in society	Working with pictures; cooperative learning strategy (think–pair–share); designing posters; viewing skills; creative writing	LP 13: Talking about the present
62	Words in Context – Individuals: the Building Blocks of Society	90	Informative text	The make-up of society	Structuring a text; organizing vocabulary; using a dictionary; translating; working with cartoons	LP 9: Word formation: suffixes; LP 20: Avoiding German-English interference
	Part A: People are People					
64	A1 Celebrating Differences	91	Photos	Looking at ourselves and others	Working with pictures; giving a presentation; taking part in a discussion	
65	A2 EXTRA What Makes Us Moral Jeffrey Kluger	93	Magazine article (extract)	Moral behaviour	Reading non-fiction; summarizing; writing an outline	
67	A3 Carrying the Fire Cormac McCarthy	95	Novel extract	Moral survival	Brainstorming; reading non-fiction; making notes; writing a summary; giving a report	LP 17: Talking about unreal situations
	Part B: Equal in Dignity and Rights?					
69	B1 The Universal Declaration of Human Rights	97	Formal document	Human dignity and rights	Doing a ranking; doing research (online)	
	B2 Living in Germany					
70	i) Satan in Heaven	98	Letters to the editor (extracts)	Xenophobia in Germany and elsewhere	Summarizing; analysing texts	
70	ii) Woher kommen Sie ursprünglich? Hasnain Kazim	99	Web article (extract)	'Civil' racism	Mediating; taking part in a discussion	
	B3 The New Gender Gap?					
72	i) The Second Sex Michelle Conlin	100	Web article (extract)	The battle of the sexes in education and employment	Cooperative learning strategy (placemat); reading non-fiction; working with charts and graphs; writing an essay	
74	ii) The Global Gender Gap CD 3.11	102	Interview	The global gender gap 2007 vs. 2009	Listening comprehension; working with charts; doing research (online); viewing skills	

3 Lead-in

75	Communicating across Cultures CD 3.12–13	104	Audio texts	Being polite	Listening comprehension; taking notes; matching; working with cartoons	
	Part C: Different Ideas about Life					
76	C1 Helping Hands	104	Logos	Making a difference	Speculating; doing research; giving a presentation	
	C2 Into the Wild					
77	i) 'Society': A Song from the Soundtrack Eddie Vedder CD 3.14	105	Song	Leaving society	Listening comprehension; taking notes; analysing a song	
78	ii) An Extract from the Book Jon Krakauer	106	Journal entry	Deliberate living	Analysing a diary entry	LP 17: Talking about unreal situations
79	iii) Two Extracts from the Film DVD	107	Feature film (extracts)	Social criticism	Speculating; viewing skills; doing research	

SB S. 60 DVD
Transkript s. TM-DVD-ROM

Lead-in

Source: *balance, 24 animationsfilme der hfbk hamburg*, 2003
Topic: The individual's role in society
Text form: Animated film
Length: 7:20 min
Skills/Activities: Working with pictures; cooperative learning strategy (think–pair–share); designing posters; viewing skills; creative writing

Didaktischer Kommentar Der Einstieg in das komplexe Thema erfolgt multimedial: Nach einer ersten Reflexionsphase und Standortbestimmung mithilfe der Poster setzen sich S mit dem Kurzfilm *balance* auseinander, um ein fundiertes Arbeiten an den folgenden gesellschaftsspezifischen Unterthemen zu fördern.

SB-DVD-ROM

Lernwortschatz
bear sth. in mind (task 4)

Unterrichtstipps Einstieg: L schreibt *society* an die Tafel, S kommen einzeln nach vorn und notieren ein Stichwort dazu: eine Gemeinschaftsmindmap entsteht. Anschließend werden die Assoziationen im Plenum diskutiert.

HA **2** S recherchieren entweder in Partner- oder Gruppenarbeit (PC-Raum) oder vorab zuhause. Im Plenum werden die Ergebnisse zusammengetragen und die sechs wichtigsten Institutionen und Organisationen ausgewählt. Die Klasse wird anschließend in sechs Gruppen aufgeteilt; jede Gruppe bearbeitet eine Institution/Organisation und erstellt gemeinsam ein Poster **(2b)**.

ALT Um mehr Ergebnisse zu erhalten, arbeiten S durchgängig zu zweit.

2a Das Ergebnis kann allgemein als Grundlage für die weitere Arbeit an den Inhalten des Kapitels sowie speziell für das Poster in **2b** dienen.

2b Hierfür können verschiedene, auch nicht computerbasierte, Formate genutzt werden: Fotos, Collagen, Skizzen, Cartoons, Bilder usw.

Linktipp: *www.wordle.net* bietet u. a. leistungsschwächeren Lerngruppen eine abwechslungsreiche Alternative (s. Info). S achten bei der Textauswahl darauf, einen inhaltlich relevanten englischen Text zu verwenden, z. B. die UN-Menschenrechtscharta.

Lead-in – The Individual in Society

4 Ein Vergleich mit den Postern aus **2b** ist denkbar, da sich die Ansichten zu einer funktionierenden Gesellschaft bereits geändert haben können. Im Gegensatz zu **2b** werden hier nur die Schlüsselwörter festgehalten; eine weitere Gestaltung des Posters ist nicht erforderlich.

> **Info**
>
> *Wordle* is a tool for generating 'word clouds' from text provided by users. The more often a word appears in the source text, the more prominently it is displayed in the word cloud. Afterwards, the clouds can be re-designed, printed out or saved onto the Wordle gallery to share with others.
>
> *Balance* (1989) depicts five individuals on a platform which they have to keep balanced so as not to fall off. They cooperate until each takes out a rod and one individual pulls a box onto the platform. They inspect the box one by one. And one by one, they fall or are pushed over the edge until one individual remains who has to maintain a balance with the box which is now out of his reach.
>
> *Christoph and Wolfgang Lauenstein* (twin brothers, born 1962), German film producers, won an Academy Award with *balance* for the best animated short film in 1990. They now specialize in animated advertisements and short films.

Lösungshinweise

1a *The first poster* uses only three words and two colours to keep the poster simple; the message is clear from both the words and the layout of the poster: society is made up of 'you' and 'me' co-existing in a defined space.
The second poster uses more colours and words. Three bigger words stand out; perhaps the poster suggests that society is made up of many individuals and that everyone is part of a 'we'. The possessive pronouns next to the word 'we' show that society is common to all and everyone has a part in shaping it.
In *the third poster*, the layout, words and message reinforce each other: the word 'imbalance' looks like it is at risk of falling over, whereas the word 'balance' looks very stable at the bottom of the poster. The colours are simple and clear and the words could define a good society: 'people live in balance together' or a bad one: 'people live in imbalance together'.

1bc Individual answers.

2a A *parliament* makes laws to ensure that life in a society follows certain rules. Law courts are the central means for dispute resolution. Charities are non-profit organizations set up to come to the aid of those in need.

2b **EXTRA** Individual answers.

3a The character in the first screenshot looks sad, alone and thoughtful. The five characters in the second screenshot are not interacting with each other at all, but facing away from each other. They seem to be looking over the edge of the platform on which they are all standing. In the third screenshot, one of the characters (maybe the one from the first screenshot) is getting ready to catch a box which has somehow landed on the platform and is sliding towards him. It might contain a treasure, food, gold, a survival kit, or just nothing. Perhaps it contains the answer to the characters' predicament. The other four characters are holding sticks in their hands, maybe weapons to keep one person from taking the box.

3bc Individual answers (for the plot in **3c**, cf. Info).

3d The characters' behaviour mirrors life in modern society. A healthy, cooperative society is thrown off balance (or rather: destroyed) by the greed and brutality of a single person. Individual answers.

Message: Society can only function when individuals work together to achieve a common goal. The film shows isolation and hopelessness as the result of a society which has failed in this respect.

4 Individual answers.

3 Words in Context

SB S. 62
▶ LSET ex. 1, 2

Words in Context – Individuals: The Building Blocks of Society

Didaktischer Kommentar

Der Text gibt Anhaltspunkte für S, mögliche Bezugspunkte des Individuums zu unterschiedlich definierbaren Gesellschaftsgefügen zu geben. Durch die Beschäftigung mit den verschiedenen Möglichkeiten für Menschen, zu Mitmenschen zu werden oder dies zu verweigern, werden S für die folgenden Themen sensibilisiert. Gleichzeitig wird das thematische Basisvokabular eingeführt und geübt.

SB-DVD-ROM

Lernwortschatz

human being (l. 1), social and geographical setting (l. 1), pattern of thought and behaviour (l. 3), influence sb./sth. (l. 3), value (l. 4), habit (l. 4), identity (l. 6), self-image (l. 6), well-being (l. 6), be aware of sth. (l. 7), be conscious of sth. (l. 8), motivate sb. (l. 8), interact with sb. (l. 9), moral (l. 9), socialize with sb. (l. 10), agreement (l. 12), tribal codex (l. 12), constitution (l. 12), democracy (l. 17), monarchy (l. 17), dictatorship (l. 17), social and political structure (l. 17), subculture (l. 19), voluntary (l. 20), superior (l. 23), inferior (l. 23), be discriminated against (l. 24), attitude (l. 25), shift (n, l. 26), circumstances (l. 27), permanent change (l. 28), conformity (l. 29), mainstream (l. 29), oppose sth. (l. 30), resort to violence (l. 32), alternative lifestyle (l. 34)

Unterrichtstipps
⚠ HA

S lesen den Text (z. B. als Hausaufgabe) und vergewissern sich, dass sie die Bedeutung der gelb unterlegten Vokabeln verstehen.

ZA

S fassen die einzelnen Absätze zusammen. Lösungshinweise:
1: The development of an individual's identity depends on the social environment he/she grows up in. 2: Rules regulate life in society and organizations and institutions help shape it. 3: Certain circumstances may lead to changes in society and in an individual's attitude towards it. 4: Some oppose society or leave it altogether.

👥 HA

2 kann als Hausaufgabe erledigt und in Partnerarbeit kontrolliert werden.

👥 ZA

With a partner, collect examples for 'grown-up bullies with money'. Then discuss the message of the cartoon in class. Lösungshinweise:
Bosses can order employees to work overtime; rich lobbyists can persuade politicians to decide in the lobbyists' interests; sponsors of large sums of money can ask for publicity. Although such dependency on money sometimes leads to conflicts, the fact that most people depend on someone else's money for their salaries makes society tolerate the general idea that 'money makes the world go round' (which could be considered as the cartoon's message).

Differenzierung
👥 👥👥 ZA

Touch–turn–talk: S wählen eines der *words in context* (Nomen) aus, umschreiben den Begriff und der Partner / die Gruppe errät ihn.

ALT

Als (Vor-)Übung für mündliche Präsentationen lesen S einen Begriff laut vor und erklären eine Minute lang, was sie damit verbinden.

3 Vorab bietet sich in Kursen mit wenig Erfahrung im Übersetzen die Bearbeitung von *LP 20: Avoiding German-English interference* an.

Info

Moore Street (shown on p. 148) is a street in central Dublin in which Moore Street Market, Dublin's oldest food market, is held.

Lösungshinweise

1a 1 be aware/conscious of sth; 2 motivate sb.; 3 interact with sb.; 4 socialize with sb.; 5 be discriminated against; 6 oppose sth.

Part A

1b

1 The advertising industry is aware/conscious of young people's interest in the Internet.
2 A cruel experiment proved that babies die when no one interacts with them.
3 If you have trouble socializing at parties, prepare some topics for small talk.
4 Thousands of people opposed the G8 summits.
5 There's a good way to motivate oneself: always believe in your own strength.
6 The constitution prohibits discrimination against people on the grounds of race, gender or religion.

2

1	adjective:	conscious	noun:	consciousness
2	noun:	agreement	verb:	agree
3	verb:	oppose	noun:	opposition
4	verb:	value	noun:	value
5	noun:	constitution	adjective:	constitutional
6	noun:	conformity	verb:	conform
7	adjective:	alternative	verb:	alternate
8	adjective:	voluntarily	noun:	volunteer
9	noun:	violence	adjective:	violent
10	adjective:	tribal	noun:	tribe

3

1 Every human being develops his or her own <u>habits</u> and <u>attitudes</u> in the course of his or her life.
2 These depend on personal <u>circumstances</u> and change constantly.
3 In a <u>democracy</u>, <u>subcultures</u> can develop freely.
4 The aims and <u>values</u> of the EU were defined in the <u>Constitution</u> of Europe.
5 A human being is influenced by the social and geographical setting they live in.

Part A – People are People

SB S. 64 **A1 Celebrating Differences**

Didaktischer Kommentar Die Arbeit mit den Fotos sensibilisiert S dafür, wie sie unterschiedliche Menschen wahrnehmen. Sie üben Bildeindrücke zu versprachlichen und sich je nach Kontext bewusst dafür zu entscheiden, welche Informationen zur eigenen Person sie preisgeben und welche nicht.

Unterrichtstipps **1c** S reflektieren in Kleingruppen ihr Umfeld, beschreiben es im Hinblick auf verschiedene Bevölkerungsgruppen und überlegen begründet, ob die in den Fotos dargestellten Personen darin Platz hätten.

2 S bringen ein Foto von sich mit, besprechen es und halten wie in **1ab** fest, welche Informationen sie ihm entnehmen können und welche nicht. Sie tauschen sich darüber aus, welche Informationen sie je nach Kontext vermitteln möchten.

2b erfolgt als Hausaufgabe oder in Stichworten.

3b S klären mithilfe eines Wörterbuchs die Bedeutung von „difference" im Kennedy-Zitat (auch „disagreement"), bevor sie sich Stichpunkte notieren für die Diskussion darüber, wie die geforderte Sicherheit heute aussehen könnte.

Differenzierung **3b** Interessierte S recherchieren John F. Kennedy und seine Zeit (Kalter Krieg), bevor das Zitat im Plenum in die Gegenwart der S übertragen wird.

3 Part A1 – Celebrating Differences

> **Info**
>
> *John F. Kennedy* (1917–1963) was President of the USA from 1961 until his assassination in November 1963. He was popular in his own country as well as abroad. His speech in West Berlin against Communism in 1963 (with the famous German phrase 'Ich bin ein Berliner') drew an extremely large audience. The quotation in **3b** is taken from Kennedy's Commencement Address at American University, Washington, D.C. on 10 June 1963. In this speech he urges young people to pursue peace in a world dominated by the Cold War.
>
> ⁎ **Linktipp:** *www.ratical.com/co-globalize/JFK061063.html* gives the complete text of the address.

Lösungshinweise

1a

A The girl looks Asian and like somebody I might see in a park near my home. From the type of clothes she is wearing it's a teenage girl from a middle-class family. She's standing on a park bench and smiling pleasantly into the camera.

B The person in picture B appears to be an Asian mother carrying her child in a special carrier on her back. She seems to be well-off, since both she herself and her child are wearing colourful clothes. She is pretty, but she is frowning at the camera. (The photo was taken in Bhutan.)

C The skinny black boy is about six years old and posing with his right foot on a soccer ball. It is hard to tell whether he is poor or not, because he is only wearing a pair of shorts. He looks friendly. (The photo was taken in Cuba.)

D The man is obviously a Buddhist monk. His head is shaven, and he is wearing the typical orange gown worn by monks. He is young, perhaps in his twenties, and quite handsome despite his large glasses. He is smiling very slightly. (The photo was taken in Thailand.)

E The elderly white woman is sitting at a table in a room. She appears to be middle-class. Her facial expression is quite pleasant, even though she is not smiling. (The photo was taken in Berlin, Germany.)

F The person in picture F is a dark-skinned man who might be from South-Eastern Europe. His short dark hair covers his head almost like a hat, and over his shoulders he is wearing a scarf. He is leading a horse that has been decorated with flowers for some kind of festival, it appears. His serious-looking face is in the shadows. (The photo was taken in Afghanistan.)

1b The photos can only tell the viewer something about the visible features of a person, and these are often open to interpretation. But most of the things that we usually want to know about an individual cannot be seen in a photo – we don't even know where these pictures were taken, because we are seeing them out of context. We can only speculate about the people's religious or political attitudes and beliefs, their social status, their education, their future prospects, etc.

1c–2 Individual answers.

3a *Favourable impact:* multicultural customs/music/food/dress; different languages and religions; a cosmopolitan world view; a generally more tolerant society
Unfavourable impact: racism; xenophobia; loss of a core culture; conflicts with the laws or religion of the host country

3b **EXTRA** While real disagreements should end in the long run, there will always be differences of attitude, skin colour, etc. in an increasingly globalized society. Safety here means the opportunity to pursue one's personal goals in life without fear of discrimination. This means there must be rules and laws to establish and guarantee equal rights, justice and order, as well as institutions to safeguard these. Safety on a global plane means that no nation should impose its political or religious ideals upon another nation, but that nations should help each other, e.g. by providing food and medical supplies after natural disasters.

Part A2 – What Makes Us Moral

3

SB S. 65
▶ LSET ex. 3

A2 EXTRA **What Makes Us Moral** Jeffrey Kluger

Source:	'What Makes Us Moral?', TIME, 21 November 2007
Topic:	Moral behaviour
Text form:	Magazine article (extract)
Language variety:	American English
Number of words:	860 words
Level:	Advanced
Skills/Activities:	Reading non-fiction; summarizing; writing an outline

Didaktischer Kommentar

Aus verschiedenen Blickwinkeln erfahren S Einzelheiten über die Faktoren, die für ein moralisches bzw. ein zeitweilig unmoralisches Verhalten der Spezies Mensch verantwortlich sind. Sie arbeiten an ihrer Lese- und Analysekompetenz und schulen ihre Schreib- und Sprechfähigkeiten.

SB-DVD-ROM

Lernwortschatz

weep (l. 2), drill (l. 5), preserve sth. (l. 6), vanity (l. 6), spoil (l. 16), grasp sth. (l. 17), comply (l. 19), hesitate (l. 20), slaughter sb./sth. (l. 29), consistent (l. 29), scatter sth. (l. 31), boot up sth. (l. 34), notion (l. 43), favour sb./sth. (l. 47), troop (l. 47), bias (n, l. 48)), delinquent (adj, l. 49), be struck by sth. (l. 50), outrage (l. 51), empathize with sb./sth. (l. 55), alien (adj, l. 55), promiscuous (l. 58), go on about sth. (l. 58), savagery (l. 65)

Unterrichtstipps

PRE-READING kann (mit höherem Zeitkontingent) auch als *placemat* (s. S. 298) durchgeführt werden.

HA Der Text kann als vorbereitende Hausaufgabe gelesen werden.

2 Zeile 40 wird als Teil des sechsten Absatzes (Zeilen 33–39) betrachtet.

Differenzierung

Je nach Klassensituation kann der Text abschnittweise behandelt werden.
Zweiteilung: *Teil 1:* Zeilen 1–40; *Teil 2:* Zeilen 41–67
Dreiteilung: *Teil 1:* Zeilen 1–16; *Teil 2:* Zeilen 17–40; *Teil 3:* Zeilen 41–67

ZA Interessierte S bereiten über einen längeren Zeitraum Beispiele zu „moralischem" oder „unmoralischem" Verhalten auch fächerübergreifend (Geschichte, Religion, Politik, Zeitgeschehen, Familien-/Schulleben) für ein Kurzreferat vor und stellen der Lerngruppe ggf. den dafür relevanten Wortschatz zur Verfügung.

3 Die Zitate eignen sich (besonders für leistungsstärkere S) auch als Grundlage für einen Aufsatz bzw. eine Stellungnahme (s. *SF 44: Writing an essay* bzw. *SF 45: Writing a comment*).

Info

Jeffrey Kluger is a senior writer for *TIME* magazine and a licensed attorney. He is the author of numerous cover stories, teaches Journalism at university and is co-author of *Lost Moon: The Perilous Voyage of Apollo 13,* which served as the basis of the movie *Apollo 13,* released in 1995.

Lösungshinweise

1a Morality is a quality that we possess from birth, but in order for us to behave accordingly, moral teaching by the community is necessary. While biology reduces us to reproducing and preserving life (that of our family), the challenge is to extend our moral behaviour to those outside our community. Conflicts and wars are the result of our failure, but it is our responsibility to extend moral behaviour to all.

3

Part A2 – What Makes Us Moral

1b To the author, human nature is capable of great empathy. On the one hand, human beings are the most caring, on the other hand, the cruellest species, killing others with no real necessity. We are paradox, and what sets us apart from other species is precisely our moral judgement and our (a)moral behaviour.

1c People do not necessarily make use of their intuitive moral feelings and especially not towards those whom they consider alien or simply different. We are morally programmed to a certain degree, but our community must still teach us to practise moral behaviour.
The 'biggest challenge' (l.41) is not just behaving morally within our family, community or workplace, but applying the same rules to 'outsiders'.

2 *Focus of each paragraph:* 1: human beings' almost unnatural kindness; 2: use of language and tools not unique to humans; 3: morality (sympathy and empathy) makes humans unique; 4: morality is an inborn quality; 5: while moral judgement is pretty consistent from one person to another, moral behaviour is not; 6: in order for us to practise the morality we feel intuitively, somebody has to teach it; 7: because of the biological need to pass on genes, it is 'natural' for humans to apply moral values only to their community; 8: humans identify with their own, not with outsiders; 9: the line between insiders and outsiders has been the premise for wars; 10: we have a moral obligation to treat everyone morally

Outline: Possible answer:
I   What Makes Us Human?
   A   Thesis 1: An almost unnatural kindness (paragraph 1)
   B   Thesis 2: Use of tools and language (paragraph 2)
   C   Answer: Morality and empathy (paragraph 3)
     1   Morality
        a   Moral judgement (felt innately) (paragraph 4)
        b   Moral behaviour (does not follow moral judgement) (paragraph 5)
        c   Moral teaching (done by community) (paragraph 6)
     2   Empathy
        a   Empathy for insiders (family/community)
           i   Sociobiological effort to pass on genes (paragraph 7)
           ii Human beings identify with community (example) (paragraph 8)
        b   Empathy for outsiders
           i   Little or none
           ii Premise for wars (paragraph 9)
II Where Should We Be Heading? ('full civilization', paragraph 10)

Morality: Our morality and our empathy distinguish us as human beings (paragraph 3), our language and our tools do not (paragraph 2). Psychology helps to show that moral judgement is an inborn quality (paragraph 4), whereas moral behaviour is not (paragraph 5). We need a community to take on the role of moral programming (paragraph 6). Since we are biologically programmed to pass on our genes, it is natural that we should apply moral values only or mainly to our community (paragraphs 7 and 8). This differentiation between 'me' and 'you' and the resulting dehumanization of the other is the premise for wars (paragraph 9). It is our (moral) responsibility to 'fully civilize ourselves' (l.65) in order to reduce and, finally, end all wars (paragraph 10).

3 Individual answers.

Part A3 – Carrying the Fire

SB S. 67
▶ LSET ex. 4

A3 Carrying the Fire Cormac McCarthy

Source:	*The Road,* New York: Alfred A. Knopf, Inc., 2006
Topic:	Moral survival
Text form:	Novel (extract)
Language variety:	American English
Number of words:	395
Level:	Intermediate
Skills/Activities:	Brainstorming; reading narrative prose; making notes; writing a summary; giving a report

Didaktischer Kommentar

Die fast archaische Darstellung der beklemmenden Situation von Vater und Sohn mit ihren Implikationen für geistig-moralisches Überleben jenseits von rein physiologischem Hungerstillen bietet Diskussionsanlässe zur Schulung der Sprachkompetenz. Darüber hinaus wird Textkompetenz geübt bei der Interpretation der Titelmetapher sowie beim Vergleich mit A2.

SB-DVD-ROM

Lernwortschatz

take one's bearings (l. 2), twilight (l. 3), pike (*AE*, l. 3), creek (*AE*, l. 4), bank (l. 5), huddle (l. 5), lighter (l. 7), scrawl (l. 30), billboard (l. 31), starve (l. 50)

Unterrichtstipps

PRE-READING Alternativ oder als Hilfestellung bei der Lösung der Aufgabe beantworten S folgende Frage: *In a large crowd, you become separated from your parents. The streets are filled with panicked adults and there is no mobile phone signal. Where your home was, there is only rubble; you cannot recognize once familiar places. How do you find your family?*
From: *The Times Educational Supplement,* 19 February 2010, p. 13

1a S notieren während oder nach der Lektüre ihre persönlichen Reaktionen und vergleichen sie mit ihren *pre-reading*-Überlegungen.

1c erfolgt alternativ als Hausaufgabe. Schon hierfür greifen S auf die *language help* zurück. S tauschen ihre Zusammenfassungen mit einem Partner aus (s.a. SF 16: Peer evaluation).

2a Stichwortartig dient die Lösung der Aufgabe zur Vorbereitung einer mündlichen Präsentation; als Hausaufgabe wird sie ausformuliert.

3a Die Aufgabe wird einzeln (z.B. als Hausaufgabe) vorbereitet und mit einem Partner verglichen. Wegen der Relevanz stilistischer Analysen für Klausuren und das Abitur findet die Auswertung im Plenum statt.

Differenzierung

Bei Nachfragen und in stärkeren Lerngruppen wird das fehlende Apostroph bei den verneinten Kurzformen der Hilfsverben thematisiert und folgende Aufgabe z.B. als Hausaufgabe bearbeitet. *Examine the negative short forms of the modal auxiliaries in the text and analyse the effect of this form of notation.* Lösungshinweis:
An apostrophe indicates that the word actually consists of two words (e.g. do not*); without the apostrophe, the negative* dont *becomes as natural as the affirmative* do. *Just like the lack of names (they are merely 'the man' and 'the boy') and the reduction of the syntax, the grammar mirrors the apocalyptic wasteland all around.*

3b Impuls: *Think of people who resist(ed) tyrants or dictators, e.g. during the Nazi regime in Germany, Christian martyrs in Ancient Rome or someone in your family or neighbourhood who stands up for moral values. Examples: Mahatma Ghandi, Aung San Suu Kyi.*

Part A3 – Carrying the Fire

> **Info**
>
> *Cormac McCarthy* (born 1933) is an internationally acclaimed American novelist, playwright and screenwriter whose work has won many awards. His most recent novels *No Country for Old Men* (2005) and *The Road* (2006) have both been made into popular films. McCarthy currently lives in New Mexico, USA, with his third wife and his son.
>
> *The Road* (2006) is set in the USA after an apocalyptic disaster has destroyed almost every living thing and tells the story of a father and son who travel southwards towards the sea in search of better living conditions. Bands of scavengers and cannibals roam the country. The son feels the urge to help other people on the way, while the father tries to protect him from harm. The novel ends with the death of the father and the boy being taken into another family who had been tracking them. *The Road* won the 2007 Pulitzer Prize and was made into a film in 2009, directed by John Hillcoat and written by Joe Penhall.

Lösungshinweise

1a Individual anwers.

1b *Setting 1:* a bridge over a dry creek in the country, away from the main road; *Setting 2:* a roadside near what used to be a town, with billboards that used to advertise things but have now been painted over

1c Father and son are walking through an apocalyptic landscape in search of shelter and food. They distinguish themselves from those who steal and kill in order to survive. They believe that they are the 'good guys' who uphold the moral values of civilization.

2a In order to survive, some people are resorting to cannibalism, but the boy is determined to stay 'good'. He doesn't judge the others' behaviour, but is shocked both by the cannibalism and his own inability to help. When he cries, it is perhaps at the thought of what people are capable of. But he makes his father assure him that they would never do such a thing, 'No matter what' (l. 56).

2b The fire stands for the values of civilization, or even of humanity itself. The carriers of the fire need to keep it alive against the temptation to give up old values when faced with starvation. It reminds me of the Olympic flame, which is carried from Olympia, Greece months before the beginning of the Games to the site at which the Games are held and burns until these are over.

3a **EXTRA** *Message / Stylistic devices A2:* While mankind is the only species that can empathize with the suffering of others, i.e. show responsible moral behaviour, this has so far not led to an end of 'savagery'. Not until our moral behaviour catches up with our moral judgement will we be fully civilized. The *enumeration* in l. 2 underlines the amount of kindness we are capable of. The *repetition* in ll. 7 and 8 ('We're the only…') underlines our uniqueness and makes the following refutation even stronger. The *metaphor* of the software that needs booting up and configurating (l. 34) and the image of 'moral grammar' (l. 36) underline the importance of moral teaching in addition to our moral judgement.

Message / Stylistic devices A3: When survival is at stake, moral behaviour quickly breaks down. The whole extract is very simple, in keeping with the bleakness of the landscape. The language in the dialogues is plain and there are short sentences only. The syntax of the narrative parts is also very simple, 'and' being the main linking word. The most remarkable stylistic device is *repetition* (e.g. 'I dont know', ll. 20/22; 'we wouldnt', ll. 54/55), which reinforces the simplicity of the dialogues. The novel extract is grounded firmly in the kind of physical as well as moral wasteland that the magazine article evokes abstractly.

3b Individual answers (cf. *Differenzierung* above).

Part B

3

Part B – Equal in Dignity and Rights?

SB S. 69

B1 The Universal Declaration of Human Rights

Topic:	Human dignity and rights
Text form:	Formal document
Number of words:	29
Level:	Intermediate
Skills/Activities:	Doing a ranking; doing research (online)

Didaktischer Kommentar

S lernen hier die grundlegenden Artikel aus der UN-Menschenrechtscharta kennen und setzen sich inhaltlich und sprachlich mit ihren Aussagen auseinander, um weitere Diskussionen über Menschenwürde und Gleichberechtigung aller Menschen in der Gesellschaft auf dieser Grundlage führen zu können.

SB-DVD-ROM

Lernwortschatz

proclaim sth. (l. 2), distinction (l. 6), dignity (l. 8), be endowed with sth. (l. 9), conscience (l. 9), spirit (l. 10)

Unterrichtstipps

PRE-READING Die Aufgabe wird bei geschlossenem SB bearbeitet, um Aspekte aus Artikel 1 nicht vorwegzunehmen.

1 L schreibt *dignity, reason, conscience, brotherhood* an. Im *think–pair–share*-Verfahren (s. S. 299) notieren S ihre Assoziationen mit den Begriffen.

ALT Alternativ vervollständigen S Sätze: *Dignity/Reason/Conscience/Brotherhood is…* Dann werden dem Partner (oder anderen Teilnehmern der Kleingruppe) die Sätze vorgelesen und die Ideen verglichen.

S suchen zu zweit oder in Kleingruppen Beispiele für *brotherhood* aus dem eigenen Umfeld.
Im Anschluss an die Klärung der Begriffe wird im Plenum überlegt, was S an Artikel 1 besonders wichtig ist oder was ihnen fehlt.

HA **2a** Der Webcode bietet einen Link zum vollständigen Wortlaut der UN-Menschenrechtscharta. Die Aufgabe kann auch als Hausaufgabe erledigt werden.

Differenzierung

2a Interessierte/Leistungsstärkere S stellen ausgewählte Artikel vor und betrachten sie kritisch oder recherchieren Menschenrechtsverletzungen in Bezug auf ausgewählte Artikel und tragen sie der Lerngruppe vor und/oder diskutieren die Notwendigkeit der Anzahl der Artikel. Leistungsschwächere S recherchieren weitere Dokumente der Vereinten Nationen und stellen diese kurz vor.

Info

Anna Eleanor Roosevelt (1884–1962) was the First Lady of the United States from 1933 to 1945 (her husband, Franklin D. Roosevelt, was the 32nd President of the USA). An advocate for civil and especially women's rights, Roosevelt was an internationally acclaimed author, speaker, politician and activist.

The picture (oil over photograph) shows Roosevelt, one of the authors, with a copy of the Universal Declaration of Human Rights in November 1949, a year after the ratification, at Lake Success, New York.

Lösungshinweise

PRE-READING Individual answers (S may be able to recycle some of the more complex ideas noted down in the Lead-in, task **4**).

1 All human beings are equal in freedom, dignity and rights. They are gifted with rational, moral minds and should behave peacefully towards each other.

Part B2 – Living in Germany

2a *Article 2:* Without exception, everyone has the rights and freedoms laid down in the Declaration.
Article 3: Everyone has the right to live a free and secure life.
Article 4: Slavery and slave trade in any form are to be prohibited.
Article 5: Torture and degrading treatment are to be prohibited.
Article 6: Before a court / In court, every person is to be recognized as a person.
Article 7: Everyone is equal before and protected by the law against discrimination.
Article 8: Whenever an individual's constitutional rights are violated, he or she is under the protection of national jurisdiction.
Article 9: Nobody may be arrested, taken into custody or exiled without reason.
Article 10: Everyone must be treated equally and fairly by independent and unbiased tribunals.

2b Individual answers.

B2 Living in Germany

SB S. 70
▶ LSET ex. 5

i) Satan in Heaven

Source:	'As Welcome as Satan in Heaven', *SPIEGEL ONLINE*, 22 January 2008
Topic:	Xenophobia in Germany and elsewhere
Text form:	Letters to the editor (extracts)
Language variety:	British English; English as a foreign language
Number of words:	395
Level:	Basic
Skills/Activities:	Summarizing; analysing texts

Didaktischer Kommentar

Anhand von Stellungnahmen zweier in Deutschland lebender Ausländer setzen S sich kritisch mit den provokanten Thesen eines Onlineredakteurs auseinander, was einer lebensnahen Schulung der Sprachkompetenz entspricht.

SB-DVD-ROM

Lernwortschatz

xenophobia (introductory text), yearning for sth. (l. 3), purity (l. 3), breed (n, l. 5), blunt (l. 15), riot (l. 16), no-go zone (l. 18), racial (l. 24), suit (l. 25)

Unterrichtstipps
ZA

S schreiben einen Leserbrief zum Thema Integration von Immigranten bzw. Leben als Ausländer (in Deutschland oder anderswo) bzw. führen die auf *SPIEGEL ONLINE* geführte Debatte in der Klasse fort (s. *SF 25: Debating*).

Differenzierung
ZA

PRE-READING Der fächerübergreifende Bezug zu Religion (Ursprung bzw. Deutung des Zitats „Satan in Heaven") wird genutzt: *Discuss whether or not the simile 'life for a foreigner is like that of Satan in heaven' is appropriate by looking at the image a) from a neutral point of view and b) from a religious point of view.*
Lösungshinweis:
The initial (neutral) response to the quote would be to conclude that Satan was admitted to heaven ('the country') without becoming part of the heavenly community ('society'), the conclusion being that foreigners in Germany have no chance of integration or of doing anything about this. From a religious point of view, Satan was himself an angel who was expelled from heaven (cf. e. g. Luke 10, 18) when he tried to assume God-like qualities. Therefore, the comparison does not work in this sense.

ZA

Interessierte S verfassen einen Leserbrief und tragen diesen vor bzw. laden ihn in ein (eigenes) Blog hoch.

Part B2 ii) – Woher kommen Sie ursprünglich?

> **Info**
>
> *No-go zones* are areas usually controlled by violent gangs, which even police are reluctant to enter or have little control of. The Stonebridge estate in Harlesden, London was once a no-go zone with gang and drug-related shootings rife in the area. A police crackdown on crime and government investment in housing and local employment has led to many improvements in the area and crime rates have fallen. The South Central area of Los Angeles is also known for its gang-related crime. Poor social conditions lead to the development of gangs and drug dealing. Here too the crime rate has fallen considerably since new measures were introduced in 2002.

Lösungshinweise

PRE-READING Individual answers (cf. *Differenzierung*).

1 *Letter 1:* Meusburger suggests that intolerance and ethnically motivated violence are worse in the USA, Great Britain or France. For him, Germany is the most tolerant country of the four. He supports his opinion by rhetorical questions concerning e.g. the number of hate crimes, murders of immigrant children and prejudice against foreigners on TV. He ends his letter by accusing the editor of prejudice.

Letter 2: In his/her three years of living in Germany, Balan has never had any trouble with skinheads. He/She is more afraid of intolerance from people of a higher social standing. Since Balan has no German friends, he/she does not feel a part of German society.

2 *Meusburger's* experience does certainly not reflect Crossland's statements. He doesn't deny xenophobic incidents or behaviour in Germany but puts the situation in the countries into perspective. Though he seems to have only second-hand experience of Britain and France, only stayed a year in the USA and his impressions therefore may not be representative, his letter has got an honest fundamental tone.

Madhu Balan is not afraid of the 'Heile Welt' mentality and 'collective xenophobia' which Crossland stated. But he/she obviously sees Germany more critically and puts forward weighty, though general, examples of Germans being hostile to foreigners, comparing life as a foreigner in Germany with that of 'Satan in heaven'. This seems to reflect Crossland's statement about the German love of 'pure breeds' and underlines the difficulty in making German friends. Balan makes no mention of the good educational conditions (completed Master studies) or the complicated job market (seeking a job). Instead, his/her letter focuses more on Germany's 'bad job of integrating its foreigners', which at least partly reflects Crossland's statements.

SB S. 71   **B2 ii) Woher kommen Sie ursprünglich?**   Hasnain Kazim

Source:	'Zu Gast bei Pessimisten', *SPIEGEL ONLINE*, 26 January 2009
Topic:	'Civil' racism
Text form:	Web article (extract)
Number of words:	157
Skills/Activities:	Mediating; taking part in a discussion

Didaktischer Kommentar

S setzen sich mit offenen und verdeckten Formen von Rassismus auseinander. Besonders durch den Textimpuls mit anschließender Sprachmittlung aber auch aufgrund persönlicher Erfahrungen erfolgt hier eine weitere Sensibilisierung für das tägliche Miteinander.

Unterrichtstipps

L weist S auf den latenten Rassismus der Frage des älteren Manns im *SPIEGEL*-Artikel hin, indem sie sie bittet, das Ergebnis der Bearbeitung von A1 noch einmal zusammenzufassen und auf diesen Text zu beziehen (auch Haut- und Haarfarbe sind nur Äußerlichkeiten, die nichts über eines Menschen Nationalität oder Muttersprache aussagen).

3   Part 3 – The New Gender Gap?

> *Hasnain Kazim* (born 1974) is the son of Indian-Pakistani immigrants to Germany. After studying Political Science, he became an editor and has been working for *Der Spiegel* since 2006. In *Grünkohl und Curry* (2009) he relates the story of his family's move to Germany, their integration and their naturalization after 16 years.

Lösungshinweise

1a Mediation
- two people standing in a queue in a Hamburg bookshop
- an elderly man behind the writer is surprised that he is buying a German book
- the writer asks what's so amazing about that
- the writer is told that he can't be German and asks where he comes from
- the writer replies 'Hamburg' / Stade / Oldenburg / Altes Land, but the elderly man is never satisfied, wanting to know where he *originally* came from
- when it's his turn to pay, the writer does so without answering
- the elderly man wanted to hear that he comes from some faraway country, because a dark-skinned person can't be German
- the writer is angry with himself for having divulged so much personal information

1b S continue their mediation from **1a** by writing an ending (individual answers).

2 Individual answers.

B3 The New Gender Gap?

SB S. 72
▶ LSET ex. 6, 7, 8

i) The Second Sex   Michelle Conlin

Source:	BusinessWeek Online, 26 May 2003; www.businessweek.com
Topic:	The battle of the sexes in education and employment
Text form:	Web article (extract)
Language variety:	American English
Number of words:	675
Level:	Advanced
Skills/Activities:	Cooperative learning strategy (placemat); reading non-fiction; working with charts and graphs; analysing stylistic devices; writing an essay

Didaktischer Kommentar

S erörtern Veränderungen zum Thema (neue) Ungleichheit zwischen Frau und Mann und bringen ihren Standpunkt in einem abschließenden Essay auf den Punkt, wobei sie ihre Schreibkompetenz schulen.

SB-DVD-ROM

Lernwortschatz

gender (heading), scholar (l. 4), inch (l. 6), admit sb. (l. 8), scholastic (l. 9), post (l. 15), label sb. as sth. (l. 29), suspend sb. from sth. (l. 30), outnumber (l. 33), reign (l. 35), BA (l. 35), master's degree (l. 36), PhD (l. 42), inherit sth. (l. 47), obstacle (l. 50), child-rearing (l. 51)

Unterrichtstipps ⚠ HA

PRE-READING Die *placemat* (s. S. 298) kann auch in Jungen- bzw. Mädchengruppen erfolgen. Alternativ bereiten S ihre Ansichten (als Vorbereitung auf den Essay in **4** mit Beispielen belegt) als Hausaufgabe vor.
Der Text (einschließlich **1**) eignet sich als unterrichtsvorbereitende Hausaufgabe.

2 Der Webcode bietet Links mit den Ergebnissen des Global Gender Gap Report der Jahre 2007 und 2009.

Part B3 i) – The Second Sex

Differenzierung
ZA HA

Zum Thema geschlechtsspezifische Berufswahl kann **KV 7** z. B. als Hausaufgabe erledigt werden. Lösungshinweise:

1 Benachteiligung abbauen (l. 3): *reduce inequality;* schlechtes Abschneiden (l. 6): *poor performance;* realistische Vorbilder (l. 11): *realistic role models;* Kult um Männlichkeit (l. 12): *masculinity cult;* falsche Männlichkeitsvorstellungen (l. 17): *false concepts of masculinity;* Kräfte messen (l. 20): *demonstrate one's strength;* angepasstes Verhalten (l. 22): *behaviour conforming to the norm;* jdn. für etwas gewinnen (l. 34): *win sb. over to sth.;* sich von Stereotypen leiten lassen (l. 37): *be guided by stereotypes;* die Zukunft liegt in … (l. 39): *the future lies in …*

2
- Girl's Day aims to get girls interested in careers that are considered 'boys' jobs'
- girls now tend to be more successful than boys academically
- many areas of education in Germany such as nursery and primary school are predominantly female professions (in pre-school education, only 3% of teachers are male)
- many boys don't have realistic male role models
- this can lead to boys performing poorly in school and developing false concepts of masculinity
- boys feel they have to demonstrate their strength which can lead to aggressive behaviour in school
- a successful new boxing programme allows boys to train and get help with their homework at the same time
- a programme aimed at unemployed men in Brandenburg retrains them for nursery and play schools
- the Government now wants to introduce a Boys' Day to win boys over to careers in care or education

3 EXTRA Individual answers.

> **Info**
>
> *The ranking in the Global Gender Gap Report:* Countries are ranked according to their gender gaps and the score they receive indicates the percentage of the gap between the sexes which has been closed.

Lösungshinweise

1 Individual answers.

2

		boys/men		girls/women	
		positive	negative	positive	negative
high school		Boys have had access to education for centuries. (implicit in l. 7)	Boys have fallen behind girls at school, and are now doing worse than they used to do. (l. 21)	Girls have made all the educational progress in the last 30 years. (l. 5)	Girls have only had access to education for the last century. (implicit in l. 7)
			Boys are developmentally two years behind girls when they start school. (l. 24)	Girls have overtaken boys in school achievements, e.g. leadership positions, academic slots, sports teams. (l. 14)	
			The education system does not suit boys' biological needs: they need more action and more breaks. (ll. 26–31)		
			'Anti-boy' culture views boys' behaviour in schools as wrong or abnormal. (l. 30)		

Part B3 ii) – The Global Gender Gap

	boys/men		girls/women	
	positive	negative	positive	negative
college	Men have outnumbered women at college for centuries. (l. 33)	The percentage of boys entering college is no longer rising. (ll. 40–43)	The percentage of girls entering college is still rising. (ll. 43–44)	
college			More girls than boys achieve BAs and MAs at universities in the USA, and the numbers are rising. (l. 35)	
work place	Ninety per cent of billionaires are men. (l. 45)			Only one woman billionaire has made her own fortune, rather than inherited it. (l. 46)
work place	Men still dominate in highest paid jobs and the leading industries. (l. 47)			Women still have to face problems like the pay gap, the glass ceiling, juggling work and children. (l. 50)

3a *The girls' 'scholastic Roman Empire' versus the boys' 'languishing Greece'*: The author is using the extended metaphor and drawing on historic events to show where this gender reversal trend is leading. She points to the changing role of the sexes by juxtaposing the (at its best) powerful Roman Empire and (at its worst) weak Greece.

3b By drawing on history, Conlin is implying that the glory days are forever over for boys just like they were when the Roman Empire started growing in importance and size. In doing so she renders the trend as inevitable as any occurrence in the past. Thus, the metaphor underlines the huge gap between girls' and boys' educational performance.

3c *Repetition*: 'every state, every income bracket, every racial and ethnic group' (l. 34)
Alliteration: 'lawsuit-leery' (l. 28); 'still-Sisyphean struggle' (l. 51)
Humour: 'As for college – well, let's just say this: At least it's easier for the guys who get there to find a date.' (l. 32); 'Still, it's hardly as if the world has been equalized: …' (l. 45)
Sarcasm: 'Hug a girl, and he could be labelled a "toucher"' (l. 29)

4 EXTRA Individual answers.

B3 ii) The Global Gender Gap

Source:	'Gender Gap Narrows in Nordic Lands', Reuters, 8 November 2007
Topic:	The global gender gap 2007 vs. 2009
Text form:	Interview
Language variety:	American English
Length:	2:24 min
Level:	Intermediate
Skills/Activities:	Listening comprehension; working with charts; doing research (online)

Part B3 ii) – The Global Gender Gap

Didaktischer Kommentar
S setzen sich mit Fakten des seit 2005 jährlich herausgegebenen *Global Gender Gap Report* auseinander und lernen die einem solchen Bericht zugrunde liegenden Parameter kennen, indem sie zwei Jahrgänge vergleichen. Ihre beim Hören und Recherchieren gewonnenen Kenntnisse fügen sie zu einer kurzen Beschreibung der Entwicklung eines (frei wählbaren) Landes zusammen.

Unterrichtstipps ZA
Fact File S recherchieren das Weltwirtschaftsforum oder das *Women Leaders Programme* und stellen es der Klasse vor.
Linktipp: www.weforum.org Das Weltwirtschaftsforum bietet auf seiner Website eine Vielzahl von (Audio-/Video-)Materialien und unter „Communities/Women Leaders and Gender Parity" mehr über das gleichnamige Programm.

Word help
Vor dem Hören machen sich S mit unbekanntem Wortschatz vertraut.

Differenzierung ZA
PRE-LISTENING Leistungsstärkere stellen die Geschichte der *gender gap*-Diskussion vor, Leistungsschwächere gestalten dazu ein Poster bzw. eine Collage. Zur gerechteren Aufgabenverteilung wird **KV 8** eingesetzt.

2 In schwächeren Lerngruppen wird eines der in **1b** genannten Länder ausgewählt, da hier schon eine gewisse Vorbereitung stattgefunden hat. Leistungsstarke S wählen eines der Länder nach Interesse, wobei es auch keines der Länder mit English als Amtssprache sein muss (UK, USA, Pakistan und die Philippinen). Der Webcode eröffnet die Länderprofile für 2009 und 2007.

Lösungshinweise
PRE-LISTENING 'Gender gap' sounds like a general term for the difference between men and women or boys and girls in different areas, e.g. income.

1a The gender gap is closing; the top nations have closed 80% of the gap, the bottom nations are halfway there.

1b *Number of countries:* 128; *Position* of Japan: 91st; the Philippines: 6th; Sweden: 1st; the UK: 11th; the USA: 31st
Smallest percentage closed: the political empowerment gap (14%)

1c EXTRA	yes	no	not given
the country's resources		X	
labour force participation rates	X		
wages	X		
literacy rate			X
number of female ministers in parliament	X		
life expectancy			X
distribution of resources	X		
policy reasons behind the distribution of resources		X	

2 Individual answers. Example: The UK reached 11th place in the Gender Gap Index of 2007 but fell to 15th place by 2009. Negative trends in employment may have been influenced by the global economic crisis, which only started to take effect in 2007, but in all areas of education attainment, the UK ranks top. On closer analysis, the data reveals that the fall in rank has less to do with falling standards in the UK and more with rising standards in other countries.

3 Communicating Across Cultures

SB S. 75 CD 3.12–13
Transkript s. TM-DVD-ROM
Didaktischer Kommentar

Communicating Across Cultures – Being Polite

S üben das dialogische Sprechen in berufs- bzw. lebensnahen Situationen sowie Grundlagen des höflichen Kommunizierens in der Fremdsprache in potenziell angespannten Situationen.

Unterrichtstipps
⚠ HA

1a kann als Hausaufgabe erledigt und im Plenum besprochen werden. Dabei bleiben verschiedene Varianten nebeneinander stehen, bevor mit der CD gearbeitet wird.

1b Im Anschluss werten S ihre in **1a** vorgestellten Formulierungen aus und erkennen, wo sie möglicherweise zu forsch, unhöflich oder unidiomatisch waren.

2a S erhalten Gelegenheit, ihre Antworten vorzutragen, bevor sie sie im Zusammenhang mit den Dialogen auf der CD anwenden.

2b Mehrere Durchgänge empfehlen sich, um möglichst vielen S die Möglichkeit zu sprechen zu geben.

Differenzierung
ZA

2 Leistungsstärkere S bereiten weitere Minidialoge vor, auf die der Rest der Lerngruppe reagiert.

ZA

S beschreiben den Cartoon und erläutern, worin sein Witz besteht; interessierte S suchen ähnliche, d.h. auf sprachlicher Über- oder Untertreibung basierende Cartoons und beschreiben sie ihren Mitschülern.
☆ **Linktipp:** www.cartoonstock.com Unter Schlagwörtern wie „exaggerate", „exaggeration" oder „understatement" finden S geeignete Cartoons.
Lösungshinweis: *The dog apparently does not want to surrender the paper without being duly thanked for it ('Oh, alright'), so the owner thanks him with exaggerated politeness by using a complex metaphorical expression. The effect of the exaggeration is enhanced by the introduction, the concluding impatient question, the man's unenthusiastic face, and of course by the fact that the addressee is a dog.*

Lösungshinweise

1a Individual answers; cf. transcript on TM-DVD-ROM for suggested answers.

2a 1E; 2A; 3D; 4B; 5E; 6C; 7A; 8D; 9E; 10B; 11C; 12A/D; 13E; 14C

2b Individual answers; cf. transcript on TM-DVD-ROM for suggested answers.

Part C – Different Ideas about Life

SB S. 76
C1 Helping Hands

Didaktischer Kommentar

S lernen weltweit operierende soziale und Umweltorganisationen kennen und präsentieren eine davon nach einer Gruppenrecherche.

SB-DVD-ROM

Lernwortschatz

human trafficking (logo)

Unterrichtstipps
👥 ZA ALT

Der Einstieg erfolgt ohne SB, um zu klären, welche Hilfsorganisationen S bereits kennen. Alternativ beschreiben S ihnen bekannte Logos während die übrigen S raten, welche Initiative sich dahinter verbirgt. Die ab **1b** zu bildenden Gruppen werden hierfür schon zu Beginn gebildet.

HA

1b Der Webcode stellt die URLs der verschiedenen Organisationen zur Verfügung. Die Aufgabe kann auch als Hausaufgabe erledigt werden.

2 Interessierten S räumt L mehr Zeit ein, um eine (v.a. regionale) Organisation fundierter und ggf. mit weiteren (multimedialen) Mitteln vorzustellen. Inhalt und Art der Präsentation werden dann von L längerfristig mit der Context Task (am Ende von C2) abgestimmt, um eine Doppelung zu vermeiden.

Part C2 – Into the Wild

Differenzierung — Leistungsschwächere recherchieren weitere Organisationen, gruppieren diese nach Art der geleisteten Hilfe (z. B. Umweltschutz) und stellen sowohl die Logos als auch die Ziele kurz vor. Künstlerisch begabte S entwerfen eigene Logos und stellen vor, was sich dahinter verbirgt. Leistungsstärkere S fungieren jeweils als sprachliche Berater oder Juroren. Eine weitere Möglichkeit der Rollenverteilung in den Gruppen besteht über die Nutzung der Rollenkarten auf **KV 8**.

> **Info**
>
> *HOW* (Helping Orphans Worldwide, founded in 2007), is a California-based non-profit organization committed to providing health and security to abused, abandoned and neglected children living in the Philippines and Vietnam.
>
> *World Vision* (founded in California in 1950) is an international partnership of Christians dedicated to working with children, families and communities to overcome poverty and injustice regardless of religion, race, ethnicity or gender.
>
> *Humantrafficking.org* (created in 2000) is a web resource to combat human trafficking, especially in East Asia and the Pacific, by bringing governments, NGOs and individuals together to cooperate.
>
> *Helping Hands* (founded in 1979) is a non-profit organization based in Massachusetts which raises, trains and places monkeys to help and accompany severely disabled people.
>
> *Save The Species Worldwide* (SSWW, founded in Washington in 2002) aims at the survival of threatened and endangered plant and animal species by raising people's awareness through wildlife documentary films, products and programmes.
>
> *Unicef* (The United Nations International Children's Emergency Fund, founded in 1946) works for the worldwide protection of children's rights.

Lösungshinweise — **1–2** Individual answers; **1b** cf. Info.

C2 Into the Wild

Didaktischer Kommentar — Anhand unterschiedlicher Materialien setzen S sich kritisch mit dem radikalen Ausstieg aus einer als defizitär empfundenen Gesellschaft auseinander. Sie üben dabei in einer Vielfalt von Übungen sowohl ihre rezeptiven als auch ihre produktiven Textkompetenzen.

> **Lernwortschatz**
>
> prospect (introductory text); deliberate (ii), pre-reading task)

SB S. 77 CD 3.14
Transkript s. TM-DVD-ROM

C2 i) 'Society': A Song from the Soundtrack — Eddie Vedder

Source:	*Into the Wild*, 2006
Topic:	Leaving society
Text form:	Song
Language variety:	American English
Length:	3:53 min
Level:	Intermediate
Skills/Activities:	Listening comprehension; taking notes; analysing a song

Unterrichtstipps — Vor dem Hören machen sich S mit unbekanntem Wortschatz vertraut: *greed* (l. 2): a selfish desire for more of sth. than is needed; *breed* (l. 9): class, kind, type

3 Part C2 ii) – An Extract from the Book

1 S erhalten etwa eine Minute Zeit, um ihre Eindrücke festzuhalten, und tauschen sich mit einem Partner darüber aus.

2a S einigen sich auf einen Satz, den sie schriftlich festhalten.

2b S notieren vorab Stichpunkte, um das zweite Hören vorzustrukturieren. Diese werden dann ergänzt und ggf. modifiziert.

Differenzierung **3** In leistungsschwächeren Kursen stellt L das Transkript (s. TM-DVD-ROM) als Kopie oder OH-Folie zur Verfügung. Alternativ versieht L den Text mit Lücken und stellt ihn S beim Hören zur Verfügung, um das Hörverstehen zu präzisieren.

Lösungshinweise **1** Individual answers.

2a The singer's general attitude is very critical of society.

2b *Statements on society:* greedy, always hungry for more, people think they're not free until they have it all; criticism of capitalism
Conclusion: he thinks he needs more space; he has to leave society

3 *The music* is repetitive and regular, exceptions are an instrumental in the middle and a woman's background vocals.
The repetition hammers it home: society is crazy and the singer has to leave it to be free. The *variation* in the refrain underlines how unreliable society is – another reason for leaving. Like the variation in the otherwise regular rhythm of the music, this could also be a sign of the singer's insecurity – and a foreshadowing of the events to come.
There is *rhyme* and *assonance* with a strong emphasis on the 'ee' sound which reoccurs constantly, e.g. in the pun 'a greed / With which we have agreed'.
Irony/Paradox: On the one hand, the singer is so critical of society that he needs to leave it (verses), on the other, he is so much a part of it that he's afraid to disagree. The paradoxical statement 'Hope you're not lonely / Without me' could either reflect his fear of leaving or (ironically) underline the importance of the individual for society.

SB S. 78 ## C2 ii) An Extract from the Book   Jon Krakauer

Source:	*Into the Wild,* New York: Anchor Books, 1996
Topic:	Deliberate living
Text form:	Journal entry
Language variety:	American English
Number of words:	99
Level:	Intermediate
Skills/Activities:	Analysing a journal entry

Unterrichtstipps S lesen den Textauszug und tauschen sich zunächst zu zweit über ungewöhnliche Layoutelemente sowie Verständnisschwierigkeiten aus; Fragen zu Wortschatz und Syntax werden im Plenum vorgetragen und geklärt.

HA **1** S notieren sich ihre Antwort (zu Hause) und vergleichen sie im Plenum mit ihren Spekulationen.

Lösungshinweise **1** 'Deliberate living' means taking what you are doing at any given moment seriously and paying attention to the details, being aware of your environment and your actions.

2 Individual answers.

Part C2 iii) – Two Extracts from the Film

SB S. 79 DVD
Transkript s. TM-DVD-ROM

C2 iii) Two Extracts from the Film

Source:	*Into the Wild*, 2006
Topic:	Social criticism
Text form:	Feature film (extracts)
Language variety:	American English
Length:	*Scene 1* 1:58 min; *scene 2* 2:05 min
Level:	Basic
Skills/Activities:	Speculating; viewing skills; doing research

Unterrichtstipps

1 S formulieren jeweils mindestens drei Fragen und halten diese schriftlich fest, bevor sie sich in Vierergruppen austauschen.

2b Nach dem zweiten Sehen haben S ein- bis zwei Minuten, ihre Eindrücke festzuhalten. Danach tauschen sie sich in der Vierergruppe darüber aus.

5 *Linktipp:* http://tifilms.com/wild/call_debunked.htm kann S als Grundlage ihrer Recherche (zweiter Spiegelstrich) dienen.

CONTEXT TASK erfolgt in Einzelarbeit (z. B. als Hausaufgabe über einen längeren Zeitraum) oder in Partner- oder Gruppenarbeit (3–4 S).

a S lassen die behandelten Themen in Partnerarbeit Revue passieren und überlegen gemeinsam, wie das Erarbeitete auf ihr eigenes Leben anzuwenden ist.

b S diskutieren zu zweit die Vor- und Nachteile der verschiedenen Formate, z. B. die benötigte Zeit oder die Anzahl der Sprecher, bevor sie sich für eins entscheiden.

Info

Christopher McCandless (1968–1992) grew up in a financially privileged environment. After graduating he cut off contact with his parents and got rid of all his valuables. Taking very few belongings (and no map or compass) with him, he set out for Alaska, working and hitchhiking along the way. He survived for four months before he died of starvation only a few miles from civilization.

Into the Wild (1996): Jon Krakauer's book made McCandless a hero to many. The story was made into a feature film of the same title by Sean Penn in September 2007; a documentary on McCandless' journey, *The Call of the Wild*, was released a month later. Both Krakauer's book and the Hollywood movie have been criticized for romanticising McCandless' fate and causing young men to risk their lives. McCandless' bus became a tourist attraction by 2002. Far from daring, critics called his behaviour dangerous and lacking common sense; McCandless could have saved himself had he informed himself of his surroundings.

Lösungshinweise

1 Individual answers. *Questions Wayne might ask:*
- Why do you want to go into the wild? (C: I'm so dissatisfied with society.)
- How do you plan to survive? (C: I'm not planning; it will all come to me when I need it.)
- What will you do if you get sick? (C: I won't, because I will be in a natural, healthy environment and not in a sick society.)
- Will you be able to protect yourself from bad weather? (C: I will find shelter.)
- When do you expect to be back? (C: I'm not coming back to this crazy society in which everybody thinks ahead instead of finding stability in the given reality.)

2a *Content:* Christopher explains his plans of going into the wild without any gadgets. He outlines what it is about 'society' that makes him sick, and when he becomes more specific as to who he means, Wayne says it's a mistake.
Atmosphere: A bar at night-time; there is no natural light, the lamps are dim. At the beginning, the atmosphere is rather cosy and casual, but then Christopher and Wayne get worked up about 'this sick society', and it becomes more tense, culminating in Wayne's reaction at Christopher's mention of hypocrites.

3   Part C2 iii) – Two Extracts from the Film

2b *Facial expressions / Gestures:* Christopher's eyes light up when he talks about his plan, Wayne's eyes are sceptical, but his face shows he is involved in the conversation. Christopher's gestures underline his words: he spreads his arm out to stress 'way out there', touches his watch as if to take it off when he says 'no watch', and growls in imitation of a wild beast. When he explains who he means by 'society', he leans forward and almost whispers, as if conspiring with Wayne against 'parents, hypocrites, politicians, pricks'.
Techniques: The camera is focused on the two protagonists in a medium close-up, switching from one to the other as they speak. From time to time the camera moves to other parts of the room. At the beginning we see the man Wayne recommends as an outdoorsman getting slapped by a young woman; when the camera focuses on Christopher's face, he shows signs of amusement; when the two men keep shouting 'society', we see a blonde woman standing in the background, watching.

3a In C2 ii), Christopher notes down 'Absolute Truth and Honesty' and 'Independence' which are reflected in iii) in Christopher's insistence on 'just living' and of his criticism of people being so bad to each other. 'Deliberate living' is expressed in explanations like 'Just be out there in it. Big mountains, rivers, sky, game.', and 'You're just there, in that moment, in that special place and time.'

3b Christopher no longer wanted to live in a society full of greed (i), in which people do not take the task or the moment at hand seriously enough to really relate to it (ii), and in which people are cruel to each other (iii). He was looking for a society that would let individuals live in the present without constantly looking for new and better pleasures, and in which people did not pressure each other through control and judgment.

4a Individual answers.

4b *Camerawork:* The first shot is a full shot of a bus. Then the camera focuses on Christopher getting up in the dark; he is first seen in medium close-up with his head down, then from behind, getting dressed, then we get a close-up of his face before we see him walking unsteadily towards the camera, and sitting down at his table. The camera then switches between his bespectacled, concentrated face in profile, and his pen writing the words 'happiness is only real when shared'. After the last stroke of the pen, there is an extreme close-up of his face, he takes off his glasses and tears fall from his reddened eyes. The scene ends with an extreme close-up of his right hand, obviously wiping the tears from his face.
Lighting: The inside of Christopher's bus is dark; the camera only occasionally allows us to see some daylight through the windows. One take is so dark we can hardly discern anything. However, the page of the book between whose lines he writes his new insight is black and white and thus a bit lighter.
Sound consists mostly of Christopher's loud and strained breathing. Only when the writing is almost finished do we hear a few strains of soft music, as if to underline the nostalgia for shared happiness.

4c In the short film *balance*, society worked only when people cooperated. The message that 'happiness is only real when shared' is very similar: Christopher wanted to experience happiness alone, just as the survivor on the platform wanted to enjoy the box all alone, but since there is nobody left to counterbalance his movements, he cannot open it without endangering himself or the box. In the same way, Christopher finds that human interaction is an essential element of happiness.

5 Individual answers.

CONTEXT TASK Individual answers.

Kopiervorlage 7: Mediation: A Day for Blokes

Read the following extract from an interview that German Minister for Family Affairs Kristina Schröder gave *DIE ZEIT* on Girls' Day 2010. Mark important expressions in Schröder's key arguments.

Schröder [Wir wissen], dass nicht mehr wie früher Mädchen, sondern Jungen die Problemkinder sind. Sie bleiben häufiger sitzen, sind öfter ohne Ausbildung, machen seltener Abitur. Die Aufgabe von Politik muss sein, diese Benachteiligung abzubauen. Bei Mädchen haben wir viel erreicht, jetzt wollen wir bei den Jungen genauso viel erreichen.

DIE ZEIT Was gedenken Sie zu tun?

Schröder Das schlechtere Abschneiden von Jungen liegt unter anderem daran, dass Kindergärten und Schulen weiblich dominiert sind. In den Kitas sind nur drei Prozent der Erzieher Männer.

DIE ZEIT Was soll daran schlecht sein?

Schröder Ich glaube nicht, dass Erzieherinnen oder Lehrerinnen Jungen bewusst benachteiligen, etwa ihnen schlechtere Noten erteilen. Tatsache aber ist, dass viele Jungen ohne Männer aufwachsen. Ihnen fehlen damit realistische Vorbilder. Mitunter entwickelt sich daraus ein Kult um Männlichkeit, der sogar Gewalt idealisiert.

DIE ZEIT Das sind Extremfälle.

Schröder Die machen uns aber große Sorgen. In der Machokultur, die wir bei einigen Migranten, aber auch zum Beispiel bei rechtsextremen Jugendlichen finden, herrscht oft die Meinung vor, ein Mann dürfe seine Frau schlagen oder er muss seine Ehre mit Gewalt verteidigen. Auf diese falschen Männlichkeitsvorstellungen muss Jungenförderung eine Antwort finden.

DIE ZEIT Jungenpädagogen warnen schon heute davor, dass Jungen heute nicht mehr Jungen sein dürfen.

Schröder Jungen haben ein natürliches Bedürfnis, ihre körperlichen Kräfte zu messen, also zu toben und zu kämpfen. Nicht jede Rauferei muss man deshalb gleich mit einem Streitschlichter unterbinden. Ebenso sehe ich in vielen pädagogischen Einrichtungen die Gefahr, das stärker angepasste Verhalten von Mädchen als Norm zu betrachten. Man sollte die latent größere Aggressivität von Jungen aber in vernünftige Bahnen lenken.

DIE ZEIT Wie zum Beispiel?

Schröder In Offenbach gibt es ein Projekt namens „Hart aber fair – Boxclub Nordend", bei dem Jungen das boxen trainieren und gleichzeitig Regeln und Disziplin üben. Daneben erhalten sie Hausaufgabenhilfe. Das kommt enorm gut an.

DIE ZEIT Wo sollen die Erzieher herkommen?

Schröder Gemeinsam mit der Bundesagentur für Arbeit wollen wir arbeitslose Männer zu Erziehern umschulen. In Brandenburg haben wir damit gute Erfahrungen gemacht. Da gibt es ehemalige Handwerker, deren Fähigkeiten heute Kitas nutzen. Diese neuen Erzieher werden sogar von anderen Bundesländern abgeworben. [...]

DIE ZEIT Wie wollen Sie die Jungen gewinnen [sich für ein pädagogisches Studium zu entscheiden]?

Schröder Zum Beispiel durch einen *Boys' Day*, den wir ab 2011 parallel zum *Girls' Day* anbieten. Seit zehn Jahren versuchen wir an diesem Tag, Mädchen für frauenuntypische Berufe zu gewinnen. Doch auch Jungen lassen sich bei der Berufswahl noch immer stark von Stereotypen leiten. Dabei werden die traditionellen Männerberufe, in denen es auf Kraft oder handwerkliche Fähigkeiten ankommt, immer weniger. Die Zukunft liegt in den Dienstleistungen – gerade auf dem sozialen Feld, das bislang von Frauen beherrscht wird, zum Beispiel in der Altenpflege.

From: Martin Spiewak, 'Ein Tag für Kerle', *DIE ZEIT* no. 17, 22 April 2010, p. 37

1 Study the expressions you marked and write down English equivalents.

2 Choose either **2a** or **2b**. Write an email in which you sum up the gist of the interview. Then ask for Jonathan's / Jenny's opinion with regard to their career plans.

a Your e-pal Jonathan wants to do something after school that would be meaningful for society.

b Your e-pal Jenny wants to be a primary school teacher, but is worried that she might not be able to keep discipline in classes with a lot of boys in them.

3 **EXTRA** Write Jonathan's (**2a**) or Jenny's (**2b**) answering email.

Kopiervorlage 8: Roles for Project Work

The four cards below describe different roles of team members during project work.
One person cuts out the cards.
Each team member chooses a card and familiarizes themselves with their role.

A The language monitor

Apart from contributing their share to the team's project, the language monitor

- makes sure everyone on the team speaks English only;
- politely corrects any mistakes they hear;
- deals with any language difficulties which might crop up (may ask teammates for help);
- checks the resources with the materials monitor;
- uses a dictionary to deal with any vocabulary problems; checks vocabulary, keywords, etc.

C The materials monitor

Apart from contributing their share to the team's project, the materials monitor

- makes sure everyone on the team has the necessary texts and resources as well as other materials (pens, highlighters, etc.);
- helps teammates decide which materials to use for the project with the project monitor;
- chooses reliable resources, makes sure they are available and checks them with the language monitor.

B The time monitor

Apart from contributing their share to the team's project, the time monitor

- makes sure everyone in the team works towards completing the task within the given time;
- draws up a time plan with the project monitor;
- keeps the team members informed about how much time is left;
- gives the team a friendly warning if it is wasting time;
- gets the team back on track if it gets carried away;
- makes suggestions on how the team could work more efficiently.

D The project monitor

Apart from contributing their share to the team's project, the project monitor

- organizes and coordinates the team's work;
- makes sure everyone on the team understands the task and keeps them 'on task';
- makes sure the work is divided equally between the team members;
- makes sure the team agrees on the form of the presentation;
- draws up a time plan with the time monitor;
- checks with the materials monitor that everyone has the materials needed;
- checks with the language monitor that there are no language problems.

Context 21 The Individual in Society: Topic Vocabulary

Word/Phrase	Memory Aid	German
ASPECTS OF IDENTITY		
background	*definition:* the details of a person's family, education and work experience	Herkunft
(to) **be emancipated**	*synonyms:* (to) be free / (to) be independent / (to) be at liberty to do sth.	emanzipiert sein
(to) **be hospitable** [hɒˈspɪtəbl ☆ ˈhɒspɪtəbl]	*word family:* (to) <u>be hospitable</u> – hospitality – hospitably	gastfreundlich sein
citizen	*collocations with* **citizen**: second class / senior ~	Bürger/in
education	*collocations with* **education**: adult/higher/secondary/state ~	(Aus-)Bildung
group identity	*other collocations with* **identity**: corporate/cultural/personal ~	Gruppenbewusstsein, Gruppenidentität
(to) **have a belief**	*other collocations with* **belief**: (to) hold/reject/share a ~	einen Glauben haben
hereditary [həˈredɪtri ☆ -teri] *(adj)*	*opposite:* acquired	erblich, angeboren
(human) rights	*other collocations with* **rights**: women's / animal / gay ~	(Menschen-)Rechte
independence	*example sentence:* Angela valued her ~ very highly and didn't like people telling her what to do.	Unabhängigkeit
(to) **protest**	*word family:* (to) <u>protest</u> – protest *(n)* – protestor	protestieren
(to) **realize your full potential**	*example sentence:* Despite being clever, Harry never **~d his full potential** and worked as a waiter all his life.	sein Potential voll ausschöpfen
shape an individual's personality	*definition:* to have a lasting effect on a person's character	die Persönlichkeit einer Person formen
shared values	*word family:* (to) value sth. / <u>value</u> / valuables *(n)* / valuable *(adj)*	gemeinsame Werte
(to) **show personality traits**	*other collocation:* (to) have personality traits	Persönlichkeitsmerkmale haben
social class	*other collocations with* **class**: upper/middle/working ~	gesellschaftliche Schicht
upbringing	*example sentence:* The cousins had a similar ~ despite living in different countries as children.	Erziehung

Context 21 The Individual in Society: Topic Vocabulary

Word/Phrase	Memory Aid	German
PERSONALITY		
(to) **be ambitious** [æmˈbɪʃəs]	*definition:* (to) be determined to be successful	ambitioniert sein
(to) **commit yourself to (doing)** sth.	*example sentence:* I **~ted myself** to helping disadvantaged children at the local youth centre every day.	sich verpflichten etwas zu tun
(to) **conform** (to sth.)	*example sentence:* Teenagers are often under pressure to ~ to their peer-group norms.	sich (an etwas) anpassen
(to) **have a positive attitude to/towards** sb./sth.	*example sentence:* Camilla has a **positive ~ towards** healthy living – she loves sport and eating well.	eine positive Einstellung jdm./etwas gegenüber haben
mainstream	*definition:* what is considered normal because it is accepted and shared by most people	Mainstream
(to) **rebel** [rɪˈbel]	*word family:* (to) rebel – rebellion – rebel [ˈrebl] *(n)* – rebellious	rebellieren
(to) **sponsor** sb./sth.	*word family:* (to) sponsor – sponsor – sponsorship	jdn./etwas fördern, jdn./etwas sponsern
subculture	*collocations with* **subculture** drugs ~ / punk ~ / youth ~	Subkultur
(to) **volunteer**	*word family:* (to) volunteer – volunteering – volunteer *(n)* – voluntary	ehrenamtlich arbeiten

4 National Identity and Diversity

Das Kapitel beleuchtet Chancen und Grenzen nationaler Identität und das durch Migration verursachte Aufeinandertreffen unterschiedlicher kultureller Wertesysteme. Verschiedene aktuelle Aspekte des Zusammenlebens in einer modernen multikulturellen Gesellschaft werden diskutiert und exemplarisch historische Entwicklungslinien verdeutlicht.

Part A – National Identity or National Stereotypes diskutiert die Wesensart nationaler Charakteristika im Gegensatz zu gängigen Klischees.

Part B – New Identities erläutert das Entstehen nationaler Identität am Beispiel Großbritanniens und der USA.

Part C – Living with Diversity gibt exemplarisch anhand von Einzelschicksalen Einblick in unterschiedliche Umgangsweisen mit kultureller Andersartigkeit.

Didaktisches Inhaltsverzeichnis

SB p.	Title	TM p.	Text Form	Topic	Skills and Activities	Language Practice
80	Lead-in DVD	114	Photos; video clip	Different aspects of national identity and cultural diversity	Working with pictures; defining terms; viewing skills	
82	Words in Context – The Character of a Nation	115	Informative text	National identity	Matching words and definitions; activating passive vocabulary; translating	LP 1: Collocations with nouns; LP 19: Using articles and quantifiers; LP 20: Avoiding German-English interference
	Part A – National Identity or National Stereotypes?					
84	A1 Oaths and Pledges	116	Oaths (extracts); pledges (extracts)	Pledging allegiance to a country	Reading non-fiction; working with statistics; doing research; giving a presentation	
86	A2 UK Stereotypes: How to Be Polite Martyn Ford; Peter Legon	118	Cartoon	Stereotypes about the English	Working with pictures; taking part in a discussion	LP 25: Expressing yourself concisely
87	A3 US Stereotypes: Loud and Boisterous, Quiet and Polite	119	Non-fictional text (extract)	Stereotypes about Americans and how to deal with them	Summarizing; mind mapping; writing an essay	LP 26–27: Connecting your thoughts
88	Communicating across Cultures CD 1.08–1.09	120	Conversations	What to say and what not to say	Listening comprehension; mediating	LP 22: Using the appropriate register
	Part B – New Identities					
89	B1 The Roots of Diversity: An Anglo-American Timeline CD 1.10–11	121	Timeline; illustrations; photos; lecture	The history of multiculturalism in the UK and the USA	Working with pictures; doing research (online); listening for gist/detail	LP 26–27: Connecting your thoughts
90	B2 EXTRA Half-Caste John Agard	122	Poem; painting	Avoiding stereotypes	Reading poetry; working with pictures	Working with non-standard English
92	B3 Hyphenated Americans Stephanie Faul	125	Non-fictional text (extract)	From melting pot to hyphenated Americans	Brainstorming; creative writing	LP 26–27: Connecting your thoughts
	Part C – Living with Diversity					
93	C1 Yaya and Nanna Nadia Wheatley	125	Short story (extract)	Coping with a multicultural background	Reading fiction; analysing style	LP 14: Talking about the past
95	C2 A Rich but Imperfect Thing Jhumpa Lahiri	127	Magazine article (extract)	Living in two cultures	Reading non-fiction; understanding imagery	LP 14: Talking about the past
97	C3 In No Other Country Barack Obama	129	Speech (extract)	The potential of diversity	Comparing texts; writing a text	
98	C4 EXTRA A Better Way of Life Petro Georgiou CD 1.12–13	131	Newspaper article (extract); radio report; cartoons	The challenge of multiculturalism	Reading non-fiction; listening for gist/detail; taking part in a discussion; working with cartoons	

4 Lead-in

SB S. 80 DVD
Transkript s. TM-DVD-ROM
Didaktischer Kommentar

Lead-in

Als theoretische Grundlage für die Behandlung der facettenreichen Themen in den verschiedenen Abschnitten des Kapitels erarbeiten S eine erste Definition der Begriffe *national identity* und *diversity*.

Unterrichtstipps

1c S diskutieren in den für **1b** gebildeten Vierergruppen.

2 Die *language help* aus **1** wird auch für **2** verwendet.

ALT

3 L teilt die Klasse in drei Gruppen, die die folgenden Aufgaben bearbeiten:
Gruppe 1: *Collect all the reasons why the group calls itself 'Diversity'.*
Gruppe 2: *How is the name 'Diversity' reflected in the group's performance?*
Gruppe 3: *Describe the mood created by the whole clip.*
Die Gruppen halten gemeinsam die gesammelten Informationen fest und bilden dann neue Gruppen, sodass in jeder Gruppe S der alten Gruppe vertreten sind, die die Informationen austauschen. Der Clip wird am Ende noch einmal betrachtet und S prüfen, ob sich ihr erster Eindruck bestätigt. Lösungshinweise:
1 The group members have different professions, ages, races, heights, and hairstyles.
2 The performance is characterized by a large number of different musical influences and dance elements; they seem to have tried to incorporate as many different influences as possible to achieve something diverse and completely new.
3 Individual answers (e.g. The mood is very positive/exciting/emotional/…)

ZA

Make a list of the (musical) influences you detect in the performance and speculate on the reasons the group had for choosing them. Lösungshinweise:
(Musical) influences: *Martin Luther King (speech, 1963): overcoming racism; 'I want you back' by The Jackson 5 (song): giving someone a chance – which is what talent shows do;* Carmina Burana *by Carl Orff (classical music, 1936): a traditional piece reused in a new context;* Chariots of Fire *by Vangelis (film soundtrack): people of different backgrounds achieving greatness by working together; 'I believe I can fly' by R. Kelly (song): achieving your dreams*
Reasons: *Individual answers.*

> **Info**
>
> *Diversity* (founded in 2007) is a street dance group that won first place in the third series of the British TV show *Britain's Got Talent* in 2009. It consists of three sets of brothers and their four best friends; all are from east London and the Essex area and between 13 and 26 years old.

Lösungshinweise

1a **A** US Capitol, Washington, D.C. (seat of the US Congress); **B** a black British policeman ('bobby'); **C** a UK postage stamp with the face of Queen Elizabeth II on it; **D** the Statue of Liberty in New York; **E** an Asian violinist; **F** The Houses of Parliament in London; **G** Sydney Opera House, Australia; **H** coffin of a US soldier with the US flag covering it; **I** two people sitting in the rain; **J** a ferry with the white cliffs of Dover behind it; **K** a statue representing justice; **L** children with the Canadian maple leaf emblem painted on their faces; **M** English football fans; **N** a cowboy in Monument Valley, Utah; **O** an Inuit with his dogs; **P** Ayers Rock /

Uluru, Australia, with an Aborigine in front of it; **Q** a teapot with the Union Jack on it; **R** a Sikh taxi driver in New York

1b *Australia*: G, P; *Canada*: L (possibly O); *USA*: A, D, H, N, (possibly O), R; *UK*: B, C, F, (possibly I), J, M, Q; *any of the countries*: E, I, K

1c Individual answers.

2 Individual answers. (National identity in all of these countries has a lot to do with multiculturalism.)

4 Words in Context

3a Diversity can refer to the fact that they are all different races, heights, sizes, ages and colours, and that they come from different walks of life.

3b Individual answers.

4 Individual answers. (Diversity can not only refer to ethnicity/race, but also to national origin, religion, education, sexual orientation, age, class, etc.)

SB S. 82
▶ **LSET ex. 1**

Didaktischer Kommentar

Words in Context – The Character of a Nation

Nutzen und Herausforderung von Multikulturalität für eine moderne Gesellschaft werden angesprochen und Grundwortschatz vermittelt. Der anschließende Übungsteil dient zur Erarbeitung, Vertiefung und Festigung dieses Wortschatzes.

SB-DVD-ROM

Lernwortschatz

culture (l. 3), tradition (l. 3), identify with sth. (l. 4), national character (l. 8), stereotype (l. 8), shared values (l. 11), ethnic and social group (l. 12), sense of belonging (l. 12), unite a nation (l. 14), member of society (l. 14), basic set of beliefs (l. 14), respect a culture (l. 15), citizen (l. 16), adopted homeland (l. 16), swear an oath of allegiance (l. 16), nationality (l. 18), ethnicity (l. 18), immigrant (l. 19), ethnic mix (l. 19), multicultural society (l. 21), diversity (l. 21), experience prejudice and discrimination (l. 23), integrate (l. 25) core culture (l. 25), assimilate (l. 27), ethnic identity (l. 28), mix of cultures (l. 30), melting pot (l. 31), homogenous whole (l. 33), salad bowl (l. 34), voluntarily segregate oneself from sth. (l. 41), be discriminated against (l. 42), ethnic ghetto (l. 43), migrant community (l. 47)

Unterrichtstipps

Einstieg: Vorab kann auf Grundlage der Karikatur die Frage: '*Melting pot*' or '*salad bowl*' – which is the more suitable image? diskutiert werden.

1ab S kontrollieren sich gegenseitig in Partnerarbeit.

ALT

4 Alternativ arbeiten S statt mit dem SB-Text mit einem zweisprachigen Wörterbuch, in dem sie die Wörter nachschlagen und die passende Übersetzung auswählen. Dabei werden die Strategien für die Auswahl besprochen und ausgewertet.

Info

'The Mortar of Assimilation – and the One Element that Won't Mix' (1889) by Charles J. Taylor (1855–1929) is an American political cartoon showing Columbia (the feminine personification of the USA) stirring the melting pot of US citizenship with 'equal rights'. 'The one element that won't mix', i.e. that refuses assimilation, is an Irishman. His sash ('Blaine Irishman') reveals that he is a supporter of James G. Blaine, Republican presidential candidate in 1884 of part-Irish descent with whom the Republican Party had hoped to gain traditionally Democrat Irish votes. The banner he is holding is that of the 'Clan na Gael', an Irish Republican organization in the USA at the time.

Lösungshinweise

1a 1 national character; 2 stereotype; 3 shared values / basic set of beliefs; 4 sense of belonging; 5 ethnic ghetto; 6 assimilate

1b Individual answers.

2a national *capital*, etc.; vague *description*, etc.; ethnic *ghetto*, etc. ; obey a *law*, etc.; shared *beliefs*, etc.

2b Individual answers.

3a The definite article has a selective function: it is used with common nouns only when referring to quite specific or definite persons or things. (*We know a lot about the lives of the members of the Royal Family.*)

4 Part A

When referring to persons or things in general, the noun is used on its own. This applies to abstract nouns (e.g. *life, death, society*), material nouns (e.g. *bread, water*) as well as to nouns in the plural (e.g. *petrol prices have risen*)

Church, school, prison, university, etc. do not need a definite article when the function of the building is referred to. If, however, the building is referred to rather than the function, there has to be a definite article. (e.g. *I am going to church* but *I am in the church*).

3b

1 Discussions of national identity are always difficult in Germany because of World War II. (Unlike 'World War II', 'the Second World War' takes the definite article because of the ordinal number, cf. 'chapter 3' versus 'the third chapter'.)
2 One of <u>the</u> biggest problems in German society is prejudice against immigrants.
3 Foreigners find it hard to follow American politics.
4 Before others criticize <u>the</u> segregation of blacks and whites in <u>the</u> USA, they ought to look at <u>the</u> problem of segregation in their own cities.
5 Germans can be proud of <u>the</u> way democracy has developed in their country.

4 EXTRA

1 <u>According to</u> a study, 92.9% of Americans are proud …
2 There is <u>a good deal of overlap</u> in the answers to the survey.
3 Visitors <u>are expected</u> to behave respectfully.
4 <u>It is generally accepted</u> that large industrial nations need immigrants.
5 Native Americans are a minority that has been <u>discriminated against</u> in the USA.

Part A – National Identity or National Stereotypes?

LSET Skill 19

SB S. 84

A1 Oaths and Pledges

Topic:	Pledging allegiance to a country
Text form:	Oaths (extracts); pledges (extracts)
Language variety:	American English; British English
Number of words:	292
Level:	Intermediate
Skills/Activities:	Reading non-fiction; working with statistics and tables; doing research; giving a presentation

Didaktischer Kommentar

Im Vergleich der Eidesformeln der vier verschiedenen Länder wird herausgearbeitet, auf welche Grundwerte die einzelnen Nationen Wert legen. In arbeitsteiliger Gruppenarbeit schulen S ihre Präsentationstechniken bzw. ihre Hörverstehenskompetenz und lernen, Verantwortung für das Lernen der Gruppe zu übernehmen.

SB-DVD-ROM

Lernwortschatz

pledge (title), allegiance (l. 4), heir (l. 5), successor (l. 5), obligation (l. 15), fidelity (l. 17), subject (l. 18), domestic (l. 20), reservation (l. 25)

Unterrichtstipps

2ab S vergleichen die Ergebnisse im Plenum.

2c S erarbeiten die Aufgabe im *think–pair–share*-Verfahren und sichern die Ergebnisse schriftlich.

3 Vorbereitend beschreiben S das Foto der kanadischen Einbürgerungszeremonie, dessen Atmosphäre auch als Überleitung zum Ton des Textes dienen kann.

Differenzierung
ZA

2d EXTRA In leistungsstarken Gruppen werden die Besonderheiten der US-amerikanischen Eidesformel kritisch diskutiert: *Is the image of a defensive democracy still appropriate today? How much can a state ask of its subjects?*

Part A1 – Oaths and Pledges

ZA **4a** **EXTRA** Leistungsstärkere S referieren über im Unterricht nicht behandelte Nationen. Politisch interessierte S informieren sich alternativ über Einbürgerungszeremonien in Deutschland und präsentieren ihre Erkenntnisse. Sie vergleichen, erörtern und bewerten Einbürgerungstests in Deutschland und ausgewählten angelsächsischen Ländern.

Linktipp: Der Einbürgerungstest
- in den USA: *http://usgovinfo.about.com/blinstst.htm*
- in Kanada: *www.v-soul.com*
- in Australien: *www.australiantest.com/free-test*
- in Großbritannien: *www.workpermit.com/uk/naturalisation/life_in_the_uk.htm*

Info

Oaths, affirmations and pledges are all formal promises. An oath is usually taken with a call for a divine power as witness whereas an affirmation is often offered as an alternative to those who object to taking an oath because of their religious beliefs. A pledge is simply a solemn promise.

American citizenship: The Oath of Allegiance is an oath taken by all immigrants to the USA. It was introduced in 1778.

Australian citizenship: Until 1949 Australians were British subjects. In 1994 the Oath of Allegiance was replaced by the Pledge of Commitment, which must be given by all new citizens.

British citizenship: Applicants for British citizenship must take an Oath of Allegiance to the monarch. Modern versions of this oath have existed since 1689. In 2003 the Citizenship Pledge to the United Kingdom was introduced.

Canadian citizenship: The Oath of Citizenship derives from the British Oath of Allegiance. Before 1947, Canadians were British subjects. The Oath of Citizenship goes back to the British Oath of Allegiance and was used even before 1947.

Lösungshinweise

1ab	Australia	Canada	UK	USA
loyalty to country	✓		✓	
loyalty to monarch		✓	✓	
loyalty to people	✓			
democratic beliefs	✓		✓	
respect for rights	✓		✓	
respect for liberties	✓		✓	
obedience to laws	✓	✓	✓	✓
fulfilment of duties as a citizen		✓	✓	
support for constitution				✓*
willingness to defend country				✓*
willingness to serve country				✓*
renunciation of past allegiances				✓*
oath taken freely, truthfully				✓*

* The five asterisked points in the American oath can be seen as specific descriptions of what is meant by the fulfilment of duties as a citizen in the British and Canadian oaths.

2a All oaths and pledges require loyalty and allegiance to the new state and form of government. They demand obedience to laws and the upholding of (democratic) rights and liberties. All four oaths are formal and solemn.

2b In constitutional monarchies like the UK, people have to swear allegiance to the king or queen as the head of state. Some nations put emphasis on the fulfillment of the duties of a citizen. The USA not only requires its citizens to renounce all allegiance to other states or sovereigns, but also demands that its citizens defend the nation and its democratic constitution against foreign and/or domestic enemies.

4 Part A2 – UK Stereotypes: How to Be Polite

2c *Australia* sees itself as a place where the people are just as important as the country itself: new citizens swear loyalty to both.

Canada puts allegiance to the monarch first, then mentions the country's laws and the duties of a citizen without mentioning any rights that derive from citizenship.

The UK separates the oath of allegiance to the monarch and the pledge, which addresses other items. The oath combines the historical position of the monarchy within the system with the benefits of a modern democracy. The monarch holds a very important position in the UK. The pledge lists rights, freedoms and democratic values on the one hand and obedience to the law, citizen duties and obligations on the other hand.

The USA demands full commitment from its citizens. It presents its political system as strong and well-prepared against any evil-doers and democracy as a system that requires effort and dedication from all its beneficiaries.

2d EXTRA The formality of the language, the emphasis on military defence and civilian service show that the oath is taken very seriously. It lists very specific requirements such as bearing arms and serving in the Armed Forces if called upon to do so. It originates from the War of Independence when the Americans were fighting the British. This war demanded utmost commitment from every inhabitant of the colonies. The USA has always accepted immigrants from different political backgrounds, often from European states where a monarchy was still the norm. The USA had to make sure that newcomers would commit themselves to the new system of democracy. This is why they made (and still make) them distance themselves from other forms of government they used to follow.

3–4 Individual answers.

Fact File

Lösungshinweise

	Australia	Canada	UK	USA
Foreign-born population in percent	24.1%	19.8%	9.7%	12.6%
Foreign-born population in figures	4,500,000	6,000,000	5,800,000	38,000,000
No. of people granted citizenship in 2006	ca. 103,000	ca. 260,000	ca. 154,000	ca. 700,000

S might find it easier to have facts and figures shown in a table, as it allows them quick access, an instant overview and straightforward comparisons.

SB S. 86

A2 UK Stereotypes: How to Be Polite

Didaktischer Kommentar

S setzen sich mit gängigen Klischees über Engländer auseinander und diskutieren Sinn und Unsinn nationaler Stereotype. Sie erarbeiten dieses Thema anhand eines Cartoons, den sie analysieren und interpretieren.

SB-DVD-ROM

Lernwortschatz

bother sb. (cartoon), evaluate sb./sth. (task 3)

Unterrichtstipps

PRE-READING Einstieg (SB geschlossen): Die Ideen werden an der Tafel festgehalten, um im Anschluss an **5** noch einmal auf die Fragestellung zurückkommen zu können.

2 S halten die Antworten schriftlich fest.

⚠ **HA** **4–5** S suchen als Hausaufgabe nach Beispielen aus Büchern, Filmen, Fernsehsendungen usw., in denen (vermeintlich) typisch englisches bzw. deutsches Verhalten dargestellt oder karikiert wird.

Differenzierung **4–5** Leistungsstärkere S halten Kurzreferate zu den mitgebrachten Materialien (s. Unterrichtstipps), in denen auch der Hintergrund der Bücher/Filme/Fernsehsendungen erläutert wird. In Vorbereitung auf **5** nehmen sie Stellung zu den in diesen Medien dargestellten Stereotypen.

Part A3 – US Stereotypes: Loud and Boisterous, Quit and Polite

ZA S denken sich eine ähnliche auf einem Vorurteil basierende Situation unter der Überschrift „Get around in German" aus. In Zusammenarbeit mit künstlerisch begabten S stellen sie die Situation für ein Postkartenmotiv dar.

Lösungshinweise

PRE-READING *Stereotypes:* The English are said to be reserved and to have a stiff upper lip; are famous for their self-discipline; eat big cooked breakfasts; boil all food / aren't famous for their cuisine; are great football players; talk about the weather all the time; don't bother learning other languages.

Origin: Some of the stereotypes originate from British history: in colonial times, when Britain ruled over large parts of the world, the Armed Forces and the Civil Service were famous for their organizational skills and their discipline. The English brought their culture and language to the world, English is the *lingua franca* now, so the English often expect to be understood by foreigners.

1 The postcard illustrates the politeness of the English. They are rarely blunt and direct. The stereotype is the basis for the humour in the cartoon. It would not work without the cultural characteristics it draws upon.

2a *1. Wrong:* A formally dressed Englishman is walking his dog beside a river, where another man is calling for help. The man on shore doesn't want to be bothered – he holds up his hand as if to say 'Leave me alone.' He walks past a lifebelt and leaves the drowning man to his fate. Even the dog puts its nose in the air, deliberately ignoring the drowning man.
2. Right: The situation is the same, but the drowning man addresses the man on the riverbank very indirectly, politely apologizing for the inconvenience. The man on the riverbank reacts to this approach and throws him the lifebelt.

2b *Message:* If you want anything from an English person, you need to be extremely polite.

3 Both situations portrayed are, of course, unrealistic. It is hard to imagine that anyone, in England or elsewhere, would allow someone to drown. It is just as unrealistic to think that a drowning man would have the time or inclination to ask for help in such a long and involved way.

4 *The message* has a certain core of truth: English people pay attention to rules of politeness, they like to be spoken to in a friendly way and avoid being blunt or direct. Thus they often regard foreigners, especially Germans, as rude.
Examples from the media: the Monty Python or Fawlty Towers TV series that ironically depict English behaviour

5 Individual answers.

SB S. 87
LSET ex. 3

A3 US Stereotypes: Loud and Boisterous, Quiet and Polite

Source:	www.edupass.org/culture/stereotypes.phtml
Topic:	Stereotypes about Americans and how to deal with them
Text form:	Non-fictional text (extract)
Language variety:	American English
Number of words:	182
Level:	Intermediate
Skills/Activities:	Summarizing; mind mapping; writing an essay

Didaktischer Kommentar S setzen sich mit Stereotypen über US-Amerikaner auseinander und evaluieren Ratschläge zum Umgang damit. Dabei erweitern sie ihren Wortschatz zum Thema „Verhalten" und weisen ihre Erkenntnisse zur Wechselbeziehung nationaler Identität und nationaler Stereotypen in einem abschließenden Essay nach.

SB-DVD-ROM

Lernwortschatz

boisterous (title), xenophobic (l. 6), generate (l. 7), distorted (l. 8), preconceived (l. 13), acquaintance (l. 15)

4 Communicating across Cultures

Unterrichtstipps

2a S arbeiten allein oder in (Zweier-)Gruppen; Einzelne präsentieren die Ergebnisse anschließend dem Plenum.

Differenzierung

3a Leistungsschwächere Lerngruppen nutzen die Listen aus **2b**, um anhand der Vorurteile gegenüber einer Nationalität Rückschlüsse auf die nationale Identität zu ziehen: *What conclusions regarding national identity can you draw from these stereotypes?* Die Antwort auf Aufgabe **2** des Lead-in („Define national identity") kann S ebenfalls als Grundlage dafür dienen.

> **Info**
> *'Cheesehead'* is the nickname for a Green Bay Packers fan (cf. photo). Green Bay is in Wisconsin, which is referred to as the 'Dairy State'.

Lösungshinweise

1a The text recommends ignoring the many stereotypes readers may have heard about Americans and suggests they keep an open mind. It claims this is important so as not to offend people and to avoid embarrassment.

1b The text admits some stereotypes may be generally true, but states that they may not apply to everyone. Whereas some Americans are louder and more boisterous in certain situations, many are quiet and polite. While some may dislike foreigners, most are friendly and hospitable. The text confirms one stereotype: Americans tend to be quite informal; they wear casual clothing and address professors by their first name.

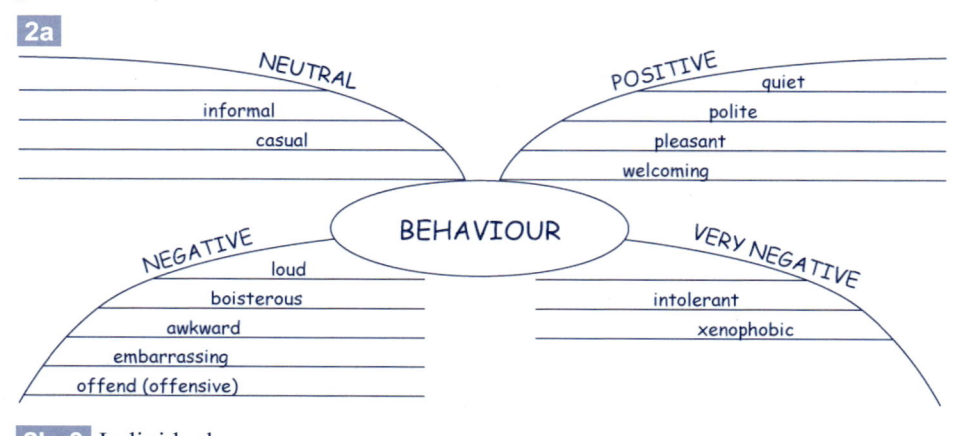

2a

BEHAVIOUR

- NEUTRAL: informal, casual
- POSITIVE: quiet, polite, pleasant, welcoming
- NEGATIVE: loud, boisterous, awkward, embarrassing, offend (offensive)
- VERY NEGATIVE: intolerant, xenophobic

2b–3 Individual answers.

Communicating across Cultures – What to Say and What Not to Say

SB S. 88 CD 1.08–09
Transkript s. TM-DVD-ROM

Didaktischer Kommentar

S werden dafür sensibilisiert, dass Deutsche im englischsprachigen Ausland in ihrer Kommunikation oftmals als zu direkt und rüde eingeschätzt werden und lernen, ihre interkulturelle Kommunikation an den Maßstäben anglo-amerikanischer Höflichkeit auszurichten.

Differenzierung

Einstieg für leistungsschwächere Lerngruppen (SB geschlossen): *What does the term 'understatement' mean to you? Explain it to a partner, giving examples*

Part B

ZA Einstieg für leistungsstärkere Lerngruppen (SB geschlossen): *Comment on British politeness and compare it to the way Germans behave. Name differences and similarities. Can you think of problems or difficulties connected with the differences? Discuss.*

Lösungshinweise

1 1a, 2a, 3b, 4a

2a Mediation Individual answers; cf. transcript on TM-DVD-ROM for suggested answers.

2b Individual answers.

Part B – New Identities

SB S. 89 CD 1.10–11
Transkript s. TM-DVD-ROM

B1 The Roots of Diversity: An Anglo-American Timeline

Topic:	The history of multiculturalism in the UK and the USA
Text form:	Timeline; illustrations; photos; lecture
Language variety:	Caribbean English
Length:	*Part 1* 4:20 min; *part 2* 4:51 min
Level:	Advanced
Skills/Activities:	Working with pictures; doing research (online); listening for gist/detail

Didaktischer Kommentar

Am Beispiel der britischen und US-amerikanischen Geschichte wird S die Entstehung einer multikulturellen Gesellschaft vor Augen geführt. Bild- und Hörmaterialien vermitteln die wichtigsten Daten der britischen und amerikanischen Geschichte seit dem 16. Jahrhundert.

Unterrichtstipps

1 wird zuhause erledigt, sofern keine Rechner mit Internetanschluss zur Verfügung stehen. Zu Beginn der Stunde werden die Ergebnisse in Fünfergruppen zusammengetragen.

2 Vor dem Hören machen sich S mit unbekanntem Wortschatz vertraut.

Differenzierung

Nachdem S die Einwanderungszahlen für vier Länder ausgewertet (Fact File **A1**), eine Kurzpräsentation zu den Einbürgerungsbestimmungen gehalten (**A1**, Aufgabe **4**) und mit der Geschichte der ethnischen Vielfalt in Großbritannien und den USA (**B1**) konfrontiert worden sind, stellen sie (ggf. arbeitsteilig zu verschiedenen Teilbereichen) Recherchen zu Kanada an (Geschichte der Kolonisation und Einwanderung), das sonst leicht mit den USA über einen Kamm geschoren wird. Anschließend werden die Ergebnisse mit dem über Großbritannien und die USA Gelernten verglichen.

ZA Interessierte S halten zu einzelnen historischen Ereignissen Referate. Sie greifen entweder auf Daten und Ereignisse dieses Abschnitts zurück oder berichten über andere wichtige Ereignisse der angloamerikanischen Geschichte, z.B.: *the struggle for independence; the triangular slave trade; immigrant biographies (e.g. Lee Iacocca, former president of Chrysler; Fiorello LaGuardia, mayor of New York; Jim Thorpe, Native American athlete)*. Der autobiografische Roman des indianisch-amerikanischen Schriftstellers Sherman Alexie sensibilisiert S für die Perspektive der *Native Americans*. S lesen *The Absolutely True Diary of a Part-Time Indian* (erschienen in der CSEL, ISBN 978-3-06-031263-4) und halten ein Referat (s. *SF 22: Giving a report on a book*).

> **Info**
>
> *The Mayflower* was the ship that transported English Protestant dissenters, better known as the Pilgrims, from Plymouth, England, to Plymouth, Massachusetts in 1620. The Mayflower is a symbol of the European colonization of North America and of religious, political and personal freedom found in the new Promised Land.

4 Part B2 – Half-Caste

> *The Brookes* carried black slaves to the USA in the 18th century. The *Brookes print* (cf. photo on timeline) was used by campaigners for the abolition of the transatlantic slave trade and has become a symbol of the struggle against slavery.
>
> *The Great Famine* (1845–1855) was a period of mass starvation, disease and emigration during which the population of Ireland fell by roughly one quarter. Approximately one million people died and a million more emigrated. The cause of the famine was a potato disease known as potato blight.
>
> *Ellis Island* (in operation 1892–1954) was the leading federal immigration station of the USA. Located in the harbour of New York City, over 12 million immigrants passed through the immigration process there. It is now a museum.
>
> *The Empire Windrush* arrived in England on 22 June 1948, transporting 492 passengers from Jamaica who wished to start a new life in Britain. The passengers were the first large group of West Indian immigrants after World War II. The ship has become an important symbol of multiracialism in the UK.

Lösungshinweise

1a Individual answers.

1b *Verb form:* colonize; (diversify); emigrate; —; immigrate; persecute; —; —
i) ... set up their <u>colonies</u>, they came into contact with the <u>indigenous</u> people.
ii) Colonization, <u>slavery</u> and waves of <u>immigration</u> ... led to ... <u>diversity</u>
iii) ... face <u>persecution</u> ..., they often become <u>refugees</u>
iv) ... more people who <u>emigrate/immigrate</u> do so for economic reasons.

2 *Message:* While diversity is an integral part of any society, certain historical events can be pinpointed which led to a more diverse USA and UK.

3 1585: Sir Walter Raleigh sails west and claims first American colony (Virginia) for Queen Elizabeth
1600: Queen Elizabeth grants East India Company a Royal Charter
1788: investigation into terrible overcrowding on the slave ship *Brookes*
1845–55: Great Famine, cf. Info
1892: Ellis Island, cf. Info
1948: British Nationality Act and arrival of *Empire Windrush* in England (cf. Info)

4 Individual answers.

SB S. 90
▶ LSET Skill 39

B2 EXTRA **Half-Caste** John Agard

Source:	*Half-Caste*, 2004
Topic:	Avoiding stereotypes
Text form:	Poem; painting
Language variety:	Caribbean English
Number of words:	217
Level:	Advanced
Skills/Activities:	Reading poetry; working with pictures

Didaktischer Kommentar

Durch die Gedichtanalyse setzen sich S mit kultureller Vielfalt auseinander sowie damit, wie der unreflektierte Gebrauch von Bezeichnungen („Mischling' = *half-caste*) auf Betroffene wirkt. Neben der inhaltlichen Auseinandersetzung steht auch die Arbeit mit der Varietät *Caribbean English* im Vordergrund.

SB-DVD-ROM

Lernwortschatz

caste (title), canvas (l. 9), overcast (l. 20), cast (v, l. 47) apologetic (task 2d), defiant (task 2d)

Unterrichtstipps
⚠ **HA**

Als Vorbereitung auf die inhaltliche wie sprachliche Erarbeitung in der Stunde lesen S das Gedicht vorab zuhause.

Part B2 – Half-Caste

2a–c Für eine ruhige und konzentrierte Erarbeitungsphase machen sich S zunächst in Einzelarbeit Notizen, bevor sie diese in ihrer Gruppe besprechen.

ALT 2c (i)–(iv) werden arbeitsteilig diskutiert und die Ergebnisse der Klasse präsentiert und besprochen.

2d Nachdem S sich das Gedicht gegenseitig vorgelesen haben, besprechen sie den Ton ihres Vortrags. Anschließend suchen sie Indizien im Gedicht, die für einen solchen Ton sprechen.

ZA
1 Research the history behind the term 'half-caste' in Australia.
2 List offensive terms for people of mixed or of a particular race and find politically correct alternatives. Lösungshinweise:
1 Cf. Info C1.
2 half-caste, half-breed, mulatto – of mixed race / of ... descent/origin; Indian – Native American; coloured/Negro/nigger – black (BE) / African American (AE)

Differenzierung ⚠ **HA**
1 In leistungsstarken Lerngruppen werden die Gruppen vorab eingeteilt und das Gedicht bzw. der jeweilige Abschnitt zu Hause vorbereitet. Die Übersetzung wird im Plenum vorgetragen.

> **Info**
>
> *John Agard* (born 1949) is a playwright, poet and children's author. He was born in Guyana and moved to the UK in 1977. He has won several awards for his work. His poetry *(Half-Caste)* features in the GCSE syllabus, which has made him popular with British pupils.

Lösungshinweise

1 *A:* Please excuse the fact that I am standing on one leg: I am a half-caste (or: I am half-cast, i.e. I have a cast on one leg). Explain what you mean when you use the word half-caste: are you saying that when Picasso mixed red and green he created a half-caste (i.e. mixed, inferior) painting?
B: Explain what you mean when you use the word half-caste: do you mean that when light and shadow mix in the sky we have half-caste weather? In that case English weather is nearly always half-caste. In fact some of those clouds are half-caste (i.e. a mixture of white clouds and dark clouds) until the sky is overcast and those spiteful clouds won't allow the sun to be seen.
C: Explain what you mean when you use the word half-caste: do you mean that when Tchaikovsky sat down at the piano and played both the black and the white keys he created a half-caste (i.e. mixed, inferior) symphony?
D: Explain what you mean. I am listening to you with the keen half of my ear and looking at you with the keen half of my eye, and when I am introduced to you I'm sure you will understand why I offer you half a hand and when I sleep at night I close half an eye and consequently when I dream I dream half a dream and when the moon begins to glow I as a half-caste human being cast half a shadow.
E: But you must come back tomorrow with the whole of your eye and the whole of your ear and the whole of your mind and I will tell you the other half of my story.

2a *A:* Agard is asking people to think about what they're saying when they use the word 'half-caste'. He asks whether you would call a painting with different colours a half-caste canvas.
B: He is showing that life consists of differences mixed together to make a whole, and if only one thing predominates (here: clouds), you lose other aspects (the sun).
C: By suggesting a symphony be played with only the black or the white keys, Agard shows how absurd it is to consider a mixture of different things as inferior.
D: Agard points out how foolish it is to regard someone as being 'half' by citing examples from his body. He does not consist of half-pieces but is a whole. The stanza ends mid-sentence.

E: Agard reverses the accusation of being 'half' by accusing the addressee of having used only half his capacity for hearing, seeing and thinking and asking him to open up the other half in order to get the true picture. Stanza 4 (ll. 49–51) takes up the sentence from the previous stanza and again ends in mid-sentence. The break is for emphasis, underlining the importance of all parts of a sentence to fully understand, hence the repetition of 'whole' in each line.

2b What Agard is rebelling against is the term 'half-caste' used as a pejorative term for someone of mixed race, as it implies they are 'half', i.e. lacking something. He opposes the implication that the mere fact of something consisting of more than one ingredient makes it less valuable, as it is with animals, where crossbreeds are often considered inferior to pure breeds. He argues that the mixture gives all these things – paintings, the weather and symphonies – something more, makes them special and exciting. This also applies to humans, and the black and white piano keys that are 'mixed' could stand for his black father and white mother. The painting's red and green colours both oppose and complement each other: the two parts could stand for adulthood (green) and childhood (red). Part of the man remains firmly in the red part, suggesting the importance of one's childhood, while the child will grow into the green part of the painting. Thus, like the poem, the painting underlines the importance of both halves to make a whole.

2c (i) Perhaps Agard chose an uneven number of stanzas (five) to make a division into two equal halves impossible. The great variety in the length of both the lines and the stanzas reflect the meaning of diversity.
(ii) Caribbean dialect is non-standard English. Agard may have chosen this for three reasons: 1) because he wanted to emphasize his own roots; 2) because it's very colourful and rhythmic; 3) because it requires the reader to look at an old situation in an unfamiliar language. Caribbean English is a blend of languages and represents English in a different form, much as Agard represents a different kind of Englishman. The fact that he mixes Caribbean and standard English – e.g. *Ah* (ll. 34, 36) / *I'm* (ll. 3, 39); *yuself/yu* (ll. 4 ff.) / *you'll* (l. 39) – makes the poem 'half-caste': in Agard's sense, richer through diversity.
(iii) With his unorthodox use of capital letters (only at the beginning of the first three stanzas and the pronoun 'I', disregarding proper names), Agard undermines the expectations of his white readers. He has decided not to conform to the rules of orthography of those whose unreflected use of vocabulary ('half-caste') he opposes.
(iv) For one, the repetition structures the poem: the three lines beginning with 'Explain yuself' (ll. 4/10/24 ff.) each introduce a new speculation of what might have been meant by 'half-caste'. The previous repetitions set the variation in ll. 32–33 more clearly apart as the beginning of something new: the second part of the poem in which the lyrical I is turning the tables on the addressee and ironically applying the 'halfness' to parts of his body.
For another, the repetition makes it clear that the lyrical I thinks the reader should be explaining himself for not properly thinking through his ideas and for using a word like half-caste without considering the implications. The repetition of 'half' in ll. 34–54 underlines its ironic use and prompts the reader to question it.

2d Individual answers, e.g. *defiant*: There is defiance throughout the poem. The repetition of 'explain yuself' indicates that it is the addressee who must defend his point of view. From l. 49 onwards the speaker is saying that all the silly examples (ll. 4–31) must be put aside and that when the reader comes to him with an open mind, he'll tell him his whole story. The 'Excuse me' at the beginning is less an apology than a way of addressing the reader that reveals the ironic stance of the poem.

4

Part B3 – Hyphenated Americans

SB S. 92 · **B3 Hyphenated Americans**   Stephanie Faul

Source:	*The Xenophobe's Guide to the Americans*, 2001
Topic:	From melting pot to hyphenated Americans
Text form:	Non-fictional text (extract)
Language variety:	American English
Number of words:	276
Level:	Intermediate
Skills/Activities:	Brainstorming; creative writing

Didaktischer Kommentar   S erweitern ihre Kompetenz im Umgang mit Sachtexten, indem sie den Ton des humorvollen Texts über amerikanisches Selbstbewusstsein und den amerikanischen Umgang mit den eigenen Wurzeln bestimmen und mögliche Lesarten ermitteln.

SB-DVD-ROM

Lernwortschatz

hyphen (title), misfit (l. 1), convict (n, l. 1), demographic (l. 2), retain (l. 3), splinter (l. 11), delusion (l. 20), descend from sb. (l. 22)

Unterrichtstipps   **3** Das Sammeln von Ideen für **3a** kann zu zweit erfolgen; **3b** eignet sich als Hausaufgabe.

Mediation *In a bar, you're talking to German friends about American national pride and the American attitude towards foreigners. Tell the others about the text you just read.* Lösungshinweise:
- Amerikaner sind stolz auf ihr Land und darauf, Amerikaner zu sein, betonen aber gern die Unterschiede zwischen sich und anderen Amerikanern
- *national pride:* Amerikaner betonen ihre Abstammung, indem sie sie mit einem Bindestrich versehen: Deutsch-Amerikaner usw.
- sie sind ihrem Ursprungsland oft nicht durch Traditionen, Sprache o.Ä. verbunden
- *attitude towards foreigners:* das Wissen um Amerika als Einwanderungsland macht Amerikaner so tolerant; alle sind potenzielle (Bindestrich-)Amerikaner

Lösungshinweise   **1** The writer uses the term 'hyphenated Americans' to describe American citizens who were born or have roots in another country. The implication is that they have both American and e.g. Indian/Irish/Polish characteristics and traditions.

2a The tone of the text is humorous (ll. 1–2 and 15–18), ironic (l. 5) and informal (ll. 9–10) throughout.

2b The effect is to amuse the reader and make them wonder if the descriptions do not have some degree of truth in them.

3 Individual answers.

Part C – Living with Diversity

SB S. 93 · **C1 Yaya and Nanna**   Nadia Wheatley

LSET ex. 4

Source:	*The Night Tolkien Died*, 1994
Topic:	Coping with a multicultural background
Text form:	Short story (extract)
Language variety:	Australian English
Number of words:	572
Level:	Intermediate
Skills/Activities:	Reading fiction; analysing style

4 Part C1 – Yaya and Nanna

Didaktischer Kommentar

In den zwei Großmüttern des Mädchens Xenia spiegelt und verdichtet sich kulturelle Vielfalt : die Einwanderin, die ihr Land verlassen und sich in fremder Umgebung zurechtfinden musste auf der einen, die Einwohnerin des aufnehmenden Landes, voller Skepsis und Vorurteile gegenüber Einwanderern auf der anderen Seite. S analysieren die Kurzgeschichte und schulen ihre Textkompetenz.

SB-DVD-ROM

Lernwortschatz

lullaby (l. 7), homesickness (l. 9), godfather (l. 13), godchild (l. 14), tracksuit (l. 20), ingredient (l. 32), parish (l. 36), squad (l. 38), murmur (v, l. 47), scarlet (l. 47)

Unterrichtstipps

2 kann in arbeitsteiliger Gruppenarbeit mit anschließender Ergebnispräsentation auf Folie oder Poster erfolgen.

3 EXTRA Wenn S mit Migrationshintergrund in der Lerngruppe sind, eignet sich diese Aufgabe, um an die Lebenswelt der S anzuknüpfen.

1c/2a *Taking the information from the Fact File on immigration to Australia into account as well as the title of the book from which the short story is taken, speculate on Wheatley's attitude to immigration.* Lösungshinweise:
'Melting Point' is a play on the term 'melting pot'. The Australian government's assimilation policy has failed as portrayed through both grandmothers. One harbours reservations of foreigners or people with foreign names (even her son-in-law), the other, an immigrant, refuses to assimilate and speaks her mother tongue whenever possible. Overall Wheatley seems critical of the government's immigration policy, calling the end result 'a big gluggy mess', while describing both grandmothers in a warm and humorous tone.

ZA Bei Interesse können Einzelne *Follow the Rabbit-Proof Fence* von Doris Pilkington Garimara (1996) lesen und vorstellen oder die Klasse den Film *Rabbit-Proof Fence* (94 min, s. Info) sehen.

Differenzierung
⚠ HA

1 kann in leistungsstarken Gruppen eigenständig vorbereitet werden.

Info

The Stolen Generation: Between 1869 and 1970, many thousands of Aboriginal children were forcibly removed from their families and placed into state- or church-owned institutions in order to 're-educate' them to become servants in white households. It is estimated that between 1910 and 1970 almost every Aboriginal family had at least one child removed from it.

Rabbit-Proof Fence (Australia, 2002; director: Phillip Noyce; screenplay: Christine Olsen) is set in 1931 in Western Australia, where the government forces two sisters and their cousin, all of mixed (white and Aboriginal) descent (so-called 'half-castes'), into an institution where they are to be educated as whites. The three girls manage to flee and walk the 1400 km to their home along the rabbit-proof fence, pursued by the 'Chief Protector of Aborigines' (Kenneth Branagh) and an Aboriginal tracker.

Lösungshinweise

1a Xenia remembers being homesick at a Brownie camp and her father fetching her home in the middle of the night. Yaya (her dad's mother) came with him and on the way home told her the story of her immigration to Australia. She remembers watching a TV interview with both Yaya and Nanna (her mum's mother).

1b The homesickness Xenia experiences (ll. 1–3) is the homesickness you experience on your first (or an early) stay away from home: suddenly you miss home and your parents. Yaya's homesickness was also for her home and her parents, but home was much farther away and she had reason to fear that she would never see it again. Yaya was in a country whose language she didn't speak; her homesickness was deeper and lasted much longer (ll. 22–23) than Xenia's.

Part C2 – A Rich but Imperfect Thing

1c *Yaya* left the Greek island of Crete for an arranged marriage when she was 17. She was very homesick and never learned to speak English very well, although well enough to be able to poke fun at Nanna's prejudices.
Nanna comes from a family that has been in Australia for generations ('dinky-di Aussie', l. 24).

2a *Yaya* can support Xenia when she is homesick because Yaya knows what homesickness is. She has never felt at home in Australia and misses her homeland.
Nanna feels part of Australia and believes that newcomers don't really belong.

2b Subtitles are used in foreign language films to translate the dialogue into the language of the country where the film is being shown. The use of the word 'subtitle' is figurative since the extract is not a film; it is literal in that Yaya either tells the story in Greek or broken English, so what we are reading is a 'subtitled' standard English version.

2c l. 13: Sydney, Australia; l. 42: English. Wheatley wants to emphasize that to this day Yaya has a strong Greek accent and pronounces very important words which she must have had to use very often in her own way.

2d Nanna uses the term 'high flyer' figuratively, to denote someone who does very well and thinks too highly of himself. Yaya picks up its literal meaning of someone in a plane flying high up in the air. Wheatley uses the wordplay to show Nanna's prejudices and highlight Yaya's well-kept secret – that her command of the English language is good enough to undermine Nanna's prejudices.

2e *Original meaning of new Australian:* someone newly immigrated to Australia from another country
- *immigrant:* someone who leaves their home country to live in another country
- *refugee:* someone who has had to leave their homeland because their life was in danger there
- *ethnic (n):* a member of an ethnic (= national/racial/cultural) group, especially one who retains this group's customs
- *high-flyer:* an ambitious person

New Australian, immigrant, refugee and ethnic are all words which describe a person's background. By using these words as terms of abuse, Nanna implies that someone does not belong, or is not an Australian because of their different origins, her reasoning being that because she has been there much longer, she is somehow 'better'. She probably uses 'high flyer' for people she thinks are trying to seem superior e. g. by the way they talk (cf. ll. 36–37).

2f Having grandmothers of different ethnic origin might be difficult for Xenia as her grandmother don't get along and she might feel caught in the middle, particularly if Nanna implies that Yaya doesn't belong there.

3 EXTRA Individual answers.

SB S.95
▶ LSET ex. 4, 5, 6, 7

C2 A Rich but Imperfect Thing   Jhumpa Lahiri

Source:	*Newsweek,* 6 March 2006
Topic:	Living in two cultures
Text form:	Magazine article (extract)
Language variety:	American English
Number of words:	589
Level:	Advanced
Skills/Activities:	Reading non-fiction; understanding imagery

4 Part C2 – A Rich but Imperfect Thing

Didaktischer Kommentar

Die Schwierigkeiten einer *hyphenated American* werden S in einem längeren autobiografischen Artikel nahegebracht. Der Text trifft die Lebenswirklichkeit der S indem er darlegt, wie komplex bikulturelles Aufwachsen gerade für Kinder und Jugendliche in der Phase eigener Identitätssuche ist.

SB-DVD-ROM

Lernwortschatz

anticipate sth. (l. 2), intense (l. 11), approve of sb./sth. (l. 14), perception (l. 17), distinguishing (l. 33), humiliating (l. 36), tangled (l. 38), sibling (l. 44), intertwined (l. 46), feel compelled to do sth. (l. 54), proficiency (l. 57), bicultural (l. 61), upbringing (l. 61)

Unterrichtstipps

2a/3 **3c** kann alternativ zuerst bearbeitet werden, indem S in Kleingruppen alle Metaphern und Vergleiche aufzählen, die ihnen auffallen. Diese werden an der Tafel oder am OH-Projektor gesammelt, bevor sie arbeitsteilig – unter Berücksichtigung von **2a** und **3ab** – analysiert und interpretiert werden. Mögliches Tafelbild:

	outmoded currency (money, l. 27)	roots (l. 37)	arithmetic (l. 41)	siblings (brother/sister, l. 44)	a rich but imperfect thing (l. 61)
characteristics	old, dirty, worthless, sentimental value only	underground, sustain a plant	logical, one right answer only	fight and love each other, have same parents	e.g. a rough diamond (precious)
image for	things important to her parents	ethnic origin	her two selves (American and Indian self)	her two traditions	bicultural upbringing

Anschließend übertragen S die mathematische Metapher aus **B2** (1 + 1 = 2) auf das Gedicht in **A2** (½ + ½ = 1) und nehmen dazu Stellung, welche Gleichung ihnen (für ihre Situation, für die des Dichters bzw. der Autorin oder allgemein für Kinder, die in zwei Kulturen aufwachsen) als die treffendere erscheint: *Which mathematical sum better illustrates the reality of growing up in two cultures?*

ZA Zur Überprüfung des Leseverstehens wird **KV 9** eingesetzt. Lösungshinweise:

1 1D; 2E; 3A; 4C; 5B

2 (T = true; F = false; NG = not given) 1T; 2F; 3NG; 4F; 5F; 6T; 7NG; 8F; 9T; 10F

Differenzierung

4b **EXTRA** Für eine persönlichere Stellungnahme schreiben bikulturelle S der Autorin einen Brief, in dem sie ihr schildern, wie sie die Situation in Deutschland erfahren: *Write a letter to Jhumpa Lahiri in which you comment on her article. Describe your own bicultural upbringing using suitable imagery.*

ZA Interessierte Klassen sehen den Film *The Namesake* (122 min, s. Info).

Info

Jhumpa Lahiri (born 1967 in London), the daughter of Bengali Indian immigrants who moved to the USA when she was three, considers herself an American. Lahiri's debut short story collection, *Interpreter of Maladies* (1999), won the 2000 Pulitzer Prize for Fiction, and her first novel, *The Namesake* (2003), was adapted into a film of the same name.

The Namesake (USA 2006, director: Mira Nair; screenplay: Sooni Taraporevala), set in the USA and India, explores the themes of immigration and biculturalism through the story of first-generation Indian immigrants Ashima, her husband Ashoke and their two American-born children.

Part C3 – In No Other Country

Lösungshinweise

1 When Lahiri was young, she lived two lives: one at home with her Bengali parents and another with her American friends.
Indian life: Indian customs, the Bengali language, Indian food (eaten with fingers), Bengali songs, Indian clothes, long trips to India in the summer
American life: the English language, which she spoke fluently and without an accent, school, English books, American music and TV

2a Most of her friends came from families whose ancestors had come to the USA many generations ago, so they had less contact with the traditional customs or languages of their countries of origin. They did not have to deal with the problem of becoming part of a new culture.

2b Lahiri has come to accept that belonging to two cultures is enriching even if you don't feel completely at home in either. It was her ability to accept imperfection that allowed her to live at peace with both her Indian and her American self.

3a A currency (money) that is no longer in use can be precious either because it is rare and has become valuable or because it reminds you of older times. While it may have sentimental value, it is worthless because you can't buy anything with it.

3b One (her Indian self) plus one (her American self) should have equalled two, according to mathematical logic, but in her eyes, when she was young, equalled zero because neither of the 'ones' was perfect. Now that she's older she realizes the 'ones' don't have to be perfect so at last one plus one equals two.

3c The images make the text interesting and illustrate otherwise rather abstract ideas e.g. ll. 15 ('hyphen'), 19 ('between two dimensions'), 27–28, 37ff. ('roots'), 40–42, 44 ('siblings').

4a In ll. 31–34 Lahiri points out typically American things such as going to (Christian) Sunday school and ice skating from which she was excluded (because her parents weren't Christian and maybe didn't know about ice skating). She feels that her strange name and her skin colour set her apart, as did the fact that she often went to India (not the norm for most American school children).

4b With maturity, Lahiri has come to accept that a bicultural upbringing is an addition, not a shortcoming. She doesn't conceal the difficulties it brings (e. g. being different, fear of not being accepted) but values both cultures as part of herself. This is relevant also for Germany: although not a traditional country of immigration like the USA, many migrants live in Germany. They may experience the imperfection of a bicultural upbringing, but hopefully bear the richness in mind also.

SB S. 97   **C3 In No Other Country**   Barack Obama

Source:	National Constitution Center, Philadelphia, 18 March 2008
Topic:	The potential of diversity
Text form:	Speech (extract)
Language variety:	American English
Number of words:	190
Level:	Intermediate
Skills/Activities:	Making notes; comparing texts; writing a text

Didaktischer Kommentar   S erarbeiten Formtypik und Stilelemente einer politischen Rede. Sie diskutieren Obamas Darstellung der eigenen Biographie und seine positive Einschätzung von kultureller Vielfalt, in der er eine Kraftquelle des Landes erkennt.

4 Part C3 – In No Other Country

SB-DVD-ROM

> **Lernwortschatz**
>
> depression (l. 5), assembly line (l. 8), inheritance (l. 11), pass on sth. (l. 11), precious (l. 12), niece (l. 12), nephew (l. 12), hue (l. 13), conventional (l. 15)

Differenzierung

2b Geschichtlich interessierte S recherchieren und erläutern Geschichte und Symbolik des 'Great Seal' (s. Info).

3a Die Diskussion kann auch als Debatte (s. *SF 25: Debating*) oder *fishbowl discussion* (s. S. 297) geführt werden: *Migration and multiculturalism – of benefit to all?* oder *Integration – dream or reality?* S wählen eine Rolle (*politician, citizen, migrant, author*), und diskutieren u. a. unter Verwendung von Argumenten aus den *Parts A–C*. Wird **C4** („A Better Way of Life") behandelt, kann die Diskussion im Anschluss daran geführt werden.

> **Info**
>
> *Barack* [bərɑːk] *Obama* (born 1961) grew up in Hawaii and Indonesia. After obtaining his law degree from Harvard, he taught Constitutional Law at the University of Chicago Law School from 1992 to 2004. He served three terms in the Illinois Senate from 1997–2004. In November 2008 he won the Presidential Election and was inaugurated as the 44th (and the first African American) President of the United States in January 2009.
>
> *The Great Seal of the USA* (created in 1782), used on certain official government documents, shows the American Eagle holding a scroll with the motto *e pluribus unum*, Latin for 'out of many, one' (cf. photo). The 13 arrows (one for each of the 13 original states) and olive branch in the eagle's talons symbolize the power of peace and of war. The shield adopts the colours of the flag which stand for purity (white), valour (red) and justice (blue).

Lösungshinweise

1 *Black:* Obama mentions his black African father (l. 1) and his black American wife (l. 10).
White: He mentions his white American mother (l. 2) and his white grandparents (ll. 4–7).
Americanness: Obama contrasts Kenya with Kansas (l. 3) to underline both his African and his American roots. He mentions specific American dates and facts: a depression, Patton's Army and World War II (ll. 4–6), a bomber assembly line at Fort Leavenworth (ll. 7–8) as well as the American universities he went to (l. 9; school *AE infml* = college or university).

2a Obama is referring to the belief that the USA, built by immigrants, is a 'land of opportunity' where there is a racial mix and each individual is equal before the law, regardless of his or her background. The USA is therefore the only country on Earth in which he could have become a candidate for the highest office in the land.

2b Obama, diversity personified because of his mixed-race background, uses the phrase to illustrate the concept of the melting pot: one united nation has emerged from all the many races that make up the population of the USA.

3a Individual answers.

3b **EXTRA** *A newspaper/magazine article* reports on a matter of current or general interest and is usually written in a more formal register and a more serious tone.
A speech is usually held to convince the audience of the speaker's view. In order to do so, the structure is generally simple and stylistic devices are used. The register and tone can be less formal.
C2: In contrast to what one would expect from such an article, Lahiri's text uses a lot of imagery, dictated less by the text form than by her profession as a writer.

Part C4 – A Better Way of Life

C3: Obama uses a lot of repetition and contrast (cf. ll. 1–3, ll. 3–9, ll. 9–10) which make the speech more dramatic. This is dictated both by the text form and by his character and profession: Obama was running for the US presidency at the time and had to come across as ambitious and strong.

SB S. 98 CD 1.12–13
Transkript s. TM-DVD-ROM
▶ LSET ex. 8

C4 EXTRA A Better Way of Life Petro Georgiou

Source:	*Sydney Morning Herald*, 26 July 2005; National Public Radio, 7 October 2004
Topic:	The challenge of multiculturalism
Text form:	Newspaper article (extract); radio report; cartoons
Language variety:	Australian English; American English
Number of words/Length:	478; *part 1* 3:59 min; *part 2* 3:14 min
Level:	Advanced
Skills/Activities:	Reading non-fiction; listening for gist/detail; taking part in a discussion; working with cartoons; writing a text

Didaktischer Kommentar

Der argumentative und subtil appellative Text fordert S zur Stellungnahme heraus. S verknüpfen die Argumente des Textes mit den vorangegangenen Texten (s. v. a. C1, in dem es auch um australische Einwanderer geht) und vertiefen so ihr Wissen. In einem Radiointerview werden authentische Positionen zur Frage der Notwendigkeit von *assimilation* und *core culture* präsentiert.

SB-DVD-ROM

Lernwortschatz

scapegoat (l. 1), perceived (l. 2), flimsy (l. 5), assert sth. (l. 7), atrocity (l. 8), proclaim sth. (l. 10), flawed (l. 12), exploit (l. 16), inherent (l. 17), predate sth. (l. 19), manifestation (l. 22), dignity (l. 29), rejection (l. 31), renounce sth. (l. 32)

Unterrichtstipps
👥 ZA

Einstieg: S arbeiten in Fünfergruppen und erweitern ggf. die in *Words in Context* geführte Diskussion um weitere Bilder: *Melting pot, salad bowl, pizza, tomato soup, quilt: note down their characteristics and discuss to what extent they qualify as an image of multi-ethnicity and multiculturalism. Agree on one image that you think is most appropriate.*

ZA

Zur Sicherung des Hörverstehens wird **KV 10** eingesetzt. Lösungshinweise: 1B; 2A; 3B; 4A; 5C; 6C; 7C

1 Je nach zur Verfügung stehender Zeit arbeiten S arbeitsgleich oder arbeitsteilig und halten die Ergebnisse an der Tafel oder auf einer OH-Folie fest.

⚠ HA ● Word help

2 Vor dem Hören machen sich S mit unbekanntem Wortschatz vertraut.

CONTEXT TASK **a** Die *language help* wird auch schon für **a** genutzt.

Differenzierung
ALT

1 Leistungsstarke S, die schnell die Textstruktur erkennen, gliedern den Text und listen die zentralen Informationen jedes Abschnitts auf.

Info

CD 1.13

The Crips (founded in 1969 in Los Angeles) are one of the most violent American street gangs and, with c. 30,000 primarily African American members, one of the largest. Involved, among others, in murders, robberies, and drug dealing, the Crips are known for their rivalry with the *Bloods*. The Bloods were founded in the 1970s when a faction of the Crips broke off, forming alliances with other gangs to form the gang now known as the Bloods. No less violent and also consisting mainly of African American males, the Bloods have spread out over the USA.

4 Part C4 – A Better Way of Life

CD 1.13 *Gunnar Myrdal* (1898–1987) was a Swedish economist known for his study of the influence of US economic policies on the discrimination of blacks. He received the Nobel Memorial Prize in Economic Sciences in 1974.

Lösungshinweise

1a Arguments against multiculturalism: causes ethnic enclaves and violent youth gangs; muddies national identity; contributes to terrorism (e. g. London bombings)

1b Western democracies are based on certain freedoms, especially of speech, movement and religion. This environment, which makes it difficult for democracies to take action against religious extremists, was not created by multiculturalism but is characteristic of a liberal democracy.

1c Australia adopted multiculturalism because in the huge wave of post-war immigration there were many people who hoped and expected to make a new life without having to give up all their old customs and traditions. Georgiou considers it a successful policy as it has given a lot to Australian culture and Australian values and through its tolerance has strengthened Australian democracy.

2 Apart from Australia, the UK, the USA and Canada are mentioned. Points made: In Australia, multiculturalism was a response to a new reality; this is seen as a positive contribution to the culture and values of the country. Like Australia, the other countries mentioned in this chapter are also traditional immigration countries that have embraced multiculturalism.

3a America as a melting pot or a salad bowl: Texts **B3** and **C3** portray America as more of a melting pot (= assimilation), **C2** as more of a salad bowl (= diversity). What it should be like: Individual answers.

3b Survey findings: Two thirds of the native-born Americans surveyed saw America as a country of many cultures and values that change as new immigrants arrive; everybody contributes (salad bowl). And two thirds of those surveyed think America should be a country where immigrants take on American values and culture (melting pot).

3c Mögliches Tafelbild:

	diversity/multiculturalism	assimilation / core culture
pro	change is necessary for continuity (CD 1.12, l. 23)	a nation needs a core culture to remain strong (CD 1.12, l. 47)
		the Protestant work ethic and individualism are part of America's core culture (CD 1.12, l. 55–57)
		immigration with assimilation is a great source of renewal (CD 1.13, l. 9–10)
con	America's core culture is under threat by immigration from Mexico which might result in a separate culture (CD 1.13, l. 1–2)	the term 'core culture' is unclear especially in the USA with its many subcultures (CD 1.13, l. 16–22)
		'culture' – which you don't choose – is the wrong word; 'creed' (a set of beliefs) – which you choose – is more important and more compatible with diversity (CD 1.13, l. 35)

3d Individual answers.

CONTEXT TASK a *Cartoon 1* illustrates the survey findings of the listening text in **3**: basically, immigration and multiculturalism are good, but the expectation is that immigrants should assimilate.
Cartoon 2 has a similar message: multiculturalism is fine as long as people (customs/traditions/foods) aren't too strange or different.

b–d Individual answers.

Kopiervorlage 9: A Bicultural Upbringing

1 Read the text 'A Rich but Imperfect Thing' by Jhumpa Lahiri. Then choose the best answer.

1 Lahiri is …
- A a hyphenated American.
- B Indian-American.
- C 'immigrant offspring'.
- D All of the above.
- E None of the above.

2 As a child, Lahiri …
- A attended school in Calcutta.
- B had no American friends.
- C attended Sunday school.
- D All of the above.
- E None of the above.

3 According to her parents, Lahiri …
- A is not American.
- B is not entirely American.
- C is not Indian.
- D All of the above.
- E None of the above.

4 In contrast to her parents, Lahiri …
- A is good at Maths.
- B speaks Bengali fluently.
- C speaks English fluently.
- D All of the above.
- E None of the above.

5 When Lahiri married, …
- A her parents were happy for her.
- B her friends were happy to come to India.
- C there was a Hindu ceremony.
- D All of the above.
- E None of the above.

2 Read the statements below and decide if they are true, false or not given in the text. Tick (✓) the correct boxes.

		True	False	Not given
1	Lahiri has no plans to leave the USA.			
2	Lahiri comes from a Bangladeshi family.			
3	As a child she only ate Indian food.			
4	Her parents did not live in Rhode Island but in Calcutta.			
5	Lahiri speaks Indian, Bengali and English.			
6	Lahiri felt neither Indian nor American as a child.			
7	Lahiri wanted to learn how to ice-skate.			
8	Lahiri has never been to India.			
9	Lahiri now feels comfortable with her two traditions.			
10	She believes that a bicultural upbringing only creates problems for children.			

Kopiervorlage 10: Assimilation or Diversity?

1 Listen to the interview in **C4**. Decide which of the following statements best reflects the views of the people interviewed. Tick (✓) the corresponding box.

1 Maria Williams believes that
- A ☐ everyone keeps the beliefs and ideas they arrived with.
- B ☐ everyone contributes their beliefs and ideas to US culture.
- C ☐ Americans are strong enough to reject other beliefs.

2 Susan Cleary believes that
- A ☐ in the past, immigrants used to give up their language in order to speak English.
- B ☐ immigrants nowadays cannot speak their mother tongue.
- C ☐ immigrants are adopting the American way of life.

3 Roberto Suro believes that
- A ☐ the USA is both diversified and unified as a country.
- B ☐ the USA wants to be both diverse and open, yet have a unified culture.
- C ☐ the USA is in the process of becoming a nation while remaining a society of individuals.

4 Prof. Huntington believes that
- A ☐ the core mainstream culture serves as a basis for American unity but that immigration is necessary to renew American society.
- B ☐ the work ethic is the basis of American culture and that immigrants don't possess this work ethic.
- C ☐ American individualism is threatened by too much immigration.

5 Prof. Huntington argues that
- A ☐ America was founded by immigrants, like President Roosevelt suggested.
- B ☐ America was founded by settlers, like President Roosevelt suggested.
- C ☐ America was founded by settlers, thereby contradicting President Roosevelt's statement.

6 Roberto Suro asks
- A ☐ whether an immigrant knows which street gang he should join.
- B ☐ whether an immigrant should not live in a suburban area of the USA.
- C ☐ which is the particular culture of the USA an immigrant is supposed to assimilate into.

7 Prof. Wolf believes that
- A ☐ America is a Judeo-Christian country.
- B ☐ Catholicism is the American creed.
- C ☐ an American creed is more important than an American culture.

Context 21 National Identity and Diversity: Topic Vocabulary

Word/Phrase	Memory Aid	German
PEOPLE IN A MULTICULTURAL WORLD		
ancestor [ˈænsestər]	*definition:* a person related to you who lived a long time ago	Vorfahre/Vorfahrin
(to) **be indigenous to** (a place) [ɪnˈdɪdʒənəs]	*example sentence:* This plant is ~ to the Amazon forest.	einheimisch sein, von einem Ort stammen
citizenship	*definition:* the legal right to belong to a particular country	Staatsbürgerschaft
descendant	*example sentence:* He claims to be a ~ of Queen Elizabeth I.	Nachfahre/Nachfahrin
emigrant	*example sentence:* After the earthquake, there were many ~s to neighbouring countries.	Auswanderer/Auswanderin
generation	*collocations:* the older/younger/future generation / generation gap	Generation
(to) **give up one's cultural/national identity**	*opposite:* (to) retain one's cultural/national identity	seine kulturelle/nationale Identität aufgeben
homeland	*synonyms:* country of origin / mother country / native land	Heimat(-land)
immigrant	*collocations:* immigrant community/family/worker	Einwanderer/Einwanderin
(to) **migrate**	*word family:* (to) migrate – migrant *(n, adj)* – migration	(ab)wandern
nationality	*example sentence:* She retained her German ~ despite living in Australia for ten years.	Staatsangehörigkeit
naturalization	*definition:* the process of making someone a citizen of a country where they were not born	Einbürgerung
of (Native American) descent	*synonyms:* of (Native American) ancestry/origin/ parentage	von (indianischer) Abstammung
refugee	*collocations:* political/economic refugees	Flüchtling
(to) **seek asylum**	*example sentence:* The family **sought** ~ in England when war forced them to leave their own country.	Asyl suchen

Context 21 National Identity and Diversity: Topic Vocabulary

Word/Phrase	Memory Aid	German
DIVERSITY IN SOCIETY		
(to) **assimilate** into/to sth.	*example sentence:* The new immigrants ~d successfully into their new community.	sich anpassen
(to) **be of mixed race/ethnicity**	*definition:* having parents who come from two different races or ethnic groups	von unterschiedlicher ethnischer Herkunft sein
(to) **be prejudiced against** sb./sth.	*example sentence:* **Being ~ against** one cultural group in a society is not acceptable in a democracy.	jdm./etwas gegenüber Vorurteile haben
(to) **be tolerant of** sb./sth.	*word family:* (to) be tolerant of sb./sth. – (to) tolerate sb./sth. – tolerance – tolerant *(adj)*	tolerant gegenüber jdm./etwas sein
(to) **discriminate against** sb.	*opposite:* (to) treat sb. fairly	jdn. diskriminieren
ethnic identity	*other collocations:* racial/religious/sexual identity	ethnische Identität
(to) **identify with** sb.	*definition:* to understand or share the feelings of another person	sich mit jdm. identifizieren
(to) **integrate**	*word family:* (to) integrate – integration – integrated *(adj)*	sich integrieren
multicultural society	*definition:* a society which includes people of different races, religions, languages and traditions	multikulturelle Gesellschaft
mutual respect	*example sentence:* Being open to different ideas is the first step towards **~ respect**.	gegenseitiger Respekt
racism	*word family:* (to) be racist – racism – racist *(n, adj)*	Rassismus
stereotype *(n)*	*word family:* (to) stereotype – stereotype *(n)* – stereotypical	Stereotyp
tension	*example sentence:* There was a lot of ~ between migrants and the indigenous population in the city.	Spannung
xenophobia [ˌzenəˈfəʊbiə]	*example sentence:* **X~** is often caused by people who don't understand different cultures or customs.	Fremdenfeindlichkeit

5 India – Past and Present

Das Kapitel stellt die größte Demokratie der Welt in ihrer überwältigenden Vielfalt vor.
Part A – From Colony to the World's Biggest Democracy zeichnet den Weg auf, den Indien seit der Kolonialisierung über die Unabhängigkeit (1947) bis heute gegangen ist und weiter geht.
Part B – Living in India: Tradition and Change hinterfragt die Bedeutung von Tradition für Inder heute: welche Entwicklungen stattgefunden haben und wie sich z. B. die Rolle der Frauen bis zum Jahr 2010 verändert hat.
Die in *Part C – India Today: Slumdogs and Millionaires* gewählte Perspektive eines jungen Slumbewohners zeigt Indien von unten und bringt S das Elend der Slums näher. S werden mit filmanalytischen Begriffen vertraut gemacht, lernen wichtige filmische Gestaltungsmittel und deren Wirkung kennen und vergleichen in Roman-, Drehbuch- und Filmauszügen die Wirkung verschiedener Genres.

Didaktisches Inhaltsverzeichnis

SB p.	Title	TM p.	Text Form	Topic	Skills and Activities	Language Practice
100	Lead-in CD 2.19–20	138	Photo; fantasy journey	Images of India	Cooperative learning strategy (think–pair–share); mind mapping; listening skills	LP 26–27: Connecting your thoughts
102	Words in Context – India – the Next Superpower?	138	Informative text	India – facts and figures	Reading comprehension; linking sentences	LP 27: Connecting your thoughts: sentence structure
	Part A – From Colony to the World's Biggest Democracy					
105	A1 Remembering Gandhi Madhur Jaffrey	139	Memoir (extract)	Memories of Gandhi	Evaluating information; doing research	
106	A2 India's Informal Economy Sara Sidner	141	Web article (extract)	Assessment of India's workforce	Reading non-fiction	
107	A3 India in Facts and Figures	142	Table of statistics	Geographic, political and demographic information	Working with facts and figures; writing a factual text	LP 26: Connecting your thoughts: linking words
	Part B – Living in India: Tradition and Change					
108	B1 Water Waits for No One Rohinton Mistry	142	Novel (extract)	Water rations	Reading fiction; creative writing	
109	B2 Store Wars Justin Huggler	144	Newspaper article (extract)	India's first nationwide supermarket chain	Reading non-fiction; doing research; writing an outline; writing a feature story	LP 25: Expressing yourself concisely
111	B3 Young Women in Transition Somini Sengupta	145	Newspaper article (extract)	Independent women	Skimming; using a dictionary; taking part in a discussion; doing research	LP 1: Collocations with nouns
113	B4 The Tata Nano CD 2.21	147	Speech (extract)	An affordable car	Listening skills; working with pictures	
114	Communicating across Cultures CD 2.22–23 DVD	148	Citations; documentary film (extract)	Understanding and making yourself understood	Mediating; writing a summary	LP 25: Expressing yourself concisely
	Part C – India Today: Slumdogs and Millionaires					
115	C1 Jamal's Story – the Book Vikas Swarup	149	Novel (extract)	Escape from a children's shelter	Reading fiction	
117	C2 Jamal's Story – the Film Script Simon Beaufoy	151	Screenplay (extract)	Escape from a children's shelter	Comparing a novel and a screenplay; analysing style	Expressing preference
118	C3 Jamal's Story – the Film DVD	152	Feature film (extract)	Escape from a children's shelter	Viewing a film; making notes	
119	C4 For One Million Rupees … DVD	153	Feature film (extract)	Jamal under interrogation	Viewing a film; taking part in a discussion	

5 Lead-in

SB S. 100 CD 2.19–20
Transkript s. TM-DVD-ROM

Didaktischer Kommentar

Lead-in

In einem Brainstorming bringen S ihre Vorkenntnisse zu Indien ein und haben Gelegenheit, ihre Ansichten zu bestätigen bzw. zu revidieren. Anders als bei den übrigen Kapiteln nähern sich S dem Thema emotional, bevor sie in *Words in Context* Überblickswissen erhalten.

Unterrichtstipps

1 wird bei geschlossenem SB bearbeitet: Um weitere Sinne anzusprechen, wird ein Räucherstäbchen angezündet, Darjeeling- oder Yogi-Tee (Chai) getrunken und/oder eine Aufnahme klassischer indischer Musik im Hintergrund eingespielt.

⚠ HA ● Word help

3 Vor dem Hören der Fantasiereise machen sich S mit unbekanntem Wortschatz vertraut.

Differenzierung

2 Leistungsstärkere S kreieren für das Bild einen eigenen Titel oder einen Werbeslogan.

Lösungshinweise

1–3 Individual answers.

SB S. 102
▶ LSET ex. 1, 2

Words in Context: India – the Next Superpower?

Didaktischer Kommentar

Ausgehend von einem Basis-Lernwortschatz werden schrittweise kontextuell Fakten und Themen miteinander verbunden. S schulen ihren Stil im schriftlichen Bereich, indem sie für verschiedene Ausdrucksmöglichkeiten sensibilisiert werden.

SB-DVD-ROM

> **Lernwortschatz**
>
> parliamentary system of government (l. 4), world's largest democracy (l. 5), subcontinent (l. 6), overpopulated (l. 7), British presence (l. 10), colony (l. 11), British Empire (l. 11), Jewel in the Crown (l. 12), Raj (l. 13), colonial period (l. 13), infrastructure (l. 14), colonial power (l. 16), Indian independence movement (l. 16), Partition (l. 20), sectarian violence (l. 21), nuclear weapons (l. 23), nuclear power (l. 24), economic superpower (l. 24), literacy rate (l. 26), growing middle class (l. 31), cheap labour (l. 33), manufacturing (l. 36), service-industry job (l. 36), call centre (l. 37), information technology (IT) (l. 39), poverty (l. 44), slum (l. 45)

Unterrichtstipps

1 kann ggf. arbeitsteilig in Partnerarbeit durchgeführt werden (Partner A ergänzt Sätze 1–4, Partner B Sätze 5–8).

2 S kontrollieren sich gegenseitig in Partner- oder Gruppenarbeit (s. a. *SF 8: Using a grammar book*).

Lösungshinweise

1 1g overpopulated; 2f Partition; 3b sectarian violence; 4a nuclear powers; 5c infrastructure; 6d economic superpowers; 7h cheap labour; 8e service-industry jobs

2a The clause is a participle construction in place of an adverbial clause. Alternatively it could be expressed 'As it covers almost an entire subcontinent'.

2b
1 The city of Bangalore, known today as a centre for high-tech industry, is the fastest-growing city in India.
2 Bangalore, serving as headquarters to two of the top three software companies in India, is called the Silicon Valley of India.
3 The Indian Space Research Organization, established in 1969 in Bangalore, has an annual budget of €573 million.
4 India's space programme, (already heavily) criticized for being too expensive, suffered a major setback in 2009 when contact with its moon orbiter was lost.
5 The exact number of Indian nuclear weapons, (widely) believed to be between 50 and 150, is a closely guarded secret.

Part A

6 India and Pakistan, claiming to need nuclear weapons for their defence, continue to build up their arsenals.

SB S. 104

Part A – From Colony to the World's Biggest Democracy

Fact File

SB-DVD-ROM

Lernwortschatz
comprise (l. 3), resent (l. 10), perceive sb./sth. (l. 11), mutiny (l. 14), administer sth. (l. 16), decline (l. 18), civil disobedience (l. 25), withdraw from sth. (l. 25), tremendous (l. 30), secular (l. 34), displace sb. (l. 35), eligible (l. 40)

Unterrichtstipps
ZA HA

An der Tafel können die fettgedruckten Schlagwörter in einer Mindmap gesammelt und von S ergänzt werden. Daraus kann sich z. B. eine Themensammlung für mögliche Referate ergeben. Die Präsentationen können im Unterricht oder auch als Hausaufgabe vorbereitet werden (s. *SF 23: Giving a presentation*). Mögliche Themen: British East India Company, the British 'Raj', Wars of Indian independence, Partition and its consequences until today, Mahatma Gandhi, India's economy, women in India, Bollywood.

Differenzierung

Leistungsstärkere S hinterfragen in Kurzform zur nächsten Stunde die Aussage „The sun never sets on the British Empire" (s. die Weltkarte zum *Fact File*). Leistungsschwächere S tragen nach der Bearbeitung in Partner- oder Gruppenarbeit die Antworten aller S vor und halten sie ggf. auf Folie oder an der Tafel fest.

SB S. 105

A1 Remembering Gandhi   Madhur Jaffrey

Source:	*Climbing the Mango Trees: A Memoir of a Childhood in India*, 2005
Topic:	Memories of Gandhi
Text form:	Memoir (extract)
Language variety:	British English
Number of words:	279
Level:	Basic
Skills/Activities:	Evaluating information; doing research

Didaktischer Kommentar

S stellen aus einem Text Probleme heraus, mit denen sich Gandhi auseinandersetzte. Durch einen weiterführenden Rechercheauftrag setzen sie sich mit verschiedenen Stationen in Gandhis Leben auseinander.

SB-DVD-ROM

Lernwortschatz
drop (l. 6), embrace sb./sth. (l. 11), hymn (l. 12), amplify (l. 18)   *Fact File:* Hinduism (l. 1), adhere to sth. (l. 1), upbringing (l. 10), reincarnation (l. 16), sacred (l. 17), caste system (l. 19), rub off on sb./sth. (l. 31), butcher (l. 35), sewage (l. 37)

Unterrichtstipps
ZA

Kombiniert mit einer Präsentation zum Thema „Religions in India" oder „The caste system of India" bringt der *Fact File* S die religiöse Vielfalt Indiens näher und bereitet sie so auf das Thema vor. Gandhi kann auch im Rahmen einer Filmanalyseeinheit (Unterrichtsmaterialien z.B. in: *Gandhi – Film Studies in the classroom*, Cornelsen, 2008, ISBN: 978-3-06-032156-8) oder in einer Schülerpräsentation über das Leben und Wirken Gandhis thematisiert werden.

Part A1 – Remembering Gandhi

Differenzierung

3 EXTRA Stärkere S können ein Motto Gandhis, z. B. „An eye for an eye makes the whole world blind", oder ein eigenes Motto für das Schulkonzept oder die Schulhomepage bearbeiten oder entwerfen.

> **Info**
>
> *Mohandas Karamchand Gandhi* (1869–1948) was married at the age of 13 in an arranged child marriage. He had five children, one of whom died shortly after birth. He left India in 1893 to work for an Indian law firm in South Africa, where he lived for 20 years. During his time there he was deeply involved in the campaign for basic rights for Indian immigrants. On his return to India he became involved in Indian politics and through his doctrine of non-violent protest (*satyagraha* – resistance to tyranny through mass civil disobedience) led the Indian nationalist movement against British colonial rule. Mahatma Gandhi (or 'Great Soul'), as he had become known, was killed by a Hindu fanatic in 1948, one year after the end of British rule.

Lösungshinweise

PRE-READING *Social and economic problems*: Indians had little practice at self-government after over one hundred years of British rule; sectarian violence between the Hindu and Muslim populations; millions of people displaced by the Partition; weak economy that had declined under the British Raj; Indian population already crippled by famines and epidemics

1a Although she was very young, she obviously knew who Gandhi was and that he stood for tolerance and humanity (l. 3). She was aware of the prayer meetings and what went on there. It is likely that these topics were discussed among family members in her presence.

1b The atmosphere was obviously quite intense: despite the crowd of people, everyone was silent, so silent in fact that they could hear Gandhi whispering (l. 18). The format of the prayer meetings was simple: Gandhi was escorted to the stage and spoke to the crowd, who listened.

1c
- global and universal unity is more important than being a nation
- everyone's God is the same, no matter what they call that God
- the Untouchables are to be treated as equals
- all faiths/religions are equal
- tolerance
- all humans are to be embraced, including Untouchables

2 *Problems facing colonial India*: Gandhi did not address the problem of poverty in words (in this extract), but by example: he came to the prayer meeting wearing the simplest of clothes, a loin cloth and a shawl (cf. l. 16). He addressed inter-faith distrust and violence by speaking of one God for all humanity, no matter what the different faiths called that God (cf. ll. 9–11). He also addressed the fact that some Hindus and Muslims wanted separate states by emphasizing that one world under God was more important than nations (cf. 9–11). He opposed the caste system by 'embracing' India's Untouchables (cf. ll. 11–12).

Why Gandhi was the right person: One big problem facing independent India was the violent disagreements between its Muslim and Hindu populations. By leading non-sectarian and non-denominational prayer meetings, Gandhi showed support for both groups and attempted to unite them. The traditional Indian caste system would have meant that many peoples' quality of life would not improve much even after the end of British rule, but Gandhi spoke for the rights of all sections of Indian society and believed that the 'Dalits' should be treated as equals. Gandhi's belief in tolerance and equality implied that he wanted independent India to be based on fairness, which undoubtedly made him a perfect leader for the independence movement.

3 EXTRA Individual answers, cf. Info.

Part A2 – India's Informal Economy 5

SB S. 106
▶ LSET ex. 3, 4

A2 India's Informal Economy   Sara Sidner

Source:	CNN International, 14 October 2009
Topic:	Assessment of India's workforce
Text form:	Web article (extract)
Language variety:	British English
Number of words:	178
Level:	Basic
Skills/Activities:	Reading non-fiction

Didaktischer Kommentar

Der Artikel beleuchtet die Situation der arbeitenden Bevölkerung Indiens. Er bringt S einen für Deutschland und andere westliche Länder eher unüblichen Teil der Volkswirtschaft nah – den informellen Sektor – und bietet Anlässe, über dessen Ursachen zu reflektieren.

SB-DVD-ROM

Lernwortschatz

fraction (l. 2), workforce (l. 5), make a living (l. 5), storefront (l. 9), union (l. 9), corporate structure (l. 9), emerge from sth. (l. 12), sheer (l. 13)

Unterrichtstipps
ZA

S recherchieren weitere Informationen zur informellen Wirtschaft und vergleichen die Ergebnisse mit Deutschland, den USA oder Großbritannien.

1 Research information about India's currency. (The official currency is the rupee, which is divided into 100 paise. €1 is equivalent to roughly 60 rupees.)
2 What happens to people in Germany when they can't find work? (In Germany, full unemployment pay is 60–67% of a person's previous income. This can be claimed for up to twelve months. Hartz IV is the name for unemployment benefits received independent of a person's previous earnings; it is usually over €300 a month plus the cost of housing and health insurance. There are also various German organizations which assist the long-term unemployed in their search for work.)
3 Examine the average wage/income per month in Germany in comparison to India. (Germany's average full-time wage per month in 2010 is €2,183; India's average full-time wage per month is estimated at €31.)
4 Explain in what case you would be prepared to visit a roadside dentist (cf. the photo next to the text).

Info

India's huge informal economy is generally made up of small businesses and family enterprises as well as the self-employed. On the one hand the informal sector enables entrepreneurial opportunity in allowing people without access to capital or training to set up small enterprises. On the other hand it restricts workers socio-economically and prevents them from having a voice in society, as these small businesses are often unregistered, leaving employees unprotected by government regulation or representation through unions.

Lösungshinweise

1 According to the text, of the roughly 500 million workers in India (cf. l. 3), approximately 95 % (= 475 million) work in the informal sector (cf. l. 5).

2 The country is extremely poor and there are no jobs. So people have had to 'create' jobs (cf. l. 13) in order to survive.

5

Part B

SB S. 107

A3 India in Facts and Figures

Didaktischer Kommentar

S verstehen statistische Daten und Fakten zu Indien und vertiefen so ihre Kenntnisse über Land und Leben. Gleichzeitig sind die Informationen Ausgangspunkt für das Verfassen eines Sachtextes über Indien. Neben dem Erstellen einer Gliederung üben S das Überarbeiten des eigenen Entwurfs, wobei die Arbeit an der Satzstruktur im Vordergrund steht.

SB-DVD-ROM

> **Lernwortschatz**
>
> sanitation (l. 14), life expectancy (l. 15), infant mortality (l. 16), enrol for / in *(AE)* / on *(BE)* sth. (l. 24)

Unterrichtstipps
ZA

S spekulieren über Gründe für die z.T. schockierenden Zahlen: *Speculate on possible reasons for some of the facts listed in the second half of the table.*
Lösungshinweise:
The relatively high mortality rate *among children is likely to be linked to the fact that 46 % of children under five are* underweight. *Starvation or malnutrition must be high in India, with tragic consequences for vulnerable young children. The large amount of deaths caused by* diarrhoeal diseases *is probably a direct consequence of poor access to* improved sanitation and water. *Although it would seem that a relatively high number of children are* enrolled in education *(for a developing country), there are still many that aren't in schools, presumably because they have child-labour jobs. Hard work in poor conditions must make life very depressing for many Indian children, and this could partially explain the country's high youth suicide rate. The low percentage of the Indian population that has a* phone, *or* access to the Internet, *implies that India is still very much part of the under-developed world whose population is, for the most part, too poor to afford new technology.*

Differenzierung
ZA

1ab Leistungsschwächere S nutzen fünf bis zehn Fakten, um einen entsprechenden Sachtext zu verfassen. Dazu können sie auf die *Language help* sowie auf *SF 37: Structuring a text* zurückgreifen.

1c Leistungsstärkere S wählen maximal zwei Fakten aus, vergleichen sie mit den Verhältnissen in Deutschland und analysieren ihre Bedeutung:
1 Name facts you find surprising and explain why.
2 Investigate reasons for the leading causes of death in India.
3 Compare the literacy rates in India and Germany. How might India's literacy rate be improved?

Lösungshinweise

1 Individual answers.

▶ LSET Skills 47, 48

Part B – Living in India: Tradition and Change

SB S. 108
▶ LSET ex. 5

B1 Water Waits for No One Rohinton Mistry

Source:	*A Fine Balance*, 1996
Topic:	Water rations
Text form:	Novel (extract)
Language variety:	Canadian English
Number of words:	505
Level:	Intermediate
Skills/Activities:	Reading fiction; creative writing

Didaktischer Kommentar

Mithilfe dieses Romanauszugs lernen S einen neuen Aspekt Indiens kennen: das Leben in einem Slum in Mumbai. Sie vergleichen den Text mit ihrem Bild von Indien und werden dafür sensibilisiert, dass Menschen in anderen Teilen der Welt keinen Zugang zu Annehmlichkeiten haben, die für sie als selbstverständlich gelten.

Part B1 – Water Waits for No One

SB-DVD-ROM

Lernwortschatz

fall on hard times (introduction), copper (l. 1), tap (l. 8), scold sb. (l. 15), retort (l. 18), queue (l. 25), obstacle (l. 33), tug (at) sth. (l. 37)

Unterrichtstipps
ZA

PRE-READING Zusätzlich zu ihrem kognitiven Wissen über Politik und Religion in Indien werden S emotional angesprochen, wenn sie sich den Wohlstand bewusst machen, in dem sie selbst leben und später leben möchten.
1 *Think about how much money you would need per day/month to live on your own.*
2 *Assess the income you would need to make your present living standard possible (family, house, car, holidays, hobbies, etc.).*
3 *Describe the photo next to the text. With a partner, brainstorm the consequences of having to get your daily water supply in such a way.*

Info

Rohinton Mistry (born 1952) is among the 20 million Indians who have left India to live abroad (despite the large number, this only represents 1.6 % of the Indian population). Born in Mumbai where he spent his formative years and completed his first degree, he moved to Canada at the age of 23. He has published four novels as well as a collection of short stories. Three of his novels have appeared on shortlists for the prestigious Booker Prize for Fiction award, and he has won various literary competitions. His books all depict aspects of Indian life, culture, religion and traditions.

Lösungshinweise

1a *They own* a mirror, a razor, a shaving brush, a plastic cup, a loata, a copper water pot, a cardboard box, a trunk, some bedding and their clothes.
They don't have a bucket.

1b Om meets the old lady when he tries to get water out of the tap later in the day. She tells him there's only water at dawn and that if he doesn't want to go thirsty he'll have to be there very early. She pours two glassfuls of the water she has stored for herself into his copper pot.
The next morning Om and Ishvar get up early to go to the tap and bump into their neighbour. They have with them the things they need to wash and brush their teeth. The man tells them they'll start a riot if they stand at the tap and wash – what they must do is quickly fill a bucket with water, then wash themselves back in their shack. When they tell him they don't have a bucket, he generously lends them one.
The old lady has explained the need for collecting water early in the morning; the neighbour explains you need to collect it in a bucket so that you don't take up too much time at the tap.

1c One learns from the extract that the shacks are bare, that the water supply is bad, but that the people are willing to help each other.

2 Possible answer: Although the text is fictional it contributes to my picture of India by showing what slum life is like. Because Om and Ishvar are new to the slums, the novelist uses other characters to give explanations concerning what to do and how to behave. However, fiction can also distance the reader because they won't necessarily appreciate that this image of India is a reality for many people.

3a People have nothing but the bare essentials – no furniture, no sanitary facilities. The neighbour tells Om and Ishvar that if they take too long at the tap a fight will break out – this suggests that people are on the verge of violence a lot of the time.
The old lady is quite gruff (though kind at heart): you have to be aggressive and assertive in order to survive.

3b Individual answers.

5 Part B2 – Store Wars

SB S. 109
▶ LSET ex. 6

B2 Store Wars Justin Huggler

Source:	*The Independent*, 6 November 2006
Topic:	India's first nationwide supermarket chain
Text form:	Newspaper article (extract)
Language variety:	British English
Number of words:	570
Level:	Intermediate
Skills/Activities:	Reading non-fiction; doing research; writing an outline; writing a feature story

Didaktischer Kommentar

Am Beispiel einer neuen indischen Supermarktkette zeigt der Artikel, wie Moderne und Tradition aufeinandertreffen. S werden geschult, Zeitungsartikel nicht nur inhaltlich zu verstehen, sondern auch analysieren zu können, für wen und warum dieser Artikel geschrieben wurde. Abschließend verfassen S selbst eine Zeitungsreportage.

SB-DVD-ROM

Lernwortschatz

throng (l. 1), drip (l. 5), be ill at ease (l. 7), company-branded (l. 8), senior executive (l. 9), grand opening (l. 9), outlet (l. 10), supply chain (l. 11), live up to sth. (l. 14), read (l. 16), dignity (l. 21), convenience (l. 29), delivery (l. 40)

Unterrichtstipps

Zum Einstieg bietet sich der Titel des Artikels an, der z. B. mit *Star Wars* in Verbindung gebracht werden könnte und illustriert, dass hier tatsächlich ein existentieller Kampf zwischen Einzelhändlern und Warenketten stattfindet.

1 *What do you associate with the title 'Store Wars'? (The headline is a reference to the iconic American film series 'Star Wars').*
2 *Good against evil: who is good, who is evil? ('Reliance Fresh' could be a symbol of goodness, selling clean produce in a well-ordered setting amidst the chaos of Indian markets. It is convenient for Indian shoppers and benefits farmers, as well as claiming it can help India's agricultural industry to thrive. 'Reliance Fresh' could also be a source of evil: it is a symbol of capitalism interfering with Indian traditions and trying to put smaller businesses out of business.)*

Diffenzierung
ZA HA

4 EXTRA Leistungsstärkere S schreiben einen kurzen Artikel zu den aufgeführten Themen und tragen ihn der Klasse vor.

Info

Reliance Industries are the largest private-sector enterprise in India. Between November 2006 (publication of the article) and today (October 2010), Reliance has opened more than 1000 stores, creating a national retail presence covering fresh produce, electronics and clothing and accessories. Angry demonstrations from some traditional street vendors and supporters of left-wing parties have led to twelve store closures in Uttar Pradesh. The conclusion could be drawn that strong traditions slow down modernization in India, or that not every society needs Western-style supermarkets. On the other hand, if 1000 stores have opened in three years, this implies that there is demand for such retail and that the Indian market is rapidly modernizing.

Lösungshinweise

1a *Available in both 'Reliance Fresh' and Western stores*: brightly coloured signs, fruit and vegetable counters with piles of oranges and carrots, rice, milk, juice bar
Only in Reliance stores: palm tree, puja flowers, hijras
Only in Western stores: frozen pizza, convenience foods

1b (i) There are so many customers because supermarkets are a novelty in India: people are curious to find out what they can buy there and how much it costs.

Part B3 – Young Women in Transition

(ii) The hijras are there because of an old Indian tradition: the owner of a new shop has to give them a cash gift. Whether they're interested in what the shop sells or not, they want to receive money.

2 At the beginning of the article, Huggler says that 'to western eyes, it was nothing out of the ordinary', but then he mentions the dripping palm tree (l. 5). He clearly wants his readers to be aware that there are similarities with the West, but also differences. From the start he emphasizes how ordinary the scene would be but for its Indian quirks. The language he uses when he comes to the hijras (cf. ll. 18–22) also shows that he feels he's describing something exotic – he even uses alliteration ('bevy of burly …', l. 18). He explains a lot of things (cf. e.g. ll. 29–33, ll. 40–42) that wouldn't need explaining if the text were written for people familiar with India.

3 Individual answers; cf. Info.

4 EXTRA Individual answers.

SB S. 111
▶ LSET ex. 7, 8

B3 Young Women in Transition   Somini Sengupta

Source:	*The New York Times*, 23 November 2007
Topic:	Independent women
Text form:	Newspaper article (extract)
Language variety:	American English
Number of words:	463
Level:	Intermediate
Skills/Activities:	Skimming; using a dictionary; taking part in a discussion; doing research

Didaktischer Kommentar

S erfahren, wie sich die gesellschaftlichen Umstände moderner Frauen in Indien verschieben, indem sie einem Text wesentliche Informationen entnehmen. S sammeln und erweitern ihren Wortschatz zum Thema Beruf und Arbeitswelt. Der Schwerpunkt liegt hierbei auf Kollokationen. Sie sammeln Argumente und diskutieren darüber, ob es in Deutschland, Europa und/oder anderen Teilen der Welt sogenannte Männer- und Frauenberufe gibt.

SB-DVD-ROM

Lernwortschatz

surge (l. 8), prompt sb. to do sth. (l. 9), unwitting (l. 11), nudge sb. (l. 11), find a footing (l. 14), defer sth. (l. 19), back-office business (l. 21), retiree (l. 23), crawl with sth. (l. 23), trudge (l. 25), cling to sth. (l. 33), dowry (l. 35), prevail (l. 36), match (l. 41), be torn (l. 43)

Unterrichtstipps

1 Je präziser S einen Inhalt reduzieren können, umso eher kann er anschließend in eigenen Worten weiterverarbeitet werden: eine Technik, die für das Erstellen eigener Texte wichtig ist.

HA

4 EXTRA Nach der Internetrecherche vergleichen S in Partnerarbeit ihre Ergebnisse und diskutieren folgende Aspekte:
1 Speculate on how your friends or family members (especially parents) would react if you were to get married at your present age.
2 Imagine your best friend were to ask you for advice on whether or not to get married. How would you react?

Info

Equal rights for women are guaranteed in India's constitution. In March 2010 the upper house of India's parliament passed a bill reserving one third of parliamentary seats and legislatures for women. Examples of women in top governmental positions include India's President Pratibha Patil, National Congress Party leader Sonia Gandhi and former Prime Minister Indira Gandhi.

5 Part B3 – Young Women in Transition

Lösungshinweise

1a 1: the dependence of Indian women on their parents/husband until recently; 2: the surging economy brings women new freedoms; 3: the sharpest changes for women in the new economy; 4: the independent lives of young women; 5: Bangalore attracts young people; 6: the new lifestyle becomes more common; 7: new lifestyle – old values; 8: new freedom, old values, new problems; 9: independence or marriage?; 10: the difficulty of making decisions

1b Young professional women in Bangalore today are much freer than their mothers could have dreamed of being. They earn their own money, live on their own in flats and are no longer forced to stay at home until marriage. Many of them have good jobs in the IT industry or lifestyle jobs associated with the boom. Although they marry maybe a year or two later than they might have done a few years ago, they are still torn between their independence and pre-arranged marriages.

2a High-tech worker, fashion designer, aerobics instructor, radio DJ

2b *High technology*: computer programmer, computer engineer, software designer, chip manufacturer, …
Back-office business: call-centre worker, telesales worker, helpline worker, virtual assistant, …

2c *Verbs*: design, DJ, programme, engineer, work, assist
Collocations: design software, work in a chip factory / manufacture chips for computers, work in a call centre, work as a telephone salesperson, work as an expert for a helpline / answer people's questions on a helpline, assist customers

2d *Jobs from B1 and B2*: tailor, vendor, shop assistant, executive, farmer, security guard, chairman, servant, cook
Verbs: sew, sell, manage, cook
Collocations: sew clothes, sell vegetables, work in a shop/supermarket, serve customers, run a company, work on a farm, cook food

2e 1) programmer / designer; 2) doctors; 3) sales assistants / vendors; 4) fashion designer; 5) DJ; 6) taught/educated; 7) engineers

2f–3 Individual answers.

4 EXTRA *Marital age* in India: 17; Turkey and Poland: 23; USA: 26; UK: 30; Germany: 31
These figures show that, of the countries compared, the average age in which young women marry is lowest in India. This suggests that traditions change slowly in India. It also shows how much pressure there is on young professional women who want more independence and a career before getting married – something women in most of Europe and the USA take for granted.

Part B4 – The Tata Nano

SB S. 113 CD 2.21
Transkript s. TM-DVD-ROM

B4 The Tata Nano

Source:	Tata Motors Ltd.; 11 January 2008
Topic:	An affordable car
Text form:	Speech (extract)
Language variety:	Indian English; British English
Length:	3:52 min
Level:	Intermediate
Skills/Activities:	Listening skills; working with pictures

Didaktischer Kommentar

S erweitern ihre Kompetenzen zur Texterschließung, indem sie einem Hörtext die wesentlichen Informationen entnehmen, und lernen, dass sie nicht jedes Wort verstehen müssen, um den Gesamtzusammenhang zu verstehen. Weiterhin analysieren S eine Illustration und lernen, die Ergebnisse zu den zuvor herausgestellten Informationen in Beziehung zu setzen.

Unterrichtstipps
⚠ HA ● Word help

1 Vor dem Hören der Rede Ratan Tatas machen sich S mit unbekanntem Wortschatz vertraut.

1a Zum Einstieg beschreiben S das Bild der Familie auf dem Motorrad und nennen ihre Assoziationen (Familienzusammenhalt, Sicherheitsbedenken, Armut, Fortschritt), bevor sie erfahren, wozu dies Bild den Vorsitzenden von Tata Motors veranlasste.

> **Info**
>
> *Tata Motors Ltd.* is the largest Indian company in the automobile industry; it took over Jaguar, the British luxury carmaker, in 2008. It has also created the Tata Nano (pictured in SB), which is currently the cheapest car in the world and went on sale in India at the beginning of 2009. In 2011, the Tata Nano should be available across certain parts of the European market, including Germany, where the estimated price is €5,000.

Lösungshinweise

1a Individual answers.

1b 1 true; 2 true; 3 not given; 4 false; 5 true; 6 not given; 7 true; 8 false; 9 false; 10 true

1c (i) People laughed and said that what he had in mind was tying two scooters together. They didn't think he could produce a cheap car that would be safe, low on petrol consumption, and meet modern emissions criteria. The latest worry was that the Nano would cause additional congestion on India's roads.

(ii) He assured his audience that the Tata Nano was a small but proper car. It had a very low price but nonetheless satisfied safety criteria, had low petrol consumption and met the emissions criteria better than many two-wheelers in India. Finally, with regard to congestion, even if the car sold 500,000 a year for the next five years it would still only represent 2.5 % of Indian traffic.

1d The photo shows a real car with a modern shape, not at all like two scooters tied together. A 624cc engine means it won't consume too much petrol, and the plastic windscreen will make it safer. On the other hand, plastic is probably one way in which he is able to keep his promise to produce a 'people's, i.e. a cheap car. Another way is by saving on sophisticated electronics (e.g. electric windows).

5 Communicating across Cultures

SB S. 114 CD 2.22–23 DVD
Transkript s. TM-DVD-ROM

Communicating across Cultures – Understanding and Making Yourself Understood

Source:	Amar C. Bakshi, 'How the World Sees America', *The Washington Post*, 2007
Topic:	An Indian call-centre job
Text form:	Citations
Language variety:	Indian English
Length:	1:02 min
Level:	Basic

Source:	Australian Broadcasting Corporation, 2001
Topic:	A Delhi-based call-centre company
Text form:	Documentary film (extract)
Language variety:	Australian English; Indian English
Length:	2:04 min
Level:	Intermediate

Skills/Activities:	Mediating; writing a summary

Didaktischer Kommentar

Anhand unterschiedlicher Hör- und Hör-/Seh-Texte setzen sich S mit zwei Varietäten des Englischen (dem indischen und dem australischen Englisch) auseinander und machen sich die Schwierigkeiten bewusst, die bei der Verständigung entstehen können. Gleichzeitig üben S das Anfertigen von Notizen sowie das Schreiben einer Zusammenfassung.

Unterrichtstipps
⚠ ZA

Als Einführung in das Thema Callcenter werden folgende Aufgaben im Plenum bearbeitet:
1 *Assess the importance of call centres for the average person.*
2 *Explain how you would react to a phone call from a call centre.*

⚠

1 L kann S entweder vorab oder im Anschluss an die Aufgabe folgenden Hinweis geben (der im Übrigen auch auf Deutsch-Muttersprachler zutrifft): *Some of the verb forms had to be changed from present progressive to simple present because in Standard English things you do habitually require the simple present. Indians often use the present progressive instead.*

⚠ HA ● Word help

2 Vor dem Sehen des Dokumentarfilmauszugs machen sich S mit unbekanntem Wortschatz vertraut.

ZA

Describe the cartoon. What point does the cartoonist want to make? Lösungshinweise:
The cartoon depicts a misunderstanding between a native English speaker and a French tourist. The tourist is attempting to ask for the time, but doesn't use the article 'the'; the native speaker replies by explaining the concept of time itself. The cartoonist's message is that, when speaking English, small linguistic mistakes can drastically alter the meaning of a sentence. (Instead of making fun of foreigners, native speakers should be tolerant and helpful, overlooking such errors.)

Lösungshinweise

1 We take more than 300–400 calls per day and we only need to make one sale ... If you try to sell the product – sometimes even if they don't want to, they'll listen to the call.
Sometimes they'll be very rude to us, they'll use bad words.
We don't want / try not to get angry at them because, you see, when we call them they're at work or busy.
We even understand their irritation because we call them and try to sell them something. But it's the job we do.

2a Mediation Individual answers.

Part C

2b Mediation
- der Callcenter-Markt ist eine der am schnellsten wachsenden Industrien der Welt
- Roys Firma bearbeitet Abrechnungen für britische und amerikanische Banken, Telefonverkäufe, etc.
- mehr als eine Million Menschen in Indien arbeitet derzeit in diesem Industriezweig, den es 1999 noch nicht gab

3
1. How can I get to the airport for very little money?
2. Where is the nearest hospital where they can help us?
3. My shoe is broken. Can you tell me where there's a shoe repair shop?
4. Excuse me, when do the shops close?
5. Where can we go to eat some good local food?
6. Where does the bus to [name of town] stop?
7. I need some information for a report. Can you tell me where the place is where they keep books – not to buy, but just to work with for an hour.
8. My dog has hurt his foot. I need an animal doctor.

4a Mediation 1 chemist *(BE)* / drugstore *(AE)* / pharmacy; 2 art gallery / museum; 3 police station; 4 supermarket; 5 tourist information; 6 cafe

4b Mediation
1. Die Dame möchte wissen, wo es eine Apotheke gibt.
2. Die Dame möchte wissen, wo die Gemäldegalerie / das Museum ist.
3. Die Dame sucht das Polizeirevier.
4. Die Dame sucht einen Supermarkt.
5. Die Dame möchte wissen, wo das Fremdenverkehrsbüro ist.
6. Die Dame sucht ein Café.

▶ LSET Skills 19, 23

Part C – India Today: Slumdogs and Millionaires

SB S. 115

C1 Jamal's Story – the Book   Vikas Swarup

Source:	*Q & A*, 2005
Topic:	Escape from a children's shelter
Text form:	Novel (extract)
Language variety:	Indian English / British English
Number of words:	632
Level:	Intermediate
Skills/Activities:	Reading fiction

Didaktischer Kommentar

Der Auszug aus Vikas Swarups Roman *Q & A* stellt S das Leben der sogenannten „Slumdogs", Kindern aus den Slums der Großstädte vor. S untersuchen Elemente der Textanalyse wie Handlung und Erzählperspektive. Darüber hinaus entnehmen sie dem Text Informationen über das Leben im heutigen Indien und fertigen Notizen dazu an.

SB-DVD-ROM

Lernwortschatz

resist sb./sth. (l. 3); fend for oneself (l. 6); run down sb.'s spine (l. 10); jigsaw (l. 12); deliberate (l. 22); maim sb. (l. 22); destiny (l. 29); be reconciled to sth. (l. 32); steady (l. 40); bolt (l. 42); wire-mesh (l. 42); tackle sth. (l. 50); clamber (l. 55); pant (l. 56)

5 Part C1 – Jamal's Story – the Book

Differenzierung

2b EXTRA Leistungsschwächere bearbeiten stattdessen folgende Aufgaben:
1 Briefly sketch out the boys' future (l. 29) if they don't escape Maman.
2 Describe the kind of beggars you have encountered in Germany. Would you give them money? Explain.
3 Give your own definition of a 'guardian angel' (l. 27). Do you have a guardian angel? Describe him or her to your classmates.

Die einzelnen Aspekte werden ggf. arbeitsteilig in Partner- oder Gruppenarbeit besprochen, um den Zusammenhang mit dem Romanauszug zu klären.

3 Jamals Aussage bietet Möglichkeiten interkulturellen Lernens:
1 In what kinds of situations would you normally call the police? Are there situations in which you wouldn't want to call the police?
2 Explain the concept of corruption. Do you think this takes place in Germany too?

> **Info**
>
> *Vikas Swarup* (born 1963) is from Allahabad, India. After graduating from Allahabad University in 1986, he joined the Indian Foreign Service and has since held posts in countries around the world, including the UK, South Africa and the USA. He is currently posted in Japan. *Q & A* was his first novel.

Lösungshinweise

PRE-READING *Tension created through*: knowledge gaps: reader doesn't know who is speaking at the beginning or what the sums refer to and wants to find out more; Jamal's feeling of horror (l.10); the toss of the coin: scary that such an important decision will be made by chance; sense of urgency created for escape extract, Maman's guards are just seconds away; the jammed bolt delays the boys' escape and heightens chance that they will be caught

1a Maman and Punnoose only see the boys as a source of income. They are prepared to hurt them so they will earn (more) money or to let them starve if they don't bring in enough money.

1b Jamal understands that Maman and Punnoose want to gouge out their eyes that night.

2a i) *Involvement*: The use of a first-person narrator draws us deeper into the story; we literally see events through his eyes. A relationship is therefore created between us and Jamal as we are able to understand how he feels and to observe the situation from his point of view. The effect is that we become personally involved in the story we are reading.
ii) *Tension*: This heightens the tension of the extract: we want Jamal to escape almost as much he does himself. With every obstacle (Salim's disagreement with the escape plan, or the boys' struggle to unscrew the fourth bolt in the window) we panic that Maman could catch them.

2b EXTRA Jamal speaks very correct and expressive English, which you wouldn't expect of a young boy from an Indian slum. He would also speak Hindi, e.g., but not English. This shows that the character is, strictly speaking, not really authentic. However, if he spoke as a 'slumdog' would speak – even if he could speak English – we would probably have difficulty understanding him and that would make the story difficult to follow.

3 It seems likely that in Delhi the two boys were in a desperate situation or in trouble with the police and were mistreated by them. The remark seems intended to suggest that the 'slumdogs' of India get little sympathy from the police.

4 The extract tells you that there's a very desperate side of India today with many people living in slums and on the streets. There's a very ruthless element in society: however low some people (like Maman) have sunk, they will look for someone else worse off (e.g. children like Jamal and Salim) to exploit.

Part C2 – Jamal's Story – the Film Script

SB S. 117   **C2 Jamal's Story – the Film Script**   Simon Beaufoy

Source:	*Slumdog Millionaire: The Shooting Script*, 2008
Topic:	Escape from a children's shelter
Text form:	Screenplay (extract)
Language variety:	Indian English / British English
Number of words:	204
Level:	Intermediate
Skills/Activities:	Comparing a novel and a screenplay; analysing style

Didaktischer Kommentar

Schwerpunkt ist der Vergleich der Drehbuchadaption eines Romanauszugs mit dem Romanauszug selbst. S untersuchen Inhalt, Form und Stil der Drehbuchadaption und wenden dabei verschiedene Elemente der Textanalyse an, um Handlungselemente herauszustellen und die Auszüge einander vergleichend gegenüberzustellen.

SB-DVD-ROM

Lernwortschatz

giggle (l. 23); rag (l. 26); fling sth. (l. 28); clutch sth. (l. 29); scramble (l. 32)
Fact File: subsidize

Unterrichtstipps

1 Für die Bearbeitung dieser Aufgabe empfiehlt sich ein gemeinsames intensives Lesen des Skripts mit S, wobei Fragen im Plenum geklärt werden.

2 S erhalten ausreichend Zeit, um sich in die Aufgaben hineinzudenken. Auf Grundlage einer Hausaufgabe kann im Plenum eine Mindmap (oder eine alternative Sicherung an der Tafel oder auf Folie) erfolgen, um die Beiträge entsprechend zu würdigen und in den Kontext zu setzen.

Lösungshinweise

PRE-READING *Content*: script focuses on the escape scene itself with little introduction; script introduces humour with Jamal's cheekiness
Layout: script focuses on dialogue: the characters' names and what they say are emphasised
Style: script not very descriptive. No vivid language, unlike the book extract; actions are described with simple sentences

1 *The relationship between the boys* is close in both the book and the script, but in the book it is Jamal who watches over Salim, while in the script Salim protects and saves Jamal.
The settings of the book extract and the script are completely different. In the book, Salim and Jamal converse in their room and escape from a bathroom. The scene in the script is set exclusively in a shack.
Action: In the book Jamal and Salim plan their escape, then we find them trying to prise open a window. In the film things happens much faster: Salim fetches Jamal, waits for his moment, throws the chloroform and they run.

2a *Tension created*: *In the novel*, tension is created through Jamal's explanation of Maman's plans to Salim. Tension also builds through Jamal's fear – 'A chill runs down my spine' – and through the toss of the coin. The tension of escape is created by the delay in loosening the fourth bolt before Maman arrives.
As there is no mention of Salim's feelings prior to the escape *in the script*, reading it doesn't inspire tension. Beaufoy relies on speed: the sign from Maman that Punnoose should blind Jamal and Salim's sudden action with the chloroform; everything moves very fast.

2b Beaufoy may have introduced a female character to create a love triangle (A likes B better than C). The story continues into Jamal's young adulthood and the friendship could develop into a love interest.

5 Part C3 – Jamal's Story – the Film

SB S. 118 DVD
Transkript s. TM-DVD-ROM

C3 Jamal's Story – the Film

Source:	*Slumdog Millionaire*, Celador Films and Channel 4, 2008
Topic:	Escape from a children's shelter
Text form:	Feature film (extract)
Language variety:	Indian English
Length:	5:34 min
Level:	Intermediate
Skills/Activities:	Viewing a film; making notes

Didaktischer Kommentar

Der Analyse eines Romanauszugs sowie der entsprechenden Drehbuchadaption wird nun eine weitere Komponente hinzugefügt: der Film selbst. S stellen den Film dem Buch sowie dem Drehbuch gegenüber und stellen Unterschiede heraus, wobei sie ihre Kenntnis filmanalytischer Fachbegriffe erproben und vertiefen.

Differenzierung

Je nachdem wie viel Zeit zur Verfügung steht und welche Vorkenntnisse S haben, kann der Film (in weiteren Auszügen oder in Gänze gesehen) Ansatzpunkte zur Reflexion von Literaturverfilmungen bieten. Vorab oder parallel werden Fachbegriffe der Filmanalyse eingeführt (s. *SF 20: Viewing a film*).

Obwohl *Slumdog Millionaire* kein Bollywood-Film ist, werfen interessierte oder leistungsstärkere S einen Blick über den Tellerrand (dieses indischen Films) und bereiten eine Kurzpräsentation vor: *Name typical features of a Bollywood movie and present them in class*. Lösungshinweise: s. Info.

1 In Vorbereitung auf die Filmanalyse in **C4** achten leistungsschwächere (oder alle) S bereits hier auf Kameraeinstellungen und Filmmusik.
1 Speculate what might have caused the director to use the chosen camera angle for the situations in which they occur.
2 Examine how the music reflects the relationship between the two main characters.

Info

Slumdog Millionaire (2008; director: Danny Boyle; screenplay: Simon Beaufoy) was a huge success, winning eight Oscars at the 2009 Academy Awards. It tells the story of a young Indian who miraculously wins the popular game show *Who Wants to Be a Millionaire?*. To convince a police inspector that he didn't cheat his way to the prize, he must explain how he knew all the correct answers by recounting certain parts of his life story.

Bollywood refers to the largest film industry in India. It produces mostly Hindi-language cinema and its name is derived from a combination of 'Hollywood' and 'Bombay' (the former name of Mumbai, the city where the Bollywood industry is based). Traditional romance and action films dominate in Bollywood, although recent growth in the worldwide popularity of Hindi cinema has lead to the introduction of more innovative story lines. Bollywood films are mostly musicals with sensational plots, memorable songs and choreographed dance sequences. They are also often highly expensive to make, with production typically costing over 100 crores (= ten million) rupees (15 million euros).

Lösungshinweise

1a Apart from minor differences between the dialogue in the film extract and the script, the director follows the script closely. The main differences are between the book (see **C2**, 'Lösungshinweise' **2a**) and both the script and the film.

1b The next scenes show the three children running through trees towards a train. Chased by Maman, Punnoose and the Villager, Salim reaches the moving train first and helps Jamal. Latika is behind them. Salim reaches out his hand and grabs hers, but, out of sight of Jamal, he deliberately lets go. Maman grabs her.

2a Individual answers.

Part C4 – For One Million Rupees …

2b *The scenes in the book* are slower and more intimate. *In the script* it is clear that the escape will be fast-paced. *The film's* combination of close-ups, dramatic lighting and camera angles emphasizes the sense of menace and makes the escape itself both frightening and fast. *A book* can develop more slowly; people's inner thoughts are best shown in written texts. *A film script* must explain what should be seen on screen. For dramatic purposes, film is the most effective of the three. A film can use images to explain, without words, what's inside a character's mind.

2c Individual answers.

2d Latika might hate Salim. If Jamal were to find out what really happened, it might alter his feelings for Salim – he might hate him for leaving Latika behind.

SB S.119 DVD
Transkript s. TM-DVD-ROM

C4 For One Million Rupees …

Source:	*Slumdog Millionaire*, 2008
Topic:	Jamal under interrogation
Text form:	Feature film (extract)
Language variety:	Indian English
Length:	5:46 min
Level:	Advanced
Skills/Activities:	Viewing a film; taking part in a discussion

Didaktischer Kommentar

S setzen sich mit einer weiteren Szene aus dem Film *Slumdog Millionaire* auseinander. Neben der inhaltlichen Analyse wenden sie ihr Wissen zur Filmanalyse im Hinblick auf filmische Mittel wie Erzählweise und Kameraeinstellung an.

Unterrichtstipps
⚠ HA ⬤ Word help

1 Vor dem Sehen des Spielfilmauszugs machen sich S mit unbekanntem Wortschatz vertraut.

ZA

Zur Wiederholung und als abwechslungsreicher Abschluss des Kapitels wird **KV 11** eingesetzt. Lösungshinweise:
Across: 1 Bollywood; 5 Partition; 6 Raj; 9 colony; 11 rupee; 14 reincarnation; 15 slums
Down: 2 overpopulation; 3 outsource; 4 Hinduism; 7 Untouchables; 8 subcontinent; 10 sectarian; 12 Gandhi; 13 caste

Differenzierung
HA ZA

S, die *Slumdog Millionaire* in Gänze gesehen haben, schreiben einen *film review* darüber; die übrigen legen einen anderen Film zugrunde, den sie kennen. Leistungsstarke arbeiten besondere sprachliche Merkmale von Filmrezensionen heraus, indem sie verschiedene Rezensionen in englischsprachigen (Online-)Zeitungen vergleichen.

> **Info**
>
> *Dhavari* in Mumbai is one of Asia's largest slums. It covers 1.75km and is home to more than a million people. Despite India's growing economy, more than half of Mumbai residents live in slums like Dhavari: in cramped housing with poor sanitation and no access to clean water. Many small workshops which produce pottery or garments can be found in the slums and contribute to India's informal economy (cf. **A2**).

Lösungshinweise

1a By chance Jamal came by a $100 dollar note. He gives it to Arvind to make up for the terrible thing that happened to him at the orphanage. This incident is not something Jamal is ever likely to forget. On the other hand, Jamal has probably seen very few 1000 rupee notes.

1b The whole exchange is ironic: When the gameshow host asks 'Jamal, get a lot of $100 bills in your line of work?' he is making fun of him: he knows that Jamal isn't well paid as a tea boy and makes a cheap joke at his expense. Jamal's answer is also ironic: 'A minimum tip for my services.' He is playing the host at his own game. But the host has the last word: 'Now I know why my cell-phone bills are so high. They tip the *chai wallah* with $100 bills.'
What they really mean: The exchange is actually about money, power, and having the last word.

2a *The wide shots (WSs)* set the scene at the beginning of the sequence. First the two WSs of the boys walking along the pipeline emphasize the length of their journey and how small they are in comparison to the world around them. The viewer appreciates that they are just two young children, alone in an unfriendly environment.
The close-up (CU) of Arvind's hand begins the scene in which he meets Jamal. CUs of his face force the viewer to see Arvind's blinded eyes; the cruelty of his situation becomes unavoidable and there is no choice but to react to it. When Jamal hands over the $100 bill, the film cuts to a WS and the action is seen from a distance, thereby accentuating once more smallness and vulnerability of the two young boys. At the same time the lighting and the strange angle of the WS add a sense of menace and make the viewer consider the people around them. One of those people might be Maman, who is a threat to Jamal.
Effect: The main effect of the WSs and CUs is discomforting: through an emphasis on realism, the audience is confronted with the everyday danger and cruelty in the boys' lives and should feel both shocked and sad.

2b *Intercutting*: The first part of the extract jumps between the TV show, the police station and a recording of the TV show. Boyle intercuts shots here in order to avoid an explanation of what happened in the show – you see the show and the interrogation together.
Flashback: The second part of the extract is a flashback introduced by Jamal saying 'Bombay had turned into Mumbai …'. We are transported back to Jamal's childhood and see him with Salim again. The sequence runs entirely in the past with no cuts to the present. Flashbacks allow film-makers to show the past rather than explain it in words, as we would have to do in real life.

2c In the first extract (**C3**) there is no music at the beginning which highlights Jamal's singing. Music starts when the escape begins. This first piece of music heightens the effect of the children running away and adds an element of fear. At the end, the music becomes soft and sad – Latika is lost.
In the second extract (**C4**) the music from the TV show heightens the tension as the audience wait for the contestant's answer. The music runs on in the police station because the recording of the show is still running. After the applause, the TV sound fades and music is next heard after the flashback in which Jamal explains why he knew the answer. Without the music you would just see two little boys walking along some pipes, but the music recalls their sad past and also Latika's fate.
The final piece of music is right at the end of the extract as Jamal runs off to find Latika. The images are even more urgent and scary because of the music.

2d *Camerawork*: In the first extract the camera shows Maman in low-angle shots, i.e. from the angle at which little Jamal sees him. This represents Maman's power over the slumdog Jamal. In the second extract, at the police station, the camera looks up at the policeman (low-angle shot) and shows how Jamal, the suspect, sees the powerful, established policeman towering over him. In the flashback sequence the camerawork mixes low-angle shots of the boys and the new buildings with very static shots of the demolition and rubbish, as if to say that poverty slows everything down.
Location: In the first extract we see the dirty, ruined hut in which Maman and Punnoose do their terrible work and the goods train, which people with no money board to travel long distances for free. In the second extract the two boys return to

Part C4 – For One Million Rupees …

Mumbai: we see slums, demolition work, construction, the market and the underpass. The dirt and rubbish everywhere show poverty.

Lighting: The first extract is in the dark, which creates a tense and frightening atmosphere. In the ruined hut there is no electric light. Salim uses the lamps to start the fire, implying the dangers of poor people's lives. At the beginning of the second extract, the two boys walk along the pipes at sunrise – the light is diffused and hazy. It looks almost romantic. But in normal daylight we see the slums, the dirt and the poverty speaks for itself.

The key scene takes place in the tunnel, which is dark with just a little natural light from the stairway. This creates a threatening mood of oppression and fear.

CONTEXT TASK Individual answers.

Kopiervorlage 11: India Crossword Puzzle

Across:
1. … is the informal term for Hindi-language cinema (and its film industry).
5. The 1947 … led to the formation of two states: Pakistan and India.
6. … is the Hindu word for 'reign' and refers to the British Empire in India.
9. India was a British … until 1947.
11. The Indian currency is called the …
14. … is one of the fundamental beliefs held by Hindus, which is based on the idea of an immortal soul.
15. Allegedly, over 40 % of the population in Mumbai live on the street or in …

Down:
2. … is a huge problem in India – there are too many people living in one area.
3. Many companies … jobs to India because labour is much cheaper there.
4. The main religion in India is …
7. The 'Dalits', members of the lower castes, used to be called … because members of higher castes believed their impurity could rub off on them.
8. Geographically speaking, India is a …
10. … violence between Hindus and Muslims led to uncountable deaths both in India and Pakistan.
12. … was a spiritual and political leader of the Indian Independence Movement.
13. The … system in India divides people into social classes.

6 The Media

S setzen sich mit Aspekten des Medienwandels und seines Einflusses auf die moderne Lebenswelt auseinander. Funktion, Formate, Gattungen und gesellschaftlicher Wirkungszusammenhang der zeitgenössischen Medienwelt kommen zur Darstellung.
Part A – Goodbye, Gutenberg? beschäftigt sich mit der zunehmenden Bedeutung des Internets zur Informationsverbreitung, den Auswirkungen auf die Zukunft der Printmedien und den Veränderungen für Nachrichtengestaltung und Nachrichtenrezeption.
Part B – Television reflektiert die Bedeutung dieses Mediums unter besonderer Berücksichtigung neuer populärer Formate und Gattungen, die Nähe zur Lebenswelt ihrer Zuschauer für sich beanspruchen.
Part C – Advertising beschreibt, analysiert und ermöglicht die Erprobung von Komponenten und Mechanismen der Produktwerbung und öffentlicher Anzeigenkampagnen.
Part D – Media Literacy warnt vor Gefahren im Umgang mit dem Internet und führt zu einer abschließenden Reflexion des eigenen Mediengebrauchs durch Auswertung eines *media log*.

Didaktisches Inhaltsverzeichnis

SB p.	Title	TM p.	Text Form	Topic	Skills and Activities	Language Practice
120	Lead-in	158	Photos; adverts; screenshots	The changing use and functions of the media	Working with pictures; cooperative learning strategy (think–pair–share); keeping a media log	LP 13/14: Talking about the present/past
122	Words in Context – Mass Media and Participatory Media	159	Informative text	The evolution and use of media	Organizing and using new vocabulary	Compound nouns; gerunds and nouns
	Part A – Goodbye, Gutenberg?					
124	A1 The Vanishing Newspaper Eric Alterman	160	Magazine article (extract)	The Internet replacing the newspaper	Reading non-fiction; summarizing; working with charts; comparing and assessing different media	LP 19: Using articles and quantifiers; connecting your thoughts: linking words
126	A2 Movable Type CD 3.01–02	162	Telephone interview (extract)	The new era of the active media user	Listening comprehension; summarizing; doing research; giving a presentation	LP 15: Talking about the future
	Part B – Television					
127	B1 New Genres DVD	163	Video clip (application video)	A talent show for future politicians	Defining terms; viewing skills; assessing a video clip; taking part in a discussion; making a video clip	LP 25: Expressing yourself concisely
128	B2 Making Reality – Faking Reality DVD	165	Feature film (extract)	Creating lifelike illusions	Viewing skills; analysing a film extract; writing an essay	LP 17: Talking about unreal situations
129	B3 The Television Tells Us The Music Tapes	166	Song	Our relationship to television	Working with cartoons; creative writing; analysing a song	LP 26: Connecting your thoughts: linking words
	Part C – Advertising					
130	C1 The Power of Images	167	Advertising posters	The effectiveness of advertising posters	Working with pictures; analysing and comparing posters; giving a presentation	
131	C2 Reaching the Audience DVD	168	Public information film; news report (extract)	The shock value in advertising: a valid means?	Analysing a TV advert; analysing a news report; taking part in a discussion; cooperative learning strategy (think–pair–share)	

6 Lead-in

	Part D – Media Literacy					
132	**D1 The Dangers of the Electronic Footprint** Hazel Parry	170	Feature story (extract)	Minding your electronic footprint	Writing a summary; analysing a text; doing a role-play; formulating general rules	
134	**D2 The Three Stages of Media Literacy** Elizabeth Thoman	171	Essay (extract)	Stages of media literacy	Summarizing an essay; defining technical terms; evaluating statistics; compiling results; evaluating a survey	
135	**Communicating across Cultures** CD 3.03	172	Cartoon; email	Using the appropriate register	Working with cartoon; analysing an email; writing an email; mediating	LP 22: Using the appropriate register

SB S. 120 ## Lead-in

Didaktischer Kommentar

S reflektieren Präsenz und Funktion der Medien in ihrem eigenen Umfeld. Sie vergleichen Bilder, die mediale Formen von früher und von heute zeigen, und ziehen daraus geeignete Schlüsse im Hinblick auf Veränderungen in der Medienwelt. Sie erstellen ein *media log*, mit dem sie ihr eigenes Medienverhalten erfassen.

SB-DVD-ROM

Lernwortschatz

associate sth. with sth. (task 1b)

Unterrichtstipps

Die zehn Bilder stellen den Einstieg dar und sollten für S ohne weiteres identifizierbar sein. Evtl. muss bei Abbildung G eine Vokabelhilfe *(friendship book)* gegeben werden.

1ab werden in einem Unterrichtsgespräch behandelt.
Für **2b** müssen so viele Blankofolien und Folienstifte zur Verfügung stehen, wie Gruppen gebildet werden.
Für Aufgabe **3** müssen **KV 12** und **13** in ausreichender Stückzahl vorliegen.

Info

Speakers' Corner: Every Sunday since the right of free assembly was recognised in 1872 in the Parks Regulation Act, people from all walks of life have gathered in London's Hyde Park to listen to those who have an opinion and who carry on an oral tradition that is becoming lost to a modern culture of email and online chat rooms. Speakers' Corner is a classless forum; anyone can participate and discuss the more provocative subjects of politics, religion, morality and current events.

OMG! My chunky just got funky is a British slogan to promote a new KitKat chocolate bar with caramel. 'OMG' is a text message abbreviation for 'Oh, my God', funky (infml) in this case stands for 'unusual'.

Lösungshinweise

1a The pictures all represent examples of media and/or media use: A: watching television (c. 1970); B: reading the newspaper (1950); C: a British billboard advertising chocolate (2009); D: a speaker in London's Hyde Park Speakers' Corner (2008); E: a profile on a social networking site; F: a British chocolate advert (1905); G: a blog; H: playing video games (2005); I: a friendship book entry; J: reading online news from a smartphone.
The most likely pairs: A and H (watching TV / playing video games); B and J (news); C and F (advertising); D and G (forms of self-expression); E and I (means of organizing and maintaining social contacts)

1b Individual answers. S will probably associate watching TV together (A) and the newspaper (B) with a different time. The friendship book (I) will be seen as being part of the lifestyle of younger pupils.

Words in Context 6

1c *Changing media and media use:* A/H: The movement is away from television as a communal experience and towards the individualized world of video games. B/J: The newspaper has been transformed from an independent medium to a part of the Internet. News is often read online now and even from smartphones. C/F: While the billboard and the advertisement obviously belong to different eras, it is interesting to observe how little the techniques of advertising posters have changed. D/G: It used to be necessary to speak in public to communicate one's convictions to a larger audience (and some people still do so for old time's sake). Nowadays a much wider audience can be reached by writing a blog.

1d Individual answers.

2a

communication	entertainment	information	self-expression
blog, email, letter, mobile phone, social networking site, Twitter	book, DVD, magazine, mobile phone, radio, social networking site, television	book, DVD, email, letter, magazine, mobile phone, newspaper, radio, television, social networking site, Twitter	blog, book, email, letter, social networking site, Twitter

2b Individual answers.

3ab Individual answers. For the media log and the media log evaluation sheet, cf. **KV 12** and **13**.

SB S. 122
▶ LSET ex. 1

Words in Context – Mass Media and Participatory Media

Didaktischer Kommentar

Der Text weist S hin auf die Entstehungsbedingungen der Massenmedien, die Rolle der Werbung, die tief greifenden Veränderungen der Medienlandschaft vor allem durch die Digitalisierung und die Konsequenzen für das Medienverhalten des Einzelnen, die sich aus den genannten Punkten ergeben. Linguistische Erscheinungen, die in den genannten Zusammenhängen verstärkt vorkommen, werden geübt.

SB-DVD-ROM

Lernwortschatz

channel of communication (l. 2), mass media (l. 3), print media (l. 8), electronic media (l. 11), publishing house (l. 16), broadcasting corporation (l. 17), broadcasting network (l. 17), advertising revenue (l. 19), periodical (l. 20), broadcasting time (l. 20), commercial (l. 21), sponsor (l. 22), target group (l. 25), mainstream (l. 28), digital revolution (l. 29), media content (l. 30), information sharing (l. 32), dissemination (l. 32), broadband Internet access (l. 33), blogging (l. 33), tweeting (l. 33), file sharing (l. 33), social networking (l. 33), smartphone (l. 35), user-generated content (l. 35), participatory media (l. 37), empowerment (l. 41), invasion of privacy (l. 42), identity theft (l. 43), copyright infringement (l. 43), Web 2.0 (l. 44), media hype (l. 46), media literacy (l. 47)

Unterrichtstipps
HA

Angesichts der Informationsdichte des Textes und der Vielzahl der neuen Begriffe sollte der Text als Hausaufgabe vorbereitet werden.

Differenzierung

In schwächeren Lerngruppen wird der Wortschatz stärker umgewälzt, z. B. indem Begriffe aus dem Text einem von mehreren Oberbegriffen (z. B. *print media, electronic media, advertising, new forms of communication, risks and dangers*) zugeordnet werden. Die Oberbegriffe können von S selbst gebildet oder von L vorgegeben werden.

6 Part A

Lösungshinweise

1 1 periodicals; 2 commercial; 3 sponsors; 4 mainstream; 5 user-generated; 6 copyright infringement

2a broadcasting time; identity theft; file sharing; advertising revenue; social networking; publishing house

2b mass/print/electronic media; broadcasting corporation; mainstream channel; information sharing; Internet access; media guru/hype/literacy, …

2c Individual answers.

3a 1 come into existence; 2 at low cost; 3 exert influence on sth./sb.; 4 all manner of content/content of any sort; 5 at will; 6 it remains to be seen

3b Individual answers.

4a The gerund 'broadcasting' means the act of transmitting a radio or television programme; the noun 'broadcast' refers to a single programme on the radio or TV.

4b Individual answers.

SB S. 124

Part A – Goodbye, Gutenberg?

▶ LSET ex. 4, 5

A1 The Vanishing Newspaper Eric Alterman

Source:	*The New Yorker*, 31 March 2008
Topic:	The Internet replacing the newspaper
Text form:	Magazine article (extract)
Language variety:	American English
Number of words:	522
Level:	Advanced
Skills/Activities:	Reading non-fiction; summarizing; working with charts; comparing and assessing different media

Didaktischer Kommentar

Am Beispiel des durch das Internet in Not geratenen Zeitungsmarktes werden die ökonomischen Folgen des Medienwandels exemplarisch aufgezeigt. Gleichzeitig wird deutlich, wie medialer Wandel die Aufbereitung, Verbreitung und Aufnahme von Nachrichten verändert.

SB-DVD-ROM

Lernwortschatz

sense of mission (l. 3), license (*n*, AE) / licence (*n*, BE) (l. 7), circulation (l. 10), vanish (l. 12), coincide with sth. (l. 14), artifact (AE) / artefact (BE) (l. 17), abandon (l. 22), rely on sth. (l. 25), end up (l. 26), stock valuation (l. 28), rapid (l. 29), on demand (l. 36)

Unterrichtstipps

3 PRE-READING Der Vergleich von Online- und Printausgaben von Zeitungen kann als Gruppenarbeit organisiert werden, wobei sich die einzelnen Gruppen mit Zeitungen unterschiedlicher Art befassen, z. B. lokal/regional/überregional, Boulevardzeitung/Qualitätszeitung. Falls vorhanden und möglich, können einzelne Gruppen ihre vergleichenden Untersuchungen auch auf verschiedene Fassungen internationaler Zeitungen ausweiten.

Differenzierung

3 Lernschwächere S bereiten das Thema „*(online) newspapers*" anhand des *Topic Vocabulary* (s. S. 178) vor.

ALT

3 Für Lernstärkere bietet es sich an, statt einer deutschsprachigen die Printausgabe einer englischsprachigen Tageszeitung zu erwerben und diese mit der Onlineversion zu vergleichen.

Part A1 – The Vanishing Newspaper

> **Info**
>
> *Newspaper formats: A tabloid* is a newspaper with pages half the size of regular papers. The term refers to newspapers that offer less serious news, short articles and many pictures. *A broadsheet*, by contrast, is printed on large paper and refers to quality newspapers. *A Berliner* is between a broadsheet and a tabloid in size. British newspapers in this format include *The Guardian*; a German example is *die tageszeitung* (taz).
>
> *Yellow journalism/press* refers to newspaper reports that exaggerate the facts to attract and shock readers. The term comes from a cartoon *The Yellow Kid* that was printed in yellow ink.
>
> *Rupert Murdoch* ['mɜːdɒk ☆ -dɑːk] (born 1931) is a leading global media executive who owns or controls a wide range of media outlets from *The Wall Street Journal* to MySpace. His empire covers television, filmed entertainment, cable network programming, book publishing, direct broadcast satellite television, magazines and newspapers in the USA, Australia, Continental Europe, the UK, Asia and the Pacific Basin. His rise has been controversial not least because of his ruthless management style. It is important to place Murdoch's quotes in the article in this context and recognize the irony in these statements: far from being a supporter of less control over news and information and the rising influence of social media, Murdoch continues to broaden his influence over the media, thus practically embodying the controlling 'godlike figure' he appears to speak disparagingly of.

Lösungshinweise

PRE-READING A wide definition of 'information' including sports, (pop) culture, local, regional, national, and international news should be allowed. *Popularity of some sources over others:* Those that are cheaper and more easily accessible (e. g. online versions) will probably be and continue to become more popular.

1a Online editions of newspapers will have replaced print editions by the middle of the 21st century.

1b *Symptoms of decline and contributing factors*: loss of advertising revenue; loss of (especially young) readers; decay of journalistic professional ethos (sense of mission); competition from the Internet; changing public expectations of the news

2a Murdoch describes newspaper publishers and editors as authoritative figures who strictly command what is or is not published. He describes the situation in religious terms: the editors and publishers are divine beings; the consumers a community of believers and the spreading of news is like spreading a religious truth.

2b The traditional consumer was passive. He received news as and when it was offered to him. The modern consumer, on the other hand, demands access to the latest news at all times, in addition to background information and the opportunity to participate.

2c Digital technology accelerates the process of spreading news. Online versions of newspapers allow for continuous updates: editions are updated several times a day and contain news tickers (a line of text with news which passes across the screen of a computer or television). Background information on a news item can be provided through links to related articles or other websites. Readers can participate via email or blog links.

3 Individual answers based on the selected paper, its print edition and online version (not to be confused with the E-Paper edition [the electronic version of the print edition]). Some less obvious answers:

Pros online version: personal news update systems can be subscribed to (RSS feeds); links to social networking sites (e. g. Facebook); web portals for regional news; spontaneous contributions to forums possible; access to older articles and archive; cheap (or free)

Part A2 – Movable Type

Cons online version: more information than needed by the general reader; immediate reactions are often emotional, sometimes more self-expression than argument; free access leads to greater significance of advertising revenue; speed of online versions may lead to a decline of journalistic virtues, e.g. superficial research; looking at a screen is a tiring and more complicated way of reading; hardware required

Pros print edition: the information published can be digested by the reader; traditional and familiar sections navigate the reader through the paper easily

4 Between 1993 and 2008 the percentage of people who read a print edition of a newspaper daily decreased from 58 to 34 per cent. Between 1996 and 2008, the percentage of people who read news online, three or more days a week, increased from 2 to 37 per cent. The steady decrease of print-reading is directly related to the increase in the reading of online editions, as obviously many who formerly read printed newspapers now turn to the online versions.

The number of people who neither read nor saw the news 'yesterday' rose from 14 per cent in 1998 to 19 per cent in 2008. This general trend can be observed within each age group with the exception of the 50- to 64-year-olds, where the percentage remained stable. The most significant change can be seen with the 65+ age group, where the percentage of those who neither read nor saw the news 'yesterday' more than doubled.

SB S.126
CD 3.01–02
Transkript s. TM-DVD-ROM

A2 Movable Type

Source:	'New Media', *Economist.com*, 20 April 2006
Topic:	The new era of the active media user
Text form:	Telephone interview
Language variety:	British English; American English
Length:	*Part 1* 3:29 min; *part 2* 4:01 min
Level:	Advanced
Skills/Activities:	Listening skills; writing a summary; doing research; giving a presentation

Didaktischer Kommentar

S entnehmen dem Telefoninterview Informationen zum Strukturwandel der Medienlandschaft durch die aktive Mitgestaltung und den Austausch medial vermittelter Inhalte seitens der Nutzer und zur damit verbundenen Neuausrichtung der Aufgaben von Mediendienstleistern. Sie erörtern die Auswirkungen der Digitalisierung (Musikindustrie, E-Book) und persönlicher Beteiligungsmöglichkeiten (soziale Netzwerke) im Medienbereich.

Unterrichtstipps

Vor dem ersten Hören machen sich S mit unbekanntem Wortschatz vertraut.

⚠ HA ● Word help

1a Zur Bearbeitung der Aufgabe hören S das vollständige Interview.

3 Die Präsentation der Gruppenrecherche erfolgt in Form einer Kontroverse. So stellen z.B. ein bis zwei S die Vorzüge des E-Book dar und zeigen Gründe auf, warum es sich durchsetzen werde. Ein bis zwei S argumentieren für das gedruckte Wort.

ALT Bei Fünfergruppen lässt sich die Präsentation als Debatte organisieren (s. SF 25: Debating).

Differenzierung

1/2 Lernschwächere S nehmen beim Hören die *word help* von der SB-DVD-ROM zu Hilfe. Lernstärkere bearbeiten beide Aufgaben nach einmaligem Hören des vollständigen Interviews. Sie erklären, warum die Wahl für den Namen eines *Weblog Publishing System* auf „Movable Type" fiel (s.a. Info).

Part B

ZA Interessierte S vergleichen die Folgen der Erfindung des Buchdrucks mit beweglichen Lettern mit der Entwicklung des Internets und des *World Wide Web* oder porträtieren Johannes Gutenberg, Bill Gates, Jerry Yang (Yahoo), Sergey Brin und Larry Page (Google) oder andere Pioniere der Mediengeschichte.

> **Info**
>
> *Movable Type* is a free blog publishing system popular with celebrity bloggers. It was developed by Mena and Ben Trott in San Francisco in 2001 and named 'Movable Type' for being as revolutionary as Gutenberg's invention 550 years earlier.

Lösungshinweise

PRE-READING Mass media (radio, television, newspapers and magazines) do not allow interactivity and presuppose a passive consumer.

1a S listen to the complete interview before filling in the table.

	mass media age	age of participatory media
role of audience	– passive consumers – one-way communication	– active creators – two-way communication
role of media companies	– produce content – own/manage copyright	– media exchange – no direct influence on content

1b The traditional era can be characterized as a system of one-way communication with inactive readers, listeners, viewers. The dawning age of participatory media creates and demands interactive communication. Modern media users will receive, create and exchange media content with other members of the audience. The difference between creators and consumers will gradually disappear.

2 C

3 Individual answers. The webcode offers links to background information on the topics for class presentations.

Part B – Television

SB S. 127
DVD
Transkript s. TM-DVD-ROM

B1 New Genres

Source:	*Canada's Next Great Prime Minister*, CBC, 2009
Topic:	A talent show for future politicians
Text form:	Video clips
Language variety:	Canadian English
Length:	*Clip* 1 0:40 min; *clip* 2 0:40 min; *clip* 3 0:40 min
Level:	Intermediate
Skills/Activities:	Viewing skills; summarizing; taking part in a discussion; producing a video clip

Didaktischer Kommentar

S knüpfen bei ihrer Beschäftigung mit dem Medium Fernsehen und seinem Verhältnis zur Lebenswelt des Publikums an ihre Erfahrungen als Zuschauer an und erarbeiten Gattungsdefinitionen zu verschiedenen Formaten. Die Bewerbungsclips sind Teil einer politischen Variante der Castingshow.

SB-DVD-ROM

> **Lernwortschatz**
>
> decision-making process (task 3b)

Unterrichtstipps
Word help

Vor dem ersten Sehen der Videoclips machen sich S mit unbekanntem Wortschatz vertraut.

Part B1 – New Genres

ALT **4 EXTRA** S präsentieren sich einer Teilgruppe oder dem gesamten Kurs direkt, ohne sich vorher aufzunehmen. Das Zeitlimit gilt natürlich trotzdem.

Differenzierung ZA Politisch interessierte S erörtern die Frage, ob Formate wie *Canada's Next Great Prime Minister* oder seine deutsche Variante *Ich kann Kanzler* ein Mittel gegen die Politikverdrossenheit Jugendlicher sein können.

> **Info**
>
> *Canada's Next Great Prime Minister* (debut 2006) is a talent show produced by the Canadian Broadcasting Corporation (CBC) and sponsored by Magna, a supplier of vehicle components. Four Canadians between 18 and 25 apply and are judged by four Canadian politicians. The show format was sold to the BBC in 2008 (the show will be called *The Next Great Leader*) and to the ZDF in 2009, who called it Ich kann Kanzler. In the 2009 show, Amy Robichaud was the winner.
> **Linktipp:** http://pdf.zeit.de/2009/17/ZDF-Kanzler.pdf Patrik Schwarz, 'Die Kanzlerkandidaten', *Zeit Online*, 16 April 2009, reports on the German show and notes the differences to the Canadian original.
>
> *Docusoap:* A subgenre of reality TV which is highly edited and therefore similar to soap operas (which is where the name docusoap comes from). In contrast to the daily soap, the majority do not use professional actors (examples include *I'm a Celebrity – Get Me out of Here!* and *Die Kochprofis*).
>
> *Reality TV:* Originally referring to shows featuring 'real' people (i.e. not actors) in real situations (police, fire-fighters, paramedics, doctors), it is now a generic term for a great variety of formats from talent shows and quiz shows (*Who Wants to Be a Millionaire?*) to voyeuristic programmes such as *Big Brother*.
>
> *Talent show:* A subgenre of reality TV in which contestants perform in their art. A jury publicly evaluates their performance. Jury decisions are complemented or replaced by the results of the public vote by phone or text message in the final rounds of the competition. Winners may receive a contract with a media firm or another valuable prize.

Lösungshinweise

1 Talent show: *Deutschland sucht den Superstar* (2002), *Germany's Next Top Model* (2006); docusoap: *Frauentausch* (2003), *Teenager außer Kontrolle* (2007); reality TV: *Das perfekte (Promi-)Dinner* (2006), *Die Super Nanny* (2004)

2a *Common features:* focus on ordinary people; no fixed script, improvised, claim to be close to reality; reveal intimate facts, voyeuristic appeal; serialized, impression of continuity; aim at viewers' identification with 'protagonists'; claim to be informational, educational, yet entertainment prevails; allow for advertising revenue (product placement); tend to be broadcast more by private TV stations than by public ones
Differences; talent show: defined aim and rules; participants compete in a particular field (singing, dancing); staged in a number of rounds; jury and audience choose the winner. *Docusoap:* observation of everyday life; extraordinary situations; concentration on few characters or a special (e.g. professional) group to allow for identification; great variety; winners usually awarded with a contract. *Reality TV:* generic term, cf. Info.

2bc Individual answers; cf. Info.

3a *Criteria for judging the quality of the presentation:* visual effectiveness (choice of setting/shots/cuts); authenticity; potential for identification; eloquence; a message beyond the self-presentation; convincing and original final statement

3bc–4 Individual answers.

Part B2 – Making Reality – Faking Reality

SB S. 128
DVD
Transkript s. TM-DVD-ROM

B2 Making Reality – Faking Reality

Source:	*The Truman Show*, USA 1998
Topic:	Creating lifelike illusions
Text form:	Feature film (extract)
Language variety:	American English
Length:	5:45 min
Level:	Intermediate
Skills/Activities:	Viewing and listening skills; analysing a film extract; writing an essay

Didaktischer Kommentar

S analysieren die zentrale Szene des medienkritischen Spielfilms *The Truman Show*, die darstellt, wie das Reality-TV die Realität, die es angeblich widerspiegelt, künstlich erzeugt, um den Protagonisten und die Zuschauer zu manipulieren. S schulen ihre Hör-/Seh-Kompetenz und setzen sie zur Medienkritik ein.

SB-DVD-ROM

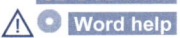

Lernwortschatz

fake sth. (title); nagging doubt (introductory text), dispel sth. (introductory text)

Unterrichtstipps
SB-DVD-ROM
Word help

Vor dem ersten Sehen machen sich S mit unbekanntem Wortschatz vertraut.

Es empfiehlt sich, den ganzen Film im Unterricht zu behandeln. Dabei ist es denkbar, mit der Analyse der hierzu ausgewählten Szene einzusteigen. S gewinnen so eine distanziertere Haltung zum Filmgeschehen.

Differenzierung
ZA

Medienaffine S vergleichen unter fächerübergreifenden Aspekten die „desillusionierenden" Techniken in *The Truman Show* mit Verfremdungseffekten des modernen Theaters und formulieren die ethischen Fragen, die der *Truman Show* und anderen Sendungen des Reality-TV gestellt werden müssen.

Lösungshinweise

1ab

Scene	Who?	What?	Where?
A: on the set (acting)	Truman, Marlon	Marlon tries to persuade Truman to accept his fate; Truman is reunited with his father.	bridge
B: behind the scenes (directing)	Christof, studio staff	Christof directs the scene, later accepts congratulations of staff.	studio
C: in front of the TV (viewing)	audience at home and in café	watches reunion scene, is very emotional	private homes, café

2a The cross-cutting between Marlon and Truman on the bridge and the studio has an alienating effect: Christof is shown as the creator of the supposedly spontaneous action. Marlon's words ('And the last thing I'd ever do is lie to you') are immediately revealed as a lie. The emotional, repetitive music (which normally has the effect of captivating the viewer) thus contributes to the alienating effect as it is regularly interrupted by studio scenes. The extract concludes with alternating shots (cross-cutting) showing the relief and professional pride of Christof and his team and the emotional response of the viewers in various locales: another strong contrast intended to distance the viewer from the emotions depicted.

2b *Camerawork:* Close-ups of Marlon and Truman precede the reunion of Truman and his father. A medium long shot and an over-the-shoulder shot delay the expected embrace of father and son. Using the crane camera, Christof employs a long high-angle shot to show both men's gradual approach to each other. Thus, he

6 Part B3 – The Television Tells Us

increases the suspense of the moment. When Christof makes his team use the button camera, the viewer sees Truman's face from a low angle through the round lens of the camera. Then he has the kerb camera employed for a long shot from a side position, rejecting his assistant's suggestion to zoom in. He wants a further retarding moment to increase the tension. The embrace is not shown directly: it is on the central screen of the studio and the picture is not quite clear. Christof's hand appears briefly on the screen. All this has a distancing effect on the viewer who is made to concentrate more on the *how* than on the *what*.

Music: Christof resembles a conductor of an orchestra when he makes the piano fade in, and the musical background contributes strongly to the success of the scene.

Effect: While the TV audience thinks it is witnessing real-life drama, the viewer of the film is forced to recognize that the emotional impact of the scene is based on calculation and cynical manipulation of Truman and the audience.

2c EXTRA Individual answers.

2d *Message:* Reality TV has nothing to do with reality but creates illusions in a sophisticated way. It exploits the actors, the non-professional participants and the audience. The driving force is economic interest.

SB S. 129
▶ LSET ex. 6, 7

B3 The Television Tells Us The Music Tapes

Source:	'The Television Tells Us', 1998
Topic:	Our relationship to television
Text form:	Song
Language variety:	American English
Number of words:	183
Level:	Basic
Skills/Activities:	Working with cartoons; creative writing; analysing lyrics

Didaktischer Kommentar S wenden das bisher über das Fernsehen und Reality TV Gelernte bei der kreativen Erschließung und Weiterverarbeitung sowie bei der Analyse eines Liedtextes an.

SB-DVD-ROM

> **Lernwortschatz**
>
> substitute for sth. (pre–reading)

Unterrichtstipps **1/3** Sowohl die produktionsorientierte Sicherung des Leseverständnisses als auch die kreative Schreibaufgabe können als Schreibgespräch (s. S. 299) gestaltet werden.

Differenzierung **1** Das Verständnis des Inhalts kann in einer Zusammenfassung gesichert werden.

ALT **3** Die Antwort erfolgt in Prosa statt in Liedform.

Lösungshinweise PRE-READING All the captions go well with the cartoon and can be justified:
1 Television shows us who we really are because it tries to show us 'real people like you and me'. This is especially true of reality TV.
2 Watching television is a substitute for reality because people prefer to sit in front of the TV to see what is happening instead of going out and doing something themselves.
3 Television gives the audience what it deserves, as programming lowers its standards to meet the viewers' demands.

1 Individual answers.

2a Televisions describe themselves as observers incapable of living themselves (l. 12). On the one hand they are conquerors (l. 3), on the other hand they depend on human beings to live their 'real life' (ll. 11, 22) and thereby feed them with information (l. 21). Only humans can stop television from further expansion (ll. 2, 4).

Their attitude is one of 'envy' (ll. 10, 30) and possibly exasperation at human beings' lethargy who spend their time watching TV and neglect their own lives (ll. 24–27). Thus, a vicious circle is created: according to the song, TV, designed to receive and broadcast information about human life, creates an audience that becomes inactive and does not provide TV with interesting material.

2b Repetition reinforces the message that the life-endangering symbiosis of television and humans has to be stopped (ll. 2, 4). People are urged to reflect on the nature of television (ll. 14, 29) to find out what the medium could contribute to human life and what effect it actually has. The original mission of television is to observe 'the real life that you live' (l. 11). This line is repeated and modified in l. 22. The progressive form 'are living' indicates that any form of life they find is temporary and can change. The immediate repetition of 'you are living' in l. 23 may be interpreted as a kind of wake-up call for the viewer to start living again or as a cynical comment on the degenerate form of human life televisions are witnessing. The repetition of the phrases 'just to sit' (l. 25) and 'just watch/Watch' (ll. 26–27) expresses lament and accuses human beings of wasting their lives.

2c The song contains sophisticated media and media consumers' criticism in a nutshell. An animated television talks to human beings, appealing to them to change their lives. A role reversal has taken place: in a variant of the Frankenstein motif, the gadget has taken over and criticizes its user. This surreal situation allows a distanced view of the TV audience and their relationship to the medium and reality. A gadget made to spread information on human life becomes an integral part of life and thus reduces the scope of real-life experience. With programmes tailored to the taste of a mass audience, programmers and viewers prevent people from fully living, enjoying or mastering their lives. The moral of this parable is that the viewer should start living again, reduce the TV to a normal gadget, to 'life size', which would enable the medium to observe real human life rather than the infinite repetition of illusions ('dream of life', l. 27)

3 Individual answers.

Part C – Advertising

SB S. 130

C1 The Power of Images

Didaktischer Kommentar

S vergleichen die McDonald's- (A) mit der Lavazza-Kaffeewerbung (B), indem sie den Aufbau analysieren und die Zielgruppe ermitteln. Abschließend erarbeiten S einen Kriterienkatalog zur Beurteilung der Wirksamkeit von Plakatwerbung.

SB-DVD-ROM

> **Lernwortschatz**
>
> create a desire (introductory text), plant sth. firmly in sb.'s mind (introductory text), consumption (task 2a/1), recommend (task 2c)

Unterrichtstipps ZA

2/3 L stellt weitere Werbeposter (für Kaffee oder andere Produkte) zur Verfügung. 2 könnte somit in arbeitsteiliger Gruppenarbeit erfolgen und die Aufstellung des Kriterienkataloges zur Wirksamkeit eines Plakats (3) wäre auf eine breitere Basis gestellt.

Differenzierung

3 Schwächeren S strukturiert L den Kriterienkatalog mit Teilüberschriften und Formulierungshilfen im Ansatz vor:
Language: a suggestive/simple/plain/witty slogan; the use of superlatives; the use of foreign words creates an impression of elegance; technical terms underline that the product is the result of scientific research, words with positive connotations/associations
Image: visual elements; design, layout; colour symbolism, warm/cool colours; perspective

6   Part C2 – Reaching the Audience

Overall effect: relation between picture and text (reinforce each other); humorous contrast between picture and slogan; strong appeal to the consumer desires; promise of social prestige; suggestive power; present an idealized world; provoke an emotional response.

Lösungshinweise

1 Individual answers.

2a **1** *Advert 1* emphasizes the stimulating and revitalizing effect of caffeine; *advert 2* evokes an image of coffee as a special, luxurious, romantic drink.
2 *Advert 1* is aimed at (blue-collar) workers. The run-down plastic-toy figure (a mechanic in a car repair shop) rests its head on its chest. A paper cup of coffee is recommended as a remedy. *Advert 2* is aimed at affluent, cosmopolitan people. A young couple – elegantly dressed – embrace passionately on a bridge in Rome in the early evening hours. Both are holding espresso cups.

2b Individual answers.

2c *Arguments for advertisement 1:* coffee reaffirmed as an everyday drink for ordinary, hard-working people; identification with the worker; coffee as a *folk drink*
Arguments for advertisement 2: win over affluent clientele; coffee as an integral part not only of everyday life but also of special occasions; appeals to everyone's secret dreams; suggests that coffee can connect you with an elegant lifestyle

3 *Criteria to evaluate advertisements, language:* informative or emotive? supportive of the message?
Picture: composition (balance of space and images); setting appropriate to product and target group(s)?; support through light and colours?; facial expressions and poses adequately chosen?
Overall effect: message: straightforward or food for thought?; mood?; presentation: clear and favourable?; target group: clear or more than one?; does it create a desire for the product?

SB S. 131
DVD
Transkript s. TM-DVD-ROM
▶ LSET ex. 8

C2 Reaching the Audience

Source:	'Separation', Quit Victoria, 5–25 July 2008
Topic:	Effect and effectiveness of a TV advert
Text form:	Public information film (TV)
Language variety:	Australian English
Length:	1:00 min
Level:	Basic

Source:	ABC News, 2 April 2009
Topic:	The shock value in advertising: a valid means?
Text form:	News report (TV)
Language variety:	American English
Length:	2:28 min
Level:	Advanced

Skills/Activities:	Viewing skills; writing the end of a TV advert; analysing a news report; taking part in a discussion

Didaktischer Kommentar

S analysieren einen kontroversen Werbespot sowie einen Nachrichtenbeitrag zu dessen Wirkung. Sie überprüfen kritisch die Objektivität der Nachrichtensendung und erweitern dadurch ihre medienkritischen Kompetenzen sowie ihr Fachvokabular.

SB-DVD-ROM

Lernwortschatz

Fact File: concern (l. 3), striking (l. 5)

Part C2 – Reaching the Audience 6

Unterrichtstipps

1 Da S mit unterschiedlichen Suchtpräventions- und Aufklärungsmaßnahmen in der Schule in Berührung kommen, ist es naheliegend, unmittelbar nach der Analyse des Werbespots Nutzen und Gefahren von Schockkampagnen zu diskutieren.

⚠ HA ● Word help

3 Vor dem ersten Sehen des Berichts machen sich S mit unbekanntem Wortschatz vertraut.

4a **KV 14** steht S auf der SB-DVD-ROM zur Verfügung.

> **Info**
>
> *Public information films* (PIFs) (on health, safety and welfare topics) are produced and distributed by the UK government's Central Office of Information (COI). COI distributes these films to all broadcast TV stations. PIFs are also shown on screens in supermarkets, universities, GP surgeries, football stadiums, pubs, trains, buses and motorway service stations. The German equivalent of PIFs are non-commercial public campaigns, including e.g. the campaign accompanying the football world championship's motto in 2006: Zu Gast bei Freunden.
> ☼ **Linktipp:** *www.nationalarchives.gov.uk/films/aboutfilms.htm* The COI features a selection of some of the most memorable and influential PIFs.

Differenzierung

2c Schwächere S erhalten zusätzliche Redemittel, um die beabsichtigte und die tatsächliche Wirkung eines Werbeclips zu beschreiben und einzuschätzen:
gripping, disturbing, alarming, provocative, manipulative, play with people's emotions, thought-provoking, change people's awareness/habits/behaviour, counterproductive

ZA

4 Interessierte S produzieren eine Reportage aus dem Schulleben und erproben die möglichen Techniken eines Nachrichtenbeitrags.

Lösungshinweise

1a Individual answers.

1b Individual answers. The actual message is 'If this is how your child feels after losing you for a minute, just imagine if they lost you for life.'

2a The large, busy, crowded train station with its bustle and the many strangers is frightening for a four-year-old.

2b Individual answers.

2c The advertisement addresses parents who smoke and has the intention of shocking them. Focusing on the child's growing fear and panic it strongly appeals to parents' sense of responsibility. They are urged to consider the consequences of smoking for their children. But does the end justify the means? Does the ad go too far by exploiting the young boy who was in real fear of losing his mother? This may provide smokers with an excuse for ignoring the ad's message. Furthermore, really addicted people may be immune to provocation. On the other hand, the clip gives serious food for thought.

3a EXTRA *Facts:* decisive bill passed by the House of Representatives authorizing the federal government to impose regulations on tobacco, reducing nicotine in cigarettes, controlling or forbidding cigarette ads, demanding bigger warnings on packets of cigarettes; Australian anti-smoking clip aired in New York aroused controversy; it is one of a number of 'shock ads' against smoking aired in New York
Opinions (in favour of the advert), Dr Frieden, New York Health Commissioner: Advert drives the message home that smokers harm their children and families; the city *(New York)* emphasizes that a child actor was employed for the film; *Prof. Stanton Glantz, University of California, San Francisco:* clear, undisguised messages make smokers give up their dangerous habit; *John McKenzie, ABC News:* global effect

Opinions (against the advert), bloggers: ruthless and inconsiderate; borders upon child abuse; highly manipulative; *Bob Garfield, Ad Age:* tears at viewer's heart, children freak out

4ab *Not used:* computer graphics (S may mention images from the video clips, though; cf. under 'inserted video clips'), animation, man-on-the-street interview
Used: anchorperson (live): moderator, reads out the news, links a news item with a report; *inserted titles:* underscore the key statements, make it easier to follow the report and identify the interviewees; *on-the-scene reporter:* provides authenticity, makes the responsible reporter visible to the audience; *voice-over:* economical means of providing the necessary information and of linking, explaining and commenting on the pictures; *sound bite:* brings in various aspects and opinions from experts; *inserted video clips:* give examples (of other 'shock ads'), intensify the message (of the original ad); *inserted web pages:* make it easier to understand and memorize specific contents, here: demonstrate the response the ad has provoked

4c The underlying function of this news report is to inform the viewers about anti-smoking measures. Although admitting arguments on both sides, the report seems to be biased as arguments in favour of the ad predominate, it inserts the shocking moments of three other New York ads, and the reporter mentions the impact of the message worldwide.

Part D – Media Literacy

SB S. 132
▶ LSET ex. 9

D1 The Dangers of the Electronic Footprint Hazel Parry

Source:	*South China Morning Star,* 12 January 2008
Topic:	Minding your electronic footprint
Text form:	Feature story
Language variety:	British English
Number of words:	366
Level:	Intermediate
Skills/Activities:	Summarizing; analysing a text; doing a role-play; formulating general rules

Didaktischer Kommentar S werden mit den evtl. gravierenden Folgen leichtsinnigen Medienverhaltens konfrontiert, lernen die Arbeitgebersicht kennen und ziehen Schlüsse für ihr eigenes Medienverhalten.

SB-DVD-ROM

Lernwortschatz

prospective (l. 17), reputation (l. 19), prospect (l. 20)

Unterrichtstipps **PRE-READING** ☼ **Linktipp:** www.emc.com/leadership/digital-universe/expanding-digital-universe.htm Hier können sich S einen *digital footprint calculator* herunterladen, um den Informationszuwachs über sie im Internet festzustellen.

ALT Einstieg: Im Vorfeld wird besprochen, welche Websites wie genutzt werden und warum S sich bei einem sozialen Netzwerk anmelden.

Differenzierung **4 Role-play** Schwächere S bereiten *role cards* mit für ihre Rolle nützlichen Redemitteln vor.

5 Formulierungshilfen für Leistungsschwächere: *media consumption: choose well/not too much; social networking: check privacy settings; downloading: rights of the copyright holder; publishing photos / personal data / opinions on the Internet; check the reliability of information from Web sources*

ZA HA S, die ihren Wortschatz zum Thema Bewerbungen erweitern oder festigen möchten, bearbeiten folgende Aufgabe, z. B. als Hausaufgabe: *The first sentence of the text*

Part D2 – The Tree Stages of Media Literacy

contains three words connected with job applications: 'résumé', 'qualifications' and 'references'. Collect more examples from the text. Consult your dictionary and include useful collocations. Lösungshinweise:
be on the shortlist (l. 3); selection panel (l. 3); chance of getting a job (l. 9); turn up for a job interview (l. 12); prospective employer (l. 17); career prospects (l. 20); prospective employee (l. 22); (influence a) recruitment decision (l. 23); HR decision-makers (l. 23); reject an applicant (l. 24); recruit (v, l. 26); CV (l. 26); candidate (l. 27)

> **Info**
>
> *Positive effects of blogs and social networking sites (SNS):* Although caution is advised on SNS and blogs, the National Literacy Trust found that among 3,000 young people surveyed in 2009, those who kept a blog enjoyed writing more than those who didn't (57 % versus 40 %). The survey also found that social networking is good for young people's self-confidence: more young people who had a profile on an SNS thought they were good at writing compared to those who did not have a profile (56 % versus 47 %).
> From: 'A write clever idea', *Times Educational Supplement*, 11 December 2009

Lösungshinweise

PRE-READING An electronic (or digital) footprint is the trace people leave online when they transmit information e.g. when registering for a social networking site, sending emails and attachments, uploading videos or digital images, but also simply when browsing the Internet: cookies stored by your web browser make it possible to collect this information.

1 Individual answers.

2 Promising job candidates may be rejected because of the negative impression made by content they have posted on the Web. A significant number of employers admit they 'google' candidates; some have rejected candidates on the basis of what they found. Many (young) people are ignorant of the consequences of their online behaviour.

3a Function of opening: introduces topic; catches reader's attention; arouses curiosity; shows dramatic example of effects of incautious behaviour: from success to failure in one click

3b Characteristic aspects: topic (matter of general interest); opening (human interest); use of quotations (experts). It comes closest to a feature story.

4 Role-play Individual answers.

5 Suggested answers, DO: choose the media you consume critically; check the privacy settings of your social networking site to see who has access to your personal data; DON'T: publish anything on the Web that you wouldn't want your future employer to see; download or copy digital material that is protected by copyright unless you have permission

SB S. 133 **D2 The Three Stages of Media Literacy** Elizabeth Thoman

Source:	Center for Media Literacy, 1995
Topic:	Stages of media literacy
Text form:	Essay
Language variety:	American English
Number of words:	230
Level:	Advanced
Skills/Activities:	Working with charts and graphs; discussing the results of a survey

6 Communication across Cultures

Didaktischer Kommentar S lernen den Begriff *media literacy* kennen. Anschließend arbeiten sie in kooperativer Form die Daten ihrer *media logs* auf, präsentieren sie angemessen und reflektieren ihr Medienverhalten kritisch.

SB-DVD-ROM

Lernwortschatz

incorporate (l. 1), inquiry *(AE)*/enquiry *(BE)* (l. 8), applicable (l. 20)

Unterrichtstipps **CONTEXT TASK** S bringen zu dieser Stunde ihre media logs mit.

a Für die Auswertung benötigt man pro S ein *Media Log Evaluation Sheet* (**KV 13**).

b Es erleichtert die Auswertung, **KV 15** auf Folie zu kopieren und die Daten von S in die entsprechenden Kästchen mit Folienstift eintragen zu lassen. Auf diese Weise sind die Daten per OHP allen zugänglich; für die Auswertung der Gruppenergebnisse wird nur noch ein Taschenrechner benötigt.
Im *SF 13, Working with graphs and charts* finden sich Hinweise auf graphische Präsentationsmöglichkeiten.

Info

The Center for Media Literacy (CML) is an educational organization that provides leadership, public education, professional development and educational resources nationally. CML is dedicated to promoting and supporting media literacy education as a framework for accessing, analysing, evaluating, creating and participating with media content.

Lösungshinweise **1a**

Stage 1	managing media consumption; making critical choices; reducing time spent on media consumption
Stage 2	skills of critical viewing: understanding how media are constructed and how they function
Stage 3	analysing economic, social and political background of the media; reflecting how the media affect public opinion; reflecting the relationship between the media and economy

1b *Possible answers, stage 1:* don't watch more than one film per evening; *stage 2:* watch films critically and think about the means that are used; *stage 3:* write a blog criticizing a dubious advertising campaign.

CONTEXT TASK Individual answers.

SB S. 125 ## Communicating across Cultures –
CD 3.03 ## Using the Appropriate Register

Didaktischer Kommentar S werden mit zwei Situationen konfrontiert, wie sie sich ergeben können, wenn sich S im englischsprachigen Ausland schriftlich oder mündlich an fremde Menschen wenden müssen. S üben, sich in solchen Situationen sprachlich angemessen zu verhalten.

SB-DVD-ROM

Lernwortschatz

addressee (introductory text)

6 Communication across Cultures – Using the Appropriate Register

Unterrichtstipps Der Cartoon kann als Ausgangspunkt für ein Gespräch über Register allgemein benutzt werden, wobei S evtl. aus eigener Erfahrung Beispiele für unangemessene Äußerungen beisteuern können.

ALT **1** S verfassen im Anschluss an die Übung eine ähnlich unangemessene E-Mail, tauschen sie mit einem Partner und schreiben jeweils eine verbesserte Fassung.

Lösungshinweise **PRE-READING** The teacher uses an expression of annoyance ('pain in the ass') that is taboo in a parent-teacher conversation. Normally, a teacher might say something like 'Your daughter is quite a challenge' or 'I sometimes find it difficult to cope with your daughter's behaviour'.

1a Relevant rules: use appropriate opening and closing phrases; state the purpose of your letter; be factual and state your point clearly; avoid colloquial expressions and short forms

1b The form of address and the sign-off are both too informal for an adult you don't know personally; Kai doesn't inform Alison who he is or mention the fact that he will be doing his internship at Radio Brighton; Kai doesn't say when he would like to have a day off.

1c Dear Ms Cooke
I have just started my internship at Radio Brighton. During the week from 7–11 September, my younger brother will be staying in London with his school class. I was wondering if it would be possible for me to have a day off during this week so that I could visit him.
Yours sincerely
Kai Kratzberg.

TM-DVD-ROM **2 Mediation** Individual answers; cf. transcript on TM-DVD-ROM.

173

Kopiervorlage 12: Media Log

Use this log to record your use of media for seven days. Do not write your name on it.

Day	Medium	Function/Use	Time spent
one			
two			
three			
four			
five			
six			
seven			
Total time spent on media consumption			

Kopiervorlage 13: Media Log Evaluation Sheet

Use this worksheet to find out how much time you, your group and your class have spent on each medium for each function/use.

Medium	Total time spent in one week		
	by me	by my group	by my class
book			
Internet			
magazine/newspaper			
mobile phone			
radio			
recorded music (CD/MP3)			
TV or DVD			
other			
Total time spent on media consumption			

Function/Use	Total time spent in one week		
	by me	by my group	by my class
communication			
entertainment			
information			
self-expression			
Total time on all functions			

Kopiervorlage 14: Elements of a News Report

Element	Used (✓)	Function
anchor (live)		
inserted titles		
computer graphics		
animation		
man-on-the-street interview *(AE)*; vox pop *(BE)*		
on-the-scene reporter		
voice-over		
sound bite		
inserted video clips		
inserted web pages		

anchor(-man/-woman) *(AE)* / **presenter** *(BE)* person who presents a radio or TV programme and introduces reports by other people
graphics *(pl)* designs, drawings or pictures
insert sth. put sth. into sth. else or between sth.
sound bite short, effective phrase taken from a longer speech
voice-over comments in a film or TV programme by sb. not seen on screen

Kopiervorlage 15: Evaluation of Media Logs

Medium	Total time spent in one week					
	Group 1	Group 2	Group 3	Group 4	Group 5	Total (1–5)
book						
Internet						
magazine/newspaper						
mobile phone / smartphone						
TV or DVD						
radio						
CD/MP3						
other						
Total						

Function/Use	Total time spent in one week					
	Group 1	Group 2	Group 3	Group 4	Group 5	Total (1–5)
communication						
entertainment						
information						
self-expression						
Total time on all functions						

Context 21 The Media: Topic Vocabulary

Word/Phrase	Memory Aid	German
(ONLINE) NEWSPAPERS		
bold type	*example sentence:* The ~ **type** used in this poster really makes the text stand out!	Fettdruck
capital letter	*opposite:* lower-case letter	Großbuchstabe
italics	*definition:* printed letters that lean to the right: *italics*	Kursivschrift
new media	*definition:* new information and entertainment technologies such as the Internet, CD-ROMs and digital television	neue Medien
print media	*example sentence:* Many people worry that new media such as the Internet will make **print** ~ like newspapers unnecessary.	Printmedien
quality newspaper / broadsheet	*definition:* a more serious newspaper traditionally printed on large paper	Qualitätszeitung
tabloid	*synonyms:* the red tops / yellow press / gutter press	Boulevardzeitung
biased ['baɪəst] **/ one-sided**	*opposite:* balanced/objective	gefärbt, tendenziös, voreingenommen
current affairs *(pl)*	*definition:* events of political or social importance which are happening at the moment	Tagespolitik, aktuelle Nachrichten
feature story	*example sentence:* A ~ **story** deals with a topic by concentrating on a particular person or on particular people.	Feature; Zeitungsreportage
heading	*defintion:* a statement at the top of a piece of text used to attract the reader's attention and to indicate the nature of the text below	Überschrift
(banner) headline	*collocations with* **headline**: (to) grab/hit/make the <u>headlines</u>	Schlagzeile
in-depth	*example sentence:* In broadsheet newspapers there tends to be more ~ reporting about events.	ausführlich, tiefgründig
letter to the editor	*example sentence:* Mrs Jones wrote a ~ **to the** ~ in reaction to the shocking article on animal abuse.	Leserbrief
news report / news story	*definition:* a written or spoken account of an event that is broadcast on TV or published in the newspapers	Bericht

Context 21 The Media: Topic Vocabulary

Word/Phrase	Memory Aid	German
(ONLINE) NEWSPAPERS		
sensationalist	*example sentence:* The ~ headlines about their area angered the local community.	sensationslüstern
(to) **write an editorial**	*other collocations:* (to) feature/print/publish/run an article/editorial / a column/comment	einen Leitartikel schreiben
OTHER/GENERAL MEDIA		
advertisement [əd'vɜːtɪsmənt☆ˌædvərˈtaɪz-] / **commercial**	*collocations with* **commercial**: show a new ~ / ~ break	Werbespot
advertising	*word family:* (to) advertise – advertisement – advertising – advertiser	Werbung
(to) **broadcast** sth.	*synonyms:* (to) air/show/transmit sth.	etwas senden
(to) **censor** sth.	*word family:* (to) censor – censor *(n)* – censorship	etwas zensieren
channel	*collocations:* change/switch (the) ~ / surf/flick/zap through the ~s	Kanal
commercial broadcaster	*definition:* TV or radio station paid for with money made from advertising during the programmes	werbefinanzierter Sender
(to) **fund** sth.	*example sentence:* In Britain the licence fee is used to ~ the BBC.	etwas finanzieren
(to) **host/present** sth.	*example sentence:* A famous model always ~s my favourite reality TV show.	etwas moderieren
hype	*synonyms:* media attention / publicity	Medienrummel
Internet access	*example sentence:* Many people still don't have **Internet** ~.	Internetzugang
licence fee *(BE)* / **license fee** *(AE)*	*definition:* the money paid for the permission to own a TV, which funds TV and radio programmes	Fernsehgebühr
on the Net	*example sentence:* I found this really helpful website **on the** ~.	im Internet
presenter *(BE)* / **anchor (-man/-woman)** *(AE)*	*definition:* the person who presents a live TV news programme, introducing reports from other people	Nachrichtensprecher/in; Fernsehmoderator/in

Context 21 The Media: Topic Vocabulary

Word/Phrase	Memory Aid	German
OTHER/GENERAL MEDIA		
public broadcasting	*definition:* TV or radio station largely paid for with money made from a licence fee or from state subsidies	öffentlich-rechtlicher Rundfunk
(to) **receive media coverage**	*example sentence:* The high-profile murder trial of a celebrity ~ed wide **media** ~.	Medienberichterstattung erfahren
(to) **record** sth.	*example sentence:* Richard ~ed everything that took place that evening, so he'd be able to remember it for years to come.	etwas aufnehmen
remote (control)	*example sentence:* Some people sit all evening with the remote control in their hand, zapping through the channels.	Fernbedienung
user-generated content	*example sentence:* Wikipedia is an online encyclopedia which is made up entirely of ~ **content**.	nutzergenerierte Inhalte

7 Global Perspectives

Mithilfe einer Vielzahl von Textsorten setzen sich S kritisch mit dem Thema Globalisation, deren Nutzen und Gefahren auseinander.

In *Part A – Case Studies in Globalization* beschäftigen sich S mit den Arbeitsbedingungen südostasiatischer Sweatshops und überdenken ihr eigenes Konsumverhalten. Filmausschnitte aus *Outsourced* fördern die interkulturelle Kompetenz.

Part B – The Globalized Economy beleuchtet positive und negative Aspekte der Globalisierung anhand von Sachtexten.

Part C – Global Ties schärft das Bewusstsein dafür, dass wir alle zur Globalisierung beitragen und ihre Vorteile nutzen. S trainieren ihr Hörverstehen und wenden neu erworbenes Wissen in der *Context Task* an.

Didaktisches Inhaltsverzeichnis

SB p.	Title	TM p.	Text Form	Topic	Skills and Activities	Language Practice
136	Lead-in	181	Photos; poem	Global interconnectedness	Mind mapping; working with pictures	
138	Words in Context – Everything is Connected	183	Informative text	Living in a globalized world	Matching words; using a dictionary; activating passive vocabulary	LP 20: Avoiding German-English interference
	Part A – Case Studies in Globalization					
140	A1 The Price Make-up of a €100 Sport Shoe	185	Photo; figures	'Needle industries' in Asia	Working with pictures	
141	A2 The Jeans Kelsey Timmerman	186	Non-fictional text (extract)	Working conditions in sweatshops	Writing; taking part in a discussion; working with charts	
143	A3 Outsourcing DVD	187	Feature film (extract)	Outsourcing business to India	Viewing a film; listening comprehension	
	Part B – The Globalized Economy					
144	B1 Global Money, Global Crisis Thomas L. Friedman	189	Newspaper article (extract)	The international financial crisis	Structuring a text; paraphrasing; using a dictionary	
146	B2 EXTRA The Butterfly Effect Thomas Hylland Eriksen	191	Non-fictional text (extract)	The implications of globalization	Reading non-fiction; working with pictures; writing a report	
148	B3 Global Protest Kevin Danaher	192	Non-fictional text (extract)	Activists against globalization	Matching; discussing; writing a comment; interpreting maps	Collocations
	Part C – Global Ties					
151	C1 Towards Peace	195	Photos	Organizations for peace	Cooperative learning strategy (group puzzle)	
152	C2 A Model Power? David Miliband CD 2.15–16	196	Speech (extracts)	New threats: a new raison d'être for the EU	Listening for gist; listening for detail	
152	C3 60 Years of the Commonwealth Paul Reynolds	197	Online article (extract)	Development of a unique association	Doing research; brainstorming; writing an essay	
153	Communicating across Cultures CD 2.17–18	198	Conversations	Negotiation and compromise	Mediating; matching; doing research; debating	

SB S. 136 **Lead-in**

Didaktischer Kommentar Fotos und Text beleuchten die Kapitelthematik aus verschiedenen Blickwinkeln und fordern S auf, ihr eigenes kulturspezifisches Wertesystem durch den Vergleich mit anderen zu relativieren.

7 Lead-in

SB-DVD-ROM

> **Lernwortschatz**
>
> How come? (l. 3), hijack sth. (l. 24), natural resources (*pl*, task 1c)

Unterrichtstipps

1a–d S tragen in Partnerarbeit die Namen der im Text genannten Länder auf der Umrisskarte (**KV 16**) ein. Um die Bearbeitung zu erleichtern, vergrößert L die Karte auf DIN-A3.

1b Die Aufgabe kann im *think–pair–share*-Verfahren gelöst werden, wobei die Intention des Textes im Plenum diskutiert wird.

ALT **2a** Gruppen à 3–4 S suchen sich jeweils ein Foto aus und erstellen in einer *placemat* (s. S. 298) für die dargestellte Person eine Biografie, in der sie die Fragen *who/what/where/when/why* beantworten. S stellen ihre Biografie in einem *gallery walk* vor und erläutern, was das Foto mit dem Thema Globalisierung zu tun hat.

Differenzierung **1a** Leistungsstärkere wählen eines der in **1a** identifizierten Länder und präsentieren in einem Kurzvortrag, welchen Beitrag zum globalen Miteinander die genannten Länder leisten.

> **Info**
>
> *Globalization* can be described as the connection of different economic systems and cultures around the globe influenced by large companies and improved communication.
>
> *Diana, Princess of Wales* (1961–1997) was married to Prince Charles from 1981 till 1996, when they divorced. She was respected for her charity work, including support for an international ban on the use of landmines, and was one of the most photographed celebrities of the last century. She and her partner, Dodi Fayed, an Egyptian business tycoon, were killed in a car accident in Paris in 1997 while being followed by paparazzi.

Lösungshinweise

1a Individual answers.

1b *Intention*: The poem aims to explain the complex issue 'globalization' in a simple way. *Tone*: The humorous, ironic tone makes the poem enjoyable and the issue of globalization more accessible / easier to understand. 'An English princess with an Egyptian boyfriend' sounds like a fairy tale, and exaggerations (ll. 11–12) further simplify the case. Not all the photographers who followed the princess were Italian and certainly not all of them were driving Japanese motorcycles, but the simpler image is funnier.

1c **EXTRA** Areas of the world missing: China (toys, technology), Russia (oil, gas), Australia (wool, meat, wine), Southern States of Africa (gold, timber) …

1d Tafelbild:

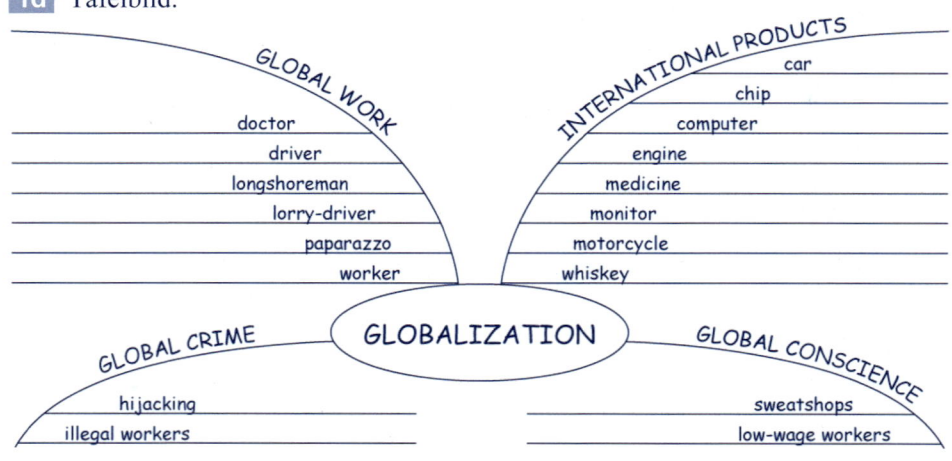

Mindmap – **GLOBALIZATION**:
- **GLOBAL WORK**: doctor, driver, longshoreman, lorry-driver, paparazzo, worker
- **INTERNATIONAL PRODUCTS**: car, chip, computer, engine, medicine, monitor, motorcycle, whiskey
- **GLOBAL CRIME**: hijacking, illegal workers
- **GLOBAL CONSCIENCE**: sweatshops, low-wage workers

Words in Context

2a

A Indian people with telephone headsets are sitting in a call centre. *Chapter title*: Many big companies have call centres in India, so a US customer may be calling an Indian call centre agent about their computer problems without even knowing it.

B An African tribal woman is drinking a can of Coca Cola and holding a little child in her arm. *Chapter title*: International brands can be found even in remote corners of the developing world.

C Mainly white people are demonstrating against capitalism in London (Big Ben is visible). *Chapter title*: The current economic system in the developed world – capitalism – causes problems in both developed and developing countries.

D A black man is eating a Chinese takeaway. *Chapter title*: Chinese food is served all around the world.

E A black nurse is looking after an old white man. *Chapter title*: People are able to move to, live and work in other countries. Sometimes they flee their country because of poverty or political motives. Thus, multicultural and multiethnic populations develop.

F Asian women in a factory are working at sewing machines. They're all using the same material so they are probably working for a big company. *Chapter title*: Big companies have their clothes manufactured in developing countries.

2b Photos A–F all show aspects of globalization – the effects of breaking down trade barriers, allowing companies to sell or produce their goods wherever they want and wherever they can make the biggest profit. Photo C represents the views of the opponents of globalization who think that this is not fair or sensible and that there are other ways in which society can be run.

2c Possible answers: Photo A: India – linked to UK or USA (who use cheap Indian call centres)

Photo B: Africa – linked to the USA (where Coca Cola comes from)

Photo C: UK – linked to the rest of the world, but especially the G8 (USA, UK, Japan, Germany, France, Russia, Canada, Italy)

Photo D: UK, USA or elsewhere – linked to Africa (where the man or his family came from) and China (where the food comes from)

Photo E: UK or USA – linked to Africa (where the nurse or her family came from)

Photo F: Asia – linked to the USA (or wherever the cheap clothes are sent to)

Words in Context – Everything Is Connected

Ausgehend vom Text setzen sich S vertiefend mit dem Thema Globalisierung auseinander. Sie bekommen einen Einblick in die Vor- und Nachteile des globalen Handels und lernen die Sichtweisen der Befürworter und Gegner kennen. S wenden verschiedene Memorierungs- und Vernetzungstechniken an und arbeiten sicher mit dem einsprachigen Wörterbuch.

Lernwortschatz

globalization (l. 1), breaking down of trade barriers (l. 1), supporters of globalization (l. 2), deregulation (l. 2), developing country (l. 5), access to world markets (l. 5), competition (l. 5), consumer (l. 6), developed country (l. 6), market forces (l. 7), supply and demand (l. 7), globalization critics (l. 8), unsafe and unhealthy conditions (l. 9), sweatshop (l. 10), earn a subsistence wage (l. 10), enjoy job security (l. 11), child labour (l. 11), trade union (l. 12), organize workers (l. 12), improve working conditions (l. 12), skilled worker (l. 14), unskilled worker (l. 14), employer (l. 15), production cost (l. 16), plant (l. 16), domestic production (l. 16), outsource sth. (l. 17), labour force (l. 18), employee (l. 18), wage (l. 19), boycott (l. 21), multinational company (l. 22), brand (l. 23), image (l. 23), bad press (l. 24), import goods (l. 25), protect the rights of workers (l. 26), globalization opponent (l. 26), fair trade (l. 27), workplace (l. 28), global economy (l. 30), financial crisis)

Words in Context – Everything is Connected

(l. 31), bankrupt sb./sth. (l. 32), government intervention (l. 33), international trade (l. 34), regulate sth. (l. 34), Group of Eight (G8) (l. 36), industrialized country (l. 36), international relations (l. 39), peacekeeping mission (l. 41), relief effort (l. 43), non-governmental organization (NGO) (l. 44), government funding (l. 46), donation (l. 47), volunteer work (l. 47)

Unterrichtstipps ⚠ HA

S lesen den Text (ggf. vorbereitend als Hausaufgabe) und stellen sicher, dass sie die markierten Begriffe verstanden haben und erklären können.

👥 👥👥 **2** kann in Partnerarbeit oder in Kleingruppen besprochen werden.

Differenzierung 👥👥 ZA

Leistungsstärkere Lerngruppen können ein Karteikartenreferat halten: S arbeiten in Vierergruppen und suchen einzeln die für sie wichtigsten fünf Begriffe/Phrasen im Text, mit deren Hilfe sie Kurzreferate über den Text halten. Danach vergleicht die Gruppe ihre Begriffe und einigt sich gemeinsam auf fünf Stichwörter. Diese werden auf je eine Karteikarte geschrieben. Die Referate werden bei geschlossenem SB gehalten.

ALT

Alternativ halten die Gruppen ein Karteikartenreferat mit den Karten einer anderen Gruppe.

Info

The World Trade Organization (WTO) is an international organization consisting of about 140 consenting member states. It was set up in 1995 and controls and deals with global rules of trade between nations. In addition to the Ministerial Committee in Geneva, Switzerland, which makes the top decisions, there are also a number of working groups and committees like the Goods Council and the Services Council. The WTO may issue trade sanctions against countries who violate the rules.

The Group of Eight (G8), is an important international forum made up of the eight economically most powerful countries (Canada, France, Germany, Italy, Japan, Russia, the UK and the USA). Founded in 1975 as the G6 (Canada joined a year later, Russia in 1998), the group has set itself the task of trying to solve world problems such as poverty. Its meetings, attended by the heads of the member countries as well as the head of the European Union, are often controversial.

The United Nations (UN) is an international organization founded in 1945 by 51 countries intending international peace and security. Today the organization with its 192 member states works in a wide range of areas from environment and refugees' protection, disaster relief and economic and social development to promoting democracy and human rights for a safe world in the future.

Doctors Without Borders (Médecins sans Frontières) is an international medical humanitarian organization working in more than 60 countries to assist people whose survival is threatened by violence, neglect, or catastrophe. In 1999 *Doctors Without Borders* received the Nobel Peace Prize.

Oxfam (Oxford Committee for Famine Relief), founded in 1942, is an international charity focused on fighting poverty and empowering impoverished individuals around the world. 13 partner organizations belong to Oxfam, working with a number of affiliates in 100 countries to provide everything from donations of clothing to legal support.

Lösungshinweise

1a break down trade barriers – stop protectionism; deregulation – relaxing of laws; earn a subsistence wage – make just enough money to survive; enjoy job security – be safe from unfair firing; globalization opponents – anti-globalization activists; labour force – workers; outsource – send jobs abroad; improve working conditions – make workplaces better; domestic production – manufacturing at home; peacekeeping mission – peace in a conflict zone

Part A

1b Individual answers.

2 1 supportive; 2 bankruptcy; 3 critical; 4 consumes; 5 employment; 6 oppose; 7 development; 8 regulatory

3 EXTRA

1 Cheap food is a <u>positive thing</u> for us, but it <u>comes at the expense of workers</u> in developing countries.
2 In most developing countries, employees <u>work</u> extremely <u>long hours</u> and don't <u>enjoy job security</u>.
3 The workers have <u>barely</u> enough money to feed their families.
4 Protest campaigns against WTO summit meetings <u>are</u> often <u>met with violence</u>.
5 The global finance system is, <u>figuratively speaking</u>, a house of cards that could collapse at any time.
6 <u>All over the world</u> activists speak up for people who don't have a say.

Part A – Case Studies in Globalization

SB S. 140

A1 The Price Make-up of a €100 Sport Shoe

Didaktischer Kommentar

Am Beispiel eines Sportschuhs werden S für die in asiatischen Sweatshops (Ausbeuterbetrieben) hergestellten Billigprodukte und deren Preise sensibilisiert. Sie schulen ihre Kompetenz, Statistiken zu versprachlichen und Informationen grafisch darzustellen.

SB-DVD-ROM

Lernwortschatz

profit (illustration), subcontractor (illustration), retailer (illustration), VAT (value added tax) (illustration), advertising (task 1)

Unterrichtstipps

Einstieg: S führen innerhalb ihrer Lerngruppe eine Umfrage zu ihrem Konsumverhalten durch: Welche Marken werden bevorzugt, wo wird eingekauft, wie viel Geld wird für Lieblingskleidungsstücke bezahlt und woher kommen die gekauften Waren?

1 L präsentiert die Abbildung ohne Zahlen sowie die Erläuterungen aus **1**. S schätzen, welchen Anteil die jeweiligen Posten am Gesamtpreis des Schuhs haben, ordnen die Definitionen den Posten zu und tragen ihre Schätzungen ein. Abschließend vergleichen sie sie mit den korrekten Zahlen.

2 wird zunächst in Partnerarbeit, anschließend im Plenum diskutiert.

Differenzierung

1 In leistungsschwächeren Lerngruppen wird der Wortschatz vorentlastet:
brand name: name given to a product by the company who produces it
labour: (physical) work
rent: the money you pay regularly for the flat or house you live in
retailer: a person or company that sells goods ([Einzel-]Händler)
subcontractor: a person or company that does part of the work for another person or company
stock: the inventory of goods a person or company sells (Lager)

ZA **2** Leistungsstärkere Lerngruppen diskutieren (z. B. in Kooperation mit dem Gemeinschaftskunde- oder Wirtschaftskurs) über Preisentwicklungen und die Faktoren, die sie beeinflussen.

Lösungshinweise

1 1 €1.50 (production costs); 2 €17 (VAT); 3 €12 (rent/stocks retailer); 4 €18 (labour costs retailer); 5 €0.50 (labour costs workers); 6 €2.50 (publicity retailer); 7 €13 (profit brand name)

2 Individual answers.

7 Part A2 – The Jeans

3a A pie chart is best because it lends itself to showing proportional parts of a whole. Tafelbild:

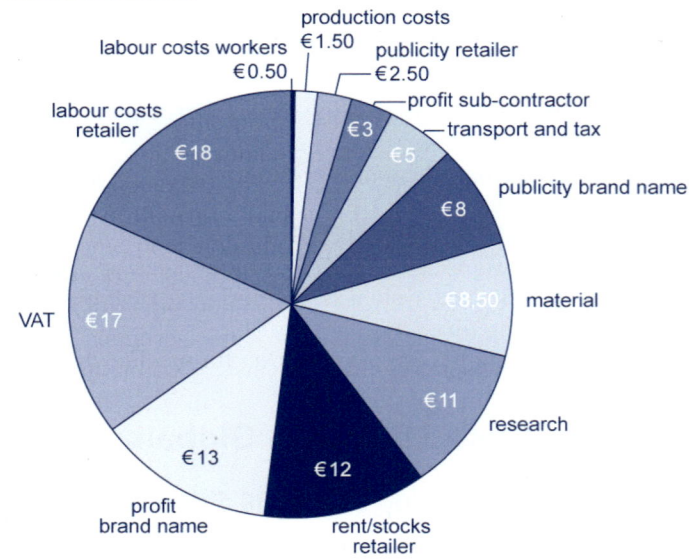

- production costs €1.50
- labour costs workers €0.50
- publicity retailer €2.50
- labour costs retailer €18
- profit sub-contractor €3
- transport and tax €5
- publicity brand name €8
- material €8,50
- research €11
- rent/stocks retailer €12
- profit brand name €13
- VAT €17

3b Individual answers.

SB S. 141
▶ LSET ex. 4, 5

A2 The Jeans Kelsey Timmerman

Source:	*Where Am I Wearing? A Global Tour to the Countries, Factories and People that Make Our Clothes*, 2009
Topic:	Working conditions in sweatshops
Text form:	Non-fictional text (extract)
Language variety:	American English
Number of words:	487
Level:	Intermediate
Skills/Activities:	Writing; taking part in a discussion; working with charts and graphs

Didaktischer Kommentar

Dieser Reisebericht sensibilisiert S für die Situation junger Arbeiterinnen in den Sweatshops Asiens, die für die westliche Bekleidungsindustrie produzieren. Ohne erhobenen Zeigefinger wird das Konsumverhalten der S auf den Prüfstand gestellt. Sie schulen ihre Schreibkompetenz, indem sie den Reisebericht als *news story* umschreiben.

SB-DVD-ROM

Lernwortschatz

freelance (*adj*, introduction), treat sb. to sth. (l. 1), uncover sth. (l. 30), be subject to sth. (l. 31), market sth. as sth. (l. 35), conscience (l. 39)

Unterrichtstipps

Einstieg: S betrachten zunächst nur den abgebildeten Buchumschlag. Sie beschreiben das Titelbild und spekulieren über den Inhalt.

ZA S werden an die niedrigen Lohnkosten erinnert, von denen sie in **A1** erfahren haben. Sie beschreiben, welche Konsequenzen für ihr eigenes Konsumverhalten sie daraus ziehen können (z. B. Boykott, Bevorzugung fair produzierter Waren). Auch über mögliche Konsequenzen eines Boykotts für Niedriglohnarbeiter wird spekuliert.

ZA **1** Vorab lesen S den Text still und notieren sich drei Verständnisfragen, die anschließend in Partnerarbeit beantwortet werden.

ALT **3** Um die durch den Text erworbenen Erkenntnisse und das Vokabular noch einmal umzuwälzen, finden S Argumente für und gegen Boykotts und tauschen diese in einer *zigzag debate* (s. S. 299) aus.

Part A3 – Outsourcing

Differenzierung

ALT — **1** Leistungsschwächere finden vorab Überschriften für die Abschnitte des Textes: Abschnitt 1: Zeilen 1–12; Abschnitt 2: Zeilen 13–26; Abschnitt 3: Zeilen 27–40.

ZA — Lesebegeisterte und am Thema interessierte S lesen das Buch von Kelsey Timmerman und stellen es dem Plenum in einem Buchreport vor.

ZA — Eine Gruppe leistungsstärkerer S stellt Fragen für ein Interview mit Kelsey Timmerman zusammen. Sie kann den Autor über seine Website http://whereamiwearing.com kontaktieren und ein Interview per E-Mail führen, das anschließend im Plenum vorgestellt wird.

> **Info**
>
> *Kelsey Timmerman* (born 1975) is a freelance writer and journalist. He has a passion for travelling and while packing for one of his trips, he came up with the idea of visiting the countries where his clothes were made, meeting and talking to the people who made them. His travelogue was published in 2009 as *Where Am I Wearing? A Global Tour to the Countries, Factories and People that Make Our Clothes.*

Lösungshinweise

1 *Summary:* Timmerman interviews Cambodian garment workers in Phnom Penh, finding out they earn as little as $45 a month, of which they send up to half to their families. He also learns that they are afraid of consumer boycotts because they mean earning nothing instead of earning too little.
Argument: Timmerman then discusses that boycotts can both cause mass unemployment and lead to improved working conditions: one should think carefully before buying or boycotting because it can have far-reaching effects.

2 Individual answers.

3 *Possible arguments for consumer boycotts*: draw attention to issues; get other organizations involved; can lead to improvements in wages and working conditions; make consumers buy more thoughtfully
Possible arguments against consumer boycotts: can cause job losses; may result in making consumer goods more expensive; we know too little about the garment business and should let the big companies organize things

4 **EXTRA** Individual answers.

SB S. 143 DVD
Transkript s. TM-DVD-ROM

A3 Outsourcing

Source:	*Outsourced*, USA, 2006
Topic:	Outsourcing business to India
Text form:	Feature film (extract)
Language variety:	American English
Length:	14:44 min
Level:	Advanced
Skills/Activities:	Viewing a film; listening comprehension

Didaktischer Kommentar

S erkennen die Bedeutung globaler Arbeitsrealität und des Englischen als Lingua franca. Sie reflektieren Klischees, Vorurteile und Stereotype, schulen ihre interkulturelle Kompetenz am Beispiel dreier Szenen aus dem Film *Outsourced* und halten ihre Eindrücke in einem *viewing log* fest.

SB-DVD-ROM

> **Lernwortschatz**
>
> supervisor (extract 1, introductory text)

Unterrichtstipps
HA • Word help

Vor dem Sehen der Spielfilmauszüge machen sich S mit unbekanntem Wortschatz vertraut.

7 Part A3 – Outsourcing

PRE-VIEWING S diskutieren die Frage aus dem SB im Plenum und berichten von eigenen Erfahrungen mit Call-Center-Gesprächen.

ZA S bearbeiten **KV 17** zusammenfassend als *post-viewing task*. Lösungshinweise:

1 1g; 2a; 3h; 4b; 5e; 6i; 7l; 8k; 9n; 10j; 11d; 12m; 13f; 14c

2 *Extract 1 (in order of appearance)*: **g** Todd says this to a caller to convince him to choose overnight shipping.; **a** Dave says this about his plans for Todd's department.; **h** Todd expresses his disbelief at his boss's announcement to move the department.; **b** Todd says this to Dave when arguing against Dave's plans.; **e** In their initial conversation, Dave tells Todd he can quit if he doesn't want to go to India.; **i** Dave gives this as a reason for moving the department.; **l** Todd asks a taxi driver in Mumbai.
Extract 2 (in order of appearance): **k** Todd introduces his 'lecture' to the call centre workers with this.; **n** Asha argues against Todd's claim that they aren't native English speakers.; **j** Todd suggests the call centre workers say this to make believe that they are in Chicago.; **d** Asha brings this up in response to Todd's claim that Americans are upset about outsourcing.
Extract 3 (in order of appearance): **m** A call centre worker explains the situation.; **f** Todd gives this order when the call centre is flooded.; **c** Dave gives this as a reason for moving the department to China.

> **Info**
>
> *Outsourced* (2006; director: John Jeffcoat, screenplay: George Wing, John Jeffcoat): Todd (Josh Hamilton), supervisor of a Seattle sales call centre, is outsourced to India and travels to Mumbai to train his replacement. Facing the chaos in the streets of Mumbai and an office paralyzed by constant cultural misunderstandings, Todd yearns to go back as fast as possible. Before long, Todd finds himself disarmed by the friendliness of his likeable replacement Puro (Asif Basra) and charmed by co-worker Asha (Ayesha Dharker) who helps him to familiarize himself with the people and customs of India. Todd realizes that there's a lot to learn for him too and in the end discovers that being outsourced may be the best thing that ever happened to him.

Lösungshinweise

EXTRACT 1

1a The company sells American souvenirs and novelties.

1b The boss is going to fire all the workers except Todd and move the telephone sales operation to India where the wages are much lower.

1c Todd decides to go to India because he doesn't want to lose his job. Although someone else will do his job as a supervisor when they are fully trained, Todd's boss tells him that the expanding company can find him another position.

2 Individual answers.

EXTRACT 2

1a He wants the call centre workers to learn about America, to sound American, make small talk and say they are in windy Chicago. Less cultural misunderstandings are supposed to increase the centre's MPI record.

1b Todd is asking the workers to lie about their whereabouts and Asha feels this is wrong.

2a When Todd says that the Indian call centre agents should sound like native English speakers, Asha points out that in fact they are, English being the official language in India. She says that they got English from the British just like the Americans and that the Indians' pronunciation sometimes is better.

2b Individual answers.

Part B

EXTRACT 3

1 She is very calm and polite with the customer who is very upset that the company he wants to buy from is actually located in India. She says that she understands his concern and offers him the contact details of an American company that makes the same American eagle. When the customer learns that the product costs over $200, he decides to buy from the Indian call centre.

2a If an office were flooded in America there would probably be all sorts of *rules and regulations* about what to do. There would be no room for *improvisation*, one would just have to wait for all the right people to come and would probably be sent home. In India a good job is something very precious so everyone tries to deal with the crisis – there's great *personal commitment* on the part of Todd's team to their employer, long working hours if necessary are a matter of course. And, as we see, the *health and safety regulations* are not as important, which means an amateur like Todd's 'consultant' can just climb a telegraph pole and connect the electricity again. In the US that would certainly have to be an electrician.

2b 'China is the new India' because the wages in China are even lower than in India. This means if he moves the operation to China his profit will be even greater.

2c Individual answers.

Part B – The Globalized Economy

SB S. 144
▶ LSET ex. 6

B1 Global Money, Global Crisis   Thomas L. Friedman

Source:	*The New York Times*, 2008
Topic:	The international financial crisis
Text form:	Newspaper article (extract)
Language variety:	American English
Number of words:	450
Level:	Advanced
Skills/Activities:	Structuring a text; paraphrasing; using a dictionary

Didaktischer Kommentar

Die Auseinandersetzung mit dem Artikel über die Ursachen der Bankenkrise in Island 2008 ermöglicht es S, ihre Textkompetenz zu schulen, indem sie die argumentative Struktur mittels eines *flow chart* darstellen.

SB-DVD-ROM

Lernwortschatz

municipality (l. 4), savings account (l. 8), withdrawal (l. 10), state ownership (l. 15), asset (l. 18), tenfold (l. 18), mortgage (l. 19), get around (l. 21), deposit (l. 22), be in charge (l. 37)

Unterrichtstipps
⚠ **HA**

1 kann als schriftliche Hausaufgabe bearbeitet und anschließend im Plenum besprochen werden.

2a S testen sich zusätzlich in Partnerarbeit, indem sie Definitionen von fünf weiteren Begriffen notieren und einem Partner vorlesen, der das entsprechende Wort aus dem Text heraussucht.

Differenzierung
⚠ **HA**

Leistungsschwächere lesen den Text vorbereitend als Hausaufgabe und erarbeiten unbekanntes Vokabular.

credit crunch: Finanz-, Kreditkrise   *interest:* Zinsen

Part B1 – Global Money, Global Crisis

Lösungshinweise

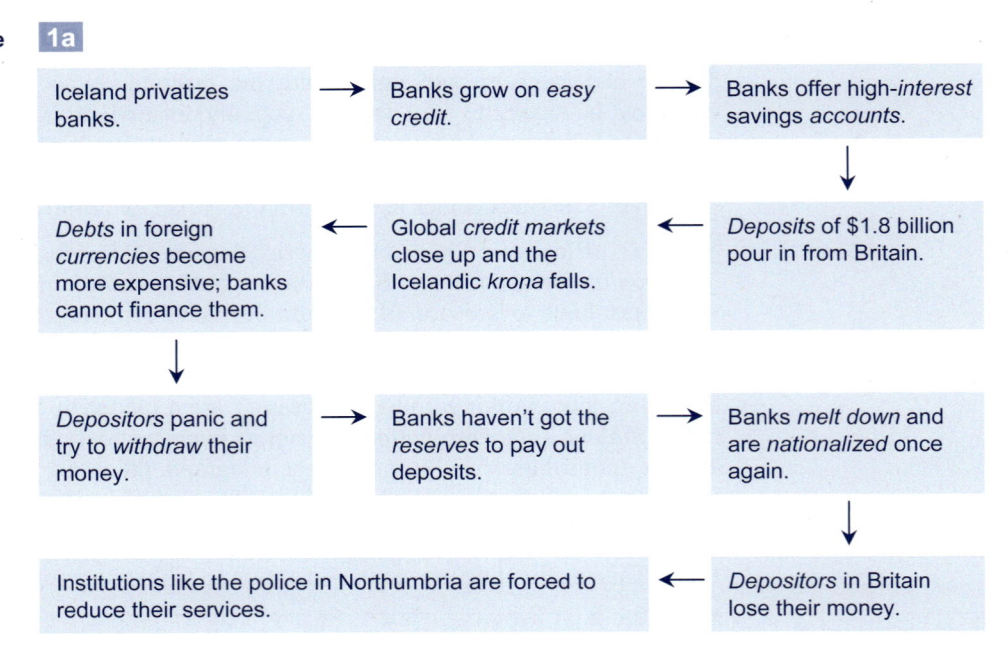

1a

Iceland privatizes banks. → Banks grow on *easy credit*. → Banks offer high-*interest* savings *accounts*.
↓
Debts in foreign *currencies* become more expensive; banks cannot finance them. ← Global *credit markets* close up and the Icelandic *krona* falls. ← *Deposits* of $1.8 billion pour in from Britain.
↓
Depositors panic and try to *withdraw* their money. → Banks haven't got the *reserves* to pay out deposits. → Banks *melt down* and are *nationalized* once again.
↓
Institutions like the police in Northumbria are forced to reduce their services. ← *Depositors* in Britain lose their money.

1b Years ago, Iceland decided to privatize its banks. This was followed by the banks growing very quickly on easy credit. They used the money to offer high-interest savings accounts; as a result, deposits of $1.8 billion began to pour in from Britain. When global credit markets suddenly closed up, the Icelandic krona fell against other currencies. Consequently, all debts that were denominated in foreign currencies became very expensive, and the banks couldn't finance their debt. Depositors panicked and tried to withdraw their money. This led to problems, as the banks didn't have the reserves to pay out all the deposits. As a result, the banks went into meltdown and were nationalized by the Icelandic government once again. Depositors in Britain lost their money, which resulted in institutions like the police in Northumbria being forced to reduce their services.

1c EXTRA

Mortgage broker gives consumer with no credit rating a subprime mortgage. → Mortgage is globalized through global banking system. → Globalized mortgages 'go sour', i.e. become worthless.
↓
Accounts in Icelandic banks are frozen. ← The resulting credit crunch hits Iceland. ← Banks worry that other banks hold toxic assets and refuse to lend them money.
↓
Depositors, including the police in Northumbria, lose their money. → Northumbria is forced to reduce street patrols.

2a
1. bank accounts for one's extra cash that always pay out good interest
2. take out money that one has put into the bank
3. banks were able to expand because they could borrow money easily and cheaply
4. money the bank pays depositors for keeping their money at the bank, amounting to 5.45 % of the deposit each year
5. the money always goes where it will earn the most money in return
6. have enough money available to pay back any amount owed

Part B2 – The Butterfly Effect 7

2b EXTRA Individual answers.

3a To Friedman, the most important fact about globalization is that everyone in the world is somehow connected to everyone else. He also claims that there is no one there to regulate the global economy. While his article certainly makes the argument that there is a high degree of interconnectedness, nowhere has he specifically said anything about the problem of regulation. So his statement about nobody being in charge is merely that: a statement, and not a conclusion.

3b The introduction of the topic goes all the way to line 14. The main body of the text, where the argument is developed, is introduced with the words 'So what's the story?' (l. 15), a clear signal that the text is about to take another direction. In line 36 the writer starts his paragraph with 'And', which is often a signal that a new topic or section is being started. 'Therein lies the central truth of globalization today' makes it clear that he is about to present his conclusion.

SB S. 146
▶ LSET ex. 7, 8

B2 EXTRA **The Butterfly Effect**   Thomas Hylland Eriksen

Source:	*Globalization: The Key Concepts*, 2007
Topic:	The implications of globalization
Text form:	Non-fictional text (extract)
Language variety:	American English
Number of words:	406
Level:	Intermediate
Skills/Activities:	Reading non-fiction; working with pictures; writing a report

Didaktischer Kommentar

Der Textauszug erklärt den in einer globalisierten Welt wichtigen *butterfly effect* (Schmetterlingseffekt). S festigen ihre Textkompetenz, indem sie mithilfe bekannter Erschließungstechniken die notwendigen Informationen entnehmen, bewerten und auf eine neue Situation übertragen.

SB-DVD-ROM

Lernwortschatz

fieldwork (l. 3), global interconnectedness (l. 12), cumulative effect (l. 23), momentous (l. 32), outcome (l. 34), relativize sth. (l. 37), exercise power over sb. (l. 38)

Unterrichtstipps

1 S tauschen sich mit einem Partner aus und vergleichen ihr Ergebnis mit einem weiteren Paar.

ALT **3** kann auch als Einstieg in diesen Text verwendet werden: S spekulieren, wie die beiden Motive der zwei mittleren Fotos miteinander zusammenhängen. Dann bringen sie die restlichen Bilder in eine sinnvolle Reihenfolge, versprachlichen sie und beschreiben so ein Beispiel für einen *butterfly effect*.

Info

Thomas Hylland Eriksen (born 1962) is a social anthropologist at the Department of Social Anthropology, University of Oslo, Norway. His professional work has largely focused on identity politics and globalization. He wrote essays and articles on numerous topics, academic and non-academic. From 1993 to 2001, he was editor of a general cultural journal covering politics, literature and culture. Eriksen is the author of a book series called *Anthropology, Culture and Society*.

The chaos theory was developed by the American mathematician Edward Norton Lorenz (1917–2008). It studies the behaviour of highly sensitive dynamical systems in which small changes in conditions can have large effects. This ripple effect is also referred to as the 'butterfly effect': even the beat of a butterfly's wing can cause a tornado on the other side of the globe.

7 Part B3 – Global Protest

Lösungshinweise

1 *Possible answer*: The butterfly effect is a way of explaining complex processes. The idea is that every action, no matter how small, has a reaction, which may be greater than the original action. That reaction becomes an action, which also has a possibly larger reaction, and so on, until something really big comes of it all: a very small cause, e.g. a nail missing in a horseshoe, ultimately results in the collapse of an entire country.

2a *Examples*: There are so many Indian restaurants in London that the city can be seen as the capital for development in Indian cuisine. The same is true for San Francisco and Chinese cooking. So many Dominicans now live in New York that you have to study them there in order to understand Dominican culture. The souvenirs bought by tourists in Norway aren't made in Norway. London has such a big Caribbean population that it can be seen as the largest 'Caribbean' city. The competition between companies in California and those in the Far East leads not only to factory closures but also to local shops going out of business. All these examples have to do with human development and customs and underline the connectedness of things, demonstrating that every action causes a reaction.

2b The rhyme portrays another example of the butterfly effect: a seemingly small event causes a chain of consequences, increasing in importance, which culminate in the collapse of a kingdom.

3a 1 Photo 3 (bird on power pole); 2 photo 6 (power plant); 3 photo 2 (L.A. airport); 4 photo 1 (L.A. airport control tower); 5 photo 4 (screen: delayed flights); 6 photo 5 (USA air traffic)

3b Everything started when a bird landed on a power pole near Los Angeles, which caused a transformer to short circuit. This in turn led to the power plant responsible for the area shutting down for about ten seconds. The resulting power outage meant that Los Angeles airport was without power briefly, emergency lights going on. It took a few minutes to restore the power, but even then air traffic control was affected. The problems at air traffic control meant that flights out of L.A. were delayed, some as long as 90 minutes. This in turn disrupted air traffic elsewhere in the country, leaving everything in chaos for the rest of the day.

4 Individual answers.

SB S. 148
▶ **LSET ex. 9**

B3 Global Protest   Kevin Danaher

Source:	Website of Global Exchange, 28 October 2007
Topic:	Activists against globalization
Text form:	Non-fictional text (extract)
Language variety:	American English
Number of words:	414
Level:	Intermediate
Skills/Activities:	Matching; taking part in a discussion; writing a comment; interpreting maps

Didaktischer Kommentar

Der Text thematisiert Nachteile der Globalisierung. S schulen ihre Kompetenz, einem Text entnommene Informationen zu strukturieren. Auf der Grundlage der bisher gewonnenen Erkenntnisse diskutieren sie Vor- und Nachteile der Globalisierung und festigen so ihre mündliche Ausdrucksfähigkeit.

SB-DVD-ROM

Lernwortschatz

proceed (l. 3), pressure sb. (l. 4), wealthy elites (l. 17), greed (l. 25), accountability (l. 28)

Part B3 – Global Protest

Unterrichtstipps
ZA

Zur Verständnissicherung visualisieren einige S die in Absatz 2 (Zeilen 9–15) genannten Zahlen in angemessener Form (s. SF 10: Working with charts and graphs).

4 S werden über die Frage „If you're not happy with the political situation you live in, what can you do?" auf Möglichkeiten der politischen Einflussnahme hingewiesen (Boykott, Demonstration, offener Brief an Politiker/in). Über Bildbeschreibungen wird zu Formen des Protests übergeleitet (s. Info).

ZA

3 S setzen sich anhand der **KV 18** mit den Argumenten eines Globalisierungsbefürworters auseinander. Anschließend können sie den Positionen der Kritiker gegenübergestellt werden. Lösungshinweise:

1a Increases in the price of grain have become a huge problem for poor Africans who generally spend half of their budgets on food. The author suggests that large-scale farms should be created on good land in Africa and other less developed countries. These farms could be managed productively by big companies to control the rises in food prices.

1b *Arguments from the text for the proposal*: Africa needs large-scale commercial agriculture to solve the problem of food shortage; This kind of farming is more suited to innovation and investment; The production of more grain would drive down the cost of food.
Arguments from the text against the proposal: Large-scale commercial agriculture is unromantic. The Western world prefers small-scale, 'human' farms; Although Africa should grow GM crops because they are drought-resistant, Europeans don't trust this kind of scientific innovation in agriculture; Both Europe and the USA have become more conscious of the environment. Small-scale farms are seen as more environmentally sustainable.
Further arguments for the proposal: Large-scale agriculture could allow many African countries to be more self-sufficient. They wouldn't have to buy as much food from other countries and could even export grain to make more money; The creation of new, bigger farms would create more jobs in construction as well as agriculture, thereby offering employment to more Africans.
Further arguments against the proposal: The solution seems like a 'second colonization' of Africa. Perhaps Westerners would feel that they shouldn't be trying to manage African countries; Large companies are commercial enterprises. It seems wrong for businessmen to be making money from the desperate situation of many poor Africans.

1c Individual answers.

2a Individual answers. *True for Germany*: preference for organic, ethically farmed produce; purchase of in-season food that has not been imported; …
Not true for Germany: large-scale industry in many parts of the country; …

2b Individual answers. Possible arguments:

Argument	Counter-Argument
Goods and people are more easily and quickly transported around the world.	Able workers leave less developed countries for higher pay elsewhere.
Free trade between countries increases.	Cheaper imports from highly industrial countries can push small local businesses out of the market.
Barriers between different cultures are reduced.	Diversity decreases due to assimilation.
More developed countries can invest in developing ones.	Richer countries can use their investments as a way to exert power and influence over poorer ones.

7 Part B3 – Global Protest

Differenzierung

2 Leistungsschwächere paraphrasieren zur Festigung der neuen Lexik die Begriffe schriftlich mithilfe eines Wörterbuches.

ZA Leistungsstärkere S analysieren die Wortwahl in Zeilen 3 („pressure"), 17–18 („a hunger for more wealth and power"), 23–25 („guns", „focus on greed") im Hinblick auf die Frage, wie neutral die Darstellung des Autors ist.

Info

Dr Kevin Danaher, an expert on the green economy and globalization, is a co-founder of the NGO Global Exchange (1988), founder and executive co-producer of the Green Festivals (2001), and executive director of the Global Citizen Center. Danaher is a frequent speaker at universities and community organizations as well as an author and editor of numerous books (e.g. *Building the Green Economy: Success Stories from the Grass Roots*, 2007).

Creative protest: The photo shows women dressed as queens protesting in Rostock, Germany, on 2 June 2007 against the G8 summit that was held in Heiligendamm near Rostock from 7–8 June 2007.

Violent protest: The photo shows protesters in Berlin-Kreuzberg burning a litter bin on 1 May 2008. Every year on 1 May, this Berlin district becomes a backdrop for multiple riots.

Pie-in-the-face protest: At the UN climate talks in the Hague, Netherlands, on 22 November 2000, US chief negotiator Frank Loy is hit in the face with a custard pie. Protestors claim that the USA is unwilling to fight global warming effectively.

Lösungshinweise

1a Danaher argues that the globalization of market forces through the World Bank, the International Monetary Fund and transnational companies is the reason for inequality. These organizations have facilitated the movement of goods and money across international borders, thereby encouraging competition between countries who must offer them better interest rates in return for larger shares of their wealth.

1b

Demands	Results for workers	Results for me
raise wages (l. 30)	higher pay	expensive goods
improve health and safety standards (l. 30)	better quality of life	expensive goods; clearer conscience
stewardship of natural resources (l. 34)	healthier and more pleasant environment	expensive goods; clearer conscience; safe environment for future generations

1c

Demands	Results for workers	Results for me
outsourcing	lose their jobs	cheap goods
low health and safety standards	low quality of life	cheap goods; guilty conscience
exploitation of natural resources	polluted environment	cheap goods; polluted environment; future generations inhabit a spoiled Earth

2a 1E; 2I; 3F; 4B; 5A; 6G; 7H; 8C; 9D

2b 1 natural resources; 2 remove barriers; 3 wealthy elites; 4 environmental pollution; 5 trade unions

Part C

3 Individual answers.

4 Individual answers; cf. Info.

5a 1 size, wealth; 2 north; 3 south, smaller; 4 richest, largest; 5 ratio

5b On the second map, the countries' size depends on their population. As a result, countries such as India, China, Indonesia and Japan appear much larger than they really are. Most of the others are considerably smaller. China is apparently the most populous country, as it is the biggest, with India not far behind. The ratio of geographic size to population is quite large for Indonesia as well. It is shown in light yellow.

5c Comparing the two maps, it becomes obvious that the richer countries are among the least populated, whereas poorer countries are overpopulated. The one exception is Japan, which appears larger than it actually is in both maps, indicating that, although somewhat overpopulated, it is extremely wealthy.

Part C – Global Ties

SB S. 151 **C1 Towards Peace**

Didaktischer Kommentar Ausgehend von vier Bildimpulsen informieren sich S in einer kooperativen Lernform über verschiedene friedenserhaltende bzw. –schaffende Organisationen und diskutieren deren Wirksamkeit.

Unterrichtstipps

1a S bearbeiten in Gruppen à 4 S je ein Foto in einer *placemat activity*. (s. Skills File 1) und beantworten die Frage ‚*What do you know and think about the photo?*' in Stichpunkten auf der *placemat*.

1b In einer weiteren Phase formieren sich neue Gruppen. S konzentrieren sich gemeinsam auf eines der Bilder und recherchieren über die dargestellte Organisation. Die Informationen werden gesammelt und schriftlich festgehalten.

1c Zurück in der ursprünglichen Gruppe (**1a**) präsentiert jeder seine Organisation und die Gruppe diskutiert gemäß Aufgabe **1e**. Die Ergebnisse werden stichwortartig in der Mitte der *placemat* festgehalten und ggf. noch einmal im Plenum diskutiert.

> **Info**
>
> The first *UN peacekeeping mission* took place in 1948. UN military observers were sent to the Middle East to monitor the Armistice Agreement between Israel and its Arab neighbours. With its missions the UN seeks to help countries in times of conflict and war. So far, there have been a total of 64 UN peacekeeping operations around the world.
>
> *The Commonwealth Games* are a multi-sports competition that takes place every four years. It involves the 54 member states of the Commonwealth and, in addition to many Olympic sports, it includes some that are only played in the Commonwealth countries, e.g. lawn bowls. The first games were held in Hamilton, Ontario, Canada, in 1930. In 2014 Glasgow, Scotland, will host the next event.
>
> *The European Union* is both a political and economic union that counts 27 member states today. Due to EU laws that are binding for all member states money, people, services and goods may move freely within the Union. 16 member states also share the euro as a currency. The EU includes several important institutions such as the European Commission or the Court of Justice of the European Union. Every five years, EU citizens can elect members of the European Parliament directly.
>
> *Doctors Without Borders*: cf. Info in the section 'Words in Context'

7 Part C2 – A Model Power

Lösungshinweise

1a 1A; 2D; 3B; 4C

1b–e Individual answers.

SB S. 152 CD 2.15–16
Transkript s. TM-DVD-ROM

C2 A Model Power — David Miliband

Source:	'Europe 2003: Model Power, Not Superpower', The Foreign and Commonwealth Office, 15 November 2007
Topic:	New threats: a new raison d'être for the EU
Text form:	Speech (extracts)
Language variety:	British English
Length:	*Part 1* 3:24 min; *part 2* 3:09 min
Level:	Advanced
Skills/Activities:	Listening for gist; listening for detail

Didaktischer Kommentar

S schulen ihre Hörverstehenskompetenz, indem sie zunächst die Themen der Rede Milibands identifizieren und ihr danach gezielt Informationen entnehmen.

Unterrichtstipps
⚠ HA ● Word help

1a Vor dem Hören der Rede: S machen sich mit unbekanntem Wortschatz vertraut. Sie lesen Überschrift, Einleitung und Themen 1–5 in **1a** und spekulieren zunächst, welche der Themen am wahrscheinlichsten in der Rede angesprochen werden und auf welche Aspekte sich Milliband möglicherweise konzentriert.

2 S vergleichen ihre Ergebnisse in Partnerarbeit.

3 wird in den Kleingruppen aus **C1**, anschließend ggf. im Plenum besprochen.

> **Info**
>
> *David Wright Miliband* (born 1965 in London) is the son of immigrants to the UK. He was educated in London, graduated with First Class Honours in Philosophy, Politics and Economics from Corpus Christi College, Oxford University, and completed a Masters Degree in Political Science at the Massachusetts Institute of Technology, where he was a Kennedy Scholar. He is a British Labour politician and has been the Member of Parliament for South Shields since 2001. From June 2007 until May 2010 he was the Secretary of State for Foreign and Commonwealth Affairs.
>
> *The College of Europe* (founded in 1949) is an independent university institute which offers students a Master's degree programme in European Studies. The College has two campuses, one in Bruges, Belgium, and another in Natolin, Poland.
>
> *Anna Politkowskaya* (1958–2006) was a Russian-American journalist well known for her coverage and opposition to the Chechen conflict. She received numerous awards for her work, among them the Amnesty International Global Award for Human Rights Journalism in 2001 and the Lettre Ulysses Award for the Art of Reportage in 2003. On 7 October 2006 she was assassinated in her apartment building in Moscow.
>
> *Hrant Dink* (1954–2007) was a journalist, editor and columnist of Turkish-Armenian descent. He was a prominent member of the Armenian minority in Turkey, best known for advocating Turkish-Armenian reconciliation and human and minority rights in Turkey. Dink was assassinated in Istanbul in January 2007 by a 17-year old Turkish nationalist.

Lösungshinweise

1 3, 5

2a He feels that his own heritage – a Belgian father, a Polish mother and himself being born and raised in the UK – reflects the idea of the European Union today.

Part C3 – 60 Years of the Commonwealth

2b Miliband thinks the EU can be a model power because it combines the strengths of its 27 member states. He sees it as a club of nations joining power and motivation, cooperating on regional levels, creating common values, rules and standards despite differences of nationality and religion. He also praises the single European market that could ensure prosperity.

3a His attitude to the EU is very positive: he thinks it can reserve as a model for the peaceful and productive coexistence of nations.

3b Individual answers.

SB S. 152

C3 60 Years of the Commonwealth Paul Reynolds

Source:	'Life at 60 for the Commonwealth', 9 March 2009
Topic:	Development of a unique association
Text form:	Web article (extract)
Language variety:	British English
Number of words:	338
Level:	Advanced
Skills/Activities:	Doing research; brainstorming; writing an essay

Didaktischer Kommentar

S entnehmen einem Artikel Informationen zum Commonwealth und schulen ihre sprachliche Kompetenz, indem sie die Inhalte in eigenen Worten wiedergeben, selbstständig recherchieren und vor der Klasse frei präsentieren.

SB-DVD-ROM

Lernwortschatz

over-ambitious (l. 2), reasonable (l. 7), be threatened by sth. (l. 31)

Unterrichtstipps

PRE-READING KV 16 kann erneut kopiert werden, damit die Länder des Commonwealth eingetragen werden können.

ALT S lesen den *Fact File*, betrachten das Logo und tragen Wissen und Erwartungen darüber zusammen, welche Funktion das Commonwealth ursprünglich hatte und wie es sich verändert hat.

Einstieg (SB geschlossen): Zur Wiederholung und Festigung des Gelernten erstellen S ein *acrostic* zu ‚globalization' oder ‚global perspectives'. Sie nutzen dazu die im *Lead-in* begonnene Mindmap.

Differenzierung
ZA

Politisch interessierte S referieren über verschiedene Länder des Commonwealth unter der Fragestellung, inwiefern diese von der Mitgliedschaft im Commonwealth profitieren.

Info

The Commonwealth is an association of 54 nations from six continents. Member nations work together on issues of development, democracy, freedom and peace. They support each other and establish common rules and values on a democratic basis. Those values are monitored and protected by the Commonwealth Ministerial Action Group (CMAG) which is a rotating group of nine foreign ministers. CMAG may report to heads of government if a member should be suspended or expelled. The head of the Commonwealth is Queen Elizabeth II. She has symbolic functions such as giving speeches, holding discussions and visiting the host country of each Commonwealth's summit. Decisions are made between the heads of government or the ministers responsible for a particular department. Three intergovernmental institutions of the association – the Commonwealth Secretariat, the Commonwealth Foundation and the Commonwealth of Learning – help implement the association's plans and decisions.

7 Communicating across Cultures

Lösungshinweise

1a The Commonwealth's first phase was the attempt to keep the British Empire alive under another name. Its second phase was marked by unrest due to problems over race relations and coups. One could view its third and present phase as being a useful organization with the role of a democratic authority over countries in its sphere of influence.

1b All member states have the same rights and voice, no matter how small or poor. The association relies on peaceful discussion and cooperation; it has no tools with which it could force nations to do what the association wants.

2a *Particular events:* Minority white rule in South Africa enforced by the National Party government ended in 1994 with the election of Nelson Mandela as president; Pakistan terminated its Commonwealth membership in 1972, in protest at the Commonwealth's recognition of Bangladesh; Nigeria was suspended from the Commonwealth following its execution of Ken Saro-Wiwa, an environmental activist and critic of the Nigerian government.
Encouraging peace and democracy: The Commonwealth requires its members to be functioning democracies that respect human rights and the rule of law. The Commonwealth can intervene diplomatically if a country turns to undemocratic methods. It can also suspend membership of a country that refuses to cooperate with the Commonwealth on issues of human rights, democracy, etc. It cannot, however, intervene militarily in another country.
The Commonwealth Parliamentary Association facilitates cooperation between legislatures across the Commonwealth, and the Commonwealth Local Government Forum promotes good governance amongst local government officials.

2b **EXTRA** 3 The Commonwealth can be best described as an alternative United Nations because its goals, too, are international security, economic development, social progress, respecting human rights and world peace. In contrast to the UN, the Commonwealth is rather a community or free association than an international organization.
(1 'the British Empire in another form' would imply the member countries are under British rule, which isn't the case.
2 'a community of English-speaking countries' is not accurate as in many countries, people don't speak English. In some countries, English is not even the official language, e.g. Mozambique: Portuguese; Brunei: Malay; Rwanda: French).

CONTEXT TASK Individual answers.

SB S. 154 CD 2.17–18
Transkript s. TM-DVD-ROM

Communicating across Cultures – Negotiation and Compromise

Didaktischer Kommentar

S schulen ihre sprachliche und interkulturelle Handlungsfähigkeit, indem sie in Gesprächssituationen, in denen es auf Verhandlungsgeschick und Kompromissbereitschaft ankommt, adäquat sprachmittelnd tätig werden.

Unterrichtipps

1 Beim Hören konzentrieren sich S auf die Frau bzw. den Mann und tragen ihre Beobachtungen in Partnerarbeit zusammen.

2a S denken sich weitere Situationen aus oder berichten von Situationen, die sie selbst erlebt haben, in denen Kompromisse ihnen dazu verholfen haben, ihre Meinung durchzusetzen. Dies erfolgt mündlich oder schriftlich unter Einsatz der Verben in **2a**.

Communicating across Cultures – Negotiation and Compromise

Lösungshinweise

1 The woman makes a number of concrete suggestions: collecting more money, putting in money and paying themselves back the following month, buying a cheaper brand of coffee and telling people to buy their own milk and sugar. She also tries to defuse the situation with a bit of humour (cf. her imitation of their colleague 'Herr Wittmann'). The man, on the other hand, is quite negative at first. Instead of coming up with an idea to solve the problem, he blames the woman for it and even points at her. He also interrupts her at one point, rejecting one of her ideas even before she is able to finish. Only at the end does he make a suggestion, i.e. that he could ask his mother to suggest a good, cheaper brand of coffee.

2a
1. The man <u>claims that</u> electronic items are too expensive and that they cost 10 to 15% less at the electronics shop.
2. The cyclist <u>offers to</u> contribute towards the costs, but only under certain circumstances.
3. The guest <u>admits that</u> he broke the mirror, but claims that it hadn't been hung up properly.
4. The man <u>regrets</u> having said what he said and says he's sorry.
5. The woman <u>suggests that</u> she (should) fetch the rolls and make breakfast every other day so that her roommate can sleep in. In return she asks him to let her use his bike on those days.
6. The roommate <u>agrees to</u> her terms.

2b **Mediation** Individual answers; cf. transcript on TM-DVD-ROM for suggested answers (in brackets).

3a 1. Somebody states what they want. 2. The other side says what they want. 3. Arguments are traded back and forth. 4. Suggestions are made for possible compromises. 5. One side or the other agrees to accept a compromise solution. 6. Somebody sums up what has been agreed.

3b
1. *Somebody states what they want*: I'd like to outline our objectives. / There are two main areas we'd like to discuss.
2. *The other side says what they want*: I'd like to outline our objectives. / There are two main areas we'd like to discuss. / I'm afraid we can't accept that. We …
3. *Arguments are traded back and forth*: Try to see things from our point of view. / That won't work for us. We'd like… / I'm afraid we can't accept that. We …
4. *Suggestions are made for possible compromises*: Perhaps we can find some middle ground here. / If you could see your way to accepting this, we would be willing to… / We'd be prepared to … provided that you …
5. *One side or the other agrees to accept a compromise solution*: That sounds reasonable. / I don't have any problems with that.
   Somebody sums up what has been agreed: Let's look at what we've agreed so far. / So, if I see things correctly, we…

4a **Role-play** Individual answers.

4b *More arguments for a minimum wage*: would lead to more equality in the world; would provide objective standards of fairness in employment
More arguments against a minimum wage: would be impossible to monitor; might provide first-world employers with an excuse to lower wages; would result in higher prices in the developing world, meaning that people without jobs could no longer afford basic services

4c Individual answers.

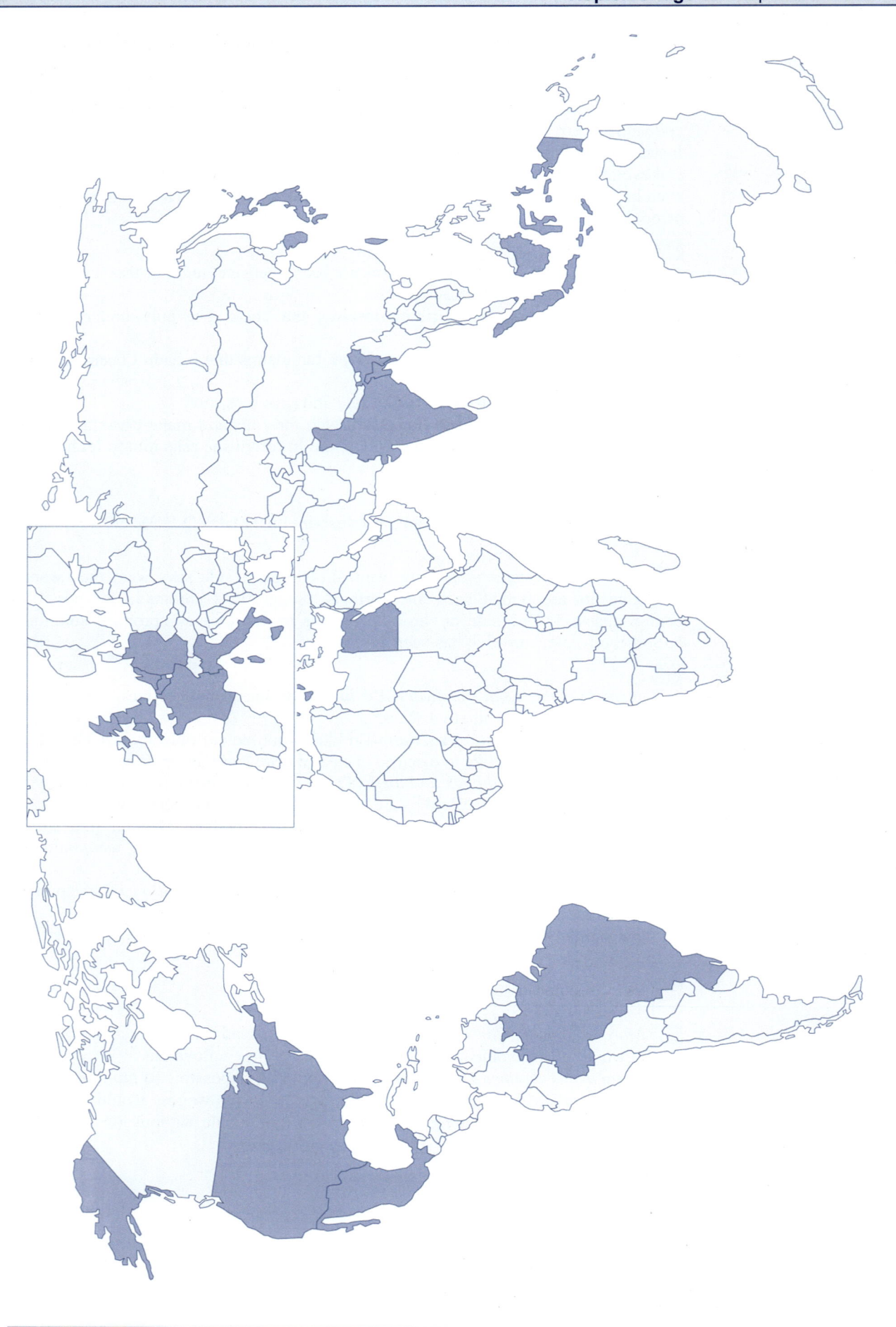

7

Kopiervorlage 16: Map of the World

Context 21 | Global Perspectives
▶ Lead-in

Kopiervorlage 17: Outsourcing

1 The following sentences are taken from the film extract you just saw. Put them in the right order.

a Offshore the whole department.
b Half our catalogue is patriotic knick-knacks.
c Twenty heads for the price of one
d Most of the products they're buying are made in China.
e Of course, you're free to quit.
f We're going up to the roof.
g For me, instant gratification isn't soon enough.
h This is some kind of weird psychological test you're pulling on me here.
i It's eight heads for the price of one.
j If anyone asks how the weather is, just say 'windy'.
k Basically, you people need to learn about America.
l Can you take me to the train station?
m Water is coming from everywhere.
n English is the official language of our government.

2 Put the sentences back into the context of the film: who says them and in what situation? Explain their meaning.

a _____
b _____
c _____
d _____
e _____
f _____
g _____
h _____
i _____
j _____
k _____
l _____
m _____
n _____

Context 21 | Global Perspectives
▶ Part A3

Read the following article by Paul Collier, Professor of Economics at the University of Oxford, and mark important passages.

The world price of staple foods has rocketed, almost doubling in the past 18 months. For consumers in the rich world this massive increase in the price of wheat or rice is an inconvenience; for consumers in
5 the poorest countries it is a catastrophe.

Food accounts for around half of the entire budget of most Africans. Of course some poor households sell food, but many are net buyers. Indeed, decades of agricultural stagnation and growing populations
10 have turned many African countries into food importers. The households that are poor and net purchasers of food are concentrated in the urban slums. These slums are already political powder kegs: rising food prices have triggered riots from
15 Ivory Coast to Indonesia, from Burkina Faso to Bangladesh. Indeed they sow the seeds of an ugly and destructive populist politics.

Why have food prices rocketed? Paradoxically, this squeeze on the poorest has come about as a
20 result of the success of globalisation in reducing world poverty. As China develops, helped by its massive exports to our markets, millions of Chinese households have started to eat better. Better means not just more food but more meat, the new luxury.
25 But to produce 1kg of meat takes 6kg of grain. Livestock reared for meat to be consumed in Asia are now eating the grain that would previously have been eaten by the African poor. So what is the remedy?

30 The best solution to a problem is often not to reverse what caused the problem. If you broke your leg by falling off a cliff, it is not a good idea to climb back up. The best solution to the rise in food prices is not to arrest globalisation. China's long
35 march to prosperity is something to celebrate. The remedy to high food prices is to increase supply. The most realistic way is to replicate the Brazilian model of large, technologically sophisticated agro-companies that supply the world market. There are
40 still many areas of the world – including large swaths of Africa – that have good land that could be used far more productively if it were properly managed by large companies. To contain the rise in food prices we need more globalisation, not less.

45 Unfortunately, large-scale commercial agriculture is deeply, perhaps irredeemably, unromantic. We laud the production style of the peasant: environmentally sustainable and human in scale. In respect of manufacturing we grew out of this
50 fantasy years ago, but in agriculture it continues to contaminate our policies. In Europe and Japan huge public resources have been devoted to propping up small farms. The best that can be said for these policies is that we can afford them.

In Africa, which cannot afford such policies, the 55 World Bank and the Department for International Development have orientated their entire efforts on agricultural development to peasant-style production. Africa has less large-scale commercial agriculture than it had 60 years ago. Unfortunately, 60 peasant farming is not well suited to innovation and investment. The result has been that African agriculture has fallen farther and farther behind.

Our longstanding agricultural romanticism has been compounded by our newfound environmental 65 romanticism. In the United States fear of climate change has been manipulated by shrewd interests to produce grotesquely inefficient subsidies to biofuel. Around a third of American grain production has rapidly been diverted into energy production. This 70 demonstrates both the superb responsiveness of the markets to price signals, and the shameful power of subsidy-hunting lobby groups. However, just as livestock are eating the food that would have been consumed by poor Africans, so Americans are 75 running their SUVs on it. One SUV tank of biofuel uses enough grain to feed an African family for a year.

In Europe deep-seated fears of science have been manipulated into a ban on both the production and 80 import of genetically modified crops. This has obviously retarded productivity growth in European agriculture. Again the best that can be said of it is that we are rich enough to afford such folly. But as an unintended side-effect it has terrified African 85 governments into banning GM lest their farmers be shut out of European markets. Africa definitely cannot afford this self-denial. It needs all the help it can possibly get from GM drought-resistant crops.

While the policies needed for the long term have 90 been befuddled by romanticism, the short-term global response has been pure beggar-thy-neighbour. It is easier for urban slum dwellers to riot than for farmers: riots need streets, not fields. And so, in the internal tussles between poor consumers 95 and poor producers, the interests of consumers have prevailed in the developing countries.

Governments in grain-exporting countries, such as Argentina, have swung prices in favour of their consumers and against their farmers by banning or 100 restricting exports. But such tariffs and export bans make investing in commercial-scale food production

Kopiervorlage 18: More Globalization?

less attractive, drive up prices further still in the food-importing countries, and discourage farmers from increasing their yields, exacerbating global food shortages.

Unfortunately, trade in agricultural produce has been the main economic activity to have resisted the force of globalisation. The cost of this is now being picked up by the poorest people in the world.

From: Paul Collier, 'Food Shortages: Think Big', *The Times*, 15 April 2008

1 **staple** basic
4 **inconvenience** annoyance
8/11 **net buyer/purchaser** sb. who buys more than they sell
13 **powder keg** Pulverfass
37 **replicate sth.** make an exact copy of sth.
38 **sophisticated,** *here* well developed
41 **swath** [swɒθ ☆ swɑːθ] *here* area, region
46 **irredeemably** unchangeably
65 **compounded** made stronger
68 **subsidy** Subvention
73 **lobby group** Interessenverband; Lobby
81 **genetically modified** gentechnisch verändert
84 **folly** stupidity
86 **lest** in case
91 **befuddled** confused
95 **tussle** conflict
110 **pick up** *here* pay

1a Summarize the text, explaining briefly the problem poor Africans face and the writer's suggestion as to how to overcome it.

b In small groups, discuss arguments for and against Collier's suggestion. Give reasons from the text and add your own ideas.

c What do you think? State your own opinion of Collier's proposal for overcoming the global food shortage.

2 Choose either **a** or **b**:

a Discuss whether the claims made in the article about 'agricultural' and 'environmental romanticism' in the Western world are true for Germany. Write a comment.

b Write an essay about the benefits of globalization. Include your own thoughts as well as potential counter-arguments to your points.

Context 21 Global Perspectives: Topic Vocabulary

Word/Phrase	Memory Aid	German
TRADE AND FINANCE		
currency	*collocations with* **currency**: single/foreign ~	Währung
economy	*word family:* (to) economize – <u>economy</u> – economist – economic	Wirtschaft
exchange rate	*definition:* the rate at which one currency can be converted into another	Wechselkurs
free trade	*definition:* trade between countries where there are no restrictions in place	Freihandel
international trade	*other collocations with* **trade**: ethical/fair/slave ~	internationaler Handel
trade barriers	*other collocation with* **trade**: ~ agreement	Handelsschranke
LIVING IN A GLOBALIZED WORLD		
(to) outsource	*synonyms:* (to) subcontract	outsourcen, auslagern
consumer	*word family:* (to) consume – consumption – <u>consumer</u>	Konsument/in, Verbraucher/in
debt relief [det]	*definition:* the practice of letting poorer nations not pay back the money they owe to richer countries	Schuldenerlass
developed country	*opposite:* developing country	Industrieland
emerging market	*definition:* country which is undergoing a process of rapid industrial growth	Schwellenland
exploitation	*word family:* (to) exploit sth./sb. – <u>exploitation</u> – exploiter	Ausbeutung
living standard	*other collocation with* **living**: ~ conditions	Lebensstandard
merger	*example sentence:* The ~ between the two companies last year was a success – they're making a profit now!	Firmenzusammenschluss, Fusion
multinational	*example sentence:* The ~ has branches all over the world, but its headquarters are in Paris.	multinationaler Konzern
poverty	*opposite:* wealth	Armut
sweatshop	*example sentence:* Mira worked in a **~shop** in Delhi making clothes for international fashion labels.	Ausbeuterbetrieb

8 The World of Work and Business

Das Kapitel beleuchtet aktuelle Entwicklungen in Wirtschaft und Arbeitswelt und bietet S ein handlungsorientiertes Training wichtiger Fertigkeiten für ihre Zukunft in der Arbeitswelt.

Part A – The Economy in a Changing World wirft ein Schlaglicht auf aktuelle wirtschaftliche Entwicklungen und deren Auswirkungen auf das Berufsleben. Ein besonderer Schwerpunkt liegt auf den Folgen der Finanzkrise und einer kritischen Auseinandersetzung mit den Stärken und Schwächen des Kapitalismus.

Part B – School's Out – What Now? führt die zum Erwerb eines Arbeitsplatzes im englischsprachigen Ausland erforderlichen Bewerbungsschritte auf und vermittelt S die für ein Bewerbungsverfahren notwendigen Fertigkeiten.

Part C – Coping in the Workplace vermittelt Fertigkeiten, die S im Rahmen einer beruflichen Tätigkeit im Bereich Wirtschaft und Geschäftswesen im englischsprachigen Ausland benötigen.

Didaktisches Inhaltsverzeichnis

SB p.	Title	TM p.	Text Form	Topic	Skills and Activities	Language Practice
156	Lead-in CD 3.04	206	Film poster; interview; magazine cover	Capitalism, the financial crisis and the future of work	Working with pictures; listening for gist/detail	LP 2: Prepositions; LP 20: Avoiding German-English interference
158	Words in Context – Present Trends in the Business World	208	Informative text	The world of work today and in the future	Translating	
	Part A – The Economy in a Changing World					
160	A1 Starting a Business Alexander McCall Smith	209	Novel (extract)	Risks and worries when starting a business	Assessing a business plan; writing an advertisement	
162	A2 EXTRA The End of the Western Economic Era? Helena Merriman	210	Web article (extract)	The global economy and its future following the financial crisis	Working with quotes; writing a summary	
165	A3 Towards a Greener Economy? Thomas L. Friedman	212	Newspaper article (extract)	The economy and the environment	Analysing a cartoon; analysing a text for stylistic devices; doing research	
167	A4 Capitalism Bill Watterson	213	Cartoon	How capitalism should not work	Working with cartoons	Finding words in a word field
168	A5 Now is the Time for a Less Selfish Capitalism Richard Layard	214	Newspaper article (extract)	The need for a more humane capitalism	Writing a letter to the editor	LP 26: Connecting your thoughts: linking words
	Part B – School's Out – What Now?					
170	B1 What Do I Want to Do?	216	Mind map	Thinking about your future	Mind mapping	
170	B2 Soft Skills Kate Lorenz	216	Web article (extract)	The importance of soft skills	Working with pictures	
172	B3 Getting the Job You Want	217	Job adverts	Job adverts	Understanding and analysing job adverts	
173	B4 A Covering Letter	218	Letter	A covering letter	Analysing a covering letter; writing a covering letter	
175	B5 A Job Interview DVD	219	Video clip	What makes a good job interview	Listening for gist/detail; analysing job interviews; conducting a job interview	
	Part C – Coping in the Workplace					
177	C1 A Business Call	221	Speech bubbles	Making a business call	Mediating; making business calls	
178	C2 A Business Letter	222	Formal letter	Business correspondence	Analysing a business letter	
179	C3 A Written Complaint	222	Fact File	A letter of complaint	Writing a letter of complaint; replying to a letter of complaint	
181	Communicating across Cultures DVD	223	Feature film (extract)	Intercultural communication	Analysing a film; doing a role-play	

8 Lead-in

SB S. 156 CD 3.04
Transkript s. TM-DVD-ROM

Lead-in

Source:	'Michael Moore vs. Capitalism', The Situation Room, CNN, 24 September 2009
Topic:	'Undemocratic' capitalism in the USA?
Text form:	Interview (extract)
Language variety:	American English
Length:	6:10 min
Level:	Intermediate
Skills/Activities:	Working with pictures; listening for gist/detail

Didaktischer Kommentar

S nähern sich dem Themenkomplex „The World of Work and Business" durch die Analyse eines Interviews zum Thema Kapitalismus und bewerten kritisch die im Interview dargestellte Sichtweise des aktuellen Kapitalismus. Anhand einer Bildanalyse beschäftigen sich S mit möglichen Zukunftsszenarien der Arbeitswelt.

SB-DVD-ROM

Lernwortschatz

accusation (task 2a), remedy (task 2a), hypocrite (task 2a)

Unterrichtstipps
⚠ HA ● Word help

Vor dem Hören des Interviews machen sich S mit unbekanntem Wortschatz vertraut.

2a Um sich zunächst auf das Globalverstehen zu konzentrieren (*listening for gist*), machen sich S beim erstmaligen Hören keine Notizen. Sie lesen sich dann Aufgaben 1–3 durch und machen sich beim zweiten Durchgang zielgerichtet Notizen (*listening for detail*).

👥 👥👥 ALT

3 Alternativ zur *silent conversation* bietet sich folgende Aufgabenstellung zum Thema „the future of work" an:
Think: *Find*
- *five jobs that don't exist yet but will 15 years from now;*
- *five jobs that won't exist anymore in 15 years;*
- *five jobs that will probably always exist.*

Pair: *Compare your list with a partner and compile one list together.*
Share: *Present your result to the class.*

⚠ HA

2b S informieren sich vorab über *Michael Moore's Action Plan: 15 Things Every American Can Do Right Now:* www.michaelmoore.com/words/mikes-letter/michael-moores-action-plan-15-things-every-american-can-do-right-now.

Differenzierung

1 Zur Hilfestellung können folgende Fragen gestellt werden:
1 *Comment on Michael Moore's facial expression.*
2 *Speculate what the demonstration in the background could be for/against.*
3 *Who could the man in the suit stand for?*
4 *What is he hiding behind his back?*
5 *Why is he waving the American flag and why is the flag so tiny?*
6 *What do you know about the causes and effects of the financial crisis of 2009?*
   (s. Fact File **A2**)

Lösungshinweise: s. unter Lösungshinweise, Aufgabe **1**.

ZA

1 Interessierte S arbeiten kreativ: *Speculate what is written on the demonstration posters and create such a poster.*

Lead-in – The World of Work and Business

> **Info**
>
> *Michael Moore* (born 1954) is an American filmmaker, author and liberal political commentator. He is the director and producer of the documentaries *Bowling for Columbine* (2002), *Fahrenheit 9/11* (2004) and *Sicko* (2007). Moore is a selfdescribed liberal who has criticized globalization, large corporations, assault weapon ownership, the Iraq War, US President George Bush and the American health care system in his books and films.
>
> *Capitalism: A Love Story* (2009; director/screenplay: Michael Moore) deals with the issues of modern capitalism and the disastrous impact of corporate dominance on the everyday lives of Americans.

Lösungshinweise

1 In the foreground of the poster is a man seen from behind. He is holding a bag of money behind his back and waving an American flag in his right hand. As he is wearing a business suit, he could be a business or banking Chief Executive Officer (CEO). His waving the flag makes him out to be a patriotic American, but his hiding money (his profits) suggests he is hypocritical. The size of the flag is an ironic statement on his real interests – those behind his back. In the background, we can see the silhouettes of a crowd of people demonstrating and waving placards against the effects of capitalism in general or perhaps against the financial crisis in particular. In the middle of the poster, director Michael Moore is standing arms crossed in front of his chest, looking at the CEO. Moore's sceptical look suggests that he knows that the man is a hypocrite.

Possible interpretation of the title: Capitalism is an economic system based on private ownership of capital. The story of capitalism may be called a 'love story' because theoretically everyone benefits from capitalism, with people becoming better off. America has always loved capitalism. The title may, however, be ironic; in reality, capitalism may lead to negative consequences; it could be seen as a love story without a happy ending.

Possible topics addressed in the film: the unpleasant sides of capitalism; the American love affair with capitalism

2a

1 *Capitalism* is a system of legalized greed; a system that guarantees that the richest 1% in America have more wealth than the bottom 95% combined; those 1% pretend that anyone who works hard can join them, but that is not the case.

2 *Accusations*: American capitalism is criminal; the American economy is based on undemocratic principles that favour the wealthy; the average American has no influence on making the changes happen he or she wants to happen; the economic system of the USA is based on the wealthy being in charge; dysfunctional health care system

Solutions and remedies: American capitalism must be replaced by democracy, an economic system run according to democratic principles that has a moral and ethical core to it; what is needed is democracy in the workplace; the economy must be controlled by the 95% of the people not in charge right now.

3 *Moore – a hypocrite?* Individual answers.

2b *Solutions*: Demand that the President and Congress immediately:
1. declare a moratorium on all home evictions.
2. expand Medicare for all Americans.
3. hold publicly-funded elections and prohibit elected officials from becoming lobbyists on leaving office.
4. ensure that each of the 50 states creates a state-owned public bank like they have in North Dakota.
5. save this fragile planet and declare that all the energy resources above and beneath the ground are owned collectively by everyone.

8
Words in Context

Make Congress and the President listen by:
1. getting into the daily habit of taking five minutes to make calls to the President, the individual's congressperson and one to each of his or her two senators.
2. taking over one's local Democratic Party.
3. recruiting someone to run for office who can win in your local elections.
4. holding vigils and marches at the local branch of a big bank that took the bailout money.
5. starting one's own media.

Things people should do to protect themselves until the economic mess is over:
1. Take money out of the bank if it took bailout money and place it in a locally-owned bank or, preferably, a credit union.
2. Get rid of all credit cards except those which one has to pay at the end of the month.
3. Not invest in the stock market.
4. Unionize their workplace so that workers have a say in how a business is run.
5. Take care of themselves and their family.

Effectiveness: Individual answers.

3 Individual answers.

4a The new workplace may be based less on your knowledge or university degree and more on what your competences and skills are. *Ten possible lessons:* 1 be flexible/mobile; 2 be creative; 3 be a team player; 4 show leadership qualities; 5 stay up-to-date on your computer skills; 6 maintain and improve your web literacy; 7 be able to deal with conflicts; 8 criticize constructively; 9 assess your progress continually; 10 gain international experience / improve your language skills

4bc Individual answers.

SB S. 158
▶ LSET ex. 1

Words in Context – Present Trends in the Business World

Didaktischer Kommentar

Der Text stellt die wichtigsten gegenwärtigen und zukünftigen Entwicklungen und Trends der Weltwirtschaft vor und erläutert deren Auswirkungen auf die Arbeitswelt der Zukunft, auf die sich S vorbereiten sollen.

SB-DVD-ROM

Lernwortschatz

emerging markets (l. 1), remain competitive (l. 4), raise the productivity of sth. (l. 4), invest in sth. (l. 6), reduce costs (l. 7), maximize profit (l. 7), multinational company (l. 7), relocate sth. (l. 7), manufacturing industry (l. 11), service sector (l. 12), part-time employment (l. 12), temporary employment (l. 12), low-skilled (l. 13), low-paid (l. 13), workforce (l. 14), highly skilled worker (l. 15), promote sb. (to sth.) (l. 19), job security (l. 19), hire and fire (l. 20), nine-to-five job (l. 21), flexi-time job (l. 22), employee (l. 23), in-service training (l. 23), meet the demands and challenges (l. 24), do business (l. 42), workplace (l. 43), work remotely (l. 44), office cubicle (l. 46), home office (l. 46)

Unterrichtstipps ⚠

S bereiten sich zusätzlich vor, indem sie Themenwortschatz anhand des *Topic Vocabulary* (s. S. 226) erarbeiten.

1–3 Um die Vokabelarbeit abwechslungsreich zu gestalten und gleichzeitig allen S die Zeit einzuräumen, die sie individuell benötigen, bietet sich die Methode des Lerntempoduetts an (s. S. 298).

Info

Emerging markets are nations with social or business activity in the process of rapid growth and industrialization. China and India are the most important emerging markets.

Part A

> *BRIC* is an acronym for the fast-growing developing economies of four large nations – Brazil, Russia, India and China. Leading economists predict that the BRIC-states as a group will overtake the G7 in 2032 and that China and India will soon be the dominant global suppliers of manufactured goods and services while Brazil and Russia will become similarly dominant as suppliers of raw materials.

Lösungshinweise

1 1 *from*; 2 *in*; 3 *to*; 4 *for*; 5 *to*; 6 *in*

2a apply for a job → have an interview for a job → land a job / hire sb. → be/get promoted → resign from a job / fire sb.

2b Individual answers.

3

1 In order to remain competitive in an increasingly globalized world, it is important for companies to invest in their employees/workforce, e.g. through in-service training.
2 In many companies in the USA, employees have no fixed workplace in their office building: they collect their things and seek out a cubicle or desk that is unoccupied. As long as they can access the necessary corporate information, it does not matter where they work.
3 Traditionally, employees would work their way up the corporate/career ladder, being promoted several times in their working life.
4 The outsourcing of jobs and capital to emerging markets in the Asian-Pacific region means that the USA is no longer the only economic superpower.
5 The service sector has absorbed many workers from the manufacturing industries, but the jobs it offers are often badly paid.

▶ LSET Skills 18, 19

Part A – The Economy in a Changing World

SB S. 160
▶ LSET ex. 4

A1 Starting a Business Alexander McCall Smith

Source:	*The No. 1 Ladies' Detective Agency*, 1999
Topic:	Risks and worries when starting a business
Text form:	Novel (extract)
Language variety:	British/Botswanan English
Number of words:	985
Level:	Basic
Skills/Activities:	Assessing a business plan; writing an advertisement

Didaktischer Kommentar

Mithilfe eines literarischen Textes eröffnet sich S zum einen ein persönlicher Zugang zum Thema Frauen in der Geschäftswelt, zum anderen ermöglicht der Text einen Perspektivenwechsel im Sinne der Interkulturalität.

SB-DVD-ROM

Lernwortschatz

run out of sth. (l. 5), stock (l. 5), blank (l. 15), start from scratch (l. 18), wince (l. 19), zip (l. 24), stroke sb./sth. (l. 32), plaster (l. 42), proprietor (l. 47), sincere (l. 59), drawer (l. 73), peer (l. 73)

Unterrichtstipps

Einstieg: Als kreative Antizipation der Geschichte schreiben S einzeln oder zu zweit eine Kurzgeschichte unter Berücksichtigung des Titels „Starting a Business". Dabei lassen sie sich vom Foto inspirieren. Anschließend werden die Geschichten in Form einer Lesekonferenz (s. S. 298) korrigiert, bevor sie in einem *gallery walk* (s. S. 298) ausgestellt werden.

1 Vorab wird geklärt, was einen *business plan* ausmacht (s. Info).

8 | Part A2 – The End of the Western Economic Era?

ZA **2b** Zur Auseinandersetzung mit dem Text notieren kreative S die Gedanken des Anwalts, der Mma Ramotswe zu Anfang der Geschichte berät: *Note down what the lawyer thinks of Mma Ramotswe's enterprise*. Dies kann in Form eines Tagebucheintrags oder eines Rollenspiels geschehen, in dem der Anwalt sich mit einem Freund über seine Begegnung mit Mma Ramotswe unterhält.

> **Info**
>
> *The No. 1 Ladies' Detective Agency* (1998–2010) is a series of eleven novels by British author Alexander McCall Smith (born 1948). The agency, founded by Mma Precious Ramotswe, is located in Gaborone, capital of Botswana. The episodic novels are as much about the adventures and foibles of different characters as they are about solving mysteries. Each book in the series follows on from the previous book. They have been adapted for radio and television.
>
> *A business plan* is a formal statement of a set of business goals, the reasons why they are believed attainable, and the plan for reaching those goals. It may also contain background information about the organization or team attempting to reach those goals.

Lösungshinweise

1 *Mma Ramotswe's business plan; business goal*: set up a ladies' detective agency called 'The No 1. Ladies' Detective Agency'
Attainability: women see more than men so it is likely that a ladies' detective agency will be successful; with her business near Kgale Hill, chosen for advertisement reasons (as a lot of people pass it), a typewriter and a qualified secretary, Mma Ramotswe feels prepared

2a Individual answers.

2b The lawyer questions whether women can be detectives (ll. 21–22); Mma Makutsi has chosen a typically female career (secretary) and expects to be told what to do (l. 62).

3 Individual answers.

SB S. 162
▶ LSET ex. 5, 6

A2 EXTRA **The End of the Western Economic Era?**   Helena Merriman

Source:	Website of the BBC, 24 September 2009
Topic:	The global economy and its future following the financial crisis
Text form:	Web article (extract)
Language variety:	British English
Number of words:	1039
Level:	Advanced
Skills/Activities:	Working with quotes; writing a summary

Didaktischer Kommentar

Anhand des Artikels über die Folgen der Finanzkrise und deren Auswirkungen auf die Weltwirtschaft verbessern S ihre Fertigkeiten im Umgang mit Zitaten und schulen damit auch ihre analytische Lesekompetenz. Die Gegenüberstellung und Bewertung der im Text präsentierten Aussagen zu Schlüsselfragen bieten eine gute Möglichkeit zur Schulung des *academic writing*.

SB-DVD-ROM

> **Lernwortschatz**
>
> implication (introductory text), rescue (l. 2), seize sth. (l. 8), witness sth. (l. 11), at the brink of sth. (l. 18), profound (l. 41), dawn (l. 53), argue (l. 57), shift (l. 63)
> *Fact File*: interest rate (l. 3), mortgage (l. 4), loan (l. 6)

Part A2 – The End of the Western Economic Era?

Unterrichtstipps Der Einstieg in die Thematik kann über ein Brainstorming zur Finanzkrise, deren Ursachen und Auswirkungen erfolgen.

1a–d Die Unterschiedlichkeit der im Text vorgestellten Positionen wird herausgearbeitet, indem einzelne S die Positionen der jeweiligen Autoren vertreten, der Klasse vortragen und anschließend einem Feld (*agree, undecided, disagree*) zuweisen, das vorher markiert wurde (z. B. verschiedene Ecken des Zimmers).

Differenzierung

1a–d S, die mit Aufgaben **1a–d** allein überfordert sind, arbeiten in Dreiergruppen: Jedes Gruppenmitglied fasst zunächst die Position eines Autors in Stillarbeit zusammen. Anschließend erstellt jede Gruppe eine Zusammenfassung des gesamten Textes.

Lösungshinweise

1ab

F. Zakaria	W.R. Mead	N. Ferguson
Question: Are we at the brink of a new financial order?		
Yes, the West will no longer dominate the world's economy. It will continue to play an important role, but there will be a shift of power towards the East (ll. 21–30).	No, crises are the rule rather than the exception. They always have and always will trigger innovations and reforms that will make the Western model even more successful (ll. 32–39).	Yes; the Western Model needs to be revised and may even be replaced by the Chinese model (ll. 40–45).
Question: Will the new economy be based on China's communist model of government?		
No; while power will shift to the non-Western countries, the new economy will be based on a Western model. He cites the example of the BRIC states to show that these economies are run very efficiently in a capitalist system (ll. 66–69).	No. The USA will remain a global power and like a 'global broker' for decades (ll. 70–73).	No. Since Chinese banks run on an increasingly Western model, their success does not prove the success of the communist model. Eastern economies (especially China) have just proven that they can control western financial institutions more efficiently than the West (ll. 57–65).

1c *F. Zakaria* thinks that while Eastern countries are gaining more power the model of economics will remain a Western one. He sees this as a new financial order because it is the first time that Eastern powers have had such a strong influence on the world's economy. He doesn't think that the economic crisis is the end of the Western era because he thinks capitalism, and not communism, is becoming stronger in the East.

W.R. Mead doesn't think the economic crisis has brought about a new financial order. He says that crises are a normal part of Western economics and that they bring about positive and innovative change. He thinks that the US will, at least for the next few decades, continue to be the world's biggest power and will act as a role model for growing countries.

N. Ferguson questions the viability of the Wall Street model and says that it needs to be revised, suggesting it could be replaced by the communist Chinese model. However he does not think that will be the case because although China is a very strong economic power, its economy has become westernized.

1d All three experts agree entirely that while global power is moving from West to East, the form of economics will remain a Western one. Mead goes along with Zakaria's assumption that the West will stay important, saying that crises lead to innovation which is what makes the Western economic model successful. Ferguson challenges the idea that the Western model will remain strong, saying that it has many faults and that a new model could soon replace it. According to Ferguson, China's economics run on an increasingly Western model. Zakaria agrees with Ferguson and underlines the BRIC states' success with capitalism.

2 Individual answers.

8 Part A3 – Towards a Greener Economy

SB S. 165 **A3 Towards a Greener Economy?** Thomas L. Friedman

Source:	*The New York Times*, 8 March 2009
Topic:	The economy and the environment
Text form:	Newspaper article (extract)
Language variety:	American English
Number of words:	533
Level:	Intermediate
Skills/Activities:	Analysing a cartoon; analysing a text for stylistic devices; doing research

Didaktischer Kommentar

Dieser Abschnitt thematisiert die enge wirtschaftliche Verflechtung zwischen China und Amerika („Chimerica"), kritisiert die moderne Wegwerfgesellschaft und das zugrunde liegende Wirtschaftsmodell und fordert vor dem Hintergrund von Finanzkrise und globaler Erwärmung eine Kurskorrektur hin zu einem nachhaltigeren Handeln aller beteiligten Akteure.

SB-DVD-ROM

Lernwortschatz

depict sb./sth. (pre-reading), addiction (l. 5), manufacture sth. (l. 8), household item (l. 8), contemptible, (l. 16), boundary, (l. 17), recession, (l. 19), physicist (l. 31), disruption (l. 43), momentous (l. 48)

Unterrichtstipps

Der Einstieg in das Thema *green economy* kann anhand kurzer Videoclips und Podcasts erfolgen, die von der Website der Vereinten Nationen heruntergeladen werden können:
www.unep.org/greeneconomy/Multimedia/tabid/1372/language/en-US/Default.aspx

3 **Linktipp:** *http://news.bbc.co.uk/2/hi/in_depth/629/629/5086298.stm* bietet Informationen zum Wasserverbrauch sowie einen *water calculator*, mit dessen Hilfe der persönliche *water footprint* errechnet werden kann.

ZA **Linktipp:** *www.storyofstuff.org* Um eine kritische Reflexion des eigenen Konsumverhaltens anzuregen und die Notwendigkeit nachhaltigen Wirtschaftens zu verdeutlichen, kann der 20minütige interaktive Videoclip *The Story of Stuff* der ehemaligen Greenpeace-Mitarbeiterin Annie Leonard eingesetzt werden, der ein kritisches Schlaglicht auf die amerikanisch geprägte Konsumgesellschaft wirft. Die animierte Dokumentation beschreibt in sieben Teilen (einzeln anzusteuern) äußerst anschaulich den Lebenszyklus eines Produkts in der Wegwerfgesellschaft. S sehen in sieben Gruppen je einen Abschnitt (*extraction, production, distribution, consumption, disposal*) und stellen der Klasse den Inhalt vor.

Lösungshinweise

PRE-READING a While the 1960s were a period of time in which the two superpowers did not communicate (they are pouting), the 1970s saw the first signs of wary rapprochement (hands are extended, but not being shaken). In the 90s both countries found themselves gripped very tightly by their partner, with the USA somewhat surprised by the strength of China's grip. Today the two countries form an inseparable bond: their economies are dependent on each other.

PRE-READING b Individual answers.

1a *Negative effects*: Our model is economically and ecologically unsustainable; we are a wasteful society driven by greed and the constant need to consume; we live at the expense of our children; we're depleting our resources and ruining our ecosphere.

1b The phrase means that once we are beyond the point of no return, our ecosystem will simply collapse and trigger an irreversible chain-reaction. In the financial crisis, the state helped banks with huge sums of money (bailout), but money alone will not repair any damage done to our environment.

Part A4 – Capitalism

1c For Thomas Friedman, the 2008 crisis marks the beginning of the end; it indicates the year in which everything began to fall apart.

2a *Stylistic device*: Repetition; the phrase 'more and more' occurs eleven times. The effect is to impress the reader with how large-scale the problems of the old-style economy are. It depends on continual growth and insists on quantity over quality.
Effect: Through the repetition the next sentence 'We can't do this anymore.' has a greater impact.

2b Other examples of repetition are the series of questions in ll. 18–19 and 49–50 (to the same effect: making what was said more forceful).

3 Individual answers.

SB S. 167

A4 Capitalism Bill Watterson

Source:	*The Complete Calvin and Hobbes*, Book Three, 2005
Topic:	How capitalism should not work
Text form:	Cartoon
Language variety:	American English
Number of words:	169
Level:	Intermediate
Skills/Activities:	Working with cartoons

Didaktischer Kommentar Durch die Analyse und Interpretation des Cartoons vertiefen S ihre Vorkenntnisse über kapitalistische Grundprinzipien. Sie erwerben die entsprechenden englischen Redemittel, um adäquat über komplexe Sachverhalte zu sprechen.

SB-DVD-ROM

Lernwortschatz

justify sth. (frame 2), supply and demand (frame 2), salary (frame 5), wage (frame 5), cut expenses (frame 7), charge sth. (frame 8), subsidize sb./sth. (frame 12)

Unterrichtstipps **2** Zum Thema Transferleistungen führen S einzeln (vorbereitend zuhause) oder in Kleingruppen (während des Unterrichts) eine Internetrecherche durch. Sie tragen Beispiele zusammen und diskutieren im Plenum über Sinn und Unsinn staatlicher Hilfen.

3 Diese Aufgabe zur Umwälzung und Vertiefung kann zuhause erledigt werden.

Differenzierung Vor allem leistungsschwächere S bereiten sich auf das Thema vor, indem sie sich das *Topic Vocabulary* erarbeiten (s. S. 226, speziell den Abschnitt „Business Matters"). Der Hintergrund von *caveat emptor* kann vorab geklärt werden (s. Info).

Kreative S erstellen eigene Comics zum Thema. Ggf. tun sie sich zu zweit zusammen, sodass künstlerisch begabte S die unterstützen, die nicht zeichnen möchten.

Info

Calvin and Hobbes is a comic strip written and illustrated by American cartoonist Bill Watterson (born 1958). It was syndicated from 1985 to 1995. It follows the antics of six-year-old Calvin and Hobbes, his stuffed tiger, who comes alive when Calvin is alone with him. The pair are named after John Calvin, a 16th century French Protestant reformer, and Thomas Hobbes, a 17th century English political philosopher. Reruns of the strip still appear in more than 50 countries.

8 Part A5 – Now is the Time for a Less Selfish Capitalism

> *Caveat emptor* (Latin, 'let the buyer beware') was first used legally in the USA in 1871. The phrase warns buyers that what they see is what they get. If the buyer finds any defects on the product or property after the purchase (unless actively concealed by the seller) they have no right to any sort of compensation. They should therefore examine the product carefully before they buy it. Today consumer rights are more protected and this rule has become less important. Goods tend to have a warranty and can often be exchanged even if they aren't faulty. The term is still used in property law where the buyer must carefully assess the quality of the property because once it is purchased they cannot seek compensation.

Lösungshinweise

1a *Words dealing with capitalism*: supply and demand, stockholder, enterprise, profit, investment, salary, wage, benefit, overhead cost, production cost, expenses, competition, caveat emptor, subsidy

1b For Calvin, 'demand' is the amount of money he wants to make either as a stockholder or a CEO or an employee (he uses it as a verb to express what he wants).
Susie's understanding of 'demand' is more in line with economic textbook theory. For her, demand is the number of people who are interested in purchasing a certain product or service.

1c In order to maximize his profit, Calvin tries to minimize his expenses, denies any responsibility for his products once they are sold; does not follow health and environmental regulations; asks his mum to subsidize him.

2a Quite obviously, Calvin's business plan is lacking substance. He isn't interested in the quality of his product and will probably not sell anything. So he turns to his mother for financial aid.

2b Subsidies are given to organisations or companies which do not make enough money so that they can afford to sell their product at a lower cost. A government or industry might choose to subsidise an organisation to raise consumer levels or to bring benefits such as social wellbeing. If Calvin was subsidised then he could sell better lemonade at a lower price and would then sell more of it.

3 According to Moore, capitalism has become 'a system of legalized greed'. It's no longer merely about goods being bought or sold. In the cartoon, we see that the purpose of Calvin's business isn't simply to sell lemonade – it's about maximizing profit for shareholders (frame 4), and paying high salaries to CEOs (frame 5). Creating a good product which people want to buy is not his aim (frame 7). Therefore, frame 4 portrays the moment where capitalism went wrong.

SB S. 168
▶ LSET ex. 7, 8, 9, 10

A5 Now is the Time for a Less Selfish Capitalism   Richard Layard

Source:	*Financial Times Online*, 11 March 2009
Topic:	The need for a more humane capitalism
Text form:	Newspaper article (extract)
Language variety:	British English
Number of words:	508
Level:	Intermediate
Skills/Activities:	Writing a letter to the editor

Didaktischer Kommentar

Der Text regt S zu einer kritischen Auseinandersetzung mit dem Kapitalismus im Hinblick auf den Fortschrittsgedanken, persönliches Glück und das Allgemeinwohl an. Diese inhaltliche Auseinandersetzung mit der Thematik bildet die Grundlage für einen Leserbrief und die Vorbereitung der Podiumsdiskussion, die beide der Schulung argumentativer Fertigkeiten dienen.

Part A5 – Now is the Time for a Less Selfish Capitalism

SB-DVD-ROM

Lernwortschatz

misery (l. 4), worship (n, l. 6), provided (that) (l. 9), accelerated (l. 13), sacrifice (l. 14), trustworthy (l. 20), rely on sb./sth. (l. 23), selfishness (l. 27), rivalry (l. 29), mutual respect (l. 30)

Unterrichtstipps

Die Karte zum subjektiven Wohlbefinden eignet sich als Einstieg in eine Debatte darüber, was unter diesem Begriff zu verstehen ist und worauf die Unterschiede zurückzuführen sind.

HA **4a** kann als Hausaufgabe erfolgen.

Differenzierung
ALT

1 Leistungsschwächere S bearbeiten statt **1a–c KV 19**. Lösungshinweise:

1 A, B, F

2 A, B, E, F, H

4b **EXTRA** Die Podiumsdiskussion kann in leistungsstärkeren Lerngruppen durchgeführt werden.

Info

Richard Baron Layard (born 1934) is a renowned British economist and a Labour life peer in the House of Lords. Layard has promoted the study of what has come to be known as 'happiness economics'. This branch of economic analysis argues that income is a bad approximation for happiness, and that other factors must be taken into account.

The Organisation for Economic Co-Operation and Development (OECD) is made up of 33 countries whose mission is to contribute to the development of the world economy by supporting sustainable economic growth, boosting employment and assisting growth in world trade and financial stability. It is one of the world's largest sources of economic and social data and is committed to democracy and the market economy. The OECD originated in 1947 as the Organisation for European Economic Cooperation (OEEC) which was founded to administer American and Canadian aid in Europe under the Marshall Plan after World War II. In 1961 the OEEC was replaced by the OECD. It has its headquarters in Paris.

Lösungshinweise

1a Progress entails the reduction of misery and the increase of personal happiness. In order to achieve progress in that sense, humanity needs to rethink its priorities. For the writer that means that we need to stop equating success with financial success and focus on the quality of personal relationships instead.

1b For the benefit of economic growth, society has sacrificed the quality of human relationships, which is the main source of personal happiness. The lack of trust can be felt everywhere, in the banking sector, the workplace, in family life and even in the playground.

1c People need to understand that the sole focus on private interest and competition is counterproductive. They need to realize that they can do better with less individualism and more team spirit, helping each other and working together, not against each other. The goal should be to humanize capitalism rather than abolish it.

2a At the beginning Layard's argument seems to support communism so this statement is important because it shows he still thinks our society should be based on capitalism. Although he talks about being less individualistic, we shouldn't go as far as communism because communist countries were inefficient and less happy and levels of trust under communism are even lower than in a democracy.

2b Individual answers.

3a *Used to connect two sentences*: so (continues the thought); in particular, most of all (refer back to ideas in the previous sentence); instead, but (offer a different perspective on what was said in the previous sentence)
Not used to connect two sentences: according to; increasingly (starts a new idea)

3b *according to*: in the view of; *so*: this is why; *in particular*: especially; *most of all*: above all; *increasingly*: more and more; *instead*: alternatively; *but*: however

4 Individual answers.

Part B – School's Out – What Now?

SB S. 170

B1 What Do I Want to Do?

Didaktischer Kommentar

Indem S ihre eigenen Schwächen und Stärken einschätzen und über die von ihnen gewünschte Zukunft reflektieren, werden sie sich darüber klar, welcher Beruf für sie geeignet ist und für welchen Beruf sie geeignet sind. Im Anschluss absolvieren S online einen authentischen *career test*, der ihnen bei der Planung ihrer beruflichen Zukunft helfen kann.

SB-DVD-ROM

Lernwortschatz

acquire sth. (introductory text), pursue a career (task 1)

Unterrichtstipps
ZA

PRE-READING S sammeln nützliche Wörter und Redewendungen in Part B, die sie später in ihrem Berufsleben, z. B. bei Bewerbungsgesprächen und für Anschreiben, verwenden können. Hierzu legen sie jeweils eine Mindmap zu den Themen *soft skills, job adverts, cover letters* und *job interviews* an und vervollständigen diese im Verlauf des Kapitels.

ZA

1b Als Ergänzung zum *career test* recherchieren S Berufe, auf die das Ergebnis ihres persönlichen *career test* passen könnte. Sie stellen diese Berufe in Form einer Kurzpräsentation vor und begründen hierbei auch, welchen dieser Berufe sie aus welchen Gründen ergreifen würden oder nicht.

Lösungshinweise

1ab Individual answers.

SB S. 170

B2 Soft Skills   Kate Lorenz

Source:	Website of AOL, 26 January 2009
Topic:	The importance of soft skills
Text form:	Web article (extract)
Language variety:	American English
Number of words:	194
Level:	Basic
Skills/Activities:	Working with pictures

Didaktischer Kommentar

S wird bewusst, welche Kompetenzen heutzutage neben rein inhaltlichen Kenntnissen in der Arbeitswelt wichtig sind. Sie erkennen, dass soziale Fähigkeiten (Soft Skills) neben den so genannten Hard Skills ein wichtiger Teil ihrer zukünftigen Karriere sind.

SB-DVD-ROM

Lernwortschatz

complement sth. (l. 2), cluster (l. 5), value sth. (l. 7), human resources (l. 11), pace (*n*, l. 12), adaptable (l. 12), work ethic (task 2)

Part B3 – Getting the Job You Want

Unterrichtstipps
ALT

1–2 Als Alternative zur Lektüre des Textes und zu den Aufgaben **1–2** kann eine freie Aufgabe gestellt werden (die alternativ aber auch nur die Aufgaben **2cd** ersetzen kann). S erarbeiten zu zweit eine persönliche Definition der Begriffe Hard und Soft Skills und erstellen anschließend eine Liste ihrer persönlichen *top ten* Soft Skills. Diese erklären sie vor der Klasse und visualisieren sie ggf. anhand geeigneter Fotos oder Abbildungen. Im Anschluss an die Präsentation können die wichtigsten Soft Skills gesammelt und an der Tafel festgehalten werden.

Lösungshinweise

1a Soft skills complement the so-called 'core competencies' and represent those social qualities, attitudes, habits and qualities that make someone a good employee and colleague.

1b Today's economy is fast-paced, service- and team-oriented, which is why companies are looking for people who are adaptable, flexible and socially gifted enough to perform well in this new job environment.

2a Individual answers (e.g.: They all improve the working conditions for employer and employees alike.).

2b *Top left*: F, possibly also C, E and H; *Top right*: I, J; *Bottom left*: E, possibly also F; *Bottom right*: B, C, G, possibly also H

2cd Individual answers.

SB S. 172
▶ LSET ex. 11, 12

B3 Getting the Job You Want

Didaktischer Kommentar

S identifizieren und klassifizieren die zentralen Informationen einer Stellenanzeige: Welcher Job wird angeboten? Wohin und an wen sollte man seine Bewerbung richten, welche Fertigkeiten und Kompetenzen sollten Bewerber/innen mitbringen?

SB-DVD-ROM

> **Lernwortschatz**
>
> promotion prospects (l. 9), be eager to do sth. (l. 10), preparatory (l. 13), tailored (l. 14), internship (l. 16), trainee (l. 16), applicant (task 1)

Unterrichtstipps

Einstieg: Vor der Auseinandersetzung mit der Stellenanzeige wird geklärt, wer Stellen ausschreibt und wo diese publiziert werden (z. B. von Tageszeitungen im Print- oder Onlinebereich oder den Unternehmen selbst).

ZA

1a–c Zur Übung suchen S in Kleingruppen ähnliche ihnen interessant erscheinende und für sie geeignete Stellenanzeigen im englischsprachigen Raum (*internships, volunteer jobs, summer jobs* usw.). Jede Gruppe erhält den Auftrag, sich auf drei Anzeigen zu einigen und diese anhand der Leitfragen zur im Buch abgedruckten Stellenanzeige zu analysieren.
Linktipp: *www.challengesworldwide.com*; *http://jobs.guardian.co.uk*; *www.volunteerabroad.com*

S mit Bewerbungsabsichten in Großbritannien oder den USA können diese (deutschen) Websites mit landesspezifischen Besonderheiten beim Bewerbungsverfahren weiterhelfen.
Großbritannien: *www.career-contact.de/laenderinfos/grossbritannien/bewerben_in_grossbritannien.php*; *www.england-jobs.de/arbeiten/bewerbungen.php*
USA: *www.career-contact.de/laenderinfos/usa/bewerben.php*

Lösungshinweise

1a
1. A full-time tour leader in US*Adventure's* new travelling programme in the USA and Canada; entry-level position with good promotion prospects
2. A 4-month internship for travel agent trainees in US*Adventure's* new San Francisco agency

8 Part B4 – A Covering Letter

1b *Tour leaders* should be responsible, adventurous, dynamic, flexible, innovative, cosmopolitan and multilingual and possess organizational as well as social skills.
Travel agent trainees should be fluent in English and one other foreign language, be service-oriented and communicative, well-organized and reliable. Advanced omputer skills are required.

1c Individual answers.

SB S. 173

B4 A Covering Letter

Didaktischer Kommentar

Der wichtigste Teil einer Bewerbung um einen Arbeitsplatz oder ein Praktikum ist das Bewerbungsschreiben. S lernen die verschiedenen Teile eines solchen *covering letter (BE)* bzw. *cover letter (AE)* kennen, analysieren den Aufbau, erwerben das notwendige Vokabular und erhalten nützliche Tipps. Als Transferaufgabe verfassen S selbständig ein Bewerbungsschreiben zu einem der beiden Jobs bei US*Adventure* (s. **B3**).

SB-DVD-ROM

Lernwortschatz

convince sb. (of sth.) (l. 3), concise (l. 7), envision sth. (l. 15), letter of reference (l. 18)

Unterrichtstipps

3 S wählen eine der Stellenanzeigen aus **B3** und verfassen einen formal und inhaltlich korrekten *covering letter*. Das Ergebnis wird der Klasse präsentiert, z. B. in einem *gallery walk* (s. S. 297). Ein Brief kann auf OH-Folie kopiert und exemplarisch besprochen werden.

Info

Application procedures in the UK/USA: When applying for a job, applicants normally provide a curriculum vitae (CV, *BE* / résumé, *AE*) and a covering letter *(BE)* / cover letter *(AE)*. Styles of CV can vary dramatically but as a rule should include the candidate's contact information, their educational history, any professional experience, and usually contact details for two referees. A referee is someone who can vouch for the candidate's character, i.e. a previous employer or someone who knows the candidate well but is not a friend or family member. Employers may then contact the referee so it is courteous to ask their permission first. Personal interests or extracurricular activities may also be included, but it is unusual to include a photo.

Lösungshinweise

1 Individual answers.

2a advert; position; apply for; pursuing; ideal; experience; currently; attended; communicative; benefit; skills; contribution; valuable; hesitate

2b Nadine is applying for a position as management intern with Broad Horizon's hotels. She is a student of Hotel, Food and Tourism at the University of East Sussex and would like to become a Broad Horizon intern due to the hotel chain's good track record and her interest in working in the hotel management sector later on.

2c Nadine has an A-level in French and has a working grasp of Spanish. She has experience abroad as an exchange student in the USA and as an au pair in Barcelona. She is creative and communicative and has good organizational skills.

2de Individual answers.

Part B5 – A Job Interview

2f

①   112 Church Street
    Brighton
    East Sussex BN1 1UD
    Tel. 08721 077 077
    nadine.monahan@resumepower.uk

② Mr James Crowley
   Human Resources Manager
   Broad Horizon Hotels
   55–57 New Mount St
   London WC1 5HT

③ 1 December 2009

④ Dear Mr Crowley
⑤ I saw your job … for the … of management intern in one of Broad Horizons' hotels and would like to … the position.
⑥ I have nearly completed my first year of studies in Hotel, Food and Tourism at the University of East Sussex and am very interested in … a career in hotel management.
   As Broad Horizons is an international company with a good track record in service, it would be an … company to give me the work … I am looking for.
⑦ As you can see from my CV, I have an A-Level in French and am … taking Spanish classes as part of my preparation for future employment, so that I will soon have a good working grasp of two foreign languages. I have also spent time abroad, first of all as part of a student exchange in Bloomington, Indiana, where I was given the opportunity of experiencing life in another country for the first time, and then as an au pair in Barcelona for thee months, where I also … a Spanish language course.
⑧ I am a very creative and … person and feel that my qualities would be a … to your company. My experience working for various university clubs is indicative of my organizational … .
⑨ I believe that I can make a positive … and be a … addition to your team.
⑩ If you feel I would be the right person to fill this position, please do not … to call me.

⑪ Yours sincerely

⑫ Nadine Monahan

⑬ Enclosure: CV, relevant certificates

1 address, phone number and email of the applicant
2 name and position of addressee, company name, address
3 date
4 salutation
5 purpose of the letter
6 reasons for applying to this particular company
7 information about one's experience
8 information about one's character and how this would benefit the company
9 closing sentence
10 contact request
11 (complimentary) close
12 signature
13 enclosure

3 Individual answers.

B5 A Job Interview

Source:	Mike Quinn
Topic:	What makes for a good job interview
Text form:	Video clip
Language variety:	American English
Length:	6:18 min
Level:	Intermediate
Skills/Activities:	Listening for gist/detail; analysing job interviews; conducting a job interview

Didaktischer Kommentar

Bei der Bewerbung um einen Arbeitsplatz ist nach dem erfolgreichen Anschreiben samt Lebenslauf meist das Bewerbungsgespräch entscheidend. Der Übungsapparat zum Thema *job interview* zielt darauf ab, S mit der Situation eines Bewerbungsgesprächs vertraut zu machen und ihnen Fertigkeiten zu vermitteln, mit denen sie ein Bewerbungsgespräch auf Englisch sprachlich und inhaltlich erfolgreich meistern können.

8 Part B5 – A Job Interview

SB-DVD-ROM

Lernwortschatz

master sth. (task 1), observation (task 3), anticipate sth. (task 4, applicant)

Unterrichtstipps
⚠ HA ● Word help

Vor dem Sehen des Videoclips machen sich S mit unbekanntem Wortschatz vertraut.

4a S nutzen die bereits analysierten und präsentierten Stellenanzeigen aus **B3** oder suchen neue englischsprachige Stellenanzeigen (s. a. **B3**, Unterrichtstipps). Sie einigen sich in Vierergruppen auf eine Stellenanzeige. Zwei S der Gruppe entwickeln als *interviewer* Fragen, die sie Bewerbern auf diese Stellenanzeige stellen würden und üben das entsprechende Auftreten des Interviewers ein. Die anderen zwei S überlegen als *applicant*, wie sie sich am Besten auf die ausgewiesene Stelle vorbereiten können: Sie antizipieren Fragen (*What strengths would you like to mention in the interview? What qualifications do you have? What do you know about the company and the job advertised?*) und bereiten mögliche Antworten vor.

Differenzierung

2a Leistungsstärkere S analysieren Miss Faulkners drei Fragen und schlussfolgern, welche Fähigkeiten und Eigenschaften diese beim Wunschkandidaten voraussetzen. Lösungshinweise: *Qualities the interviewer/company is looking for: ability to work in a team, commitment, dedication to the job, perseverance*

Info

Application procedures in the UK/USA: If a candidate's application is successful, they will be invited to move onto the next stage of the selection process. The selection process varies depending on the company and position:
Assessment centres are becoming a more and more common way to select candidates. Successful applicants will be invited to attend with other candidates and asked to complete various tasks to judge different skills such as teamwork or presenting information. This can last between a few hours and two days.
A panel interview is when the candidate is interviewed by a group of people, perhaps from different departments in the company. Candidates may be asked about their skills and experience and their strengths and weaknesses.
Psychometric tests are formal and usually timed tests used to measure skills such as logic or numerical skills or even to test the suitability of the candidate's personality for the position. It is always a good idea for the candidate to inquire about the format of the interview in advance so that they can prepare accordingly.

Lösungshinweise

1a–c Individual answers.

2a The applicants are applying for a call centre job (cf. transcript l. 13: '… my previous job I was working in *another* call centre').

2b *Interviewer's questions*: cf. transcript on the TM-DVD-ROM, ll. 25, 30, 42 (girl; 'The Bad!') and ll. 11, 21, 31 (boy; 'The Good!'; the questions are highlighted).

2c *Applicants' answers*: cf. transcript on the TM-DVD-ROM, ll. 27, 32, 45 (girl; 'The Bad!') and ll. 13, 23, 34 (boy; 'The Good!').
Differences between applicants: Applicant 1 has no qualifications whatsoever and does not really answer any of the questions she was asked.
Applicant 2 is qualified for the job and answers every question the interviewer asks.

3a *Preparation*: Applicant 1 wasn't prepared at all. She came late and forgot to turn off her mobile. She remembered to bring her CV, but kept it folded up in the back pocket of her jeans.
Applicant 2 was prepared, on time and had his CV ready in a folder.
Possible questions and answers: The girl's answers prove she didn't think about the interview at all before actually coming.

Part C

The boy seems to have anticipated possible questions and prepared answers.
Behaviour and body language: Applicant 1 shows her lack of interest in everything related to the job apart from the money. She is rude, answers her mobile, talks badly about Miss Faulkner's clothes, and even asks the first question. She chews gum, sits back in her chair, bobs up and down, plays around with her hair, hardly looks at the interviewer and refuses to shake hands.
Applicant 2 is punctual, shakes hands with the interviewer, only sits down when asked to, and expresses his interest in his body language too: he sits straight in his chair, legs firmly planted on the ground.
Content: Applicant 1 has nothing substantial to say except for her interest in herself ('Team? … Me, I'm number one').
Applicant 2 shares relevant information without praising himself.
Language: Applicant 1 is very colloquial ('yeah' instead of 'yes', 'application thing or whatever it is' instead of the correct term).
Applicant 2 is absolutely adequate. He uses one informal term ('stats' for 'statistics') and explains another abbreviation (AP), but is otherwise neither too formal nor too informal.
Dress code: Applicant 1 expresses her lack of interest in the job interview in the choice of her clothes, too: she seems to be wearing what she always wears.
Applicant 2 apparently took more care in choosing his clothes: he did without jeans and is well dressed without being overdressed.

3b *Adjectives*: With both applicants, the interviewer is equally *friendly* and *polite*, yet *professional* and *aloof*: Applicant 1: except for audibly clearing her throat when Melissa speaks badly about her, she is *composed* and *courteous*, going as far as to say '… it was a pleasure to meet you' at the end.
Applicant 2: The interviewer uses almost the exact same words towards Sweeney; she is a professional who doesn't let her feelings get the better of her.

3c *Adjectives and expressions for the applicants' attitude and behaviour:*
Tafelbild:

Applicant 1 (Melissa)	Applicant 2 (Sweeney)
unprepared, unqualified, vain and conceited, overconfident, overestimating her own abilities, impolite, ill-mannered, uninformed, inattentive, uninterested, not dressed appropriately	well-prepared, qualified, experienced, reasonable, polite, confident, well mannered, informed, attentive, interested, focused, dressed appropriately

3d Individual answers.

4ab Conducting an interview: Individual answers (cf. *Unterrichtstipps*).

Part C – Coping in the Workplace

SB S. 177

C1 A Business Call

Didaktischer Kommentar

Part C vermittelt S sprachliche Kenntnisse und Kompetenzen für eine erste Tätigkeit in der Wirtschaft. Anhand einer praktischen Mediationsübung lernen S geschäftliche Telefongespräche sprachlich angemessen zu führen.

Differenzierung

1 Mediation Zunächst sammeln S im Plenum weitere plausible Situationen für ein geschäftliches Telefonat (z. B. *information and catalogue request, customer complaint, job application enquiry*), bevor sie zu zweit ein Telefongespräch vorbereiten und die Fragen des Anrufers festhalten. Anschließend erfolgt ein Partnerwechsel, sodass leistungsstärkere S möglichst spontan auf Fragen antworten, die sie selbst nicht vorbereitet haben. Leistungsschwächere S spielen den Anrufer und stellen die vorbereiteten Fragen.

Part C2 – A Business Letter

ALT In leistungshomogenen Paaren oder leistungsschwächeren Lerngruppen fertigen S vorab Notizen für den Angerufenen an (keine ganzen Sätze) und nutzen diese während des Gesprächs.

Lösungshinweise

1 Mediation

1 The Utah Tour Company, Charles Hartfield speaking.
2 Good morning, my name is … and I am calling from USAdventure. Are you responsible for business enquiries?
3 Yes, that's correct. How may I help you?
4 I am calling on behalf of USAdventure. We offer small group adventure tours throughout North America for a younger international crowd and are currently looking for suitable travel agencies to sell our trips. I was wondering whether your agency would be interested in doing so?
5 Yes, we might indeed be interested. Would you be so kind as to send me your catalogue or brochure and any further relevant information material? I would like to go over your suggestion in more detail.
6 Certainly, I will be happy to send you everything you need. Would you please spell your name for me and tell me the mail (*AE*; *BE* postal) address you would like me to send the material to?
7 Of course. It's Charles Hartfield, H-A-R-T-F-I-E-L-D at The Utah Tour Company, 331 Pilgrim Street, Salt Lake City, UT 84101.
8 Thank you very much for your time, Mr Hartfield. I'll send the catalogue and brochures straight away.
[9 I look forward to receiving them. Thank you for calling. Goodbye.]

SB S. 178

C2 A Business Letter

Didaktischer Kommentar

Schon früh in ihrem zukünftigen Arbeitsleben werden S einen englischen Geschäftsbrief verfassen müssen. In dieser Übung sollen sie daher Struktur und Aufbau eines Geschäftsbriefes analysieren, bevor sie selbst einen schreiben.

SB-DVD-ROM

Lernwortschatz

inquiry (*AE/BE*) = enquiry (*esp. BE*) (introductory text), broaden sth. (letter, paragraph 1), favourable terms (letter, paragraph 2)

Lösungshinweise

1a

a company address of person sending the letter (sender)
b company address of person receiving the letter (addressee)
c reference (numbers and/or letters indicating where the information is filed)
d date
e subject matter
f salutation
g purpose and main body of the letter
h terms and conditions
i contact request
j closing sentence / ending
k (complimentary) close
l signature
m enclosure

1bc Individual answers.

SB S. 179

C3 A Written Complaint

Didaktischer Kommentar

Im Anschluss an die Analyse des Geschäftsbriefes schreiben S selbständig einen Geschäftsbrief (Reklamation) und wenden die in **C2** erworbenen Kenntnisse und Fertigkeiten an.

SB-DVD-ROM

Lernwortschatz

measure (l. 8), threaten sth. (l. 12)

Communicating across Cultures

Unterrichtstipps
👥 ZA

In Partnerarbeit entwickeln S ein Szenario, das jemanden zu einer Beschwerde veranlassen könnte. Das Szenario sollte Namen und Adresse derjenigen Person oder Firma enthalten, an die sich die Beschwerde richten soll, sowie stichwortartige Informationen, aus denen der Hintergrund der Beschwerde hervorgeht. Jedes Team bereitet dies auf einer OH-Folie vor und stellt es im Anschluss der Klasse vor. Die Klasse einigt sich auf die zwei besten Szenarien. S schreiben einzeln oder in Partnerarbeit einen *letter of complaint* gemäß der erlernten Regeln und unter Anwendung des Themenvokabulars. Ideen und Beispiele:
- *Complaint to an airline about a flight that was cancelled by the airline itself without being refunded*
- *Complaint about terrible conditions and service at an expensive holiday resort*
- *Complaint to a credit card company about charging the credit card for services never received*
- *Complaint to an airline about lost and/or damaged luggage (not refunded)*

ALT — **CONTEXT TASK** S mit konkreten Vorstellungen für ein Auslandsjahr stellen hierfür ihre Bewerbungsunterlagen zusammen.

Lösungshinweise

1a Possible answers: 1 not enough sightseeing; 2 too much physical exercise; 3 dangerous activities (rafting); 4 too little information on the surrounding area; 5 inexperienced guide; 6 time lost due to accidents; 7 bad weather; 8 misleading brochure; 9 bad organization; 10 unfriendly cotravellers

1b *Possible compensation*: three-day trip or its value in money

1c - **CONTEXT TASK** Individual answers.

SB S. 181 DVD
Transkript s. TM-DVD-ROM

Communicating across Cultures – Intercultural Communication

Source:	Gecko Films, 2003
Topic:	Cultural misunderstandings
Text form:	Feature film (extract)
Language variety:	Australian English; English as a foreign language
Length:	3:16 min
Level:	Intermediate
Skills/Activities:	Doing a role-play; analysing a film

Didaktischer Kommentar

Ziel dieser Einheit ist es, S für kulturelle Unterschiede zu sensibilisieren und diese wertneutral zur Kenntnis zu nehmen. Dafür wurde die Metapher des Eisbergs gewählt, weil dadurch der Zusammenhang zwischen Oberflächen- und Tiefenstrukturen besonders deutlich darstellbar ist.

Unterrichtstipps

1 Die erste Aufgabe kategorisiert kulturelle Unterschiede basierend auf dem Konzept der *cultural dimensions* von G. Hofstede, E. Hall und anderen.
☆ **Linktipp:** *www.clearlycultural.com/geert-hofstede-cultural-dimensions*

ALT **1** Statt oder vor Bearbeitung von **1** kann folgende Aufgabe gestellt und die (Un-)Einheitlichkeit der Antworten in der Klasse festgehalten und auf kulturelle Unterschiede zurückgeführt werden: *You are riding in a car driven by your best friend in a zone where the speed limit is 30 kph. You notice that he is driving 60 kph. He ignores your warnings and laughs. Suddenly he hits – and kills – a pedestrian. You are the only witness.*
Your friend's lawyer says that he may not have to go to prison if you testify that the car was traveling at normal speed.
1 What would you do?
  a I would testify in his favour to honour our friendship.
  b I would tell the truth.

8 Communicating across Cultures – Intercultural Communication

2 How do you think people from the following countries would decide?

Country	% who wouldn't lie	% who would lie
USA	93	7
UK	91	9
Germany	87	13
France	73	27

Country	% who wouldn't lie	% who would lie
Singapore	69	31
Greece	61	39
South Korea	37	63
Venezuela	32	68

2c Role-play Um S das Umschreiben des Dialogs zu erleichtern, kann L das Transkript kopieren und verteilen (s. TM-DVD-ROM).

> **Info**
>
> *Japanese Story* (2003; director: Sue Brooks; screenplay: Alison Tilson): Sandy Edwards (Toni Collette) reluctantly meets Japanese businessman Tachibana Hiromitsu as he arrives in Perth, Western Australia, to visit mines. After an awkward start as the two struggle to understand each other's cultural differences, they embark on a desert affair which ends in tragedy: Hiromitsu dives into a swimming hole that is too shallow and dies.

Lösungshinweise

1 Invidvidual answers.

2a *Awkward moments*: Possible answer: seven: first meeting (surprise at seeing a woman?); no business card from her – instead, she shows disrespect for his by putting it in the back pocket of her trousers; handshake (not expected on his side); suitcase (who should carry it); when he gets into the back of the car instead of the front; in the car; talking with the boss

2b Suggested answers:

Shot No.	Name	Behaviour	Expectations	Cultural Assumptions
1 (at airport)	Sandy	extends hand	informal greeting (handshake)	people in Japan shake hands too
	Hiromitsu	bows, presents business card	formal exchange of business cards	people in Australia exchange business cards too; ignoring a business card is impolite/ignorant; Sandy must be of low status
2 (getting into car)	Sandy	waits for him to take his suitcase; looks annoyed	expects a man to carry his own luggage	a woman shouldn't have to carry things for a man
	Hiromitsu	waits; doesn't offer help	expects Sandy to carry his luggage	guests should be treated with respect
3 (in car)	Sandy	makes small talk	small talk	small talk as icebreaker
	Hiromitsu	pretends not to speak English	to be left alone	rigid hierarchy; Sandy is not his equal so he won't talk to her
4 (at work)	Sandy's boss	exchanges business card, shows proper respect, speaks Japanese	routine exchange of business cards; wants him to feel respected and welcome	Japanese want to be treated the Japanese way
	Hiromitsu	exchanges business card, feels uncomfortable	a private trip; pleasure, not business	Japanese is used for business, English for pleasure

2c Role-play Individual answers.

Kopiervorlage 19: Reading Comprehension

1 Which of the following could be considered to be progress, according to the writer:

- A reducing misery
- B increasing happiness
- C creating wealth
- D innovating society
- E worshipping money
- F creating a more humane society

Explain how the phrases you ticked might be considered progress. How might this be achieved?

_____
_____
_____
_____
_____
_____

2 Which of the following do not make us happier, according to the writer:

- A massive wealth creation
- B accelerated economic growth
- C making sacrifices
- D human relationships
- E increased efficiency
- F productivity growth
- G trustworthy behaviour
- H competition between individuals

Explain why they do not make us happier.

_____
_____
_____
_____
_____
_____

Context 21 The World of Work and Business: Topic Vocabulary

Word/Phrase	Memory Aid	German
APPLYING FOR A JOB		
aptitude test	*definition:* a test which determines a person's ability	Eignungstest
covering letter *(BE)* / **cover letter** *(AE)*	*definition:* a letter containing additional information not to be found elsewhere in a job application, usually stating the applicant's motivation for the job	Begleitbrief, Anschreiben
CV *(BE)* / **résumé** *(AE)*	*example sentence:* Sarah almost forgot to add her ~ to her application for the internship in the PR firm.	Lebenslauf
(job) interview	*word family:* (to) interview – interviewer – interviewee – <u>interview</u> *(n)*	Vorstellungsgespräch
references	*word family:* (to) refer (to) – <u>reference</u> – referee – referral	Referenzen
work experience	*example sentence:* Paul found that despite his excellent qualifications a complete lack of ~ **experience** ultimately counted against him.	Berufserfahrung
ON THE JOB		
blue-collar worker	*definition:* a worker who does physical work in industry	Arbeiter/in
white-collar worker	*other collocations:* <u>white-collar</u> crime/job	Angestelle/r
boss	*example sentence:* Due to his strict leadership style the ~ was not a popular man among the workers.	Vorgesetzte/r
career ladder	*example sentence:* A university degree is considered to be a good way to climb up the ~ **ladder**.	Karriereleiter
(to) do an internship	*example sentence:* Many students arrange to **do an** ~ at a company during the summer holidays.	ein Praktikum machen
employer	*word family:* (to) employ – employment – <u>employer</u> – employee	Arbeitgeber/in
freelance	*example sentence:* Journalists often work ~ for several companies.	freiberuflich
(to) get a promotion	*other collocations:* (to) deserve a / (to) recommend sb. for <u>promotion</u>	befördert werden
(to) hire sb.	*synonyms:* (to) recruit sb. / (to) appoint sb. / (to) employ sb.	jdn. einstellen

Context 21 The World of Work and Business: Topic Vocabulary

Word/Phrase	Memory Aid	German
ON THE JOB		
(to) **do an apprenticeship**	*definition:* to train as an apprentice and learn a profession on the job	eine Lehre absolvieren
(to) **negotiate** (**with** sb.) (**for/about** sth.) [nɪˈgəʊʃɪeɪt]	*definition:* (to) discuss sth. in order to reach an agreement	(mit jdn.) (über etwas) verhandeln
(to) **sack** sb.	*synonyms:* (to) dismiss / (to) fire sb. *(infml)* / (to) give sb. the sack / (to) let sb. go	jdn. entlassen
salary	*definition:* the money earned by professional employees, generally paid monthly	Gehalt
wage (*also:* **wages**)	*collocations:* decent/minimum wage	Lohn
workplace	*example sentence:* The new regulations greatly improved safety in the ~ for all.	Arbeitsplatz
BUSINESS MATTERS		
asset	*example sentence:* My assets include savings, property and shares.	Vermögen
bailout	*definition:* act of giving capital to a company or country, in order to save it from bankruptcy or insolvency.	Rettungsaktion
advertising	*word family:* (to) advertise – advertiser – advertising – advertisement	Werbung, Werbe-
consumption	*example sentence:* The ~ of oil tends to increase in winter when the weather gets colder.	Konsum, Verbrauch
credit crunch	*definition:* an economic crisis in which it becomes suddenly difficult and expensive to borrow money	Finanzkrise
customer	*collocations:* customer service/satisfaction/complaints	Kunde/Kundin
(to) **deposit money**	*example sentence* The dictator deposited most of his money into a foreign bank account so it could not be traced.	Geld einzahlen
economic boom	*other collocations:* post-war/consumer/property/baby boom	Aufschwung, Steigerung
interest	*collocations:* earn/pay/yield/gain/receive ~	Zinsen

Context 21 The World of Work and Business: Topic Vocabulary

Word/Phrase	Memory Aid	German
BUSINESS MATTERS		
(to) **make a profit**	*opposite:* (to) make a loss	einen Gewinn erzielen
mortgage	*example sentence:* It is usual for people to take out a ~ on a house when they buy one.	Hypothek
productivity	*word family:* (to) produce – product – producer – productivity	Leistungsfähigkeit, Produktivität
profit margin	*example sentence:* Fast food outlets have been reporting an increase in their ~ **margins** since the global economic crisis started.	Gewinnspanne
recession	*example sentence:* After years of high unemployment, Britain started to recover and emerged from ~.	Rezession
sales	*collocations:* strong/annual/domestic/overseas sales	Umsatz
share	*collocations:* (to) acquire / (to) hold (fml) / (to) issue / (to) deal in shares	Aktie
stock market	*definition:* a public market where shares in companies are traded	Aktienbörse
stockbroker	*example sentence:* She has a very low opinion of ~s since she lost her money in the credit crunch.	Börsenmakler/in
stockholder	*example sentence:* The ~s are gathering for the company's annual general meeting.	Aktionär/in, Anteilseigner/in
supply and demand	*example sentence:* If the ~ **and demand** are unequal, the price can go up or down.	Angebot und Nachfrage
(to) **transfer money**	*example sentence:* No bank fees are charged any more for transferring money within the Eurozone.	Geld überweisen
VAT (value added tax)	*example sentence:* One of the first moves of the new British government was to raise ~ to 20%.	Mehrwertsteuer
(to) **withdraw money**	*example sentence:* The easiest way to withdraw money is from a cash machine.	Geld abheben
work ethic	*definition:* a set of values based on the belief that hard work is beneficial	Arbeitsethos

9 Science, Technology and the Environment

Das Kapitel thematisiert wesentliche Aspekte in den Bereichen Wissenschaft und Technik, Klimawandel und alternative Energien.

Part A – Living in Wonderland: Modern Technology ermöglicht eine differenzierte Auseinandersetzung mit der Bedeutung moderner Technologien und deren Auswirkungen auf unsere Gesellschaft.

Part B – Cracking the Code: Genetics zeigt am Beispiel der Präimplantationsdiagnostik und gentechnisch veränderter Lebensmittel zwei Möglichkeiten für die Nutzung von Gentechnik.

Part C – The Challenge of Climate Change wirft einen differenzierten Blick auf den Klimawandel sowie auf Strategien zum Umgang mit der Erderwärmung, erläutert die Bedeutung alternativer Energien und zeigt auf, welchen Beitrag jede/r einzelne zur CO_2-Verminderung leisten kann.

Didaktisches Inhaltsverzeichnis

SB p.	Title	TM p.	Text Form	Topic	Skills and Activities	Language Practice
182	Lead-in	230	Cartoon; photos	Environmental problems; scientific innovation	Analysing a cartoon; writing a dialogue	
	Part A – Living in Wonderland: Modern Technology					
184	A1 Getting Connected Thomas L. Friedman	231	Newspaper article (extract)	The effects of modern communication technologies	Reading non-fiction; writing a dialogue; analysing stylistic devices; paraphrasing	-ing forms
	A2 In Our Image: The Age of Robotics					
186	i) The Three Laws of Robotics Isaac Asimov CD 3.05	233	Interview (extract)	Robots with safeguards	Listening comprehension	LP 12: Using modal verbs
186	ii) Designing Robots for People Cynthia Breazeal	234	Web feature (extract)	Man-machine communication	Reading non-fiction; writing a summary; giving a presentation	
188	Words in Context – The Scientific Revolution	235	Informative text	Consequences of the scientific revolution	Translating	LP 20: Avoiding German-English interference Word formation; LP 2: Prepositions; LP 1: Collocations with nouns
	Part B – Cracking the Code: Genetics					
190	B1 How Designer Children Will Work DVD	236	Diagram; video	Pre-implantation genetic diagnosis / Embryo screening	Viewing skills; working with diagrams	
191	B2 Born for a Purpose Jodi Picoult CD 3.06-07	238	Novel (extract); interview	The downside of saviour siblings	Reading fiction; creative writing; listening comprehension; discussing ethical issues	
192	B3 GM Food – Does Anybody Want It? Maha M. Alkhazindar et al.	240	Fictional case study	The pros and cons of genetically modified food	Doing research; argumentative writing; debating	
194	Communicating across Cultures	241	Non-fictional text	Dealing with technical English	Dealing with scientific texts	LP 9: Word formation: suffixes
	Part C – The Challenge of Climate Change					
196	C1 Take AIM at Climate Change DVD	242	Music video	Strategies to cope with climate change	Viewing skills; analysing and assessing a music video	
197	C2 The Future of Energy – the Energy of the Future George Monbiot	244	Speech; chart; graph	The end of the fossil fuel age	Analysing stylistic devices; mediating; analysing charts and statistics; doing research	
199	C3 EXTRA Science to the Rescue? Oliver Tickell	246	Newspaper article (extract)	Geo-engineering	Summarizing; scanning; working with charts; mediating; doing research; making a poster	

9 Lead-in

SB S. 182 — **Lead-in**

Didaktischer Kommentar

S nähern sich dem Themenkomplex „Science, Technology and the Environment" über die Analyse eines Cartoons zum Thema Atomkraft. Anschließend beurteilen sie die Bedeutung bestimmter Technologien für unsere Gesellschaft und spekulieren über verschiedene Zukunftsszenarien.

Unterrichtstipps
ALT
ZA

2 S berichten der Klasse anschließend über die auf dem Foto ihrer Wahl dargestellte Erfindung. Alternativ beschreiben sie ihren Gegenstand (z. B. „Without this, it would not be possible to …"), während die übrigen S die Erfindung erraten.

> **Info**
>
> **A** *Light bulb:* The first successful incandescent light bulb was developed by Thomas Edison between 1878 and 1880. Before that time, gas was the main source of artificial light. Light bulbs are powered by electricity of which only a small percentage is used to create light. The rest comes off as heat. For this reason many countries are beginning to phase out incandescent light bulbs and replace them with more energy-efficient electric lights.
>
> **B** *Engine:* The internal combustion engine uses a fossil fuel and oxygen from the air to create small controlled explosions that keep the engine in motion. In the second half of the 19th century, different forms of engines were developed by inventors throughout Europe, primarily in Italy and Germany. Being smaller and lighter than the steam engines they replaced, they made the automobile possible. The widespread use of engines in industry and vehicles means that more pollution is expelled into the atmosphere.
>
> **C** *Satellite:* The first man-made satellite was the Russian Sputnik, launched in 1957. The Soviet success shook the USA out of its post-war complacency and made space flight a high priority. Satellites are now used in many areas of research, navigation and observation. Satellites have changed the way we live: global positioning systems can help navigation and observation satellites can monitor weather patterns. However, satellites are also used in military operations to locate missile aims.
>
> **D** *Battery:* The first battery of modern times was the Voltaic pile, invented by Alessandro Volta in 1800. Like its 19th century successors, the Voltaic pile was a wet cell battery; it consisted of liquid electrolytes in a glass jar, making it impractical for portable use. The first modern dry cell batteries were developed shortly before 1900. Most modern portable devices use batteries, e.g. mobile phones, torches, music players and laptops. A rechargeable battery lasts much longer than a disposable battery. The chemicals used in batteries are dangerous and when a battery is disposed of, these chemicals can leak into the environment. There are now many initiatives to encourage battery recycling.
>
> **E** *Transistor:* Canadian physicist Julius Lilienfeld patented a device for a transistor in 1925, but there is no evidence that Lilienfeld ever built such a device or investigated its properties. William Shockley of AT&T's Bell Labs is generally credited with being the first to realize the potential of semiconducting crystals in 1947. The transistor replaced the cumbersome vacuum tube and made microelectronics possible. Almost all electronic devices today use transistors.
>
> **F** *Lens:* The oldest known lenses are 3000 years old. They were presumably used as magnifying glasses or to start fires. The first reading glasses were invented in the 13th century. They were followed by the microscope in 1590 and the telescope in 1608. Photographic lenses were developed in the mid-19th century and today there are many types of lenses such as wide-angle, fish-eye and telephoto lenses for taking different kinds of photographs.

Part A

Lösungshinweise

1a The cartoon shows a man with his sleeves rolled up standing in front of a large desk. There is a man sitting in an office chair behind the desk. Through the large window, a nuclear power plant can be seen. The setting is presumably the office of the manager of the plant. The man on the right is probably an employee, an engineer perhaps. From his posture and his facial expression you can see that he is worried. Presumably he has just expressed his concern over the still unsolved problem of nuclear waste disposal. The manager is sitting back in his chair, smiling.

1bc Individual answers.

1d The chief executive officer (CEO) waves his employee's concerns aside. He represents the interests of his firm, a power company. They make their money by producing and selling electricity from nuclear power. Disposing of nuclear waste costs a huge amount of money, but brings no profits. Instead of being interested in solving the problem (cf. his reply), the CEO pretends that his company is doing the next generation a favour by leaving them a major problem to solve. The opposite is true: his company rakes in the profits today, but leaves the problems for others to solve. The cartoonist is criticizing the lack of responsibility on the part of corporations that exploit the planet for profit and leave it to coming generations to cope with the after-effects of their actions.

2 Cf. Info; *changed our lives:* individual answers.

3 Individual answers.

Part A – Living in Wonderland: Modern Technology

SB S. 184
▶ LSET ex. 1, 2

A1 Getting Connected   Thomas L. Friedman

Source:	*The New York Times*, 1 November 2006
Topic:	The effects of modern communication technologies
Text form:	Newspaper article (extract)
Language variety:	American English
Number of words:	486
Level:	Intermediate
Skills/Activities:	Reading non-fiction; writing a dialogue; analysing stylistic devices; paraphrasing

Didaktischer Kommentar

Der Text beleuchtet die Auswirkungen der modernen Technologie auf unser Leben von zwei Seiten: die weltumspannenden Möglichkeiten der Telekommunikation einerseits und die Hemmnis echter Kommunikation zwischen Anwesenden durch eben diese Möglichkeiten andererseits. Der anekdotische Charakter des Textes bietet Anlässe, das eigene Verhalten zu reflektieren.

SB-DVD-ROM

Lernwortschatz

approach (l. 4), dashboard (l. 17), column (l. 19), relate sth. (l. 27), label sb./sth. (as sth.) (l. 32), accessible (l. 35)

Unterrichtstipps

S führen, z.B. in Vorbereitung auf das Thema, einen Selbstversuch durch und verzichten 24 Stunden auf technische Geräte jeder Art. Anschließend berichten sie über ihre Erfahrungen.

1a Zur Vorbereitung auf das Rollenspiel halten S die Fakten stichwortartig fest. Anschließend bilden sie Fragen (Partner A) bzw. Aussagesätze (Partner B) aus den Stichworten. Durch den Rollentausch üben beide S Frage- und Aussagesätze.

1b L weist ggf. auf die Verwendung des Gerundiums mit *for* hin *(... is used/useful for ...ing)* sowie auf die Verwechslungsgefahr mit dem *to*-Infinitiv (Zweck eines Gegenstands: *for* + *gerund*; Absicht einer Handlung: *to* + *infinitive*).

Part A1 – Getting Connected

Differenzierung Schwächere Lerngruppen werden auf den anspruchsvolleren zweiten Teil vorbereitet, indem die Lektüre nach Z. 26 unterbrochen wird. So erhalten S Gelegenheit, ihr Verständnis der Situation zu artikulieren und ihre Erwartungen an den zweiten Teil des Textes zu äußern *(Why do you think Friedman writes about this incident? What conclusions might he draw?)*.

> **Info**
>
> *Thomas L. Friedman* (born 1953) has worked as a journalist for *The New York Times* since 1981. He has written extensively on international affairs, the world economy and the Middle East. Friedman has received three Pulitzer Prizes for his work and is the author of several best-selling books on globalization and related topics. His twice-weekly column in *The New York Times* is syndicated to ca. 100 newspapers worldwide.

Lösungshinweise

1a

Questions	Answers
Where did you arrive in Paris?	At Charles de Gaulle Airport.
Who met you there?	A driver sent by a friend of mine.
How did you recognize him?	He was carrying a sign with my name on it.
Did you notice anything strange about him?	Yes, he was talking the whole time, although he was standing alone.
How do you explain this behaviour?	When I got closer, I saw that he was wearing a wireless headset. I guess he was talking to someone on the phone.
Did you talk to him at all?	Yes, after we got into the car I asked him if he had the address of my hotel. When he said he didn't, I showed him the address.
What did he do during the trip?	He was still talking on the phone, and he had a DVD running on the GPS screen.
What did you do during the trip?	First I tried to finish a column on my laptop, but I couldn't concentrate. So I listened to music on my iPod.

1b *Device and its use: mobile phone (with wireless headset):* communicating with people who are not present; *GPS navigation system:* finding your way when travelling by car; *DVD player:* entertainment; *laptop:* processing files, entertainment (music, video); communicating (via email, chat); *iPod* (= MP3 player): entertainment.
Except for the GPS (which has no relevance for communication), all these devices can also hinder communication with people who are present.

1c *Part 1:* Friedman relates the story of his taxi ride from Charles de Gaulle Airport in Paris to his hotel (ll. 1–21).
Part 2: The author comments on his observation that modern communication technology doesn't necessarily bring people closer together (ll. 22–31).
Part 3: Friedman quotes the opinion of technologist Linda Stone that many people today suffer from 'continuous partial attention' (ll. 32–38).

2 The author uses the past progressive in the first example and a gerund in the second.
Further examples, past progressive: The driver was carrying a sign with my name on it (ll. 3–4); he was talking to himself (ll. 4–5); He was driving, talking on his phone and watching a video. I was riding, working on my laptop and listening to my iPod (ll. 24–25)

Part A2 – In Our Image: The Age of Robotics

Further examples, gerund: He nodded and went on talking (l. 9); I followed as he kept talking on his phone (ll. 12–13); I showed him the address and he went back to talking on the phone (ll. 14–15); while he went on talking, driving and watching the movie (ll. 20–21)

Effect: The past progressive is more like a description, whereas gerunds seem more active: they underline how busy the driver is.

3

1 *Antithesis / *paradox: One side-effect of having permanent access to electronic forms of communication can be that we are no longer present for the people in our physical surroundings. The paradox points out that striving for a goal (connectedness) can lead to its opposite (isolation). The antithesis (far feels near / near feels far) makes it more memorable.
2 *Juxtaposition: It seems unnatural that two people sitting together in a car for one hour and who speak the same language do not talk to each other. The juxtaposition leaves it to the reader to draw his conclusions from Friedman's presentation of the facts before the author draws his own conclusions.
3 *Antithesis/*paradox: While connected to people who are far away, we lose contact with our immediate surroundings. The antithesis underscores that everything has two sides.
4 *Paradox: Our virtual presence via modern telecommunications (e.g. in chat rooms) can seem more real to us than our real physical location. The paradox is meant to provoke the reader into realizing that our use of telecommunications may be taking us in the wrong direction.

4 Individual answers.

▶ LSET ex. 3

A2 In Our Image: The Age of Robotics

SB S. 186
CD 3.05
Transkript s. TM-DVD-ROM

i) The Three Laws of Robotics   Isaac Asimov

Source:	'Isaac Asimov Speaks with Terry Gross', Website of The New York Times, 25 September 1987
Topic:	Robots with safeguards
Text form:	Interview (extract)
Language variety:	American English
Length:	4:19 min
Level:	Intermediate
Skills/Activities:	Listening comprehension

Didaktischer Kommentar Einem Interview entnehmen S, welche Überlegungen Asimov zu seinen Vorstellungen vom Verhältnis zwischen Mensch und Maschine gebracht haben. Die drei Robotik-Gesetze weisen auf eine fast spielerische Weise auf die ethischen Probleme hin, die mit dem Eintritt intelligenter Roboter in den menschlichen Alltag verbunden sind. Somit bereitet das Interview die Auseinandersetzung mit den realen Überlegungen der Entwicklerin Cynthia Breazeal in A2 ii) vor.

Unterrichtstipps PRE-READING Ein Ausschnitt aus der berühmten Schöpfungsdarstellung Michelangelos ist im SB-Kapitel „The USA – Dreams and Struggles" in B1 zu finden; vgl. auch die Info dazu im TM, **B1**. S können diese Aufgabe in einer *placemat activity* (s. S. 298) bearbeiten.

⚠ HA ● Word help Vor dem Hören machen sich S mit unbekanntem Wortschatz vertraut.

Differenzierung **1** Vorab wird in schwächeren Lerngruppen das Verständnis der Vokabeln *humanoid* (hier: *a machine that behaves like a human*; Satz 4) und *safeguards* (*sth. that prevents accidents*; Satz 5) sichergestellt. Schwächere Lerngruppen erhalten zweimal Gelegenheit, sich den Interview-Ausschnitt anzuhören. Erst beim zweiten Hören wird Aufgabe **1** bearbeitet.

9 Part A2 ii) – Designing Robots for People

> **Info**
>
> *Isaac Asimov* (1920–1992) was born in the Soviet Union. When he was three, his Jewish parents emigrated to the USA. Asimov grew up in Brooklyn, New York, and went on to study Chemistry at Columbia University, New York. He wrote a large number of fictional and non-fictional books dealing with science and technology, but is best known for his science-fiction novels. Together with Arthur C. Clarke and Robert Heinlein, Asimov is generally regarded as one of the major writers of science fiction in the 20th century.

Lösungshinweise

PRE-READING Relationship between man and machine: The artist parodies Michelangelo's famous representation of the creation of Adam in the Sistine Chapel. In the modern version, man plays the role of God by making a creature in his image. One possible interpretation is that as creators, human beings will have to accept responsibility for the race of creatures they have made to serve them. It is also conceivable that the author is suggesting that man is overstepping his boundaries by playing God and that, like Dr Frankenstein, he will one day regret it.

1 Wrong statements: 2, 3, 4, 6

2a Corrections:

2 Asimov first used the Three Laws of Robotics in a short story.
3 Asimov invented the word 'positron'.
4 When Asimov began writing, humanoid robots made of metal were already standard features of science fiction.
6 Asimov thinks that science-fiction films are far behind printed science fiction.

2b *First Law:* A robot may not injure a human being or, through inaction, allow a human being to come to harm.
Second Law: A robot must obey any orders given to it by human beings, except where such orders would conflict with the First Law.
Third Law: A robot must protect its own existence as long as such protection does not conflict with the First or Second Law.

3

1 The robot must enter the burning house and attempt to rescue the child without regard for its own safety.
2 If the robot observes that there are people in or around the building, it is not allowed to detonate the bomb. The robot must destroy itself if necessary to fulfill its mission.
3 The robot must not allow a human being to come to harm through inaction, i.e. it must intervene. At the same time, it is not allowed to harm the aggressor. Its difficult task would be to protect the victim from further injury, if necessary stopping the attacker by force, but without inflicting any injury on the attacker.

SB S. 186 **ii) Designing Robots for People** Cynthia Breazeal

Source:	Public Broadcasting Service, 1 March 2005
Topic:	Man-machine communication
Text form:	Web feature (extract)
Language variety:	American English
Number of words:	426
Level:	Intermediate
Skills/Activities:	Reading non-fiction; writing a summary; giving a presentation

Didaktischer Kommentar S ermitteln anhand des Textes die Prinzipien, die die Entwicklerin Breazeal für die künftige Interaktion zwischen Menschen und Robotern als wichtig ansieht.

9 Words in Context

SB-DVD-ROM

Lernwortschatz

interact (l. 1), interface (l. 11), application (l. 15)

Unterrichtstipps

PRE-READING S entwickeln – z. B. in Kleingruppen – ihre eigenen Ideen zu der Aufgabe, die sich Breazeal stellte: *How should robots be designed so that people can use them in everyday life? Make a list of principles that you think are important.* Dies wird später mit den Ergebnissen von Aufgabe 1 verglichen.

3 Inspiration für weitere Anwendungsbereiche von Robotern können sich S auf der amerikanischen Website der Firma iRobot®: *www.irobot.com/index.cfm?i=us* holen.

Info

The Media Laboratory of the Massachusetts Institute of Technology (MIT), where Cynthia Breazeal is a professor, was founded in 1985. Fields of research include multimedia and digital technology, applications for the disabled, and man-machine communication.

Lösungshinweise

1a Individual answers, e.g. 1: The ideal interface for interaction of robots and people; 2: Robots as part of a new social technology; 3: Breazeal's vision of human-robot relationships

1b Individual answers.

1c In order to function in a social environment, robots have to be designed to interact with human beings. Most people are not technicians and want an interface they can easily relate to. For this reason, robots need to be equipped with emotional intelligence. Such robots could perform socially useful tasks such as helping the elderly to lead independent lives longer. Breazeal arrived at these ideas by applying a blind person's relationship with their guide dog to the relationship between a human being and a robot. It should ideally be both: a (cognitive, physical) help and an emotional support.

2a 1 layperson; 2 motivation; 3 bizarre; 4 genuinely; 5 pragmatic

2b–3 Individual answers.

SB S. 188
▶ LSET ex. 4, 5, 6

Words in Context – The Scientific Revolution

Didaktischer Kommentar

Der eingeführte Wortschatz dient dazu, eine intelligente Teilnahme an der gesellschaftlichen Diskussion um die Rolle von Wissenschaft und Technik zu ermöglichen. Die Übungen konzentrieren sich auf den allgemeinen technischen Wortschatz sowie auf die Sprache gesellschaftlichen Diskurses. Morphologie und Kollokationen bilden den Schwerpunkt.

SB-DVD-ROM

Lernwortschatz

hypothesis (l. 2), empirical data (l. 3), pure science (l. 4), basic research (l. 4), applied science (l. 5), engineering (l. 5), implement new discoveries (l. 6), major advances (l. 6), breakthrough (l. 8), progress (l. 11), state-of-the-art technology (l. 11), come under fire (l. 13), ethical (l. 14), genetically modified (l. 14), call for a moratorium (l. 15), deployment (l. 15), long-term effects (l. 15), unforeseen consequence (l. 17), controversy (l. 18), moral objection (l. 19), tamper with nature (l. 19), major challenges (l. 21), strike a balance (l. 21), global warming (l. 22), depletion of natural resources (l. 22), loss of biodiversity (l. 23), threaten sb./sth. (l. 23), quantify sth. (l. 24), environmental impact (l. 25), carbon footprint (l. 25), greenhouse effect (l. 27), sustainability (l. 27), renewable energy sources (l. 28), conservation (l. 29), rise to the challenge (l. 32), deal with the consequences of sth. (l. 32)

9 Part B

Unterrichtstipps S lesen den Text einzeln (ggf. als Hausaufgabe) und schlagen die Bedeutung und Aussprache der markierten Wörter im ein- oder zweisprachigen Wörterbuch nach.

Differenzierung In schwächeren Lerngruppen kann es sinnvoll sein, den neuen Wortschatz nach Wortfeldern zu sortieren, z. B. *science and technical progress, controversy*. Alternativ dazu lassen sich die neuen Begriffe nach Themen in einer Mindmap organisieren, z. B. *pure science, engineering, genetics, climate change*.

Lösungshinweise

1

1	verb:	modify	noun:	*modification*
2	noun:	deployment	verb:	*deploy*
3	noun:	controversy	adjective:	*controversial*
4	noun:	objection	verb:	*object*
5	noun:	depletion	verb:	*deplete*
6	noun:	sustainability	adjective:	*sustainable*
7	adjective:	renewable	noun:	*renewal*
8	noun	conservation	verb:	*conserve*

2 *Positive*: challenge (l. 21), progress (l. 11)
Negative: depletion (l. 22), tamper (l. 19), unforeseen (l. 17), threaten (l. 22)

3

1 In the 20th century basic research led to several breakthroughs in science.
2 Especially large biotech companies have come under fire in the USA and Europe.
3 Studies of the long-term effects are necessary before the deployment of genetically modified plants.
4 The term 'carbon footprint' serves to quantify the impact of our actions on the environment.

4a 1 on; 2 in; 3 on; 4 surrounding; 5 for; 6 to

4b strike a balance; driving force; push back the frontier; a change in attitude; natural resources

Part B – Cracking the Code: Genetics

SB S. 190 **B1 How Designer Children Will Work**
DVD
Transkript s. TM-DVD-ROM

Source:	'Embryo Screening', *The New York Times* website, September 2006
Topic:	Pre-implantation genetic diagnosis / Embryo screening
Text form:	News report (video)
Language variety:	American English
Length:	5:43
Level:	Basic
Skills/Activities:	Viewing skills; working with diagrams

Didaktischer Kommentar S werden mit Grundbegriffen der Genetik vertraut gemacht und erläutern ein Schaubild, das die Technik der Präimplantationsdiagnostik (PID) beschreibt. Auf der Grundlage eines Films, in dem es um die Auswahl eines Embryos mittels PID geht, artikulieren sie die Vor- und Nachteile des Verfahrens und diskutieren die moralischen Konsequenzen.

Part B1 – How Designer Children Will Work

SB-DVD-ROM

Lernwortschatz

gene (term 1), genome (term 2), chromosome (term 3), uterus (term 4), in vitro (term 5), cloning (term 6), nucleus (term 8), genetic engineering (term 9), stem cell (term 10), hereditary (definition e)

Unterrichtstipps
⚠ HA ● Word help

2 Vor dem Sehen des Berichts machen sich S mit unbekanntem Wortschatz vertraut.

1b S tauschen ihre Texte im Anschluss aus und überprüfen die sachliche Richtigkeit der Angaben.

2a Vor- und Nachteile der PID können in einer Debatte diskutiert werden *(s. SF 25: Debating)*.

Differenzierung

1 S, denen die Begriffe 1–10 weitgehend unbekannt sind, benutzen ein Wörterbuch und halten die Begriffe samt Definitionen fest, damit sie ihnen für die weitere Arbeit am Kapitel zur Verfügung stehen.

2a Weniger leistungsstarke Lerngruppen sehen das Video einmal bevor sie Vor- und Nachteile festhalten.

Info

Pre-implantation genetic diagnosis (PGD) or *embryo screening* was considered illegal in Germany under the Embryo Protection Act of 1990 until the Federal Court ruled in July 2010 that PGD could be legally used in conjunction with reproductive medicine (in a case analogous to that of the Kingsbury family). In the UK, it is permitted in certain cases in clinics that are licensed and monitored by the Human Fertilisation and Embryology Authority. In the USA as well as in several European countries, there are little or no government regulations limiting the use of PGD. The most common use of the technology is for screening out embryos that carry a potentially lethal gene. Recently, there has been some interest, especially in the USA, in using PGD to choose the baby's gender.

Lösungshinweise

PRE-READING 1e; 2f; 3i; 4h; 5d; 6c; 7b; 8a; 9j; 10g

1a First the mother-to-be is given fertility drugs so that she produces multiple eggs. These eggs are removed from her uterus and fertilized in vitro through artificial insemination. The fertilized eggs become embryos, which are now examined for genetic defects. One embryo that is free from any genetic defects is then re-implanted in the uterus and develops into a healthy baby that is born naturally.

1b Individual answers.

2a *Benefits:* Parents have children that will not develop a dangerous disease later in life; using PGD to avoid a cancer death in the family gives people control over their lives and the lives of their children; the cancer gene will eventually die out because it is no longer passed on.
Problems: The treatment is painful, expensive and time-consuming; there can be religious or ethical objections; health insurance may not pay for the treatment; the same technology can be used to avoid children with obesity or other hereditary conditions that are not fatal.

2b Individual answers.

2c
- *Reason for the Kingsburys worrying about future children's health:* Chad carried a mutated gene that often led to colon cancer in midlife. The chances were 50% that his children would have this gene.

9 Part B2 – Born for a Purpose

- *Risk of dying of cancer for persons with same gene mutation as Chad:* Not all people with the gene develop cancer; if the cancer is diagnosed early enough, there is a 90% chance of survival.
- *How family and friends reacted:* Many people didn't understand what the Kingsburys were doing; some criticized the idea for religious reasons.
- *Who paid:* The Kingsburys had to finance the treatment with $10,000 of their own money.
- *How Kingsburys feel:* They are sure they did the right thing and want to have a second child with PGD.

SB S. 191
CD 3.06–07
Transkript s. TM-DVD-ROM
▶ LSET ex. 7

B2 Born for a Purpose Jodi Picoult

Source:	*My Sister's Keeper,* New York: Atria Books, 2004
Topic:	The downside of saviour siblings
Text form:	Novel (extract) / Interview
Language variety:	American English
Number of words:	453
Level:	Basic

Source:	'Jodi Picoult on *My Sister's Keeper*', Bill Thompson's Eye on Books
Topic:	Discussion about Picoult's novel
Text form:	Interview
Language variety:	American English
Length:	8:13 min
Level:	Intermediate

Skills/Activities:	Analysing a fictional text; creative writing; listening comprehension; discussing ethical issues

Didaktischer Kommentar

Durch die Perspektive eines *saviour sibling* erkennen S, dass die ethische Beurteilung der PID auch das gesunde Kind berücksichtigen muss, das auf diese Weise entsteht.

SB-DVD-ROM

> **Lernwortschatz**
>
> fill sb. in (l. 3), multiply (l. 8), vacation (v) (l. 10), distinction (l. 12), file for divorce (l. 14), flattering (l. 18), precious (l. 22), hook up sth. (l. 21), bargain for sth. (l. 24)

Unterrichtstipps ZA

Einstieg: In Partner- oder Kleingruppenarbeit erzählen sich S, ob sie Geschwister haben und wie sie sich mit ihnen verstehen. Auch, ob sie jemanden kennen, der Leukämie (Blutkrebs) hat oder hatte sowie die Folgen und der Umgang mit der Krankheit können in diesem geschützten Rahmen besprochen werden.

3 S, die mit dem Roman oder dem Film vertraut sind, berichten anschließend über den Auslöser und den Verlauf der Handlung.

⚠ Word help

4 Vor dem Hören machen sich S mit unbekanntem Wortschatz vertraut.

ZA

5 Interessierte S setzen sich mit den ethischen Fragen im Film Gattaca (USA 1997) auseinander, in dem die PID in der Mittel- und Oberschicht zur Regel geworden ist, damit nur die besten Gene weitergegeben werden. Der Klasse wird darüber Bericht erstattet *(s. SF 22, Giving a report on a book or film.)*

Differenzierung ALT

2a In schwächeren Lerngruppen wird die Aufgabenstellung vereinfacht: *Compare the tone in the first part of the text (ll. 1–18) and the second part (ll. 19–33). Which is funnier and which is more serious? Give reasons.*

4 EXTRA kann von S übernommen werden, die den Roman bzw. den Film kennen.

Part B2 – Born for a Purpose

> **Info**
>
> *Jodi Picoult* [piː'koʊ] (born 1966) is an American author of a number of best-selling works of young adult fiction. She is married and lives in New Hampshire with her husband and three children.
>
> *My Sister's Keeper* (2004) tells the story of Anna, conceived to save her sister Kate, who is suffering from leukaemia. When she turns 13, Anna is expected to donate a kidney to save her sister's life. She consults a lawyer and finds support for her struggle to resist her parents' wishes. A film based on the novel was released under the same title in 2009.

Lösungshinweise

PRE-READING *Reasons for wanting children:* Individual answers, e.g. not wanting your family line to die out; love of children; because most people have them, …

1a Anna concludes from her observations that babies are born mainly by accident: because people thought nothing would happen, because the situation got out of control, because of faulty contraceptive, because a wife wanted to make her husband stay; but never, it seems, because the couple wanted a child.

1b On the one hand, Anna registers her parents' eagerness to underline her special status; on the other hand, she sees through it (ll. 28ff.) to realize that she, unlike other children, is an instrument of someone's will, created to serve a specific purpose. This realization seems to fill her with misgivings (ll. 29–33), as if she had no right to existence beyond her usefulness to her sister.

2a The tone of the first part of the text is humorous. Anna exaggerates ('while other families seemed to multiply before your eyes', l. 8) and quotes her father's comment on the good fortune of her classmate Sedona. Anna uses ironic detachment when she lists the reasons why people have babies. The use of colloquial speech ('I'm telling you', l. 15), exaggeration ('a thousand other reasons', l. 18) and understatement ('that really aren't very flattering', l. 16) underscores the ironic tone of the passage.

The second half of the text is more serious in tone. It becomes clear that the ironic detachment also applies to Anna and her existence ('little embryonic me', l. 25; 'I'd still be floating up in Heaven or wherever', l. 29) as well as to the well-intentioned explanations of her parents ('all the usual stuff', l. 22). Anna tries to appear sophisticated and cool, but can't completely hide the undercurrent of insecurity.

2b The beginning is one of the most important parts of a novel as it sets the tone, introduces the reader to the situation and the main characters, and it becomes obvious how the story is narrated. Picoult chooses a first-person narrator, who is introduced in the first paragraph. The first-person narrator is ideal for such a beginning, because we see the world through their eyes and the reader immediately sympathizes with the character and wants to find out more about them. This effect is amplified by the way the narrator addresses the reader directly in ll. 30–32.

3 a–c Individual answers.

4a Jodi Picoult began thinking about the issues connected with embryo screening while researching eugenics for an earlier novel. She learned about a family whose daughter had been cured of leukaemia using the blood of her baby brother, who had been born for this purpose. Picoult began thinking about the consequences it might have if the illness required multiple donations from the younger child over a longer period. When her own son Jake required medical attention for three years to save his hearing, Picoult witnessed the strain that a sick child imposes on a family. Thinking about the conflicting interests involved in a case like that of Anna Fitzgerald, Picoult got the idea of using multiple narrators to present the different sides of the conflict. The title came to her early one morning while she was jogging with a friend.

4b–5 Individual answers.

9

Part B3 – GM Food – Does Anybody Want It?

SB S. 192
▶ LSET ex. 8

B3 GM Food – Does Anybody Want It? Maha M. Alkhazindar et al.

Source:	National Center for Case Study Teaching in Science, February 2001
Topic:	The pros and cons of genetically modified food
Text form:	Case study (fictitious)
Language variety:	American English
Number of words:	652
Level:	Intermediate
Skills/Activities:	Doing research; argumentative writing; debating

Didaktischer Kommentar

Anhand einer fiktiven Reportage über die Zerstörung einer Versuchsanlage setzen sich S mit der Kontroverse um genetisch veränderte Lebensmittel auseinander. Die verständnislose Haltung der Betroffenen im Text fordert zur Stellungnahme heraus. S sammeln Argumente für und gegen die Anwendung von Gentechnik im Lebensmittelbereich und führen eine formelle Debatte darüber.

SB-DVD-ROM

Lernwortschatz

overcast (l. 1), gloomy (l. 1), mutilation (l. 5), wrench (l. 7), test pilot (l. 7), tread (l. 7), debris (l. 11), survey sth. (l. 11), rash (l. 11), breeding techniques (l. 15), pesticide (l. 17), plentiful (l. 19), crop (l. 19), sift through sth. (l. 22), drought (l. 23), yield (l. 32), underway (l. 38), vaccine (l. 38), diarrhoea (l. 38), inoculate sb./sth. (l. 40), take your cue from sb. (l. 45), steer clear of sb./sth. (l. 48), merger (l. 50)

Unterrichtstipps
ZA

Um den thematischen Wortschatz zu sammeln und zu sortieren, werden die wichtigsten Begriffe des Textes zusammengestellt (z. B. in einer Mindmap mit den Oberbegriffen *agriculture, genetics, big business*).

2–3 Der Webcode bietet URLs mit Hintergrundinformationen zu Nutzen und Risiken gentechnisch veränderter Lebensmittel.

Differenzierung
HA

In schwächeren Lerngruppen wird der Text zu Hause vorbereitet.

ZA

Karteikartenreferat: Zur stärkeren Auseinandersetzung mit dem Text sowie zur Festigung des Wortschatzes wählen S fünf Schlagwörter aus dem Text und erstellen eine Inhaltsangabe des Textes mit diesen Begriffen.

Info

Genetic engineering makes it possible to develop plants with qualities they might never have acquired naturally, as characteristics can be transferred from one species to another, even from animal to plant and vice versa. Plant breeders have been changing the genetic make-up of plants for thousands of years. The result is that today none of the plants that are grown as food crops in the world occurs in nature. Critics fear that introducing 'unnatural' life forms may cause uncontrollable damage to the environment. Plants present a particular problem, as their genetic material is transmitted by pollen, which is difficult to contain. Genetic modifications could then be spread around the world. Also, it is often claimed that large biotech firms are interested in gaining control over world food production by making farmers dependent on their products and by acquiring the patent rights for a large number of common food plants than in reducing hunger in the world.

Lösungshinweise

1a Individual answers.

1b *Pro genetic engineering:* GM crops can flourish with less pesticide, thereby benefiting the environment (ll. 15–20); they can be engineered for higher yields (ll. 31–36); vaccines could be introduced into common food crops so that children are automatically protected against common diseases (ll. 37–38).

Communicating across Cultures

2a *Con GM foods:* danger of gene flow through cross-pollination (modified genes of GM plants are transferred via pollen to non-GM plants); possibility of allergic reactions to GM substances or of new diseases; risk of uncontrollable damage to environment caused by manipulated life forms; biotech firms create new varieties that are unable to reproduce, making farmers who buy the seed dependent on one firm, which can then dictate the price

2b–3 Individual answers.

SB S. 194 ## Communicating across Cultures – Dealing with Technical English

Didaktischer Kommentar S werden mit den Eigenheiten englischer Fachbegriffe konfrontiert. Anhand von Übungen zur Wort- und Begriffsbildung lernen sie Techniken der Texterschließung kennen, die anhand eines authentischen Textes erprobt und vertieft werden (s. a. *SF 4: Dealing with unknown words*).

Unterrichtstipps **1** L achten auf die korrekte Aussprache und Betonung, v. a. auf den Unterschied bei Nomen und Adjektiven *(biólogy – biológical)* und weisen darauf hin, dass die Nomen *physics, genetics* usw. nicht zählbare Nomen *(uncountable nouns)* sind.

Differenzierung **3–4** Die Entscheidung, ob diese als EXTRA markierten Aufgaben für einen Kurs geeignet sind oder nicht, ist eine Frage des Schwierigkeitsgrades (Fachvokabular), und des (mathematisch-naturwissenschaftlichen) Interesses der S.

Lösungshinweise **1**

Field	Person	Adjective
biology	biologist	*biological*
psychology	*psychologist*	*psychological*
genetics	*geneticist*	genetic
climatology	*climatologist*	*climatological*
biochemistry	*biochemist*	*biochemical*
meteorology	meteorologist	*meteorological*
astronomy	*astronomer*	astronomical
geology	*geologist*	geological
science	*scientist*	*scientific*

2

German: compound	English: adjective + noun
Strukturanalyse	structural analysis
Umwelttechnik	environmental technology
Genmanipulation	*genetic* modification
Kernspaltung	*nuclear* fission
Industriezeitalter	industrial age
Erdanziehungskraft	*gravitational* force

9 Part C1 – Take AIM at Climate Change

3

a random access memory (adjective + noun + noun): a form of computer *memory* that can be *randomly accessed* (irregularly or without deciding to beforehand).

b acquired immune deficiency syndrome (participle + adjective + noun + noun): an *acquired syndrome* (one that you get from somebody) in which your *immune* system displays *deficiencies*, i.e. doesn't function properly

c attention-deficit hyperactivity disorder (noun + noun + noun + noun): a *disorder* characterized by *hyperactivity* and an inability to pay *attention* for longer periods

d ozone layer *depletion* (noun + noun + noun): the depletion (reduction in the amount) of *ozone* in the *layer* of the atmosphere in which it normally occurs

e embryonic stem cell research (adjective + noun + noun + noun): *research* on *stem cells* found in *embryos*

f universal mobile telecommunications system (UMTS) (adjective + adjective + noun + noun): a *system of mobile telecommunications* (not bound to fixed locations) that operates *universally* (everywhere or that can be used for any kind of multimedia application)

4a

Function	Colour	Phrase
main topic	pink	glacial and fluvioglacial deposition
main categories	yellow	glacial deposits / till
sub-categories	blue	lodgement till; ablation till
explanations	orange	material dropped by actively moving glaciers; deposits dropped by stagnant or retreating ice
examples	green	erratics, drumlins, moraines

4b Fluvioglacial or meltwater deposits (yellow) can be subdivided into prolonged drift (blue), in which the material is very well sorted (orange), e.g. varves and outwash plains (green), and ice-contact stratified drift (blue) such as kames and eskers (green), which are more varied in character (orange).

4c

```
   glacial deposits/till              fluvioglacial deposits
(e.g. erratics, drumlins, moraines)   (= meltwater deposits)
        ↓         ↓                         ↓              ↓
  lodgement   ablation              prologed drift    ice-contact
     till        till               (e.g varves,     stratified drift (e.g.
                                    outwash plains)   kames, eskers)
```

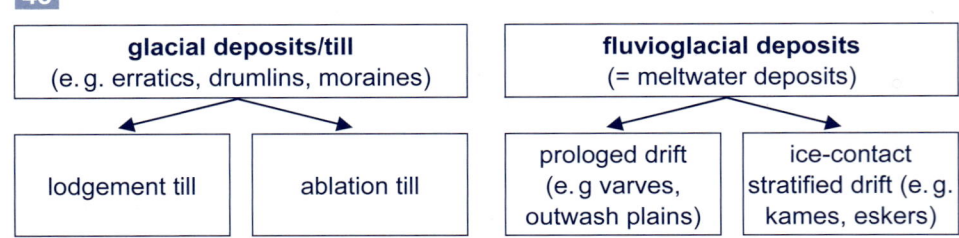

Part C – The Challenge of Climate Change

C1 Take AIM at Climate Change

Source:	Website of Passport to Knowledge, January 2009
Topic:	Strategies of dealing with climate change
Text form:	Music video
Language variety:	American English
Length:	4:25 min
Level:	Basic
Skills/Activities:	Viewing skills; analysing and assessing a music video

Part C1 – Take AIM at Climate Change

Didaktischer Kommentar S wiederholen und festigen anhand des Musikvideos ihr Grundwissen zum Thema Klimawandel. Sie lernen die drei Hauptstrategien im Umgang mit den Folgen der globalen Erwärmung kennen und wenden dieses Wissen exemplarisch an. S analysieren das Video und beurteilen dessen Wirksamkeit.

Unterrichtstipps
⚠ HA ● Word help
👥 ZA

Vor dem ersten Sehen des Videoclips machen sich S mit unbekanntem Wortschatz vertraut.

KV 20 stellt den zum Thema Ursache und Wirkung des Klimawandels (Part C) notwendigen Wortschatz bereit und hilft, das Grundwissen zu vertiefen. sie eignet sich auch als Grundlage für ein *jigsaw puzzle* (s. S. 297) oder eine *placemat activity* (s. S. 298). Die Kopiervorlage kann schwarz/weiß kopiert werden, steht auf der TM-DVD-ROM aber auch in Farbe zur Verfügung.

Differenzierung **2** Leistungsschwächeren S stellt L das Transkript zur Verfügung. Zur Verständnissicherung fassen S einzelne Zeilen in eigenen Worten auf Englisch oder Deutsch zusammen: Zeilen 7–8, 9–10, 35–36, 52–53.
2b Interessierte S überlegen, welches Medium sie am wirksamsten finden, um auf den Klimawandel aufmerksam zu machen.

Unterrichtstipps **2a** Beim ersten Sehen des Musikvideos achten S v.a. auf den Inhalt; dazu kann zunächst nur der Ton abgespielt werden.

2b Um die Wirksamkeit des Videos als Medium zu beurteilen, kann für diese Aufgabe der Ton ausgeschaltet werden, bevor es beim dritten Mal mit Bild und Ton abgespielt wird.

Lösungshinweise **1a** The acronym stands for the three main strategies of dealing with climate change, A = adapt; I = innovate; M = mitigate; cf. **1b**.

1b Picture A: mitigate. Improving the thermal insulation of houses helps to mitigate the effects of global warming because better insulation is an effective way to save energy and reduce CO_2 emissions.
Picture B: adapt. Countries like the Netherlands need to employ strategies of adapting to the effects of climate change (rising sea levels, flooding) by building floating houses, etc.
Picture C: innovate. Electric, battery-driven cars (like the Tesla Roadster in the picture, whose battery consists of hundreds of notebook batteries) do not require any fossil fuels at all.

2a The video juxtaposes images of the polar regions (icebergs, polar bears) with images of how climate change will affect us. One of the singers raises the question about the conntection, so the lead singer explains that the melting of the polar ice caps will lead to rising sea levels (verse 1, ll. 15–16) which 'will be felt at the equator' (verse 2, l. 8). Rising sea levels will affect all coastal regions of the USA and major urban areas like Florida or New York (verse 2, l. 11). The polar regions are crucial to understanding the world's climate. Experts are able to deduce the history of the Earth's climate by drilling into the ice, measuring its thickness and analyzing its composition (verse 4, l. 8).

2b Using a music video may be seen as effective because
- music videos are a *popular format* most students (who are the main target group) are familiar with;
- it combines *popular music* (rap, hip hop),
memorable song lyrics (the acronym 'aim' is repeated in every chorus, the lyrics are easy to understand because of the colloquial language that is used) and
powerful images (e.g. contrasting glaciers and polar bears with smoking chimneys and natural hazards) and turns this into a memorable multimedia mix;

9 Part C2 – The Future of Energy – the Energy of the Future

- The use of stylistic devices underlines the message of the song.
- it uses a *question and answer-pattern* (like in early blues music): Individual members of the chorus ask everyday questions which are taken seriously and answered by the lead singer in an easy-to-understand way;

It may be seen as ineffective by students for the following reasons:
- It is too obviously *didactic* and *well-meaning*.
- The artists have been commissioned to compose the song, so it lacks *authenticity* and *passion*.
- There is very little that is really *original* or *eye-catching* in the video.

SB S. 197
▶ LSET ex. 9

C2 The Future of Energy – the Energy of the Future   George Monbiot

Source:	Speech to the Climate March, 3 December 2005
Topic:	The end of the fossil fuel age
Text form:	Speech, charts and diagrams
Language variety:	British English
Number of words:	291
Level:	Intermediate
Skills/Activities:	Analysing stylistic devices; mediating; analysing charts and statistics; doing research

Didaktischer Kommentar

S vertiefen ihr Grundwissen über alternative Energien, indem sie die beiden Diagramme auswerten und analysieren und dabei relevante sprachliche Strukturen einsetzen. Die Rechercheaufgabe ermöglicht kooperative Unterrichtsformen und eine intensive Auseinandersetzung mit den Chancen und Risiken der jeweiligen Energiequelle.

SB-DVD-ROM

Lernwortschatz

circumstance (intro), be constrained by sb./sth. (l. 6), precede sb./sth. (l. 7), surplus (l. 9), available (l. 9), fortunate (l. 14), inhabit sth. (l. 14), replace sth. (l. 18), take sth. for granted (l. 21).

Unterrichtstipps

4 Um die erworbenen Fertigkeiten im Umgang mit Diagrammen zu festigen, werden solche Darstellungsformen regelmäßig in den Unterricht integriert.
Linktipp: www.eia.doe.gov/oiaf/ieo/world.html Hier finden sich weitere Diagramme zum Thema Energien.

5 Die SWOT-Analyse (**KV 21**) ist im deutschen Sprachraum noch relativ unbekannt, wird aber im englischen Sprachraum schon seit längerer Zeit von Unternehmen und auch Lehrkräften erfolgreich eingesetzt, da sie sich sehr gut dazu eignet, komplexes Denken und *academic writing* zu schulen. Aufgrund der Bestimmung und Abwägung von Stärken und Schwächen gegenüber Chancen und Risiken ist diese Form zur Analyse komplexer Sachverhalte geeignet: zur Planung, Problemlösung oder Herbeiführung von Entscheidungen, auch auf privater Ebene.

Differenzierung

3a Leistungsschwächere S bearbeiten folgende Aufgabe vorab zu zweit: *Look up the four words and explain their meaning to your partner in your own words.*

Part C2 – The Future of Energy – the Energy of the Future

> **Info**
>
> *George Monbiot* [ˈmɒnbiəʊ] (born 1963) is an English writer, known for his environmental and political activism. He writes a weekly column for *The Guardian*, and is the author of a number of books.
>
> *The Climate March* in London has been held annually since 2005 to coincide with the United Nations Climate Talks. The March is organised by the group 'Campaign against Climate Change' (CCC) to call for immediate action on climate change. George Monbiot is Honorary President of the campaign group.
>
> *Renewable energy* is generated from natural resources that are naturally replenished (renewed): e.g. sunlight, wind, rain, tides or geothermal heat. When comparing the processes for producing energy, there remain several fundamental differences between renewable energy and fossil fuels. The production of oil, coal, or natural gas fuel requires a great deal of complex equipment, physical and chemical processes, while alternative energy can be produced with basic equipment and naturally basic processes. Wood, the most renewable and available energy, actually releases the same amount of carbon when burnt as it would emit if it degraded naturally, but, of course, the time frame is very different: when wood burns it emits carbon in one go, while degradation takes place over a long time period.

Lösungshinweise

1a *Sample timeline:*

Past (ecological constraint)	Present	Future (ecological catastrophe)
• dependent on ambient energy • human lives were dominated by nature ('happenstances of ecology') • widespread fear	• abundant energy from fossil fuels • rise of agricultural and economical productivity • higher standard of living	• energy shortage (depletion of fossil fuels) • consequences of global warming

1b With these words, Monbiot wants to illustrate that our whole lifestyle is based on the concept of cheap and abundant energy; a concept that can no longer be sustained. By creating the image of a pile balanced on a ball he voices his concern that this era will probably not come to an end smoothly but with a crisis, meaning huge problems and sacrifices for everybody on this planet.

2 *Stylistic device:* metaphor. A metaphor is a very effective device because it creates in the mind of the reader a very powerful and vivid image of a complex situation, making it easily accessible and instantly understandable. In this case, the reader or listener can almost feel the instability of the mass balanced on the ball.

3a surplus: positive; interlude: neutral; impending: negative; diversity: positive

3b By using words with negative connotations, Monbiot expresses not only his attitude toward the past ('fear of hunger, predation, weather', l. 4) but also about the future ('ecological catastrophe', l. 15, 'impending shortage', l. 17). Words with positive connotations are used to describe the era of abundant energy which will come to an end quite shortly. Ironically, it is the failure of the people living in this interlude between ecological constraint and ecological catastrophe to come up with a more sustainable way of living which will lead to energy shortage and cause dramatic climate change.

Part C3 – Science to the Rescue?

4 According to the charts, global energy consumption will continue to increase. The demand for all forms of energy will rise steadily. Chart 1 shows that in the near future the world will still depend on fossil fuels such as coal and natural gas. Since all of these energy sources emit CO_2, it seems likely that the goal of limiting global warming to 2 °C by the year 2100 may be out of reach, which would have devastating effects on our environment. Both charts indicate a growing demand for renewables. There is a striking difference between OECD and non-OECD members with regard to energy sources used for generating electricity. In OECD states, hydropower seems to have reached its limit, whereas wind and other renewable sources such as solar energy will be used increasingly to generate electricity. In non-OECD states, the picture is quite different: hydropower will grow in absolute terms. By the year 2030, non-OECD members will generate more electricity from renewable sources than the richer nations.

5 Individual answers. The webcode offers links for background information on the topics for class presentations.

SB S. 199
▶ **LSET ex. 10**

C3 EXTRA Science to the Rescue? Oliver Tickell

Source:	'Geo-engineers, too, have a vital role in saving the planet', *The Guardian*, 4 September 2008
Topic:	Geo-engineering
Text form:	Newspaper article (extract)
Language variety:	British English
Number of words:	563
Level:	Advanced
Skills/Activities:	Summarizing; scanning; working with charts; mediating; doing research; making a poster

Didaktischer Kommentar

Der Text führt in das umstrittene Konzept des *geo-engineering* ein. Eine Sprachmittlungsübung gibt S die Möglichkeit, mittels Lernen durch Lehren aktiv zu überprüfen, inwieweit sie diesen komplexen Sachverhalt verstanden haben und versprachlichen können. In der *Context Task* steht die Frage im Zentrum, welchen Beitrag jeder Einzelne zum Klimaschutz leisten kann. S überprüfen gängige Vorstellungen und vergleichen diese mit Statistiken, um zu einer realistischen Einschätzung der Vorschläge zu kommen.

SB-DVD-ROM

Lernwortschatz

combat sb./sth. (l. 3), maintain sth. (l. 5), imply sth. (l. 10), deforestation (l. 14), enhance sth. (l. 16), retain sth. (l. 16), amplify sth. (l. 19), thaw (l. 27), immediate effect (l. 36), inflict harm (l. 41)

Unterrichtstipps

Die zwei Farben des Tortendiagramms beziehen sich auf den primären (blau) und den sekundären CO_2-Fußabdruck (ocker): Der primäre bezieht sich auf die von uns direkt zu beeinflussenden CO_2-Emissionen (durch das Verbrennen fossiler Brennstoffe in Haushalten und im Verkehr). Der sekundäre misst die sich aus dem Verbrauch (Herstellung und Entsorgen) der von uns genutzten Produkte ergebenden CO_2-Emissionen. Beide zusammen ergeben den vollständigen Fußabdruck.

✶ **Linktipp:** www.uhv.edu/green/Goals.aspx Auf der Homepage der University of Houston – Victoria finden sich neben der Quelle für das Tortendiagramm auch weitere Anregungen zu umweltfreundlichem Handeln, die z. T. auch an Schulen umgesetzt werden können.

CONTEXT TASK a Diese Präsentation der Ergebnisse erfolgt als *gallery walk* (s. S. 297). Dazu erhalten je fünf S einen Lösungshinweis, den sie dann möglichst frei den Gruppen präsentieren, die von Station zu Station gehen.

Part C3 – Science to the Rescue?

Linktipp: *www.zerofootprintkids.com/kids_home.aspx* bietet einen sehr schülerfreundlichen carbon calculator, *http://news.bbc.co.uk/2/hi/in_depth/629/629/5086298.stm* bietet Informationen zum Wasserverbrauch sowie einen water calculator, mit dessen Hilfe der persönliche *water footprint* errechnet werden kann.

ZA Für S, die wissenschaftlich arbeiten möchten oder ein wissenschaftspropädeutisches Seminar an der Schule besuchen, bietet **KV 22** Richtlinien für das Bibliographieren sowie eine praktische Aufgabe. Die KV ist kapitelübergreifend einsetzbar. Lösungshinweise:
- Anderson, John: 'Mistakes and Models', in: *English Teaching Professional*, issue 67, 2010, pp. 34–47
- Bhutto, Fatima, 'The Teetering State', *New Statesman*, 23 August 2010
- Monbiot, George, 'A Modest Proposal for Tackling Youth', website of Monbiot, 28 August 2010. www.monbiot.com/archives/2010/06/28/a-modest-proposal-for-tackling-youth
- Rowling, Joanne K.: *Harry Potter and the Philosopher's Stone*, London: Bloomsbury, 1997
- Swan, Michael: *Practical English Usage*, 3rd edition, Oxford: Oxford University Press, 2005

Differenzierung ZA

In leistungsstarken bzw. technisch versierten Lerngruppen kann eine von L oder S gewählte Dokumentation zum Thema Geo-Engineering Grundlage einer komplexen Mediationsaufgabe werden. In arbeitsteiliger Einzel- oder Gruppenarbeit vertonen S ein deutsches Video mittels frei verfügbarer Software wie dem Windows *Movie Maker* auf Englisch (bei sechs S/Gruppen fünf Minuten je S/Gruppe). Leistungsschwächere wählen ein englisches Video und vertonen es auf Deutsch. (Es kann z. B. bei einer Suchmaschine „Geo-Engineering" eingegeben und gezielt nach Videos gesucht werden.)

> **Info**
>
> *The Kyoto Protocol* is a protocol aimed at fighting global warming. It was initially adopted in 1997 in Kyoto, Japan and entered into force in 2005. Industrialized countries committed themselves to a reduction of four greenhouse gases (carbon dioxide, methane, nitrous oxide, sulphur hexafluoride) and two groups of gases (hydrofluorocarbons and perfluorocarbons) by 5.2 % from the 1990 level.
>
> *Kyoto 2* is an alternative framework for a new climate agreement intended to replace the Kyoto Protocol. Its aims are to stabilize greenhouse gases in the atmosphere at a level that would prevent interference with the climate system, while addressing the needs of poor countries.
>
> *Geo-engineering* is used to refer to methods intended to deliberately manipulate the Earth's climate to counteract the effects of global warming from greenhouse gas emissions. Some geo-engineering techniques include carbon dioxide air capture and ocean iron fertilization. To date, no large-scale geo-engineering projects have been undertaken. Some limited tree planting and cool-roof projects are already underway, and ocean iron fertilization is at an advanced stage of research, with small-scale research trials and global modelling having already been completed.

Lösungshinweise

PRE-READING Cf. Info.

1a Correct answer: 2

1b 1 The author mentions the Royal Society because of a special edition of its journal dedicated to geo-engineering. If an established and well-renowned organisation publishes a journal on this topic, then it must be taken seriously.
2 Doug Parr's name is used to show that there is serious opposition from NGOs like Greenpeace to the idea of geo-engineering.

Part C3 – Science to the Rescue?

3 John Latham is a physicist who proposes an approach (raising the reflectivity of marine clouds to reduce global warming) that the author sympathizes with. By presenting a scientific approach, Tickell adds further credibility to his article.

1c

```
┌─────────────────────────┐        ┌─────────────────────────┐
│ Higher temperatures     │───────▶│ More sunlight is        │
│ cause Arctic ice to     │        │ absorbed. (l. 25)       │
│ melt.                   │        │                         │
└─────────────────────────┘        └─────────────────────────┘
          ▲                                    │
          │                                    ▼
┌─────────────────────────┐        ┌─────────────────────────┐
│ Due to the greenhouse   │        │ The ground temperature  │
│ effect the temperature  │        │ rises, so permafrost    │
│ of the atmosphere       │        │ thaws.                  │
│ rises. (ll. 26, 33)     │        │                         │
└─────────────────────────┘        └─────────────────────────┘
          ▲                                    │
          │                                    ▼
┌─────────────────────────┐        ┌─────────────────────────┐
│ Methane concentration   │◀───────│ Methane escapes from    │
│ in the atmosphere       │        │ normally frozen regions │
│ increases.              │        │ into the atmosphere.    │
│                         │        │ (l. 27)                 │
└─────────────────────────┘        └─────────────────────────┘
```

2 The author appreciates Greenpeace's support for renewable energies but he does not share their optimism and is convinced that a preventive strategy alone will not be enough. He thinks that it is high time to embrace the idea of actively mitigating the effects of global warming because the feedback loop has already been triggered. It is wise to insure ourselves against this possibility by supporting geo-engineering as long as we can be sure that such measures are thought through and won't have unforeseen adverse effects on our climate. That is why he supports Latham's suggestion: it is inexpensive, benign and reversible at any given moment.

3 Mediation Als Geo-Engineering werden Vorschläge bezeichnet, die aktiv ins Klima eingreifen, um der Erderwärmung durch Treibhausgase entgegenzuwirken. Im Gegensatz dazu steht die Reduzierung von Treibhausgasen z. B. durch die Umstellung auf erneuerbare Energien. Die zwei erfolgversprechendsten Geo-Engineering-Methoden sind: 1. Sulfataerosol in die Stratosphäre einzuführen, um das Sonnenlicht zu reflektieren und 2. die Reflektivität von Meereswolken zu erhöhen, indem ultrafeine Salztropfen als Wolkenkondensationskerne dienen.

CONTEXT TASK **ab** 1 *Rating:* 5. The aviation industry claims it contributes only 6% to global emissions, but independent experts think the figure may be nearly twice that high. No other form of transportation comes even close to that figure, so stay on the ground if you possibly can.
2 *Rating:* 2. Not as smart as it appears: manufacturing a car produces an average of 15 tonnes of waste and 75 million cubic metres of polluted air. Neither buying a car nor driving one – any car – is in any sense of the word environment-friendly.
3 *Rating:* 5. Standby uses anywhere between 10–60% of the electricity consumed by an appliance, so turning appliances completely off makes good sense. If everyone in the UK did so, they would save enough electricity to power 2.7 million homes. Turning down the thermostat by one degree saves 230 kg of carbon dioxide a year.
4 *Rating:* 3. Food production and transportation accounts for 25–30% of the UK's carbon dioxide emissions. The CO_2 emissions caused by one New Zealand kiwi fruit flown to Europe weigh five times as much as the fruit itself. The average shopping cart of food has enough 'food miles' behind it to reach the moon.
5 *Rating:* 2. Every 16 minutes, the sunlight falling on the Earth's surface delivers enough energy to meet current energy demands for a whole year. But in terms of return for your investment, better windows and insulation make more sense than photovoltaic panels on the roof. Solar collectors for hot water can save energy during the summer months.

cd Individual answers.

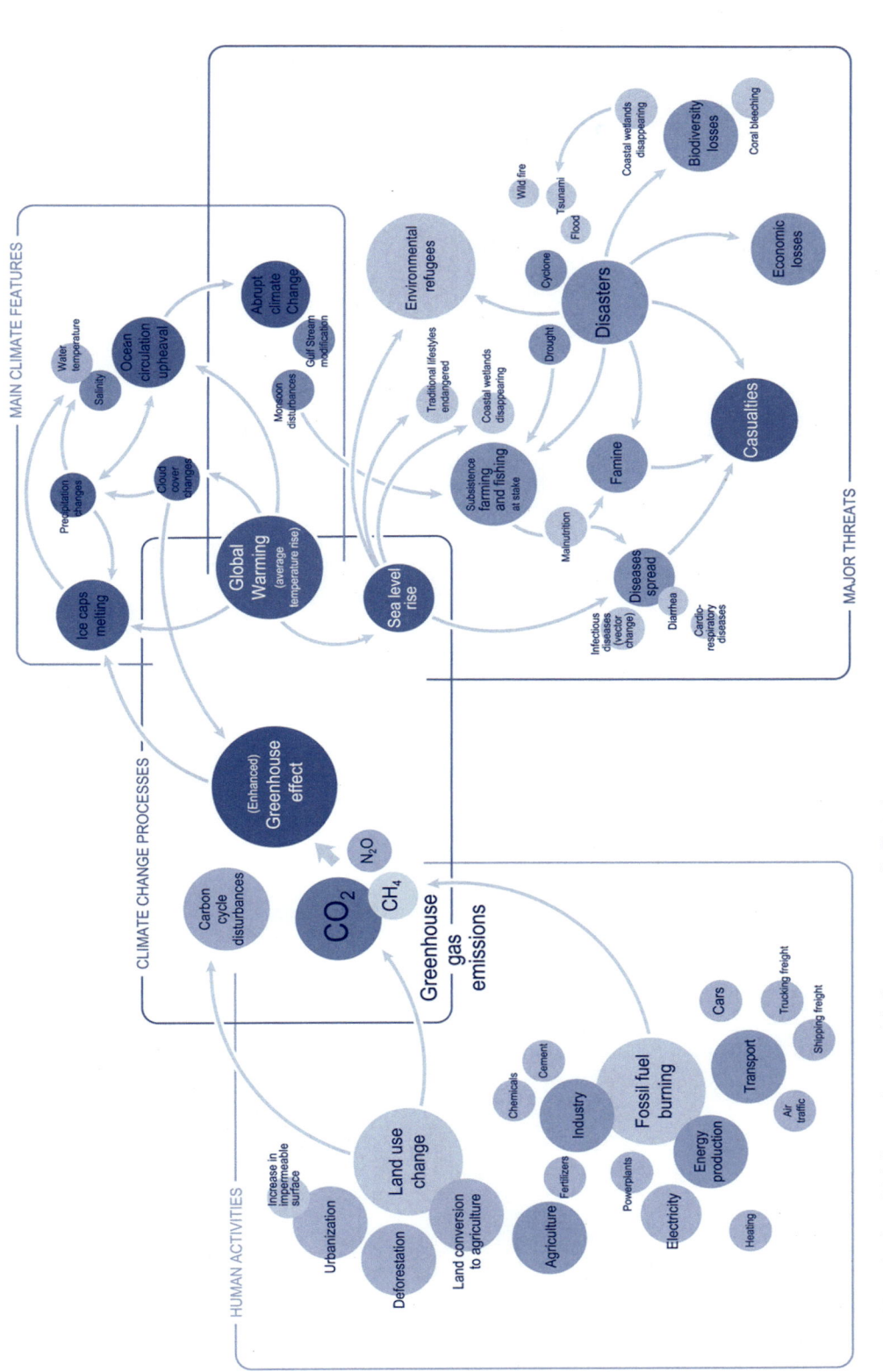

Kopiervorlage 20: Climate Change – Global Processes and Effects

MAIN CLIMATE FEATURES
- Water temperature
- Salinity
- Ocean circulation upheaval
- Abrupt climate change
- Monsoon disturbances
- Gulf Stream modification
- Precipitation changes
- Cloud cover changes
- Ice caps melting
- Global Warming (average temperature rise)
- Sea level rise

MAJOR THREATS
- Wild fire
- Tsunami
- Flood
- Coastal wetlands disappearing
- Biodiversity losses
- Coral bleaching
- Cyclone
- Environmental refugees
- Disasters
- Economic losses
- Drought
- Traditional lifestyles endangered
- Coastal wetlands disappearing
- Subsistence farming and fishing at stake
- Famine
- Casualties
- Malnutrition
- Diseases spread
- Infectious diseases (vector change)
- Diarrhea
- Cardio-respiratory diseases

CLIMATE CHANGE PROCESSES
- (Enhanced) Greenhouse effect
- Carbon cycle disturbances
- CO_2
- CH_4
- N_2O
- Greenhouse gas emissions

HUMAN ACTIVITIES
- Increase in impermeable surface
- Urbanization
- Deforestation
- Land use change
- Land conversion to agriculture
- Agriculture
- Fertilizers
- Powerplants
- Electricity
- Heating
- Chemicals
- Cement
- Industry
- Fossil fuel burning
- Energy production
- Transport
- Cars
- Trucking freight
- Shipping freight
- Air traffic

From: http://maps.grida.no/go/graphic/climate-change-global-processes-and-effects1

Language help
- … influences / leads to / is responsible for / results in / is a result of / …
- … barely / (in-)directly / seriously affects …
- The reason for … is (that) …
- Several factors contribute to …
- There is a connection/relationship/link between … and …
- In order to assess/determine/study/ discover/find/identify/understand the **cause/consequences** of …
- The real cause of the problem lies in …
- The positive/beneficial/negative/ disastrous/harmful/major/principal/ likely/potential/possible **effects** of …
- aggravate a problem
- minimize/reduce the **effects** of …
- foresee/predict the **consequences** of …

Context 21 | Science, Technology and the Environment
Part C1

Kopiervorlage 21: Doing a SWOT Analysis

Topic	
Strengths	**W**eaknesses
Opportunities	**T**hreats
Conclusion/Suggestions:	

Language help

Strengths/Opportunities:	**Weaknesses/Threats:**
▪ advantage/benefit/merit ▪ big/great/clear/considerable advantage	▪ … is/causes a problem ▪ poses/presents a threat ▪ a(n) acute/enormous/grave/serious/significant/ complex problem ▪ face / be confronted with a problem/challenge ▪ address/approach/tackle/solve/overcome a problem

Context 21 | Science, Technology and the Environment
► C2, task 5

Kopiervorlage 22: Writing a Bibliography

There are two kinds of bibliographies. One shows all the literature that you have quoted in your work. The other lists literature relevant to your topic that you consulted even though you didn't use it in your work ('Works consulted'). There are several different ways to organize a bibliography. For simplicity's sake, this guide offers one possibility. If you choose a different system, remember to be *consistent*.

1 A bibliography should be in *alphabetical order*.

2 *The information about a book* should be given in this order:
- **The author:** Give the surname first, then the first name.
  If there are two authors, put 'and' between their names.
  If there are more than two authors, list only the first one and add 'et al.' (Latin: 'and others') after the first author.
- **The title:** Give the complete title of the book, including subheadings, in italics.
- **The place of publication and publisher:** The place where the book was published is put next, then the name of the publisher.
- **The date of publication:** The date of publication is next.
- **The page number(s):** Last, give the exact page number(s) if you are indicating a particular quote. In a general bibliography ('Works consulted'), the page number is not necessary.

Examples (note the punctuation):
▶ Thomson, A.J. and Martinet, A.V., *A Practical English Grammar*, Oxford: OUP, 1980, p. 7
▶ Schwarz, Hellmut et al. *Context 21*, Berlin: Cornelsen, 2010

3 *The information about a magazine article or text in an anthology* should be given as above, except:
- **The name of the text or article:** This comes immediately after the author and is given in inverted commas. If the text is taken from an anthology, the editor's name and title of the anthology follow next after 'in'.
- **The name of publisher and place** are not given when articles are taken from magazines, newspapers, etc., but the date of publication (or issue number) is given.

Examples (note the punctuation):
▶ Blake, William, 'The Little Vagabond', in: Wu, Duncan (ed.): *Romanticism. An Anthology*, Oxford, 1994, p. 73
▶ Reeves, Richard, and Leighton, Dan, 'The Republican Moment', *New Statesman*, 25 April 2010, pp. 22–25

9

Kopiervorlage 22: Writing a Bibliography

4 *Online sources* must be treated like any other source. You need to list the exact URL as well as the date on which you accessed the site:

> Example (note the punctuation):
> ▶ Corbett Dooren, Jennifer, 'Concussions Rise Among Student Athletes', website of *The Wall Street Journal*, 31 August 2010
> http://online.wsj.com/article/SB10001424052748704323704575461831955174258.html
> (6 September 2010)

Task:

The following bibliography has got mixed up. Rewrite it according to the guidelines as best you can – there are a couple of extra points you will have to think about.

- *English Teaching Professional*, 2010, issue 67, pp. 34–47. Mistakes and Models by John Anderson
- Practical English Usage by Michael Swan. 3rd edition. Published in Oxford by OUP: 2005
- Rowling: *Harry Potter and the Philosopher's Stone* (1997, Bloomsbury, London)
- Article title: The Teetering State, in the magazine 'New Statesman', author: Fatima Bhutto, date: 23rd August, 2010
- 28 June 2010: www.monbiot.com/archives/2010/06/28/a-modest-proposal-for-tackling-youth, A Modest Proposal for Tackling Youth, George Monbiot, website of Monbiot. Seen on 22 September.

Rewrite it here first before typing it up:

_____
_____
_____
_____
_____
_____
_____
_____
_____

Context 21 Science, Technology and the Environment: Topic Vocabulary

Word/Phrase	Memory Aid	German
SCIENCE		
advances	*example sentence:* Recent ~ in technology have drastically improved the speed with which we can communicate with one another.	Fortschritte
AIDS	*definition:* 'Acquired Immune Deficiency Syndrome' – a condition in which the body is unable to protect itself from infection	AIDS
antibiotics	*example sentence:* The doctor prescribed her a course of ~ and the infection was gone in less than a week.	Antibiotika
breakthrough	*collocations:* a dramatic/major/significant ~	Durchbruch
cancer	*example sentence:* Five years passed and she was given the all-clear – she had finally beaten ~!	Krebs
chemotherapy [ˌkiːməʊˈθerəpi]	*definition:* a common course of treatment for cancer patients	Chemotherapie
diabetes	*word family:* <u>diabetes</u> – diabetic *(n, person)* – diabetic *(adj)*	Diabetes, Zuckerkrankheit
discovery	*word family:* (to) discover – discoverer – <u>discovery</u>	Entdeckung
DNA (deoxyribonucleic acid)	*definition:* a chemical in the cells of animals and plants carrying genetic information	DNS (Desoxyribonukleinsäure)
ethics *(pl)*	*definition:* moral principles that control how one behaves in a certain context	Ethik
experiment	*word family:* (to) experiment – <u>experiment</u> *(n)* – experimental	Experiment
foetus *(BE)* / fetus *(AE)*	*example sentence:* Smoking or consuming alcohol during pregnancy can harm a developing ~.	Fetus
genetic disorder	*other collocations with* **disorder**: eating/mental/nervous <u>disorder</u>	genetische Störung
HIV	*example sentence:* With over 5 million infected people, South Africa is the ~ capital of the world.	HIV
IVF (in vitro fertilization)	*definition:* a process which fertilizes a female egg outside the woman's body before being put in her uterus to develop	In-vitro-Befruchtung
laboratory [ləˈbɒrətri ☆ ˈlæbrətɔːri]	*example sentence:* The animal rights activists protested outside the ~.	Labor

Context 21 Science, Technology and the Environment: Topic Vocabulary

Word/Phrase	Memory Aid	German
SCIENCE		
(medical) treatment	*synonyms:* care/therapy	(medizinische) Behandlung
medicine	*definition:* a substance taken to cure an illness or relieve the symptoms of it	Medikamente
(to) **operate on** sb.	*word family:* (to) operate – operation – operator	jdn. operieren
painkillers	*example sentence:* After waking up with a headache, Ralph took a couple of ~ to be able to go to work.	Schmerzmittel
(to) **research**	*word family:* (to) research – research *(n)* – researcher	forschen
sperm bank	*other collocations with* **sperm**: sperm donor / sperm count	Samenbank
symptom	*synonyms:* indication/sign	Symptom
test-tube baby	*synonym:* IVF baby	Retortenbaby
tumor	*example sentence:* After months of painful headaches she went to the doctor and was told she had a brain ~.	Tumor
TECHNOLOGY		
(to) **crash**	*example sentence:* I lost a lot of my work when my computer ~ed unexpectedly.	abstürzen
identity theft	*other collocations with* **theft**: data/petty/car/identity theft	Identitätsdiebstahl, -betrug
(to) **invent** sth.	*word family:* (to) invent – invention – inventive – inventor	etwas erfinden
keyboard	*definition:* a device with which one can enter information into a computer	Tastatur
memory stick	*synonym:* flash drive / USB drive / pen drive / thumb drive *(AE)*	USB-Stick
monitor	*example sentence:* He spent too much time in front of his computer ~ playing computer games.	Bildschirm
robotics	*definition:* the science of designing and operating robots	Robotik, Robotertechnik
state of the art	*opposite:* out of date / obsolete	auf dem neusten Stand der Technik

Context 21 Science, Technology and the Environment: Topic Vocabulary

Word/Phrase	Memory Aid	German
TECHNOLOGY		
Wi-fi (wireless fidelity) ['waɪfaɪ]	*example sentence:* My favourite cafe had free ~ for paying customers and was popular with the students in the neighbourhood.	WLAN (wireless local area network)
wireless	*definition:* telecommunications transmitted through electrowaves and without a wire connection	Funk-
ENVIRONMENT		
(to) **become extinct**	*synonym:* (to) die out	aussterben
carbon footprint	*definition:* a measurement of the daily amount of carbon dioxide produced by a person or company	CO_2-Bilanz
climate change	*example sentence:* The extinction of mammoths has been attributed to ~ change rather than to hunting by humans.	Klimaveränderung
deforestation	*opposites:* afforestation/reforestation	Entwaldung, Waldabbau
(to) **destroy the ozone layer**	*opposite:* (to) repair the ozone layer	die Ozonschicht zerstören
emission	*example sentence:* The council took measures to reduce exhaust pipe ~ in the city centre.	Ausstoß, Emission
famine	*definition:* a lack of food in a region for a period of time	Hungersnot
flood	*opposite:* drought [draʊt]	Überschwemmung
fossil fuels	*definition:* fuels made up of natural materials, usually dead organisms which have decomposed over millions of years (e.g. coal or oil)	fossile Brennstoffe
global warming	*other collocations with* **global**: global economy/finance/business	Erderwärmung
greenhouse effect	*definition:* an increase in gases like carbon dioxide around the Earth that results in trapped heat and a gradual rise in temperature	Treibhauseffekt
oil spill	*example sentence:* The ~ spill in the Gulf of Mexico far exceeds any other in living memory.	Ölpest, Ölkatastrophe
(to) **pollute** sth.	*opposite:* (to) clean sth.	etwas verschmutzen
power station	*other collocations with* **station**: police/fire station	Kraftwerk

Context 21 Science, Technology and the Environment: Topic Vocabulary

Word/Phrase	Memory Aid	German
ENVIRONMENT		
radioactive fallout	*other collocation with* **fallout**: political fallout	radioaktiver Niederschlag
renewable energy	*opposite*: non-renewable energy	erneuerbare Energie
sewage ['suːɪdʒ]	*definition*: used water and human waste, disposed of and transported away via sewers	Abwasser
solar panel	*definition*: a flat object consisting of solar cells with the purpose of collecting energy from the sun	Sonnenkollektor
solar power (or ~ **energy**)	*other collocations with* **power**: wind/water power	Sonnenenergie (oder ~kraft)
sustainable	*opposite*: unsustainable	nachhaltig
toxic	*example sentence*: Be careful to wear gloves and a mask when handling ~ chemicals.	giftig, toxisch
water supply	*example sentence*: The ~ **supply** has been affected by the earthquake.	Wasserversorgung
wildlife	*example sentence*: She dedicated her life to raising awareness and conserving endangered ~.	wild lebende Tierarten

10 The World of English

Das Kapitel beleuchtet die historische Entwicklung der englischen Sprache, ihre Ausbreitung als Lingua franca und die Folgen ihrer universellen Verwendung sowohl für nicht-englische Sprachen und Kulturen als auch für das Englische selbst. Der eigene Lernprozess bildet dabei den zentralen Bezugspunkt für S.
Part A – The History of English bietet einen vereinfachten Überblick über die Entstehung, die Ausbreitung und die reiche Lexik der englischen Sprache.
Part B – Linguistic Imperialism problematisiert exemplarisch das Verhältnis von Sprache und Weltsicht und zeigt daran das Erbe des einstigen *British Empire* auf.
Part C – The Future of English beschreibt Szenarien der möglichen Entwicklung und Varianten des Englischen.

Didaktisches Inhaltsverzeichnis

SB p.	Title	TM p.	Text Form	Topic	Skills and Activities	Language Practice
202	Lead-in Doug Lansky; Martyn Ford and Peter Legon	258	Photos; non–fictional texts (extracts)	The spread of English	Working with pictures; correcting texts; reading non-fiction; comparing grammatical structures; taking part in a discussion	
204	Words in Context – English, English Everywhere CD 2.07-10	260	Informative text; citation	Varieties of English	Activating vocabulary; reading non-fiction; mind mapping; listening comprehension	LP 20: Avoiding German-English interference
	Part A – The History of English					
206	A1 Words, Words, Words	261	Non-fictional text; graph	The history of the English language	Reading non-fiction; working with charts and graphs; using a dictionary; cooperative learning strategy (group puzzle); doing research; giving a presentation	LP 22: Using the appropriate register; LP 25: Expressing yourself concisely; LP 3: Idioms
	Part B – Linguistic Imperialism					
208	B1 The Language of Power – the Power of Language Daniel Defoe; Lloyd Jones	263	Novels (extracts)	Linguistic imperialism	Reading fiction; comparing novels; creative writing	
211	B2 That's Not Cricket DVD	264	Documentary film (extract)	The Empire's heritage	Making notes; viewing a film; matching words and definitions; doing research; giving a presentation	LP 3: Idioms
212	Communicating across Cultures DVD CD 2.11-14	265	Documentary film (extract); conversations	Communicating in a world of Englishes	Viewing a film; doing research; giving a presentation; taking part in a discussion	LP 25: Expressing yourself concisely
	Part C – The Future of English					
213	C1 How English is Evolving into a Language We May Not Even Understand Michael Erard	267	Web article (extract)	Globalized English	Reading non-fiction; analysing a text; writing a comment	LP 15: Talking about the future
215	C2 On Protectionism Stephen Clarke	268	Novel (extract); photos	The need for and the effectiveness of linguistic protectionism	Reading fiction; analysing a text; writing a formal letter	
217	C3 Rettet das Englische Eckhard Fuhr	270	Newspaper article (extract)	EU appeal to adopt a European language apart from English	Mediating	LP 20: Avoiding German-English interference

10 Lead-in

SB S. 202   **Lead-in**   Doug Lansky; Martyn Ford and Peter Legon

Source:	*Signspotting – Absurd and Amusing Signs from Around the World*, 2005
Topic:	The spread of English
Text form:	Non-fictional text (extract)
Language variety:	Australian English
Number of words:	96
Level:	Basic

Source:	*The How to be British Collection*, 2005
Topic:	The spread of English
Text form:	Non-fictional text (extract)
Language variety:	British English
Number of words:	127
Level:	Basic

Skills/Activities:	Working with pictures; correcting texts; reading non-fiction; comparing grammatical structures; taking part in a discussion

Didaktischer Kommentar

Die Materialien dieser Doppelseite vermitteln eindrücklich die globale Verbreitung des Englischen. S reflektieren sowohl ihre persönliche Motivation für das Englischlernen als auch Schwierigkeiten, die sich durch die Verbreitung des Englischen ergeben.

SB-DVD-ROM

Lernwortschatz

stubbornness (text 1, l. 5), straightforward (text 2, l. 3), fuss (text 2, l. 6)

Unterrichtstipps

1 erfolgt bei geschlossenem Schülerbuch.

2 Aus zeitökonomischen Gründen können die Aufgaben in arbeitsteiliger Partnerarbeit erfolgen.

3c Es ist ratsam, Grammatiken beider Sprachen zur Verfügung zu stellen.

Linktipp: *http://www.kombu.de/twain-2.htm#x1* Zur Vertiefung und humorvollen Illustration lässt sich Mark Twains „The Awful German Language" heranziehen.

4 Zur Einteilung der Gruppen nehmen S auf einer Linie die Position ein, die ihrer Meinung entspricht: Das rechte Ende der Linie steht für Zustimmung, das linke Ende für Ablehnung. In ihren Gruppen sammeln S Argumente.

Differenzierung

3a Leistungsstärkere S erforschen die Herkunft des Begriffs Lingua franca.

3c S mit Migrationshintergrund erläutern Unterschiede zwischen ihrer Muttersprache und dem Englischen.

Info

English as a first language is spoken by roughly 330 million people, as many as 510 million including speakers of English as a second language, and more than one billion including those who speak English as a foreign language.

'Lingua franca' originally referred to a language composed of Italian, French, Greek, Spanish, Turkish and Arabic used in Mediterranean ports between the 11th and 19th centuries. Its literal meaning is 'Frankish language'. During the Renaissance, Arabs applied the word Franks to all Europeans.

Lead-in – The World of English

Lösungshinweise

1a academic and professional reasons, travelling, computer and Internet

1b Individual answers.

2a *Sign from Myanmar*: Due to wrong word formation / a misplaced gerund, the sign says that tourists have to have their feet amputated before they are allowed to enter the temple. It should read 'Footwear prohibited' or 'Wearing shoes prohibited'.
The sign from New York implies that Canada could be part of the luggage. The sentence structure creates ambiguity; a relative clause or a clearer participle construction would make the message clear: 'All international travellers with luggage – including those travelling to or from Canada – please go to ticket counter for check-in'.
Sign from Tanzania: Due to a problem of word formation, this sign implies that objects and people cannot be seen anymore. The abstract noun 'invisibility' has to be replaced by a phrase to make the warning clear: 'Be aware of sudden poor visibility' or 'Attention! Poor visibility'.
The sign from Tibet is ambiguous: 'unorganized' can mean disorganized or chaotic, but the reception centre probably wants to support tourists travelling without a tour operator. A different adjective would clarify: 'The Lhasa reception centre for independent travellers'.
Sign from Kenya: This sign would seem to address literate elephants. Lexical and syntactic changes are necessary to make the message correct and meaningful: 'Only two elephants can be led across the bridge at a time'.

3a A 'lingua franca' is the language used by people with different native languages to communicate with one another.

3b The statement that, in contrast to other languages, English has only one pronoun for the second person seems serious and informative (ll. 3–4). However, the adverb 'democratically' in l. 5 indicates that the text is more than a linguistic description; 'unnecessary fuss' (l. 6), the describing prepositions as 'a great help in global positioning systems and personal orientation programmes' (ll. 8–10) and the examples chosen to illustrate that English has a vast vocabulary and is rich in synonyms (for 'mad',' drunk', and 'to describe the weather' ll. 11–13) give the text an ironic, satirical tone. Overall, the text mixes humour with fact, and is therefore not meant to be taken too seriously.

3c *Suggested answers*: German has more inflections for cases, verb forms, number; English has strict syntactic word-order rules; English differentiates between adjectives and adverbs

3d *English as a lingua franca:* The resistance of native speakers of English to learning foreign languages as well as international travel have led to a spread of English.
Top Tongue: The structure of the language – its grammatical clarity and lexical variety – has led to a spread of English.

3e Regional varieties of English and different levels of proficiency might cause misunderstandings at various levels. English is often reduced to a simplified means of communication, which may lead to carelessness. The dominance of the English language prevents people from learning other foreign languages, but above all, native speakers of English are reluctant to learn foreign languages.

4 Individual answers.

10 Words in Context

SB S. 204 CD 2.07–10
Transkript s. TM-DVD-ROM
► LSET ex. 1, 2, 3

Words in Context – English, English Everywhere

Source:	'English, English, Elsewhere', International Dialects of English Archive
Topic:	Varieties of English
Text form:	Citation
Language variety:	British English; Australian English; Canadian English; South African English
Length:	0:51 min; 0:35 min; 0:28 min; 0:38 min
Level:	Basic
Skills/Activities:	Activating vocabulary; reading non-fiction; mind mapping; listening comprehension

Didaktischer Kommentar

Der Text benennt Formen und Folgen der weltweiten Verbreitung des Englischen, führt damit insgesamt in das hier behandelte Themenspektrum – Geschichte, Funktion und Zukunft des Englischen im globalen Sprachensystem – ein und legt den Grundstein zum Aufbau eines Themenwortschatzes.

SB-DVD-ROM

Lernwortschatz

global language (l. 2), vast vocabulary (l. 2), grammar (l. 2), mark sth. (l. 3), ending (l. 4), inflection (l. 5), gender (l. 5), case (l. 5), auxiliary (l. 6), modal auxiliary (l. 6), preposition (l. 6), word order (l. 6), spread of English (l. 11), varieties of English (l. 12), English-based pidgins and creoles (l. 13), contact language (l. 14), mother tongue (l. 17), ethnic identification (l. 18), speech community (l. 19), Black English (l. 20), antagonism towards the English language (l. 22), linguistic imperialism (l. 24), official language (l. 25), dominant language (l. 27), endanger sb./sth. (l. 29), extinct (l. 30), linguistic and cultural diversity (l. 30), communication technology (l. 35), lexical invasion (l. 36), hamper communication (l. 39), protective measure (l. 43), the world language system (l. 46), high proficiency level (l. 47)

Unterrichtstipps

S lesen den Text in Kleingruppen oder in Partnerarbeit. Sie vergewissern sich, ob sie die markierten Begriffe erläutern und ggf. übersetzen können. Zur Festigung sollte auf das Vokabular während der Behandlung des Kapitels wiederholend eingegangen werden. Der Text kann als Grundlage für ein Glossar zu *language and communication* dienen, das S im Laufe des Kapitels ergänzen (s.a. *Topic Vocabulary* S. 272). Ggf. kann das Glossar auch als Wandposter gestaltet werden.

HA **1/2/5** können als Hausarbeit erledigt werden.

3–4 Es empfiehlt sich die Arbeit in Kleingruppen.

4 Die Erstellung des *A to Z* kann aus zeitökonomischen Gründen arbeitsteilig erfolgen, indem jede Gruppe einen spezifischen Abschnitt des Alphabets behandelt. S suchen in einem Brainstorming nach Anglizismen und ziehen erst zur Ergänzung Hilfsmittel zurate. Sie überprüfen, ob es sich um offiziell in die deutsche Sprache aufgenommene Worte oder um gruppenspezifische Modewörter handelt.

Linktipp: Diese Seiten bieten alphabetisch geordnete Anglizismen in der deutschen Sprache an: *http://denglish.ini.hu/*
http://www.www-kurs.de/denglisch.htm

HA **6** Je nach Möglichkeit individuelles Hören der Beispiele und Bearbeitung der Aufgaben in Einzelarbeit, anschließend Besprechung im Plenum. Kann auch als Hausaufgabe erledigt werden.

Linktipp: Das International Dialects of English Archive bietet Audio- und Textbeispiele verschiedener Dialekte und Akzente des Englischen unter *http://web.ku.edu/~idea/index.htm.*

Part A

Differenzierung
ZA

6 Leistungsstärkere Lerngruppen können weitere Beispiele der Website *http://web.ku.edu/~idea/index.htm* hören und anschließend folgende Aufgabe lösen: *Describe the impact of personal biographies on the different ways English is spoken worldwide.* Dabei soll deutlich werden, dass Region, Herkunft und Bildung zu individuellen Redeweisen führen. S halten Kurzberichte im Plenum.

Lösungshinweise

1 1 vast vocabulary; 2 word order; 3 modal auxiliaries; 4 antagonism towards the English language; 5 lexical invasion; 6 endanger

2 1 Above all, political and economic developments are responsible for the spread of English.
2 Many contact languages developed during the slave trade.
3 For millions of people, English is the mother tongue.
4 Languages allow for communication and the expression of ethnic identity.
5 Even languages can become extinct; as biodiversity is endangered, so is cultural diversity.
6 Too many varieties of English may hamper communication.
7 Experts regard protective measures as useless.

3 Individual answers.

4 *Possible answers*: Assessmentcenter, Brainstorming, Callcenter, Dancefloor, …

5

Singular	Plural	Singular	Plural
crisis	crises	mouse	mice
criterion	criteria	potato	potatoes
(at a) crossroads	crossroads	sheep	sheep
food	foods (types of food)	spacecraft	spacecraft
foot	feet	thief	thieves
knife	knives	toe	toes
means	means		

6a Recording 2 comes closest to Received Pronunciation, there are only slight variations in the quality of the vowels. Recording 3 differs a great deal from RP: different stress pattern of individual words ('horizon'); melodious way of speaking; accent-based different pronunciation of [r]; softening of [t] in 'pot of gold'; slight tendency to shorten diphthongs and vowels. Recording 4 is relatively far from RP but hardly distinguishable from American English: strong r–coloration; vowels in 'pot' and 'bath'.

6b The resemblance of recording 2 to RP indicates that this sample is Australian. Australia is a relatively young country, a former British penal colony, so a lot of Australians have British ancestors. Recording 3 seems to be influenced by another language: Afrikaans, the language introduced by Dutch settlers in the 17th century. Therefore the speaker of recording 3 must be South African. The similarity of recording 4 to American English reflects the historical and geographical proximity of American and Canadian English; so the speaker is obviously Canadian.

SB S. 206

Part A – The History of English

▶ LSET ex. 4, 5

A1 Words, Words, Words

Didaktischer Kommentar Der Text vermittelt grundlegende Informationen zur Geschichte des Englischen von den altenglischen Anfängen bis hin zur Industriellen Revolution. Die Grafik illus-

Part A

triert darüber hinaus die weltweite Ausbreitung des Englischen in Form von Varietäten. Sie kann als Grundlage für vertiefende Rechercheaufträge dienen.

> **Lernwortschatz**
>
> superiority (box: Middle English)

Unterrichtstipps

Der Text kann als Hausarbeit vorbereitet werden.

2 Die Aufgabe kann entweder als Hausarbeit oder als Partnerarbeit im Unterricht gelöst werden. Als Hilfsmittel hierzu empfiehlt sich das *Oxford Advanced Learner's Dictionary* mit CD-ROM (8. Auflage 2010, ISBN: 978-0-19-479909-6), das Registerangaben und Informationen zur Wortherkunft enthält.

Linktipp: *www.etymonline.com* Das Online Etymology Dictionary liefert Erklärungen zur Entstehung englischer Wörter.

3 Linktipp: *www.askoxford.com/worldofwords/history* empfiehlt sich für die Bearbeitung des Gruppenpuzzles. Die Website fasst die Entwicklungsphasen des Englischen kurz und verständlich zusammen.

4 Die schriftliche Ausformulierung kann in Gruppenarbeit erfolgen, wobei S in ihren Stammgruppen aus **3** bleiben, sodass in jeder Gruppe ein Experte für einen Themenbereich vertreten ist. Alternativ kann die Aufgabe auch als Hausarbeit erledigt werden.

Differenzierung

3 Leistungsstärkere Gruppen beschäftigen sich zusätzlich mit den *varieties of English*.

Lösungshinweise

1a sheep – mutton; cow – beef; pig – pork; calf – veal; hen – poultry

1b The Anglo-Saxon words refer to the (living) animals; the Norman-French words refer to the types of meat that come from the various animals.

1c EXTRA The Anglo-Saxon language reflects the world of farming; the Norman-French words belong to the cultural sphere of the cuisine. They reflect a higher social status.

2a ask – inquire; start – commence; answer – respond; dead – deceased; buy – purchase

2b 1 My mother <u>asked</u> me: 'What's the time?' / The leader of the opposition <u>inquired</u> about the background of the government's decision.
2 The ceremony is scheduled to <u>commence</u> at 10 o'clock. / Let's <u>start</u> with the job straightaway.
3 The President of the United States of America was not willing to <u>respond</u> to the journalists' urgent questions. / Thanks for <u>answering</u> my email.
4 My father is <u>dead</u>. He died from a heart attack 25 years ago. / We have gathered here to mourn for our <u>deceased</u> friend.
5 Let's <u>buy</u> some chocolate. / These luxurious objects can only be <u>purchased</u> from a specialist producer.

3 Individual answers.

4 *Possible answer*: A <u>vast vocabulary</u> is the most important feature of the English language. It allows for precise reference to things and ideas; with its <u>numerous synonyms</u> it allows for stylistic variations and the expression of <u>fine differences of meaning</u>. Since the impact of the Scandinavian and Norman-French languages on English it has been full of <u>word twins</u>: two words for the same thing due to <u>different origins</u>, i.e. <u>etymologies</u>.

Part B

5 EXTRA All these phrases are idiomatic in German too: Vanish into thin air – sich in Luft auflösen; be in a pickle – in der Patsche sitzen; the wish is father to the thought – der Wunsch ist Vater des Gedankens; in the end, truth will out – am Ende kommt die Wahrheit ans Licht; make a virtue of necessity – aus der Not eine Tugend machen; beggar all description – jeder Beschreibung spotten; we have seen better days – wir haben schon bessere Tage gesehen; flesh and blood – Fleisch und Blut; with bag and baggage – mit Sack und Pack; brevity is the soul of wit – in der Kürze liegt die Würze

Part B – Linguistic Imperialism

SB S. 208
▶ LSET ex. 6, 7

B1 The Language of Power – the Power of Language
Daniel Defoe; Lloyd Jones

i)

Source:	*Robinson Crusoe*, 1719
Topic:	The English teacher
Text form:	Novel (extract)
Language variety:	British English
Number of words:	473
Level:	Intermediate

ii)

Source:	*Mister Pip*, 2006
Topic:	The English student
Text form:	Novel (extract)
Language variety:	New Zealand English
Number of words:	792
Level:	Intermediate

Skills/Activities:	Reading fiction; comparing novels; creative writing

Didaktischer Kommentar

Der Vergleich der beiden Texte führt auf lebendige Weise in das Thema Sprache und Weltsicht ein. S vergleichen die unterschiedlichen Haltungen und Strategien der Sprachvermittler und setzen sich kreativ mit den geschilderten Kulturbegegnungen und ihrer Wirkung auf die Beteiligten auseinander.

SB-DVD-ROM

> **Lernwortschatz**
>
> i) *Robinson Crusoe*: be shipwrecked (introductory text), cannibal (introductory text), slumber (l. 1), enclosure (l. 3), humble (l. 5), disposition (l. 5), subjection (l. 8), servitude (l. 8), submission (l. 9), likewise (l. 14), delighted with sb./sth. (l. 16), handy (l. 17), diligent (l. 19), savage (l. 22)
>
> ii) *Mister Pip*: atrocious (introductory text), explicit (l. 13), woolly (l. 17), stunned (l. 21), stir (l. 22), incidentally (l. 25), make the acquaintance of sb. (l. 30), rooster (l. 33), convict (n, l. 45), file (n, l. 46), quicksand (l. 54), corpse (l. 60)

Unterrichtstipps

PRE-READING S können zusätzlich darüber sprechen, welche Erinnerung sie an das erste Gespräch mit Muttersprachlern der gelernten Fremdsprache haben. S mit der entsprechenden Erfahrung können zudem dazu Stellung nehmen, wie das Reisen in Länder, deren Sprache man nicht spricht, sich unterscheidet von Reisen in Länder, in denen man sich mit seinen Sprachkenntnissen verständigen kann.

Differenzierung

2 In leistungsschwächeren Lerngruppen sollte mithilfe von Aufgabe **2** zunächst der eine, dann andere Text in arbeitsteiliger Gruppenarbeit untersucht werden. Anschließend werden die Ergebnisse zusammengetragen und ausgewertet.

Lösungshinweise

i)

1 The words that Robinson teaches Friday indicate the unequal nature of their relationship. Firstly, Friday's name is a reference to the day Robinson saved him. It is as if his life started at that point, that he came into existence the day he met Robinson. 'Yes' and 'No' imply that Friday does have the ability to make choices, but the fact that he knows Robinson as 'Master' makes it clear that he is in an inferior position and must do what Robinson tells him to. Finally, it is revealed that Friday only learns the names of things Robinson wants. This further emphasizes that theirs is a servant/master relationship.

ii)

1 Matilda hears English literature for the first time. Through the first chapter of 'Great Expectations' she gains an insight into 19th-century England and in this way develops an idea of another world different to the one she is living in.

2a *Robinson Crusoe*: fictitious, uninhabited island; *Mister Pip*: Bougainville Island, Papua New Guinea

2b *Robinson Crusoe*: First-person narrator; the teacher's point of view: Crusoe describes the stages of Friday's linguistic development from sign language to verbal communication.
Mister Pip: First-person narrator; the pupil's point of view: Matilda describes her first encounter with the English language and English literature. Direct speech and images make her narrative vivid.

2c *Robinson Crusoe*: Crusoe thankfully notes the 'humble, thankful disposition' (l. 5) of the 'creature' (l. 30). In his very first speech he reinforces this disposition and establishes a hierarchical relationship.
Mister Pip: Matilda describes Watts as a modest, unobtrusive man who disappears behind the language and literature he offers to the children. From the very beginning he establishes a relationship based on mutual trust (ll. 1–6).

2d *Robinson Crusoe*: Crusoe explicitly tells the reader his thoughts and feelings with the help of precise verbs and nouns: 'I was greatly delighted' (l. 16), 'pleasure' (l. 28), 'satisfaction' (l. 29), 'love' (l. 30). He is relieved not to be alone anymore
Mister Pip: Explicit and implicit rendering of thoughts and emotions: fascination (ll. 10–11), surprise (ll. 17–19, 38), confusion (ll. 18–19), total absorption (ll. 20–23), curiosity (ll. 49–54), intellectual stimulation (l. 49–60)

2e *Robinson Crusoe*: At first Crusoe teaches words and phrases to define their social relationship and words and phrases useful for cooperating effectively to survive on the isolated island.
Mister Pip: Mr Watts chooses an aesthetic approach to introduce the English language to the children. Matilda is equally impressed by the sounds of the words, the story these words help to convey, and the evocation of Victorian England.

3 Individual answers.

B2 That's Not Cricket

Source:	Mandeep Bedi
Topic:	Cricket rules
Text form:	Documentary film (extract)
Language variety:	British English, Australian English, Jamaican English
Length:	2:47 min
Level:	Basic
Skills/Activities:	Making notes; viewing a film; matching words and definitions; doing research; giving a presentation

Didaktischer Kommentar

Der Clip verdeutlicht, dass das *British Empire* neben der englischen Sprache auch eine Reihe von anderen Traditionen und Gewohnheiten exportiert hat. Cricket wird als Breitensport präsentiert, der auch Eingang in die englische Sprache gefunden hat.

10 Communicating across Cultures

> **Info**
>
> *Cricket* is said to have first been played in southern England in the 16th century. By the end of the 18th century, it had become the national sport. The expansion of the British Empire led to cricket being played overseas – particularly in India, Australia, New Zealand, South Africa – and by the mid-19th century, the first international matches were being held. The International Cricket Council (ICC), the game's governing body, currently has 104 member countries. It has a lot of its own terminology, for example the players who use the bats to hit the balls are called the 'batsmen'.
>
> *Polo* is a team sport played on horseback with the aim of scoring by getting a small ball into the opponents' goal using a mallet. Each team consists of four players. It originated in Persia 500 BC or earlier and was exported to India and other parts of Asia. The British took it up during the time of the Empire, modified it and made it popular in Great Britain. Polo is still played in the UK, the USA, India, Australia, Canada, Pakistan, Argentina, Brazil, Chile and Iran.
>
> *Rugby* is a team sport played with an oval ball. To score, the ball is put down on the field in a specific area of the opponent's half or by kicking through the opponent's goal. There are several forms of rugby, e.g. Union, League, Tag. 'Predecessors' developed in Greece, Wales and Ireland. The rules of the game were formulated at Rugby Public School in the 19th century. Rugby is very popular in England, Scotland, Wales, Ireland, Australia, France, Italy, South Africa, New Zealand and Argentina.

Unterrichtstipps HA Word help

Vor dem Sehen des Filmauszugs machen sich S mit unbekanntem Wortschatz vertraut.

1 Vorschläge und Beobachtungen können nach Bearbeitung der jeweiligen Aufgabe in Kleingruppen oder im Unterrichtsgespräch ausgetauscht werden. Die Gruppen können ihre Ergebnisse im Plenum präsentieren, das diese ergänzt.

Differenzierung ZA

Interessierte S stellen einen Vergleich zwischen Cricket und Baseball an und halten der Lerngruppe eine Kurzpräsentation.

Lösungshinweise

1 Individual answers.

2 1e; 2b; 3a; 4c; 5d

3 EXTRA Individual answers; cf. Info.

SB S. 212 CD 2.11–14
Transkript s. TM-DVD-ROM

Communicating across Cultures – Communicating in a World of Englishes

Source:	*The Adventure of English. The life story of a remarkable language*, Volume 4, Episode 7, UK, 2003
Topic:	The development of Australian and Jamaican English
Text form:	Documentary film (extract)
Language variety:	British English; Australian English; Jamaican English
Length:	6:34 min / 1:55 min
Level:	Basic
Skills/Activities:	Viewing a film; doing research; giving a presentation; taking part in a discussion

Didaktischer Kommentar

S beschäftigen sich mit zwei Varianten des Englischen, dem *Australian English* und *Jamaican patois*. In einer Hörverstehensaufgabe werden sie mithilfe von Redemitteln dazu ermutigt, sprachliche Missverständnisse zu vermeiden bzw. aufzuklären. Abschließend erstellen S einen Leitfaden für die Vorbereitung auf einen Auslandsaufenthalt.

10 Communicating across Cultures

Unterrichtstipps
⚠ HA ● Word help

Vor dem Sehen der Dokumentarfilmauszüge machen sich S mit unbekanntem Wortschatz vertraut.

👥 **1** kann in arbeitsteiliger Partnerarbeit erledigt werden; ein S konzentriert sich auf australisches, der andere auf jamaikanisches Englisch. Anschließend werden die Ergebnisse ausgetauscht.

ZA **1** *Post-viewing*: Das Hör-Sehverstehen der Filmausschnitte kann mithilfe von **KV 23** abgefragt werden. Lösungshinweise:

A 1b, c; 2b, c; 3b, c

B b, d, g, h, i, j

⚠ 👥 **3** S besprechen in Kleingruppen folgende Fragen: *Have you ever found yourself in a situation with native speakers in which you understood very little or nothing at all? Did you ask the others to explain what they were talking about? How did they react?*

4 EXTRA kann als *jigsaw puzzle* (s. S. 297) bearbeitet werden. S präsentieren den Leitfaden als Poster und stellen diese anschließend im Klassenzimmer aus.

Differenzierung
ZA

S mit entsprechender Erfahrung können über Schwierigkeiten mit britischen Varietäten wie zum Beispiel Schottisch oder Irisch berichten.

Lösungshinweise

1a *Possible answers, Australian English*: The development of Australian English is closely linked with Australia's history as a former British penal colony. It is close to British English but integrated Aboriginal words, e.g. for plants and animals: kangaroo, dingo, koala, wallaby, wombat etc.
Jamaican English: Jamaica was first a Spanish colony and later became British. African slaves worked on its plantations which greatly influenced Jamaican English. It is one of the many English-based Creole or patois varieties in the Caribbean. It is a mix of Native American, Spanish, English, and West-African languages.

1b *Possible answer, Australia*: late emancipation from the colonial past; wave of nationalism in 1972; facing a new future of its own as a multicultural society; first Australian dictionary; different pronunciation, vocabulary and abbreviations from British English; today Standard British English is more and more rejected in Australia; Australian English is very popular
Jamaica: Independence from the West Indies in the 1960s; total rejection of colonial past; campaigns to make the local Creole/patois language as socially acceptable as Standard English; pronunciation, rhythm, grammatical 'simplification'; question expressed by intonation: no inversion, no form of 'to do'; different vocabulary and phrases: 'How go on?' for 'How are you?'; Jamaican English is popular in everyday life; not officially taught at schools; Standard English is still the norm

2a 1e; 2b; 3a; 4d; 5c

2b abbreviations, rising intonation at the end of statements

3a Sorry, what's that?; Sorry, what did you say is going on …?; Sorry, you'll have to help me here. What's a …?; Sorry, you've lost me. Could you say that again, please?

3b Individual answers.

4a *Possible answers*: problems of language: misunderstandings caused by mistakes in pronunciation, vocabulary, register, grammar; problems of non-verbal communication: gestures, facial expressions, body language; wrong assessment of social situations: dress code, formal/informal behaviour; religious and national/regional traditions and customs

Part C

4b *Possible advice*: get hold of examples of speech from the country you are going to visit (DVD, audio, radio-station podcasts, practise listening comprehension); make a note of characteristics of spoken English in the country, remember them; find out about dictionaries for your country/region of interest, get hold of paperback versions; check the websites of embassies and cultural institutions; read guidelines and tips about employers, educational institutions, organizations you are working for or with; get as much information as possible on the society you will live in (history, ethnic and social mix, religion); find out how people generally greet each other and how to respond

Part C – The Future of English

SB S. 213
▶ LSET ex. 8

C1 How English Is Evolving into a Language We May Not Even Understand   Michael Erard

Source:	Wired Magazine, issue 14.04, April 2006
Topic:	Globalized English
Text form:	Web article (extract)
Language variety:	American English
Number of words:	742
Level:	Advanced
Skills/Activities:	Reading non-fiction; analysing a text; writing a comment

Didaktischer Kommentar   Am Beispiel von *Chinglish* erhalten S Einblick in die Entstehung und Struktur einer Variante des Englischen. Gleichzeitig erfahren sie etwas über die Gefährdung des Englischen als Weltsprache, die von seiner Ausbreitung und der Entfaltung regionaler Varianten ausgeht.

SB-DVD-ROM

Lernwortschatz

transgression (l. 7), poke fun at sb./sth. (l. 8), curse (n, l. 26), flash drive (l. 36), ultimate (l. 44), do away with sth. (l. 48), evolve (l. 52), fracture (v, l. 54), mingle with sth. (l. 57)

Unterrichtstipps

1 S lösen die Aufgaben in Einzelarbeit und vergleichen ihre Lösungen anschließend mit einem Partner.

2 Für die Lösung der Aufgabenteile empfiehlt sich Partner- oder Kleingruppenarbeit.

Differenzierung

1 Leistungsstärkere S fassen statt der kompetenzorientierten Leseverstehensaufgabe die Hauptaussagen des Textes zusammen.

Lösungshinweise

1a G, A, F, E, B, D, C

1b 4, 7

2a The tone of the text is ambiguous. On the one hand, it seems to be light-hearted, even humorous, starting with 'funny' Chinglish phrases. On the other hand, there are several elements which render the text serious: the title implies that English is threatened; the main body of the text is introduced with two successive sentences starting with the question: '[But] what if …' (l. 10). The questions are provocative and evoke connotations of fear that native speakers may lose control of their language (ll. 13–14). The author mentions that native speakers will soon be outnumbered by people who are learning and using the language (ll. 15–18). Further examples of a more serious tone include ll. 48 and 54. The conclusion of the text is again humorous, paradoxical and yet pessimistic (ll. 59–60).

Part C2 – On Protectionism

2b *Possible answer*: The author does not dramatize the situation (his article consists of descriptive and humorous passages). Overall the tone is not negative. Erard seems to accept the fate of English as a natural evolution and even points out potential positive consequences, e.g. its becoming simpler, more practical ... Therefore the article functions more as a description of a potential development for the English language.

2c *Possible answer*: The author predicts that global English might develop into a new world standard of simplified English which could become a language distinct from the 'classical standards' of English. The scenario is realistic, but global pressure will guarantee comprehensibility; the writer does not describe a new situation, as existing varieties are already a challenge for speakers of English when travelling around the world. Also, dialects and other regional variants of English within the UK and the USA (or other parts of the world where English is the first language) already differ considerably.

SB S. 215
▶ **LSET ex. 8**

C2 On Protectionism   Stephen Clarke

Source:	*Merde Happens*, 2008
Topic:	The need for and the effectiveness of linguistic protectionism
Text form:	Novel (extract)
Language variety:	British English
Number of words:	509
Level:	Intermediate
Skills/Activities:	Reading fiction; analysing a text; writing a formal letter

Didaktischer Kommentar

Der satirische Text knüpft indirekt an die in *Part A* vermittelten Informationen zum wechselvollen Verhältnis von französischer und englischer Sprache an. Die satirische Dimension des Textes erlaubt eine kritische Erörterung über den Sinn, die eigene Sprache per Dekret vor der Einflussnahme fremder Sprachen zu bewahren. Bei der Reflexion sollten der Einfluss des Englischen auf das Deutsche und sprachpuristische Versuche, die deutsche Sprache zu schützen, bedacht werden.

SB-DVD-ROM

Lernwortschatz

severe (l. 4), challenged (l. 6), dismissive (l. 16), have sb. on the defensive (l. 14), clinching (*adj*, l. 14), trumpet (v, l. 17), huff (l. 17), entrepreneur (l. 24), slump (l. 26), moan (l. 32)

Unterrichtstipps

Die Behandlung der in diesem Text aufgeworfenen Problematik bietet die Möglichkeit zu fächerübergreifender Projektarbeit. Denkbar ist die Zusammenarbeit mit den Fächern Deutsch (wobei die *pre-reading*-Aufgaben ausgeweitet werden können) oder Französisch.

ZA

2b S informieren sich darüber, in welchen Ländern Französisch gesprochen wird und welche Unterschiede es zwischen den Varietäten gibt.

Differenzierung
ZA

Leistungsstärkere S recherchieren die Inhalte des Toubon-Gesetzes (vgl. Info) und präsentieren diese im Plenum.

Info

French: Since 1635 the development of the French language has been influenced by the Académie Française. In its history, it has promoted linguistic reforms and has exerted a conservative influence. The Academy itself as well as other groups have tried to contain the influence of English on French. One of the most recent and controversial regulations is the so-called Toubon Law of 1994, named after the Minister of Culture at that time: a detailed decree on the usage of the French language in public.

Part C2 – On Protectionism

> *English*: Although the development of English has not been controlled by an Academy, there have been attempts to regulate developments in the history of the English language. The 18th century saw the first measures taken in lexicography (Samuel Johnson, 1709–1784), grammar (Robert Lowth, 1710–1787) and pronunciation (John Walker, 1732–1807). Jonathan Swift, author of *Gulliver's Travels* (1726), proposed the foundation of an academy to correct and 'ascertain' the English tongue in 1712. The most famous fictional example of a prescriptive linguist is Professor Higgins in Bernhard Shaw's *Pygmalion* (1912), who is said to have been inspired by the phonetician Professor Daniel Jones, who compiled an influential *English Pronouncing Dictionary*. The recurrent idea of an academy has never materialized, thus the development of the English language is characterized by a collusion of regulation and natural dynamics.

Lösungshinweise

PRE-READING *Further examples: shoppen, zappen, chillen, downloaden, jmd. pushen, relaxen, Swimmingpool, T-Shirt, Slogan, Touchscreen, Software, App, live, Livestream, Podcast, Outsourcing, Interview*
How English affects German: Some of the examples given are English-sounding words which do not exist in the English language (*Handy, Beamer*). Others (*simsen, downgesized*) demonstrate how English-based verbs assimilate the grammatical system of marking person and tense, leading to awkward-sounding hybrid forms. Grammatical phenomena like the s-genitive (*Hanne's Teestube*) or changes of word order in subordinate clauses (*Wir machen einen Ausflug, weil das Wetter ist schön.*) have influenced both written and spoken German.

PRE-READING *Pro*: English words replace German ones that are just as precise as the more fashionable English ones; interference of English with the German language at levels of vocabulary, word formation, grammar, pronunciation
Con: The German language has a long tradition of absorbing and integrating foreign language elements into its system, e.g. from Latin and French. It was enriched by these influences; a great deal of English loans are just fads; in certain fields (e.g. computer science) English fills semantic gaps

1 The language inspector bureaucratically insists on getting rid of all English words from the menu, fearing misunderstanding (ll. 8–9) and lexical invasion; the tea-room owner points out that there is no room for misunderstandings: the food referred to is on display (l. 7), a lot of English words have already been integrated into French (ll. 11–12) and the differences of certain words in both languages are very small (l. 42).

2a Logic makes it extremely unlikely that the word 'cheese' can be misunderstood as 'chaise', English: 'chair'. The reference to the minute differences between French and English words for food underlines that they are etymologically closely related: The English word 'sausage' derived from the Old Northern French 'saussiche', and 'salad' goes back to Old French 'salade'. In other words, the English expressions are nothing but French loans.

2b The situation of modern English and French contrasts with that of the Middle Ages: When England was conquered by the Duke of Normandy in 1066, Norman French became the dominant language in England. English was nearly eradicated on its own soil. It reasserted itself in the 14th century, enriched by the French lexical influence. Today the French feel that their language is endangered by Anglo-American influence. French has lost some of its importance as an international language, yet French does not belong to the endangered languages.

3a The French garden on the left embodies the ideal of controlling and bettering nature: order, symmetry and geometrical forms dominate this garden. It can be compared to the rigorous regulatory, normative traditions of French language policies. The English landscape garden on the right, by contrast, appears to be natural. But just as the garden, the English language was shaped by human

Part C3 – Rettet das Englische

intervention and manipulation, though there is no official body controlling it and limiting the freedom of its speakers.

3b Individual answers.

SB S. 217
▶ LSET ex. 10

C3 Rettet das Englische Eckhard Fuhr

Didaktischer Kommentar

Der Text gibt einen Einblick in die Kultur- und Sprachenpolitik Europas, die versucht, neben Englisch als führender Verkehrssprache, einzelne Regionalsprachen in den Institutionen der EU zu stärken. Dieser Ansatz berührt S unmittelbar, da er sich im Fremdsprachenunterricht ihrer Bildungsgänge niederschlägt.

Unterrichtstipps
ZA

PRE-READING ✵ **Linktipp:** *http://ec.europa.eu/education/languages/languages-of-europe/index_en.htm* S rufen die Website der EU-Kommission zur Sprachenpolitik auf, um sich einen Eindruck von der Bedeutung des europäischen Konzeptes der Mehrsprachigkeit zu verschaffen. In diesem Rahmen kann Themenvokabular zur Sprachenpolitik erarbeitet werden: *multilingualism, linguistic diversity, adopted language, eurocentrism, migration, (migratory) background, promote and protect regional/national/minority languages*

HA

1 Mediation Die Mediation kann als schriftliche Hausaufgabe erledigt werden.

Differenzierung

1 In leistungsschwächeren Lerngruppen erfolgt die Ausarbeitung in heterogenen Kleingruppen in Form von Schreibkonferenzen (s. S. 299).

CONTEXT TASK Schwächere Lerngruppen erhalten einen Fragenkatalog.
Past:
How long I have learnt English at school:
Forms of language acquisition outside school:
Occasions I have used English abroad:
Exchange programmes:
Work experience:
Competence levels I have reached:
Future:
When and where I will have to use English:
In which personal situations:
In which professional situations:
Areas I have to improve:
What I can do to improve my language skills:
Language certificates needed in order to take up certain subjects at particular universities:
Technical terms I have to learn (Business English, Scientific English …):

Lösungsvorschläge

1 Mediation *The EU commission's initiative*: Representatives of Europe's intellectual elite demand an end to English as the main European lingua franca.
Europeans should see their linguistic diversity as a blessing and not as a burden. Europeans ought to be encouraged to communicate in their own languages. In order to improve the standard of and increase the motivation for foreign language learning, the EU commission and its think tank launched a campaign recommending European citizens 'adopt' at least one language which they learn as a 'second mother tongue'.
Consequences: Paradoxically, reducing the impact of English will be to its advantage: it will be protected as a valuable language of culture and saved from being viewed as international gibberish.
Intention: The author fully endorses the initiative and suggests that, due to considerable immigration, people might also turn to Arabic, Mandarin, and other non-European languages with the intention of giving the English language time to recover.

2 – CONTEXT TASK Individual answers.

Kopiervorlage 23: Reading Comprehension

A Australia: Tick the correct statements; more than one statement may be correct.

1   In the 1970s …
- A   Australia looked back to its colonial past.
- B   Australia had plans to create a multicultural society.
- C   the first Australian dictionary was published.

2 The Macquarie Dictionary …
- A   did not help Australian English to emancipate from British English.
- B   contributed to making Australian English accepted and official.
- C   was an expression of taking pride in the independence of Australian English.

3 Australians …
- A   still cling to British English.
- B   may think British English sounds funny.
- C   dislike the Queen's English because they think it is artificial.

B Jamaica: Tick the correct statements.

- A   Jamaicans were willing to continue some of the colonial traditions.
- B   There has been a movement to make the Jamaican Creole as legitimate as Standard English.
- C   Patois is considered to be of lower status.
- D   If you want to bring your ideas across to the people in an emotional way you should use the Jamaican patois.
- E   Jamaican is the language of people who cannot write.
- F   Jamaican English is now accepted in official education.
- G   Some people think that children who are taught in patois will have fewer opportunities internationally.
- H   According to the Jamaican interviewee Anglo-Saxons can only think in terms of monolingualism.
- I   According to the Jamaican expert speaking two or more languages is the real achievement.
- J   According to the Jamaican expert the fact that English is the international language is pure historical chance.
- K   According to the narrator the varieties of English have not yet achieved equal status to English.

Context 21 The World of English: Topic Vocabulary

Word/Phrase	Memory Aid	German
accent	*collocations:* broad/thick/foreign/posh <u>accent</u>	Akzent
anglicization	*example sentence:* The ~ of placenames was common in Ireland.	Anglisierung
broken English	*definition:* English spoken/written with many mistakes	gebrochenes Englisch
Creole	*definition:* a language formed from a European language and the local tongue	Kreolisch
lingua franca	*definition:* a shared language used for communication purposes when the speakers have different first languages	Lingua franca, Verkehrssprache
loanword	*example sentence:* L~s are instantly recognizable in Japanese, as a different script is used to write them.	Lehnwort, Fremdwort
mother tongue	*synonyms:* first language / native tongue	Muttersprache
native speaker	*collocations:* <u>native</u> city/country/land/language	Muttersprachler/in
official language	*example sentence:* Maori is still an ~ **language** of New Zealand, even though less than 5% speak it.	Amtssprache
pidgin	*definition:* a highly simplified language developed as a means of communication for speakers without a language in common	Pidginsprache
Received Pronunciation (RP)	*example sentence:* R~ P~ is the standard accent of English in England and is also known as the Queen's English.	britische Standardaussprache
second language	*other collocations:* colloquial/flowery/offensive <u>language</u>	Zweitsprache
second-language acquisition	*synonym:* second-language learning	Zweitspracherwerb
slang	*example sentence:* Many learners of English like to flavour their language with ~ to make it more authentic.	Slang
Standard English	*definition:* a term referring to whatever form of English is the norm in a particular anglophone nation	Standardsprache
world language	*example sentence:* It is mainly thanks to colonialism that English is the major ~ **language** today.	Weltsprache

ns- und Verarbeitungsweisen des Werkes Shakespeares zu.
11 Shakespeare

Dieses Kapitel gibt einen Einblick in das Leben und das Werk William Shakespeares vor dem Hintergrund ausgewählter Aspekte der Geschichte, Politik und Theaterhistorie der elisabethanischen Zeit. Besondere Bedeutung kommt dabei der produktiven Umsetzung der Dramen und Lyrik sowie der Vielfalt der Adaptions- und Verarbeitungsweisen des Werkes Shakespeares zu.

Part A – Background. Die in eine Präsentation mündende Gruppenarbeit erforscht Aspekte zu Shakespeares Leben, der Zeitgeschichte, dem elisabethanischen Weltbild und dem Theater Shakespeares.

Part B – Drama führt über Ausschnitte aus *A Midsummer Night's Dream*, *Julius Caesar* und *Othello* in zentrale Themen der Dramen Shakespeares und deren Gestaltung ein.

Part C – Versions of Shakespeare demonstriert und diskutiert verschiedene Auffassungen der Wiedergabe und Adaption Shakespeares.

Didaktisches Inhaltsverzeichnis

SB p.	Title	TM p.	Text Form	Topic	Skills and Activities
218	Lead-in	274	Photo; pieces of dialogue	Shakespearean language and theatre	Collecting information; making dialogues
220	Words in Context – Shakespeare, His Theatre and His Time	276	Informative text, photo	The life and times of Shakespeare	Structuring and applying vocabulary
	Part A – Background				
222	A1 Watching a Play in Shakespeare's Theatre DVD	278	Feature film (extract)	The theatre and its audience in Shakespeare's time	Viewing comprehension; note taking
222	A2 Researching the Background to Shakespeare's Plays	279	Photos; illustrations; websites	Background to Shakespeare's life, time and plays	Doing research; doing project work; giving a presentation; preparing a quiz
	Part B – Drama				
224	B1 Love: A Midsummer Night's Dream CD 3.08	280	Drama (comedy; extract)	Confusion among lovers in a wood	Analysing drama; performing a dramatic scene; writing a text
226	B2 Power and Ambition: Julius Caesar CD 3.09	282	Drama (tragedy; extract)	The assassination of Caesar due to fear he may become a tyrant	Analysing speeches; performing a scene; analysing stylistic devices; writing an essay
228	B3 Revenge: Othello CD 3.10	284	Drama (tragedy; extract)	Iago sows suspicion in Othello's mind about Desdemona, Othello's wife	Analysing drama; performing a dramatic reading; speculating on plot; identifying conflict in plays and films
	Part C – Versions of Shakespeare				
230	C1 Comparing Two Shakespeare Productions DVD	286	Film (extract); documentary (extract)	Realistic vs. expressionistic adaptations of Shakespeare's work	Viewing, analysing and comparing film extracts
231	C2 A Shakespeare Comic Strip Oscar Zarate	287	Comic	Iago sows suspicion in Othello's mind about Desdemona, Othello's wife	Working with comics
232	C3 Sonnets and the German Shakespeare	288	Poems; newspaper article (extract)	Two German translations of sonnet 29; how Shakespeare's sonnets might have come into existence	Reading poetry; mediating
235	Communicating across Cultures	291	Shakespeare quotations	Dealing with different cultural values	Dealing with cultural differences; analysing quotations; doing a role-play

11 Lead-in

SB S. 218 **Lead-in**

Didaktischer Kommentar Auf der Doppelseite werden ein Foto eines Shakespeare-Theaters sowie sprachliche Impulse in Shakespeare-Englisch und in modernem Englisch in Form von Sprechblasen gegeben. S verstehen die Sprechblasen, ordnen sie einander zu und verarbeiten sie zu einem Dialog. Die Materialien des *Lead-in* erlauben S zu Beginn des Kapitels, ihr Vorwissen zu Shakespeare und seinem Werk zu äußern, weitere Aspekte aus Bild- und Sprachimpulsen hinzuzufügen und so die Scheu vor dem großen Namen Shakespeare und dem Umgang mit seinem Werk abzubauen.

SB-DVD-ROM

Lernwortschatz

lad (photo)

Unterrichtstipps **1a** L sollte vorbereitete Zettel austeilen und S ihren jeweiligen Satz laut sagen lassen, sodass schon erste Vermutungen über die Zuordnungen gemacht werden können. Hierbei können auch mögliche Verständnis- oder Ausspracheprobleme geklärt werden.

3ab Die Aufgaben zur Erschließung des Bildmaterials (**3a**) und zur Reaktivierung des Vorwissens (**3b**) sind gut als Gruppenarbeit möglich. In diesem Zusammenhang können auch Formen des Sammelns und *note-taking* nochmals wiederholt werden (s. a. *SF 3: Making and taking notes*). S sollten über die Notwendigkeit dieser Sammlung für die *Context Task* informiert werden.

3c kann sowohl mündlich oder auch schriftlich (z. B. als Hausaufgabe) erfolgen.

Differenzierung **1a** L kann Sätze in Shakespearean English gezielt leistungsstärkeren S zuweisen, um das Zuordnen der Paare zu erleichtern.

Im Anschluss an Aufgaben **1–3** bearbeiten *early finishers* oder interessierte S **KV 24** mit Shakespeare-Zitaten, die Eingang in die Alltagssprache gefunden haben (z. B. als Hausaufgabe). Lösungshinweise:

	Shakespeare Quote	German Equivalent	Source
1	I will wear my heart upon my sleeve.	Ich werde mein Herz auf der Zunge tragen.	*Othello*, Act I, Scene 1
2	Something is rotten in the state of Denmark.	Etwas ist faul im Staate Dänemark.	*Hamlet*, Act I, Scene 4
3	All that glisters is not gold.	Es ist nicht alles Gold was glänzt.	*The Merchant of Venice*, Act II, Scene 7
4	All's well that ends well.	Ende gut, alles gut.	*All's Well That Ends Well*
5	It smells to heaven.	Es stinkt zum Himmel.	*Hamlet*, Act III, Scene 3
6	too much of a good thing	zuviel des Guten	*As You Like It*, Act IV, Scene 1
7	It's all Greek to me.	Ich verstehe nur Bahnhof.	*Julius Caesar*, Act I, Scene 2
8	Love is blind.	Liebe macht blind.	*The Merchant of Venice*, Act II, Scene 6

Info

Shakespearean English: The Elizabethan Age was a time of great innovation and progress: major changes in social, political, scientific, as well as linguistic fields were commonplace during this period. It was during this time that early modern English developed. The language contained a huge variety of words of different origin (Anglo-Saxon, French, Latin, etc.) and had an extremely flexible grammatical structure as well as rules for spelling. Even the spelling of names was not fixed: 'Shakespeare' as we write it today was only canonized in the 19th century.

Lead-in – Shakespeare **11**

> Shakespeare made verbs out of nouns *(to child)*, created opposites by using prefixes *(to unsex, to unchild)* or simply made up words for the sound of them *(hurly-burly, hugger-mugger, kickie-wickie)*. Not all the words that are attributed to him, e.g. in the Oxford English Dictionary, were really invented by him however – he just wrote many of them down for the first time. A great number of them have subsequently become idioms or sayings in the English language.
>
> What sometimes makes it hard for us to read and understand Shakespeare is that:
> - some words have completely disappeared (*forsooth* = honestly; *aye* = yes; *thou* = you)
> - others have now acquired a different meaning from what they meant in Shakespeare's time (*pregnant* = full of, clever; *silly* = innocent; *fat* = glistening with sweat)
> - there were no fixed rules concerning word order ('to yon cart was our horse hitched')
> - some verbs still had archaic endings *(thou hast; thou dost; he hath; thou art)*
> - words or syllables could be left out, sometimes for reasons of the metre *(e'en; ne'er; we will to bed)*
>
> Shakespeare used all the opportunities that this 'new' language offered him, because in his day the emphasis of theatre was usually upon hearing rather than watching a play. The effect of his play therefore had to be created largely by words rather than by anything else.

Lösungshinweise **1ab**

Shakespearean phrase	English equivalent
Alackaday! Out upon it!	No way, forget it!
Aye, by my life.	Yes, honest!
Come hither, my dearest!	Over here, love!
Fare ye well!	Have a nice day.
Fie, fie! Shame on you!	That's so unfair.
Hearken! What a flibbertigibbet and hurly-burly yonder!	Listen. What's going on over there?
Hence!	Go!
I will keep my word with thee!	Trust me.
Nay, yet there is more in this.	Hang on, there is something else, isn't there?
Thou lik'dst not that.	You didn't like that, did you?
What dost thou think?	What do you suppose?
What news, my sweet wench?	What's up, dear?

1c *Possible answer:* A young girl, who has escaped from home without her parents knowing, is looking for her friends. She finally meets them in the streets and is called over by them:

Friends: Come hither, dearest!
Girl: Good wenches and fine lads!
Friend 1: What's up, sweet wench?
Girl: I hate my parents. Fie, fie! Shame on them! They wouldn't let me out.
Friend 2: Hearken! What a flibbertigibbet and hurly-burly!
Girl: I must hence! I'm sure my parents are coming.
Friend 3: Thou lik'dst not that! But out upon it, I don't think it's them.
Girl: Fare ye well! I have to go.

11 Words in Context

2 EXTRA *Possible answers:*
Differences between modern and Shakespearean English are:
- words that are no longer in use *(hither, yonder, aye, nay …)*
- words newly formed for onomatopoetic reasons *(hurly-burly, flibbertigibbet)*
- pronouns like *thou*, *thee* and *ye* alongside *you*
- different word order: *'Thou lik'dst not that!'* (no compulsory do/did)
- archaic exclamations *(alackaday, hearken)*
- extensive greetings and forms of address *(good wenches and fine lads)*

3a *Possible answers:* open air theatre; audience can sit on balcony-like rows of seats overlooking the scene *(amphitheatre)* or stand in front of the stage; wooden construction; stage scenery extensively painted to resemble stone, marble, etc.; stage protruding into the audience; stage is 'protected' by a kind of roof; two entrances visible at the back of the stage *(entrance, exit)*; balcony overlooking the stage

3bc Individual answers.

SB S. 220
▶ LSET ex. 1

Words in Context – Shakespeare, His Theatre and His Time

Didaktischer Kommentar

Mithilfe des Textes informieren sich S über Shakespeares Wirken, sein Theater und das Zeitgeschehen. In den Übungen festigen sie die erworbene Lexik, um zu den genannten Bereichen eigene Erkenntnisse und Meinungen ausdrücken zu können.

SB-DVD-ROM

Lernwortschatz

be rated as sth. (l. 1), playwright (l. 2), comedy (l. 3), tragedy (l. 3), history play (l. 3), Elizabethan Age (l. 5), Golden Age (l. 5), achievement in the arts (l. 6), struggle for sth. (l. 7), threats from foreign powers (l. 7), traditional world view (l. 10), old dogma (l. 14), master of one's own fate (l. 15), predetermined (l. 16), profit (l. 19), upheaval (l. 20), invest in sth. (l. 22), produce a play (l. 22), popular form of entertainment (l. 24), draw sb. to sth. (l. 24), spectator (l. 25), playhouse (l. 26), open to the sky (l. 26), stage (l. 27), scenery (l. 28), performance (l. 30), speech (l. 32), expression (l. 33), gesture (l. 33), hold sb.'s attention (l. 33), learn one's lines (l. 35), transcript (l. 36), role (l. 36), dialogue (l. 37), monologue (l. 37), character (l. 38), stage direction (l. 38), replica (l. 43), antiquated (l. 44), theme (l. 45), timeless (l. 46)

Unterrichtstipps

S lesen den Text in Einzelarbeit (ggf. als Hausaufgabe). Anschließend können sie in Partnerarbeit versuchen, die unbekannte Lexik zu klären, ehe sie ein Wörterbuch zu Rate ziehen. L sollte die richtige Aussprache bestimmter Wörter sicherstellen.

Nach erneuter Lektüre können S selbst *comprehension questions* zum Text formulieren, die sie anderen S stellen.

1 dient der Sammlung und Strukturierung der Lexeme. S können den Wortschatz auch in Listenform anstatt in einer Mindmap sammeln. L sollte sie ermutigen, die Sammlung über den vorgegebenen Wortschatz hinaus weiterzuführen.

HA **2/3** sind als Hausaufgabe geeignet.

5 Die Aufgabe bietet Gelegenheit, eine persönliche Stellungnahme zur Wirkung von schauspielerischen Darbietungen abzugeben. Einer fünfminütigen Besinnungsphase, in der S ihre persönlichen Präferenzen schriftlich notieren, kann eine Diskussion in der Gruppe folgen. Diese gerät besonders lebhaft, wenn sich S bei ihren Beiträgen auf konkrete Darstellungen aus Film und Fernsehserien beziehen.

Differenzierung

4 Diese Aufgabe kann gut in Gruppenarbeit erledigt werden: Entweder arbeiten Kleingruppen (à 3 S) arbeitsteilig an je einer Teilaufgabe und tragen ihre Ergebnisse im Plenum vor, oder der Kurs wird in „Spezialisten" für Aufführungspraxis, Weltanschauung und Unterhaltungsbetrieb eingeteilt.

Words in Context – Shakespeare, His Theatre and His Time

Lösungshinweise

1 Individual answers.

2 1 spectators; 2 gesture; 3 stage directions; 4 struggle for sth.; 5 dogma; 6 role; 7 predetermined; 8 transcript – replica

3 *Possible answers:*
1 The Elizabethan era was a Golden Age, but also a time of <u>upheaval</u>.
2 *As You Like It* is a comedy, while *Hamlet* is a <u>tragedy</u> and *Henry V* is a <u>history play</u>.
3 Elizabethans did accept some traditional views, yet they were keen to discover new truths beyond the old <u>dogmas</u>.
4 Some playhouses lost money, but others made huge <u>profits</u>.
5 While a few private playhouses were indoors, the public ones were <u>open to the sky</u>.
6 Audiences were seldom bored, as the actors knew how to <u>hold their attention</u>.
7 The actors were not trusted with a complete playscript, so they <u>learned their lines</u> from <u>transcripts</u>.
8 Elizabethan theatre put elegant costumes and realistic props on stage, but the stage itself was almost empty of <u>scenery</u>.
9 Shakespeare's themes are timeless, though at first the language might seem <u>antiquated</u>.

4

	THEN	NOW
the ways a play is performed	playhouses open to daylight – platform stage – hardly any scenery – spectacular costumes, realistic props – groundlings standing around the stage on three sides – audience took a lively part – actors only have a transcript of their own role to rehearse	normally indoor theatres – typically 'proscenium arch', i.e. stage framed by arch and curtain – generally some furniture and/or scenery – costume is realistic rather than spectacular – audiences generally sitting in front of the stage – audience does not usually participate in the performance – actors get the whole play to learn from
the ways people see society and the world	traditional world view with Earth as centre of cosmos – God/church as an authority – fixed rank generally accepted as the basis of society's order – curiosity and eagerness for discovery – profit motive	solarcentric view of cosmos – religion widely disputed as an authority – social mobility – curiosity and eagerness for discovery – profit motive
the role of theatre as entertainment	theatre a hugely popular form of entertainment – seen as a business venture that could yield handsome profits – 2500-strong audiences from all walks of life – audience participation expected	theatre as an art form is generally of minority interest – needs generous subsidy from the state or private/corporate sponsors – smaller audiences are the rule – audiences largely drawn from the educated middle classes – audience normally silent

5 EXTRA Individual answers.

11 Part A

Part A – Background

LSET Skill 19

SB S. 222
DVD
Transkript s. TM-DVD-ROM

A1 Watching a Play in Shakespeare's Theatre

Source:	*Shakespeare in Love*, 1998
Topic:	The theatre and its audience in Shakespeare's time
Text form:	Feature film (extract)
Language variety:	British English
Length:	6:33 min
Level:	Intermediate
Skills/Activities:	Viewing comprehension; note taking

Didaktischer Kommentar

Der kurze Filmausschnitt bietet nicht nur einen anschaulichen Einstieg in die Theaterpraxis der Shakespeare-Zeit, sondern auch einen Eindruck der Bevölkerung des elisabethanischen London. S erhalten Gelegenheit, die bisher erworbenen Kenntnisse zu verbalisieren und das Gesehene auf dieser Grundlage zu interpretieren.

Unterrichtstipps

Das Foto kann als Einstieg verwendet werden; S sollten nach den beiden vorhergegangenen Illustrationen aus dem *Lead-in* und den *Words in Context* erkennen, dass die Kamera hier von der Bühne eines elisabethanischen Theaters aus über die Schauspieler hinweg ins Auditorium blickt.

HA · Word help

Vor dem ersten Sehen des Spielfilmauszugs machen sich S mit unbekanntem Wortschatz vertraut.

PRE-VIEWING Partnerarbeit kann das Sammeln der Fakten beschleunigen.

First Viewing: Zur Sicherung des Globalverstehens sind die *five W's (who, what, when, where, why)* nützlich. Die Liste der von ihnen erkannten Charaktere kann an der Tafel festgehalten und im Klassengespräch spekuliert werden, was es mit diesen auf sich hat. S sollten verschiedene Charaktere erkennen, obwohl sie sie vielleicht nicht namentlich nennen können.

1b S halten stichwortartig Informationen zu den Schlüsselwörtern fest; die sieben Beobachtungsschwerpunkte können zwischen Gruppen bzw. innerhalb von Gruppen aufgeteilt werden. Dann findet die erste Rückmeldung in den Gruppen statt, ehe im Plenum das Detailverständnis gesichert wird.

Differenzierung

1b Eine Möglichkeit zur Differenzierung besteht in der Menge der Beobachtungsschwerpunkte, die L einzelnen S zuweist.

> **Info**
>
> *The Curtain Theatre* was an Elizabethan playhouse located in Curtain Close in London which opened in 1577 and staged plays until about 1622. It became the main acting venue for Shakespeare's company 'The Lord Chamberlain's Men' and some of his most famous plays, such as *Romeo and Juliet* and *Henry V* were performed here for the first time. Shakespeare's company changed venues in 1599 when the Globe Theatre, which was built as a replacement, was ready for use. The Curtain Theatre features in the film *Shakespeare in Love*.

Lösungshinweise

1a *Characters in the extract:*
- the audience, among them common people, aristocrats, etc.
- the priest who is trying to prevent people from entering the 'godless' show
- William Shakespeare
- the producer who keeps assuring Shakespeare 'it will be all right'
- the actors: Juliet (the boy-actor whose voice has just broken); Juliet's nurse
- the stammering speaker of the prologue
- Lady Olivia and her nurse
- Lady Olivia's husband Lord Wessex

Part A2 – Researching the Background to Shakespeare's Plays

1b *The audience:* are streaming into the theatre in an excited mood; they are obviously from different social classes, with the common people gathering around the stage as groundlings, the aristocracy on one of the three upper levels; they take an active part in the play and are quick to respond to the different turns of the action.
The priest: represents Puritan principles and is fanatically opposed to the show but is ignored by the theatregoers, whose enthusiasm to enter the theatre literally sweeps him along into the building as well.
The actors: are all men; putting a woman on stage could mean prison for the company; the female roles are played by boys until their voices break; the nurse is played by an older man who puts on a false high voice and is obviously the audience's favourite; the costumes are rich and spectacular.
The action: after the prologue, the action begins with a conflict between four young men.
The playhouse: can accommodate a great number of people; the stage is large and mostly covered by a roof resting on two large pillars.
Backstage: there are problems: the speaker who stammers during the prologue and the boy playing Juliet whose voice has just broken.
The 'drama' offstage: Lady Olivia takes on the role, but when her husband arrives, furious, it becomes clear that there is more trouble ahead.

SB S. 222

A2 Researching the Background to Shakespeare's Plays

Didaktischer Kommentar

Dieser Abschnitt bietet Quellen, die S helfen, den historischen Abstand zu Shakespeare zu überwinden, indem sie mehr über seine Zeit erfahren. S müssen sich selbst einen von vier Aspekten mithilfe des Online-Materials erarbeiten. Dies bietet Gelegenheit zur Übung einer Reihe wichtiger Fertigkeiten: selbstständige Texterschließung mit Informationsentnahme, Recherche, *working with dictionaries*, Visualisierung und Präsentationstechnik. S entnehmen dem Material eine Auswahl von Gebrauchswortschatz, den sie im Plenum teilen und lernen.

Unterrichtstipps

Es empfiehlt sich, auf die Vorbesprechung des Projektes genügend Zeit zu verwenden, sodass S genau wissen, was von ihnen verlangt wird. Ohne Zuhilfenahme eines Wörterbuches sind die Aufgaben nur schwer zu schaffen.
Die Arbeit sollte grundsätzlich in vier Phasen ablaufen: 1. Sichten und Erschließen des Materials. 2. Erstellen der Präsentation. 3. Präsentieren der Arbeit. 4. Beantwortung von Quiz-Fragen anderer S und Übernahme der gesammelten Lexik.
Zu jedem Thema wird eine Präsentationsform empfohlen, daneben sind natürlich auch *gallery walks* (s. S. 297), PowerPoint-Präsentationen usw. möglich.
Je nach Leistungsfähigkeit des Kurses wird ein Zeitrahmen vorgegeben.

Der Webcode bietet URLs mit Hintergrundinformationen zu den vier von S zu recherchierenden Themen. Wenn keine Gelegenheit besteht, die Materialien online im Unterricht zu bearbeiten, sollten S die entsprechenden Seiten zuhause ausdrucken und mit in den Unterricht bringen. Entsprechendes gilt für zusätzliches (Bild-)Material, das recherchiert werden soll.

Differenzierung

Innerhalb der Gruppen kann durch die Verteilung der Themen differenziert werden: Das Thema *Biography* ist weniger anspruchsvoll, das Thema *Elizabethan world view* etwas fordernder als die beiden übrigen Themen.

Lösungshinweise

Individual answers. Possible answers:
Shakespeare's biography: born in Stratford-upon-Avon near Birmingham (1564); son of a glovemaker; attended local school; married Anne Hathaway; three children, son Hamnet died; 'lost years' without record; by 1592 re-emerged as an actor, writer and shareholder in theatre in London; wrote about 36–40 plays of different genres and a number of poems, notably sonnets; commercially successful; retired to Stratford in 1614 and died in 1616

Part B

The historical background: Tudor dynasty victorious in the civil wars called the Wars of the Roses; new era; break with Rome by Henry VIII, Elizabeth I's father; Renaissance with learning, inquiry, exploration; expansion in trade; conflict with Spain; spirit of nationalism; new economy spells end of feudalism with mass unemployment but wealth for the new class of bourgeois; cultural life greatly enriched; London swells to a metropolis; the capital is a vibrant city full of commerce, crime, culture and opportunities for entertainment

The Elizabethan world view: Elizabethan era a time of upheaval; longing for order; the Great Chain of Being a hierarchical system ranging from God and angels through men, animals and plants to minerals; each category has certain qualities: man located in a key position between God and nature, and is therefore critically important (anthropocentricism); there is a ranking within the classes too, i.e. monarch at top (so monarchy is natural and prevents return to chaos); links between humours and elements; links between order of universe (macrocosm) and man (microcosm)

Shakespeare's theatre: There were several London playhouses in use during Shakespeare's time, e.g. the Theatre, the Rose, the Curtain, the Swan, and the Globe. They were all in fierce competition with one another and each tried to make performances increasingly spectacular by using props, costumes, special effects, fireworks and music to accompany the acting. The Globe Theatre was one of the most popular theatres at this time, and very large audiences attended the performances, where they often took an active part in the plays – shouting out and commenting loudly on the action. Theatres were disapproved of by city officials who often petitioned to have them closed down – this explains why the Globe is situated south of the Thames, away from the centre of London and St. Paul's Cathedral in the illustration. It is also located close to the 'Bear Garden' which hosted bear-baiting and other spectator sports and was the rival form of entertainment in Shakespearean London.

▶ LSET ex. 3, 4, 5, 6

Part B – Drama

SB S. 224
CD 3.08

B1 Love: A Midsummer Night's Dream

Source:	*A Midsummer Night's Dream* (III, ii)
Topic:	Confusion among lovers in a wood
Text form:	Drama (comedy; extract)
Language variety:	British English
Number of words / Length:	338 / 3:10 min
Level:	Intermediate
Skills / Activities:	Analysing drama; performing a dramatic scene; writing a text

Didaktischer Kommentar

Im Ausschnitt aus dem *Sommernachtstraum* begegnen S den Verwirrungen der Liebe, die zu einem handfesten Streit zwischen den Liebenden führen. Es gilt, diesen Konflikt und die leidenschaftlichen Beweggründe der Handelnden sowie die Komik dieser Szene zu verstehen. Durch Analyse, aber auch durch eigenes Nachspielen erhalten S Zugang zum ersten Shakespeare-Text in diesem Kapitel.

SB-DVD-ROM

Lernwortschatz

desire sb. (l. 22), modesty (l. 30)
Fact file: supernatural

Part B1 – Love: A Midsummer Night's Dream

Unterrichtstipps

PRE-READING Vor dem Lesen des Dramenausschnittes sollte das *Who is Who* geklärt werden. Dazu kann der Einführungstext gemeinsam gelesen und zur Sicherung das erste Diagramm erläutert werden. Die Bearbeitung des zweiten Diagramms erfolgt in Einzel- oder Partnerarbeit. Das Verständnis kann durch Vergleich der Ergebnisse mit einem anderen Tandem oder im Plenum gesichert werden.

PRE-READING Die zweite *pre-reading*-Aufgabe eignet sich als kurze schriftliche Einzelarbeit. Nach dem Lesen der Szene ist es sinnvoll, die Übereinstimmung mit dem tatsächlichen Szenenverlauf zu überprüfen. Da es sich hier um die erste Begegnung mit einer Shakespeare-Szene handelt, kann L zur Sicherung die Befindlichkeit der vier Liebenden von S anhand des zweiten Diagramms erklären lassen.
Nach einem ersten *listening for gist* erhalten S Zeit, den Text anhand der Annotationen nachzuvollziehen und das Verständnis zu sichern. Es empfiehlt sich, den Text ein zweites Mal zu hören, ehe mit den Aufgaben begonnen wird.

> **Info**
>
> *A Midsummer Night's Dream* (ca. 1595) is one of Shakespeare's most frequently performed and best-loved plays. It belongs to the genre of romantic comedy and with its combination of supernatural elements and the universal theme of unrequited love which ultimately ends happily, it has appealed to audiences across the world since its first performance. The play has inspired numerous adaptations over the years and some quotations from the play have since become common sayings in English, such as 'The course of true love never did run smooth' (Act 1, Scene 1).

Lösungshinweise

PRE-READING Tafelbild:

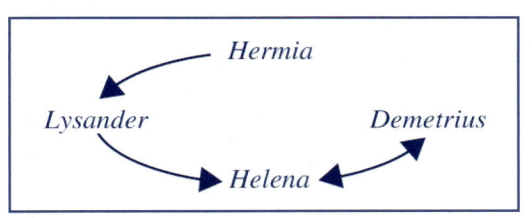

```
            Hermia
           ↙      ↘
    Lysander      Demetrius
           ↘      ↙
            Helena
```

PRE-READING Individual answers. (The text the students write should express the girls' dismay at the turn of events, possibly their sadness and jealousy and their suspicions on how the new constellation may have come about.)

1a Lysander tells Hermia that he hates her, he insults her *(cat, burr, vile thing, serpent, tawny Tartar, loathed medicine, hated poison)* and does everything he can to hurt her. He tells her that he never wants to see her again and that he now loves Helena.

1b *ll. 3–4:* 'Why have you become so rough? What has come over you, my love?' – Hermia is dismayed and shows her hurt feelings; she appeals to her lover to help her understand him.
l. 7: 'Are you playing a joke on me?' - Hermia is hopeful that there is an easy explanation to the shocking change in her lover.
ll. 14–20: 'Hating me is the worst thing you can do to me. But why do you hate me? What has happened? Aren't we both the same people we were? I am as beautiful now as I was. Last night you still loved me, and since then you have left me. Please God that you have not really left me.' – Hermia is deeply hurt by Lysander's words, and tries to reasons with him that his transformation is illogical. But she begins to fear that he is serious about leaving her.

2 Helena is taller than Hermia.
Helena insults her friend by calling her a *'puppet'*. Hermia is furious and accuses Helena of comparing her rival's stature unfavourably with her own, thus winning Lysander's affection. She feels 'put down' so that Helena can appear all the greater. She tells the taller girl that she can still reach high enough to scratch her eyes out.

11   Part B2 – Power and Ambition: Julius Caesar

In passing, she calls Helena a 'painted maypole', hinting that her tall rival puts on too much make-up.

3 Individual answers.

4 EXTRA *Five possible words/phrases:* jealousy – romantic love gone sour – rivals for the love of – end of love – jilted lover

5a *Conflicts include:*
- Lysander's frustration with Hermia following him
- Hermia's dismay at her lover's shocking treatment of her
- Helena's indignation at Hermia
- Lysander leaving his lover Hermia and suddenly becoming Demetrius's rival in his love for Helena
- Hermia's indignation at Helena's presumed wooing of Lysander
- on a meta level: the conflict between what the characters think is true and what the audience knows to be true

5b EXTRA Individual answers.

SB S. 226
CD 3.09

B2 Power and Ambition: Julius Caesar

Source:	*Julius Caesar* (I, ii and III, ii)
Topic:	The assassination of Caesar due to fears he may become a tyrant
Text form:	Drama (tragedy; extract)
Language variety:	British English
Number of words / Length:	353 / 2:41 min
Level:	Advanced
Skills/Activities:	Analysing speeches; performing a scene; analysing stylistic devices; writing an essay

Didaktischer Kommentar

Im zweiten Dramenauszug geht es um den Tyrannenmord an Julius Caesar. S analysieren und erproben die Wirkung kunstvoller Rhetorik, indem sie selbst die Verse deklamieren. Anschließend wird der Konflikt des Tyrannenmordes vor dem eigenen und dem elisabethanischen Hintergrund diskutiert.

SB-DVD-ROM

Lernwortschatz

assassinate sb. (introductory text)

Unterrichtstipps

Einstieg (SB geschlossen): L klärt, welches Vorwissen zu Julius Caesar S aus dem Geschichtsunterricht haben (ggf. als Hausaufgabe zur Vorentlastung). Vor der Lektüre sollten S den Einleitungstext genau lesen und verstehen, damit Situation und handelnde Figuren zu identifizieren sind.
Hinweis: Um S für das unterschiedlich gestaltende Lesen in Aufgabe **2** nicht vorweg zu beeinflussen, kann L darauf verzichten, die CD beim ersten Lesen der Szene mitlaufen zu lassen.
Der Text lässt sich gut zweiteilen, indem man die Szenengrenze nach Zeile 23 als Einschnitt nutzt. Es empfiehlt sich jeweils, zunächst das Grobverständnis zu sichern, ehe S sich mithilfe der Annotationen die Details erschließen.

Differenzierung

Zur Sicherung des Verständnisses können die Szenenhälften arbeitsteilig in Partnerarbeit oder in Kleingruppen erschlossen werden, indem S eine sinngemäße Transkription in drei Sätzen zu einem Teil erstellen und vortragen.

Lösungshinweise

PRE-READING The question aims to have students reflect on the justification of a people ridding itself of a tyrant by killing him; e.g. Stauffenberg's attempt to take Hitler's life.

Part B2 – Power and Ambition: Julius Caesar

1a Caesar has become too powerful, like a giant that rules over Rome and renders all other men weak and meaningless. This goes against the tradition of the state and is shameful to those inheriting a great republican tradition.

1b Caesar's speech indeed confirms Cassius' claims: He sees himself as the greatest man not only in Rome or even the world, but in the entire universe, comparing himself to the northern star. He believes he is infallible and is therefore deaf to the requests and the reasoning of his countrymen.

2 Individual answers.

3 *Stylistic devices Cassius employs:*
- *metaphor*: 'bestride' (l. 5) illustrates Caesar's power as he steps across Rome like a giant.
- *simile*: 'like a Colossus' (l. 6) is a reference to the Colossus of Rhodes, an ancient statue of the Greek God Helios; Caesar moves about Rome like a godlike giant.
- *contrast*: 'Colossus' and 'petty' (l. 6) together highlight the effect the power of Caesar has over the 'underlings'; 'not in our stars but in ourselves' (ll. 10–11) emphasizes the point that it is up to the individual to decide how to live.
- *rhetorical questions*: 'What …?' (l. 12), 'Why …?' (l. 13), 'Upon what …?' (l. 19) involve the audience in the development of the ideas; 'When went there by an age, since the great flood …?' (l. 22) evokes the whole of history as witness to how unusual Caesar's hubris is.
- *parallelism*: 'Write them …' (l. 14), 'Sound them …' (l. 15), 'Weigh them …' (l. 16), 'conjure with 'em …' (l. 16) create a rhythm that makes the audience listen and emphasizes the point.
- *alliteration*: 'grown so great' (l. 20) appeals to the ear and makes the phrase more memorable to the listener.
- *exclamation*: 'Rome, thou hast lost …!' (l. 21) heightens the drama of the utterance.

Stylistic devices Caesar employs:
- *repetition*: 'I' (ll. 28–42): hammers home the fact that Caesar sees himself as the centre of the universe; 'constant' (l. 30, l. 42, l. 43).
- *contrast:* 'I – you' (l. 28) creates a clear division between the one and the many. 'move' (ll. 28–29) and 'constant' (l. 30): the repetition of movement emphasizes the constancy; 'all … every one – but one' (ll. 34–35): Caesar draws a clear division between himself and everyone else.
- *anaphora* 'if' (ll. 28–29): Caesar emphasizes the conditional so that the 'but' which follows contrasts with it all the more strongly.
- *simile*: 'constant as the northern star' (l. 30): Caesar uses a cosmological comparison to justify his right to rule.
- *alliteration*: 'fix'd … fellow … firmament' (ll. 31–32): the sounds link the ideas and help to fix them in the listeners' subconscious.
- *comparison*: 'firmament' (l. 32) and 'world' (l. 36): the Elizabethans would recognize the reference to the order of the universe being repeated in the order of the world – the traditional world view of the Chain of Being would vindicate Caesar's argument.
- *hyperbole*: 'Wilt thou lift up Olympus!' (l. 44): the climax shows Caesar at the height of his hubris.

4a EXTRA Caesar compares himself to the northern star and draws his own authority as a ruler from his comparable status within the world of men. This is an argument the Elizabethans would have been familiar with since it tallies with the world view of the Chain of Being. It also echoes the divine right of a king to his role, which was the view of most people of the time. In the upheavals that accompanied the Elizabethan age, Caesar's evocation of constancy would sound attractive to many among Shakespeare's audience. His mention of 'place' and 'rank' would have been understood as a reference to social hierarchy, possibly in the sense of predetermination through birth.

Part B3 – Revenge: Othello

4b EXTRA Individual answers.

5 *Elements of conflict:* Caesar as a ruler who commands absolute power in his empire and is planning to become king of Rome; conspirators who feel this is unjust to them as Romans and a disgrace to the proud tradition of the Republic; the question of the means to be used to remove Caesar: Is the act of assassination really justified and where will it lead?

SB S. 228
CD 3.10

B3 Revenge: Othello

Source:	*Othello* (III, iii)
Topic:	Iago sows suspicion in Othello's mind about Desdemona, Othello's wife
Text form:	Drama (tragedy; extract)
Language variety:	British English
Number of words / Length:	303 / 2:32 min
Level:	Advanced
Skills/Activities:	Analysing drama; performing a dramatic reading; speculating on plot; identifying conflict in plays and films

Didaktischer Kommentar Im dritten Dramenauszug geht es um Iagos infamen Plan, Othello zu Misstrauen und Eifersucht anzustacheln. S erfahren die manipulative Macht Iagos, indem sie selbst darstellerische Mittel im Spiel erproben. Noch einmal sammeln und benennen S dramatische Konflikte, die zum Abschluss von *Part B* in anderen bekannten Werken identifiziert werden.

SB-DVD-ROM

Lernwortschatz

revenge (heading), envy (introductory text)

Unterrichtstipps Einstieg (SB geöffnet): L kann S über die beiden Figuren auf der Illustration und über den Inhalt ihres Gesprächs spekulieren lassen. Anschließend werden kurz die Fragen des *pre-reading* behandelt.
Zu Beginn der Lektüre sollte L darauf hinweisen, dass Othello mit seinen Eingangsworten auf Desdemona Bezug nimmt, die eben die Bühne verlassen hat.
Das erste Lesen kann ohne CD erfolgen, damit S den Text in Aufgabe **3a** unbeeinflusst vorspielen können.

ALT S können den Text still lesen, da der Inhalt bereits durch die Einleitung vorgegeben ist.

4 EXTRA Es ist nicht wichtig, dass S die Entwicklung der Konflikte richtig einschätzen, ein kreativer Umgang mit dem Material ist hier sogar wünschenswert. L kann im Anschluss an die Aufgabe klären, wie die Handlung tatsächlich weitergeht.

5 S werden sicher zu jedem der gesammelten Konflikte eine Entsprechung in ihnen bekannten Filmen oder Theaterstücken finden. Eine Möglichkeit diese Beispiele zu diskutieren, ist, diese zum Beispiel in komödienspezifische und tragödienspezifische Konflikte einzuteilen. Dies kann gut in Gruppenarbeit erledigt und anschließend im Plenum besprochen werden.

Differenzierung Es bietet sich an, Tonaufnahmen von den Darstellungen der Gruppen zu machen, damit S eine direkte Rückmeldung zu Aussprache und Lesegestaltung erhalten.

Part B3 – Revenge: Othello

Lösungshinweise

1a Othello calls Iago 'full of love and honesty' (l. 36) and considers him to be somebody who carefully reflects on what he says before speaking. Othello seems to value Iago's advice highly.

1b Iago does not immediately state his 'suspicion', but merely drops hints thus arousing Othello's own suspicion. He pretends to be reluctant to say anything against the lieutenant, but then arouses the general's fears again by stating: 'Men should be what they seem' (l. 42). In this way, it is up to Othello to force him to say more, and Iago can retain a pretence of innocence and uninvolvement.

2 It hints that Othello's balanced state of mind and sense of well-being rests on this love. If he loses it, he will not be able to maintain order both within himself and as a general of the army. [This is very important in the context of the Elizabethan world view, for Othello as foremost general in Venice would not be able to keep the entire system under control.]

3 Individual answers.

4 **EXTRA** *Othello – Iago:* Iago is successfully sowing the seeds of jealousy, but must not appear keen to denounce Cassio in order not to arouse suspicion. The audience knows what his plans are, Othello does not. Othello is very impatient and wants Iago to speak plainly.
Iago – Desdemona: Iago is accusing Desdemona of deceiving her husband. Once she finds out, he will have to face her.
Iago – Cassius: Iago is envious of Cassius's promotion to lieutenant. Like Desdemona, Cassius will be enraged when he hears about the rumours Iago is spreading.
Othello – Desdemona: Desdemona is innocent and will be shattered when her husband confronts her with the lies about her infidelity.

5 *The list might include these conflicts:*
- conflicts to do with people falling in and out of love
- conflicts on account of jealousy and rivalry
- conflicts between seeming and being
- conflict of awareness (i.e. the audience or one of the characters knows more than other characters on stage)
- conflicts of identity (people changing from what they were, e.g. Lysander changing from the devoted lover to someone who callously rejects Hermia,)
- conflicts of role (e.g. Caesar is not fulfilling his role as emperor correctly)
- conflicts of conscience and ethics (people acting against their better judgement, e.g. Iago pretends to act against his better judgement when he 'reveals' Desdemona's infidelity to Othello, or the conspirators in *Julius Caesar* having to decide whether an assassination is justified or not)
- social conflicts, for example between people of different status (or colour, e.g. Othello)
- conflicts caused by ambition and envy
- conflicts based on innocence and experience
- the conflict of order and disorder

Part C

Part C – Versions of Shakespeare

SB S. 230
DVD
Transkript s. TM-DVD-ROM

C1 Comparing Two Shakespeare Productions

Source:	*A Midsummer Night's Dream*, 1999
Topic:	Bottom is lured into Titania's bower
Text form:	Feature film (extract)
Language variety:	British English
Length:	3:11 min
Level:	Advanced

Source:	*Staging Magic*, BBC, 1981
Topic:	Presenting fairies in modern theatre
Text form:	Documentary (extract)
Language variety:	British English
Length:	3:31 min
Level:	Intermediate

Skills/Activities:	Viewing, analysing and comparing film extracts

Didaktischer Kommentar S vergleichen zwei Inszenierungsansätze zum *Sommernachtstraum*: einerseits Szenenausschnitte aus der berühmten Peter Brook-Theaterproduktion mit der Royal Shakespeare Company aus dem Jahre 1970, andererseits eine Hollywood-Verfilmung von 1999. Der krasse Kontrast zwischen den beiden Ansätzen soll S zu einer Stellungnahme bewegen wie sie sich „ihren" Shakespeare vorstellen.

Unterrichtstipps Einstieg: S reflektieren zunächst ihre eigene Vorstellung einer Shakespeare-Inszenierung. L kann sie darum bitten, sich bei geschlossenen Augen eine Szene auf der Bühne vorzustellen und diese zu beschreiben. Als Vorgabe kann hier eine der gelesenen Szenen dienen, zu der S Details zu Kostümen und Bühnenausstattung beschreiben.

HA Word help Vor dem ersten Sehen des Spielfilmauszugs machen sich S mit unbekanntem Wortschatz vertraut.

ZA S betrachten die beiden Fotos und vergleichen sie. Der Vergleich gibt ihnen sofort deutliche Hinweise, dass den beiden Versionen unterschiedliche Ansätze zugrunde liegen.

ZA Vor dem ersten Sehen sollte L zur Orientierung die unten stehende Info zum jeweiligen Clip referieren.

Differenzierung Je nach Interesse des Kurses kann die Frage der theatralischen Umsetzung weiter verfolgt werden. S können sich zum Beispiel Gedanken machen, wie eine Inszenierung von *Julius Caesar* im Stil Peter Brooks aussehen könnte oder wie sie die Feen in *A Midsummer Night's Dream* bei einer Schulaufführung gestalten würden.

> **Info**
>
> *Hollywood version:* The clip from the film introduces us to a group of artisans who are in the wood that night along with the lovers. The group is practising a play for a festival at court. We meet Bottom, who was left behind when one of the fairies put asses' ears on his head as a joke and his friends ran away in terror. Titania, the Queen of the fairy kingdom, wakes up in her bed and falls in love with Bottom. As in the case of the other lovers, magic makes her fall in love with the wrong person.

Part C2 – A Shakespeare Comic Strip

> *Peter Brook's stage version:* The second clip is from a documentary that shows some short scenes from a famous theatre production of the play. We see the lovers lost and confused in the wood and being tricked by the fairies. There is also a scene from the fairy court, where Titania is charmed to sleep and then made to fall in love with the first thing she sees upon waking. Understanding the whole of the dialogue is not as important as noting how the director tries to present the magical events on stage.

Lösungshinweise

1 Individual answers.

2a

Look out for …	Hollywood version	Stage version 1970
costume	Bottom: realistic clothes, fairies: fantastic costumes	simple colourful costumes, non-realistic
scenery	'realistic' forest background, flowery decoration	empty white box, two doors, trapezes
sound	classical opera music from record player, sound effects off	eerie music made by twirling plastic tubing on stage
effects	magical effects like Bottom being whisked up to Titania's bed, twinkling stars	conjuring tricks like spinning plates; charming of Titania conveyed by intensity of acting and audience's imagination
props	'realistic' props – food, plates, painting, record player, flowers, etc.	functional props: stilts, wands, spinning plates, trapezes, swings
lighting	lighting denoting nighttime	bright white light
acting, movement	acting 'in character', realism	'artificial' expression conveys the inner situation; actors openly 'play' with elements of the stage

2bc–3 Individual answers.

SB S. 231 **C2 A Shakespeare Comic Strip** Oscar Zarate

Source:	*William Shakespeare's Othello*, 1983
Topic:	Othello, III, iii: Iago sows suspicion about Desdemona, Othello's wife
Text form:	Comic
Language variety:	British English
Number of words:	131
Level:	Intermediate
Skills/Activities:	Working with comics

Didaktischer Kommentar

Von den verschiedenen Medien, in denen Shakespeare heute verfügbar ist, sollen S die Form des Comics kennen lernen. Daran ist zu erkennen, dass das Schaffen des *Bard* immer wieder neu rezipiert und interpretiert wird. S sollen sich eine Meinung dazu bilden, ob diese Fassung als legitime Form der Deutung gelten kann.

11 Part C3 – Sonnets and the German Shakespeare

Unterrichtstipps Einstieg (SB geöffnet): Da Dialog und Handlung bereits aus *Part B* bekannt sind, können S zunächst spontane Reaktionen zu dieser Shakespeare-Fassung äußern.

1a Um die Aufgabe reizvoller zu gestalten, können S versuchen, das Bild bei geschlossenem Buch aus dem Gedächtnis zu rekonstruieren. Die Übung kann auch als eine Wiederholung der Fertigkeit der Bildbeschreibung genutzt werden (s. a. *SF 9: Working with pictures*).

2 Als Vorbereitung auf die Diskussion bietet sich die *think–pair–share*-Methode an. Die Argumente der S lassen sich gut mithilfe einer *Placemat* verschriftlichen.

Differenzierung
ZA KV 25 bietet weitere ausgefallenere Versionen von Shakespeare. Je nach Leistungsstärke und Motivation des Kurses können S im Rahmen des *creative writing* (s. a. *SF 39: Creative writing*) auch eigene Versionen schreiben (Aufgabe 2).

Lösungshinweise **1a** Individual answers.

1bc The comic uses similar devices to a film camera, so these frames might be seen as stills. The perspective of each frame focuses our attention, as do the foreground and background elements. Colours are used to great effect to create a very vivid and vibrant atmosphere. The relatively dark lighting and the concealing curtains convey a sense of secrecy and menace. The words are in speech bubbles, but they keep to the original text. The setting of the scene is completely open to the artist's imagination however; in this case they have chosen to highlight Othello's African background, giving the scene a potent exoticism. Images of hunting, spears and masks complement the nature of the action; there is a sense that something dark and violent is going to emerge from the conflict. The bird of prey adds power to the figure of Othello, as these only belonged to people of high rank. The varying visual perspective given on the character speaking the lines may suggest either honesty or dishonesty, especially because sometimes the speaker is not even in the frame.

SB S. 232 ## C3 Sonnets and the German Shakespeare

Source:	Sonnet 29
Topic:	Love offering joy in a world of trouble
Text form:	Poem
Language variety:	British English
Number of words:	115
Level:	Intermediate

Source:	Sonnet 29 (Markus Marti; Friedrich Bodenstedt)
Topic:	Sonnet 29 in German
Text form:	Poems
Number of words:	90; 85

Source:	*Die Welt*, 28 October 2009
Topic:	How Shakespeare's sonnets might have come into existence
Text form:	Newspaper article (extract)
Number of words:	586

Skills/Activities:	Reading poetry; mediating

Didaktischer Kommentar Ein weiterer Teil des Werkes von Shakespeare besteht aus den Sonetten, zu denen es eine Fülle deutscher Übersetzungen gibt. Nach der Analyse des Sonetts 29 und der Einordnung des dort dargestellten Liebeskonzepts in die bereits kennen gelernten erhalten S Einblick in zwei Übersetzungsbeispiele, die sie vergleichen und mit eigenen Übersetzungsversuchen ergänzen.

Part C3 – Sonnets and the German Shakespeare

SB-DVD-ROM

Lernwortschatz

outcast (l. 2)

Unterrichtstipps Nach der Lektüre der Einleitung beschreiben S die Shakespeare-Darstellung. Sie spekulieren anhand des Bildes (z. B. in Partnerarbeit) über Themen, die dann anhand des nachfolgenden Textbeispiels verifiziert werden können.

1a L sollte den Text als Kopie zur Verfügung stellen, damit S bei der Analyse und Strukturierung des Sonetts (z. B. in Kleingruppen) möglichst nahe am Text arbeiten und diesen markieren können.

3a Die beiden deutschen Versionen sollten laut vorgetragen werden. Unter Umständen kann sich eine sprachlich schwierige Situation ergeben, da in englischer Sprache über die deutschen Texte gesprochen wird. L sollte darauf achten, dass dies dennoch konsequent umgesetzt wird, da nur so das zur Analyse notwendige Vokabular auf Englisch verwendet wird.

5 Mediation Da im Mediationstext weitere Informationen und Mythen zur Entstehungsgeschichte der Sonette genannt werden, kann statt mit Aufgabe **1** auch mit Aufgabe **5** begonnen werden.
Bezüglich der Mediation liegt für S die Hauptaufgabe im Dekodieren des humoristischen Grundtons, der im Zieltext einer objektiven Zusammenfassung weichen muss.

Differenzierung Leistungsstärkere, interessierte S können einzeln oder in Kleingruppen eine Präsentation zum Sonett-Zyklus Shakespeares anfertigen und dabei ggf. auch die Informationen des Mediationstextes integrieren. Die Präsentation kann als Einführung in die Stunde vorgetragen werden. Gleiches gilt für Aufgabe **2**, die auch fächerübergreifend mit den Fächern Deutsch oder Französisch behandelt werden kann.

ZA **Linktipp:** *http://pages.unibas.ch/shine/index.html* („Sh:in:E – Shakespeare in Europe") Weitere Sonette und deren deutsche Übertragungen können hier erschlossen werden. Weniger leistungsstarke Gruppen können Originaltexte oder Übersetzungen als Textpuzzle bearbeiten, bei denen sie nur die Reihenfolge des Textes erstellen müssen.

Info

Shakespeare's work in German: The relation between Shakespeare and Germany has always been a fruitful, but also controversial one. In the beginning Shakespeare's plays came to Germany as puppet theatre. Shakespeare in the original and in translation served as an example for many German writers and fostered the development of a genuinely German national literature. Not until 1741 *(Julius Caesar)* and 1758 *(Romeo and Juliet)* were the first plays translated into German. From 1762 to 1766 Christoph Martin Wieland published the first more or less complete edition, accomplished using a French-English dictionary for help. The most famous German version is probably the so-called 'Schlegel-Tieck' translation (1797 to 1840), which is still performed on stages today. Yet their translation was not the product of collaborative work as the name would suggest but rather the subject of a long-term argument between the writers. Schlegel, Tieck, Tieck's sister Dorothea and a friend called Baudissin nevertheless produced the classical German Shakespeare. To date, Shakespeare's complete works have been rendered in German at least 40 times along with countless other versions of individual plays. Examples include such writers and translators as Rudolf Alexander Schröder with his baroque Shakespeare, and Erich Fried or Frank Günther in contemporary times. The sonnets in particular have been the focus of interest for many German writers and translators, resulting in at least 200 translations, including more than 60 translations of the complete cycle.

11 Part C3 – Sonnets and the German Shakespeare

> *Sonnet 29:* The sonnet is divided into two sections (ll. 1–8 and 9–14); the speaker complains about his present state in the first two quatrains (ll. 1–8) and then recalls the joy of his lover in the third quatrain and the couplet (ll. 9–14). It is widely believed that the loved one is a young man. The interesting thing about this sonnet is that it is not about the lover but about the speaker's state of mind.
>
> *Friedrich Bodenstedt* (1819–1892) was a German poet, professor of languages at Munich University, and theatre manager in Meiningen.
>
> *Markus Marti* (born 1955) is a lecturer of English literature and culture at the University of Basel.

Lösungshinweise

PRE-READING There are images of nature (snail, cherry, bird), love (embracing couple, Cupid's arrow which has pierced Shakespeare directly in the heart), metapoetical aspects (laurel as the sign of distinction as a poet). He looks through the bird's eye which suggests that he has a 'bird's eye view' on the world, meaning he understands how the world works and how things fit together in the overall picture. The arrow could also be identified as a quill, with which he writes straight from his heart. Rich clothing indicates that he writes about noble people, and that as a professional writer he has earned enough money to afford his own rich clothing.

1a In the beginning the speaker is sad about his fate. He feels lonely and pities himself and his existence. At the end he changes his opinion because he realizes that loving his lover makes him more powerful and rich than any king in the world.
l. 1–4: Alone and Poor
l. 5–8: Wishing to Be Somebody Else
l. 9–12: Thinking of the Lover
l. 13/14: The Lover Makes All the Difference

1b There are three quatrains (abab/cdcd/efef) and one rhyming couplet (gg). This structure mirrors the development of the author's feelings.

1c The concept of love in the sonnet is one of fulfilled or requited love as a consolation for loneliness and a rather desolate life. Love is depicted as hope and inspiration in contrast to jealousy and distrust in love in *Othello*, love for your country, self-centred love and hunger for power in *Julius Caesar* or love and madness/sexuality and foolish love in *A Midsummer Night's Dream*.

2 EXTRA *Suggested elements:*
- 14th century Italy witnessed the birth of the sonnet; Petrarch's sonnet cycle *Il Canzoniere* about his idolized beloved Laura is the best-known example of this time.
- France took over the Italian model with the so-called Pléiade (group of poets around Pierre de Ronsard and Joachim du Bellay founded in 1549).
- English versions appeared in the first half of the 16th century (Sir Thomas Wyatt, Henry Howard, Earl of Surrey, Sir Philip Sidney, Edmund Spenser).
- Shakespeare did not invent the sonnet but drew on various sources and created his own form and content by adapting an existing form (cf. also humorous forms as in Sonnet 130).
- Sonnets became very popular in Germany too, but unlike in other countries the German poets (e.g. Andreas Gryphius), focused on religion, war and politics as topics probably because of experiences of the Thirty Years' War.

3a Left: Markus Marti; right: Friedrich Bodenstedt
The left-hand version seems to be more contemporary because of its more colloquial tone. The sentences sound more fluent, as if spoken in conversation, whereas the right-hand version often uses inversion and starts the lines with the objects rather than the subjects or verbs of a sentence. In the left-hand version you also find more modern words like 'erfolgreich' and 'Selbstachtung'.

Communicating across Cultures

3b *Five aspects:*
1. Line 1 is rendered more or less literally in Bodenstedt, even starting with the exact German translation of the first word: 'when' – 'wenn'. Although it gives all of the same information, Marti's translation is much freer and completely changes the grammatical construction of the line so that the speaker becomes an active subject: 'ich hab kein Geld …'
2. In Line 2, Bodenstedt chooses to leave out the fact that the speaker is crying, whereas Marti includes this: 'ich wein' alleine'.
3. The idea of the speaker's wish to be 'featur'd like him' (l. 6), referring to an object of envy, is conveyed by Marti who writes 'möchte ich … des anderen Gesicht'. The adjective 'hochgeboren' in Bodenstedt's version doesn't portray the speaker's desire to look like someone else.
4. The complicated concept in line 8, that the speaker is unhappy with things that usually make him happy, is translated fully by Bodenstedt. Marti, however, simplifies the line so that the speaker is merely unhappy with the things he owns.
5. Like in line 2, Bodenstedt changes line 12 so that the speaker is not singing, he is 'helljubelnd' instead. Marti translates the second half of this line almost word for word.

Closer to the original: Although Marti does take some liberties in rendering Sonnet 29 into German, his version is actually closer to the original than Bodenstedt's. He uses modern, sometimes colloquial, language to give us exactly the same information as Shakespeare. Bodenstedt, however, slightly changes the meaning of some lines by introducing new words that aren't translations of the English.

In general Bodenstedt's version keeps more strictly to the original wording and structure. Nevertheless Marti manages to create a fluent, harmonious and poetic German sonnet.

4 Individual answers.
Original endings:
Bodenstedt: So macht Erinnerung an Dein Lieben reich,
           Daß ich's nicht hingäb' um ein Königreich.
Marti: An deine Lieb zu denken, macht mich gleich
           so reich, ich tausch's nicht für ein Königreich.

5 – CONTEXT TASK Individual answers.

SB S. 235

Communicating across Cultures – Dealing with Different Cultural Values

Didaktischer Kommentar

Über die in **1** und **2** gebotenen Situationen können S erkennen, dass sich kulturelle Missverständnisse aus verschiedenen Regeln oder Auffassungen zu bestimmten alltäglichen Handlungen oder aber über eine Werte-Veränderung über lange Zeit hinaus ergeben. Dabei ist die gezeigte Verhaltensweise oft nur Ausweis einer tiefer liegenden Grundüberzeugung, die es vorurteilslos zu ergründen gilt. Ziel der Behandlung dieser Beispielsituationen ist, dass S solche Aspekte in ihre Überlegungen mit einbeziehen und bei Missverständnissen in der Lage sind, solche zu erkennen und sich dafür in adäquater Weise zu erklären und/oder zu entschuldigen.

Differenzierung
ZA

Linktipp: *www.macmillanenglish.com/readers/studentsite/Shakespeare%27s%20World.htm* Für interessierte S, die sich intensiv mit Shakespeare und seinem Leben befasst haben und befassen möchten, bietet die *web quest* unter der angegebenen URL eine abwechslungsreiche Aufgabe zum Abschluss des Themas.

Lösungshinweise

1
1. The apology should mention that the custom in Germany is almost the exact opposite: not opening a present more or less immediately would be considered impolite.

11 Communicating across Cultures – Dealing with Different Cultural Values

2 The explanation should refer to German history, the legal situation in Germany with the swastika being banned and consequently how sensitive Germans are about the subject.

3 Here the pupils should mention aspects like the more liberal view concerning clothes in their home country or express the idea that no offence was intended.

2

Elizabethan times	modern times
parents decide about their daughter's future and select their husbands; daughters are obliged to accept their parents' / father's decision even up to the point of life and death	it is more or less up to the daughter who she wants to marry if at all; by law parents are not allowed to use any form of force or violence
murder is explained as a way in which to restore honour in society which has been violated by an (imagined) offence	honour cannot be restored by killing somebody; honour has become a more personal concept rather than a social one
power, the right to rule and thus authority was considered to be invested by God *(dei gratia)* and could therefore not be taken away by a human being	society has developed into a meritocracy where an individual can receive things because they have worked for them rather than being awarded them by a certain birthright
as a result of their lower status in society women were being expected to obey and serve their husbands	in today's society there should be equality of the sexes
asking for and taking revenge ('an eye for an eye') was an accepted principle of justice	revenge has been replaced by punishment e.g. in prison which should also rehabilitate the prisoner and prepare him/her for a new start

3 EXTRA Individual answers.

Kopiervorlage 24: Phrases from Shakespeare

Many quotes from Shakespeare's plays found their way into our daily language.
Read the following quotes.

1 I will wear my heart upon my sleeve.

2 Something is rotten in the state of Denmark.

3 All that glisters is not gold.

4 All's well that ends well.

5 It smells to heaven.

6 too much of a good thing

7 It's all Greek to me.

8 Love is blind.

1 Find a German equivalent for the quotes above.

_____
_____
_____
_____
_____
_____
_____
_____

2 Which phrases have you used before? If so, state in which context you have used them.
Then exchange your ideas in class.

_____
_____
_____
_____
_____
_____
_____
_____

Read the condensed versions of *Julius Caesar* und *Othello*.

Cassius: Brutus, we're planning to kill our best friend, Caesar. Wanna help?
Marcus Brutus: Because I love Rome more, I will.
(They all stab Caesar.)
Julius Caesar: Et tu, Brute? In that case, I'd better die.
(The nation mourns, and everybody commits suicide.)

From: Samuel Stoddard and David J. Parker, 'Julius Caesar Ultra-Condensed', 1996–2010;
www.rinkworks.com/bookaminute/b/shakespeare.caesar.shtml

Iago: Your wife's cheating on you.
Othello: She is? *(kills wife).*
Damn – she wasn't really.

From: Ric F. Barker, 'Othello Ultra-Condensed', 1996–2010;
www.rinkworks.com/bookaminute/b/shakespeare.othello.shtml

1a Write down your spontaneous reaction to these versions.

b Discuss your reaction and with a partner.

c In class, discuss
- whether or not these ultra-condensed versions capture the spirit of Shakespeare's plays;
- the pros and cons of condensing plays in this manner.

2 Write your own 60-second Shakespeare of either *A Midsummer Night's Dream* or another play by Shakespeare that you know.

Context 21 Shakespeare: Topic Vocabulary

Word/Phrase	Memory Aid	German
THE MAN		
(to) **be innovative**	*synonyms:* creative/imaginative/inventive/original	innovativ
(to) **be inspired by** sth.	*other collocations:* (to) <u>be inspired by</u> a landscape / trip / person / work of art	von etwas inspiriert sein
(to) **coin a word**	*example sentence:* Shakespeare **~ed** many **words** which are still in use today.	ein Wort prägen
genius	*example sentence:* The ~ of a writer lies in his ability to put into words what the rest of us feel.	Genie
patron ['peɪtrən]	*definition:* a person who gives money and support to artists or writers	Förderer/Förderin, Mäzen/atin, Gönner/in
playwright ['pleɪraɪt]	*synonym:* dramatist	Dramatiker/in
poet	*example sentence:* Shakespeare is famous as a ~ and playwright.	Dichter/in
THE WORK		
comedy	*word family:* comedy – comedian – comic *(adj)*	Komödie
history	*example sentence:* Comedies, tragedies and **~ies** are different genres of plays.	Historiendrama
tragedy	*definition:* a serious play with a sad ending	Tragödie
act	*definition:* one of the major divisions of a play	Akt
line	*example sentence:* The most famous ~ of the play is spoken by the main character in the first act.	Zeile
scene	*example sentence:* The dramatic opening ~ of the play grabbed the audience's attention.	Szene
bawdy	*example sentence:* The ~ humour of the play made the audience roar with laughter.	derb
blank verse	*definition:* unrhymed verse / rhymeless verse	Blankvers
prose	*opposite:* poetry	Prosa
(to) **provide comic relief**	*synonyms:* (to) provide humour / (to) lighten the atmosphere / (to) relieve the tension	für humoristische Auflockerung / befreiende Komik sorgen

Context 21 Shakespeare: Topic Vocabulary

Word/Phrase	Memory Aid	German
THE WORK		
pun	*synonyms:* wordplay / play on words	Wortspiel
sonnet ['sɒnɪt]	*definition:* a poem that has fourteen lines and a fixed rhyme scheme	Sonett
THE STAGE		
actor/actress	*word family:* (to) act – actor/actress – act *(n)* – acted *(adj)*	Schauspieler/in
audience	*definition:* the people who watch a play, concert, etc.	Zuschauer
costume	*definition:* the clothes an actor wears on stage when performing in a play	Kostüm
curtain	*example sentence:* As the ~ fell on the last scene of the play, the audience applauded loudly.	Vorhang
fool	*example sentence:* In Shakespeare's plays, the ~ is often a clever person of low social status.	Narr
leading role	*opposite:* supporting role	Hauptrolle
(to) learn your lines	*example sentence:* The scene was ruined because the actress had not **~t her lines**.	seinen Text lernen
play	*collocations:* (to) watch / (to) perform / (to) direct / (to) produce a play	Theaterstück
playhouse	*synonym:* theatre	Theater
prop	*definition:* an object used by actors on stage when performing in a play	Requisit
(to) rehearse (for) sth.	*word family:* (to) rehearse (for) sth. – rehearsal – rehearsed *(adj)*	etwas proben, etwas einstudieren
scenery	*example sentence:* The ~ was painted to look like a castle.	Kulisse
stage	*word family:* (to) stage – stage *(n)* – staged *(adj)*	Bühne
theatre company	*example sentence:* The ~ **company** went bankrupt when its patron stopped funding it.	Theaterensemble

Group Activities

⚠ Cooperative learning strategies are marked with an *asterisk.

Double Circle
(Kugellager, Karussell)

▶ This is a useful way of developing one's discussion skills. It can also be used to revise keywords/phrases/dates/names.

1. The class is divided into two groups. One group forms an outer circle, the other an inner circle; the two groups face each other.
2. The students in the inner circle discuss the given topic with the student facing them (time: c. 3 minutes).
3. The students in the outer circle then move two places to the right.
4. Topic and class size allowing, students can report on the results after talking to three to five students. In order to do so, students may take notes.

Fishbowl

▶ Useful for giving feedback.

1. Groups of four or five discuss the pros or cons of a topic.
2. A discussion group is then formed with one student from each group joining a circle of chairs. One student is the moderator; the others become the audience and watch the discussion.
3. The moderator starts the discussion by asking one student their opinion. The moderator ensures that everyone gets a turn and no one dominates the discussion.
4. The audience should take notes and can contribute by asking questions in the final ten minutes of the discussion.
5. Once the discussion is over, the discussion group says how they felt and the audience comments on the discussion: e.g. content (was there anything missing?), articulation and discussion habits.

*Gallery Walk

▶ Useful for collecting, discussing and presenting ideas/answers/results.

1. Several different tasks are written on pieces of paper and distributed around the classroom.
2. Students form groups of four or five.
3. Groups move from station to station, taking three to five minutes at each station to
   – brainstorm and collect different ideas and solutions and note them down,
   – reflect on other groups' ideas and note down their reactions to them.
4. Once back at the station they started out at, each group organizes the information collected, discusses it and presents it to the class.

`ALT` 5. Alternatively, the results are commented on in a class discussion.

Hot Seat

▶ Useful for working out the motivation of characters in literary texts.

1. Four or five students make notes on a character from a story they have read.
2. The rest of the class notes down questions they would like to ask that character.
3. The group elects one group member to sit in the hot seat (S1). S1 should not have any notes at his/her disposal.
4. The class asks S1 questions about the particular character, addressing him/her as that character.
5. A moderator can select people to ask questions.

*Jigsaw Puzzle
(*Experten- oder Quergruppen)

▶ Useful for dealing with different tasks or for presenting results.

AAAA ⇨ $A_1B_1C_1D_1$ CCCC ⇨ $A_3B_3C_3D_3$

BBBB ⇨ $A_2B_2C_2D_2$ DDDD ⇨ $A_4B_4C_4D_4$

Group Activities

1. The class is divided into groups of four or five S, labelled e.g. A–D.
2. Each group deals with a different task. Each group member notes down the results (e.g. on a poster).
3. Students then form new groups so that each group includes members from all initial groups. One group's results are discussed. The student from this particular group (the 'group expert') explains the group results to the other students and answers questions.
4. Upon a signal from the teacher, the next task is dealt with. The new group expert presents the results.
5. The activity is over when all results have been presented.
6. As a follow-up, the most important results are collected in class.

*Exhibition Method
(*Ausstellungsmethode)

Variant 1:
▶ This method involves more activity, as groups move from station to station. Instead of each student taking notes and presenting the results in their group one by one, each initial group here displays its results on a table or on the wall. Only then are new groups formed according to the above pattern. Each group moves from one group's results to the next, with the group expert explaining the results to the other group members.

*Text Jigsaw

Variant 2:
▶ Instead of individual aspects of an issue, different text extracts are dealt with. This activity trains reading and listening comprehension as well as speaking skills.

Learning speed duet
(Lerntempoduett)

▶ Useful for exercising, acquiring knowledge or finding solutions. The activity offers S the possibility to work individually and to compare with a partner. The allotted time (c. 30 minutes) can thus be used optimally by every student.

1. Students work on task 1 on their own.
2. Students who have finished the task meet at the blackboard/whiteboard and compare their work.
3. This procedure is repeated for task 2.
4. Students who have finished both tasks can work on a third one which the other students can do as homework.

Marketplace
(Milling Around-Activity; Marktplatz)

▶ Useful for looking at different aspects of an issue and for discussing, forming and justifying one's opinion.

1. Students receive a task that is to be solved within a time limit. (The teacher gives an acoustic signal.) They move around the classroom freely.
2. Students form groups of two or three to discuss the topic, justifying their opinion (and taking notes). They then swap partners.
3. This is repeated until students have collected the necessary information.
4. The results are presented and evaluated in class.

*Placemat

▶ Useful for brainstorming in a group.

1. The given topic or question is written in the middle of a piece of paper (DIN A3 or larger).
2. Students form groups of four. Each writes down at least three ideas on the topic in one of the four corners of the placemat.
3. The group discusses all the ideas. The best or most important ideas are written under the topic in the middle of the placemat.

*Reciprocal Reading
(Lesekonferenz)

▶ Using the four strategies outlined below, reading comprehension is promoted, monitored and evaluated.

⚠ Reading strategies have to be pre-taught.

Group Activities

1. In groups of four, students read the same text (extract) at the same time.
2. Then
   - one student asks questions about the text, concentrating on the most important facts.
   - one student tries to resolve inconsistencies and clarify what was misunderstood or not understood. Difficult parts are read carefully, focusing on the meaning of a word or sentence in the context.
   - one student summarizes the main facts in one or two sentences.
   - one student speculates on what will happen and compares this to the actual ending.
3. The results are shared in the groups.
4. In a next step, a new text extract can be read with S swapping tasks.

Role-Play

▶ Useful for understanding somebody else's position, e.g. to train communication skills and interactive phrases, for better understanding of a character etc. A role-play can either be guided, with structures and chunks given, or free.

1. The pair/group decides who is going to play which role.
2. The pair/group considers the situation it is going to act out. Details about the characters (age, appearance) and how they might act (personality) can be noted down.
3. [ALT] The teacher hands out role cards. Alternatively, students make their own role cards.
4. The pair/group rehearses the situation before presenting it to the class, but does not write down lines or a script for the role-play.

*Think-Pair-Share / *Think-Square-Share

▶ Useful for brainstorming, for structuring a discussion or arguments, or for evaluating a discussion.

1. Students work on their own to collect ideas or information, taking notes.
2. Students share ideas or information with a partner (or, as in think-square-share, in a group of four), adjusting their notes and agreeing on the best ideas.
3. Students discuss their results with another pair or the whole class, completing their notes.

*Writing Conference / Round Robin
(Schreibgespräch, Schreibkonferenz, Graffiti, Rundgespräch, Blätterlawine)

▶ Useful for collecting and developing ideas and arguments. The activity should be done in silence.

1. The class receives a topic and is divided into groups of four or five.
2. On a piece of paper, each group member reacts to the topic by collecting ideas (keywords, opposites, etc.) within a given time limit.
3. The paper is passed on to the next person in the group who reacts to what has been written (again within the time limit).
4. This continues until everyone in the group has reacted to every original statement (and the comments on it) and the papers have been returned to the original student.

Zigzag Debate
(American Debate)

▶ Useful for discussing ideas/opinions.
1. Students make two rows according to the argument, e.g. pro-con.
2. S1 presents his/her argument.
3. S2 (in the opposing row) repeats the argument and presents his/her counter-argument to the next S on the opposite side, and so on.

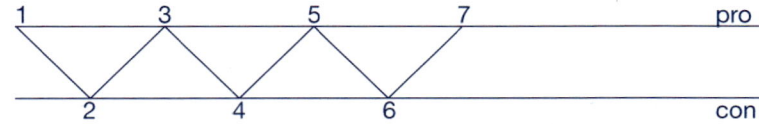

```
1     3     5     7         pro
 \ / \ / \ / \
  X   X   X
 / \ / \ / \ /
   2    4    6           con
```

It is important that any argument is presented only once. Students should make sure that they have prepared enough arguments in their group.

Quellenangaben

Quellenangaben für Transkripte und Kopiervorlagen

Global Perspectives: A3 'Outsourcing', from OUTSOURCED © 2006 Shadowcatcher Entertainment LLC. All rights reserved; **B3** 'More Globalization?', © Paul Collier, Oxford; **C2** 'Model Power?', © D. Miliband / The Foreign and Commonwealth Office;
India – Past and Present: B4 'The Tata Nano', © Tata Motors Ltd, Mumbai; **Communicating across Cultures** 'Task 1: Understanding Indian English', © Amar C. Bakshi in 'How the World Sees America' (www.washingtonpost.com/america); **Communicating across Cultures** 'Task 2: Mediation', reproduced by permission of the Australian Broadcasting Corporation and ABC Online. © 2001 ABC. All rights reserved; **C3** 'Jamal's Story – The Film', © Celador Entertainment Ltd; **C4** 'For One Million Rupees …', © Celador Entertainment Ltd;
The Individual in Society: B3 i) 'Mediation: a Day for Blokes', © Martin Spiewak: Ein Tag für Kerle, DIE ZEIT, Nr. 17, 22.04. 2010; **B3 ii)** 'The Global Gender Gap', © Reuters; **C2 i)** 'Society: A Song from the Soundtrack', Musik & Text: Jerry Joseph Hannan © Record High Publishing, SVL:Wintrup Musikverlage Walter Holzbauer; **C2 ii)** 'Two Extracts from the Film, task 2', from INTO THE WILD © River Road Entertainment;
The Media: A2 'Movable Type', © The Economist Newspaper Limited, London (2010); **B1** 'Canada's Next Great Prime Minister, 2009 competition', © CBC Canada, 2009; **B2** 'The Truman Show', © Paramount Pictures Corp. All rights reserved. THE TRUMAN SHOW Courtesy of Paramount Pictures; **C2** 'Reaching the Audience', © abc NEWS Videosource;
National Identity and Diversity: Lead-in 'Diversity', © Freemantle Media; **C4** 'A Better Way of Life', © 2004 National Public Radio®;
Science, Technology and the Environment: A2 'In Our Image: The Age of Robotics', transcribed from the New York Times podcast "Isaac Asimov speaks with Terry Gross", 1987. © Copyright 2010. All rights reserved by New York Times Syndication Sales Corp. This material may not be copied, published, broadcast or redistributed in any manner; **B1** 'How Designer Children Will Work', transcribed from The New York Times video: "Embryo Screening" by Erik Olsen. © Copyright 2010. All rights reserved by New York Times Syndication Sales Corp. This material may not be copied, published, broadcast or redistributed in any manner; **B2** 'Born for a Purpose', EYE ON BOOKS interview with author Jodi Picoult / © Eye on Books / Bill Thompson; **C1** 'Take AIM at Climate Change', © Geoff Haines-Stiles Productions Inc.;
Shakespeare: A1 'Watching a Play in Shakespeare's Theatre', © Courtesy of Universal Clip Licensing LLLP; **C1** 'Comparing Two Shakespeare Productions – Hollywood Version', footage from 'A MIDSUMMER NIGHT'S DREAM' Courtesy of Twentieth Century Foy. All rights reserved; **C1** 'Comparing Two Shakespeare Productions – Stage Version', © Open University Worldwide Ltd.; **C2** '60-Second Shakespeare', © 1996 – 2010 by Samuel Stoddard;
The UK – Tradition and Change: A4 'Britishness', © BBC Radio 4 / Matthew d' Ancona; **B6** 'The USA II', © Courtesy of Universal Clip Licensing LLLP; **C3** 'Popular Culture: Songs', © Universal Music 2008; **C4** 'Scottish Festivals', © edfest tv. Republic Productions Ltd;
The USA – Dreams and Struggles: Lead-in 'Task 3: Proud to Be an American', Musik & Text: Beyoncé Giselle Knowles, © Sony Music Entertainment; **A2** 'Lynching Will Maxie', Used by permission of Viking Penguin, a division of Penguin Group (USA) Inc.; **A3** 'Civil Rights', © Reprinted by arrangement with The Heirs to the Estate of Martin Luther King Jr., c/o Writers House as agent for the proprietor New York, NY. © 1963 Dr. Martin Luther King Jr; copyright renewed 1991 Coretta Scott King; **C2** 'Dissident is Patriotic', © 2004 Sundance Channel L.L.C. and Courtroom Television Network L.L.C.; **D3** 'Smalltown Americans', © Bill Bryson interview "Smalltown Americans" 24 July 1999: Audio and transcript from The Savvy Traveler® © (p) 1999 American Public Media. Used with permission. All rights reserved; **D5** 'Ignorant Citizens', © USA Today. July 2, 2009. Reprinted with permission.
The World of English: Words in Context 'English, English Elsewhere', © International Dialects of English Archive / © Paul Meier, Theatre and Film Department, University of Kansas, Lawrence, KS; **B2** 'That's Not Cricket', © Mandeep Bedi; **Communicating across Cultures** 'Task 1: Watching a video about Australian and Jamaican English', © 2002 and 2003 ITV Productions Limited. Licensed by ITV Global Entertainment Limited / © written and presented by Melvyn Bragg;
The World of Work and Business: Lead-In 'Task 2', Courtesy CNN; **B5** 'Job Interview', © Mike Quinn; **Communicating across Cultures** 'Intercultural Communication', © 2003 Gecko Films

Fotos/Illustrationen

Global Perspectives: Lead-in 'Map of the World', Dr. Volkhard Binder, Berlin; **Science, Technology and the Environment: C1** 'Climate Change – Global Processes and Effects', © UNEP/GRID-Arendal;

Titelfoto: Gettyimages / © David Madison

Alle Copyrightvermerke zu *Vorschläge zur Leistungsmessung* befinden sich auf der DVD-ROM.